Temporary Agency Work and the Information Society

Temporary Agency Work and the Information Society

Reports given at the International Conference held on 28–29 April 2003 at the Royal Flemish Academy, Brussels, and sponsored jointly by the Academy, the Euro-Japan Institute for Law and Business, and the Society for International and Social Co-operation.

Editors: R. Blanpain and R. Graham

Contributors
Wilfried Beirnaert
Roger Blanpain
Eva Casado Alarcon
Michele Colucci
Jan Denys
Chris Engels
Ronnie Graham
Tadashi Hanami
Frank Hendrickx
Antoine Jacobs
Gillian Morris
Junko Nakayama
Birgitta Nyström
Willem Plessen
Miguel Rodriguez-Pinero Royo
Alexander Samorodov
Sabine Smith-Vidal
Willy van Eeckhoutte
Dieuwke Visser
Manfred Weiss

2004
Kluwer Law International
The Hague/London/New York

A.C.I.P. Catalogue record for this book is available from the Library of Congress.

ISBN 90-411-2252-4

Published by:
Kluwer Law International
P.O. Box 85889, 2508 CN The Hague, The Netherlands
sales@kluwerlaw.com
http://www.kluwerlaw.com

Sold and Distributed in North, Central and South America by:
Aspen Publishers, Inc.
7201 McKinney Circle, Frederick, MD 21704, USA

Sold and distributed in all other countries by:
Extenza-Turpin Distribution Services Limited
Blackhorse Road, Letchworth, Hertfordshire
SG6 1HN, United Kingdom

Printed on acid-free paper

Printed and bound in the Netherlands.

Table of Contents

List of Contributors

Wilfried Beirnaert, *Unice*
Roger Blanpain, *Universities of Leuven and Tilburg, President of the International Society for Labour Law and Social Security*
Eva Casado Alarcon, *CIETT*
Michele Colucci, *University of Salerno, Italy*
Jan Denys, *Labour Market Expert, Randstad, Belgium*
Chris Engels, *University of Leuven, Belgium*
Ronnie Graham, *European Court of Justice*
Tadashi Hanami, *President, Japan Institute for Labour*
Frank Hendrickx, *Universities of Leuven and Tilburg*
Antoine Jacobs, *University of Tilburg, The Netherlands*
Gillian Morris, *Brunel University, UK*
Junko Nakayama, *researcher, Employment Sector, ILO*
Birgitta Nyström, *University of Lund, Sweden*
Willem Plessen, *Randstad Group, The Netherlands*
Miguel Rodriguez-Piñero Royo, *University of Huelva, Spain*
Alexander Samorodov, *senior labour economist, Employment Sector, ILO*
Sabine Smith-Vidal, *Allen&Overy, France*
Willy van Eeckhoutte, *University of Gent, Belgium*
Dieuwke Visser, *Randstad Group, The Netherlands*
Manfred Weiss, *University of Frankfurt, Germany, President of the International Industrial Relations Association*

1. Introductory Remarks: The Evolving Attitude Towards Temporary Agency Work

Roger Blanpain

A Diversified Labour Market

This International Conference on Temporary Agency Work, hosted by the Royal Flemish Academy, Brussels, is a follow up to our comparative study of Temporary Work (1993)[1] and the International Conference, organized in Leuven (1998) concerning the role of private employment agencies, then focussing on ILO Convention No. 181 (1997) and the decision of the European Court in the Job-Centre case of 1997.[2]

The timing of this Conference seems to me almost perfect, given the ongoing discussion on the proposed European Directive on working conditions for temporary workers (2002) and the major developments which have taken place in the labour market in many countries over the last years.

This debate *de facto* goes further than the issue of temporary work in a strict sense, as it involves the nature and the form of the employment relationships in the XXIst Century.

Indeed, one of the main questions is whether work should be performed by employees, contracted by the employer for that purpose, or whether the same work could also be performed by employees of another enterprise. In other words, is generalized leasing of employees something which makes sense from the point of view of HR management and which is acceptable under both labour law and social justice considerations?

Indeed, today we talk of a labour market which has become increasingly diversified. How far can and will this diversification go and how acceptable is it to the various actors and interests involved?

An Evolving Attitude

The mere raising of this question indicates that the attitude towards agency work in the EU Members States and in other countries, like Japan, has evolved enormously over the last 40 years. Let's look at this development as a whole, and put forward a broad-brush analysis.

---

1. Kluwer Law International.
2. 'Private Employment Agencies', in: *Bulletin of Comparative Labour Relations*, 1999, No. 36, p. 403 (ed. Roger Blanpain).

R. Blanpain & R. Graham (eds.), Temporary Agency Work and the Information Society, 1–6

Forbidden Fruit

Initially, temporary work was practically outlawed. I remember that the ILO received a question from the Swedish Government whether or not temporary agency work (in the form of secretarial help) had to be considered as placement of workers for payment and thus as contrary to ILO Convention 96 regarding fee-charging placement. The ILO secretariat answered yes: such placement was prohibited. This meant that temporary work was outlawed, partially or totally in many countries, including Japan, Sweden, Italy and Spain.

One way around the ILO's legal position on this matter was to consider temporary workers as self-employed, as was done for the first recognized use of temporary workers in Belgium, at the occasion of the Brussels World Fair of 1958.

In any case, many trade unions were hostile to temporary work – and some still are – as it undermines, so they say, the situation of permanent workers by providing cheaper labour, while temporary workers do not always benefit from equal treatment.

The opinion of the ILO that temporary work constitutes the prohibited placement of workers for a fee was, however, quickly set aside. Indeed, at the end of the 1960s and beginning of the 1970s, a theory was developed according to which temporary work constitutes a triangular relationship: namely that the temporary work agency is the employer of the temporary worker putting him at the disposal of a user undertaking, delegating part of the managerial authority to the user. Under that model, there is no placement, since the user is not the employer.

This opinion was endorsed by the European Court of Justice in the *Manpower* case (1970), in which a French temporary worker, performing for a German user, was considered to be an employee of the French temporary work agency, with the consequence that, in conformity with Directive No. 1408/71 of 1971, French social security contributions were to be paid in France, since the temporary worker was engaged for an assignment of less than 12 months.

Accepted?

Very, very slowly, the idea of temporary work became accepted, as a way to accommodate a changing labour market, which was showing the first marked signs of diversification.

The opinion still prevailed that the labour market should remain the monopoly of the State, of the Government. I still remember that I was the only member of an EU working party, established at the beginning of the 1980s to examine the possibility of enacting a European Directive on Temporary Work, who was of the opinion that private employment agencies should play a role in the labour market. All other members, professors and civil servants, said: no, that monopoly is part of the prerogatives of the Government. Labour is indeed not a commodity!, they said.

But diversification of the labour market became so widespread and wide-ranging that Governments had to allow, *de facto* or *de jure*, certain forms of private agency activities in recruitment, headhunting, temporary work, outplacement, and other selection activities, though mostly in a very restrictive way.

I vividly recall the discussions in the 1980s concerning outplacement, where the question was whether outplacement constituted placement or not. The outplacement agencies had to prove that the provision of their services did not lead to a job with a given employer, but were only aimed at helping a redundant employee to find a new job. It was absurd to proceed on the basis that providing workers who had been made redundant with a job constituted a criminal activity.

The Breakthrough

Finally, as a result of the many different needs to be accommodated, the job market became so diverse that public employment agencies could, in all honesty, no longer respond to the challenges and demands of employers and employees.

A real breakthrough came with the judgement of the European Court of Justice in the *Job Centre* case (1997) concerning the prohibition of temporary work in Italy, where as a consequence 'fake subcontracting' was flourishing. The Court judged that the Italian regulation, prohibiting temporary work, was contrary to freedom of competition, since the public employment service was not capable of satisfying the needs of the labour market.

At the same time, the ILO, after careful analysis of the workings of labour markets, came to the conclusion that Convention 96 on fee-paying employment agencies was outdated. So the door to private employment agencies was opened wide with the adoption of Convention 181 on private employment agencies (1997).

A European Directive?

The proposed European directive on the working conditions of temporary workers (latest version 28 November 2002) confirms this trend. The aim of the proposed directive is 'to establish a suitable framework for the temporary use of temporary work to contribute to the smooth functioning of the labour and the employment market' (Article 2b). 'Member States are asked to review any restrictions or prohibitions on temporary work for certain groups of workers, sectors or areas of economic activity in order to verify whether specific conditions underlying them still obtain. If they do not, Member States should discontinue them' (Article 4).

Full Recognition? A Growing Number of Services

At present, the diversity of the labour markets and the role of private employment services are fully recognized. Indeed private agencies perform a growing number of services, namely for:

1. **enterprises**, where private agencies provide help regarding:
   a. manpower needs
      – replacement of workers
      – peaks in production
      – shortage of certain qualifications;
   b. vocational training;
   c. control of labour costs;
   d. HR management
      – recruitment of permanent workers
      – administrative aid
      – social secretariat.

2. **employees**, where help is provided:
   a. for those looking for a (temporary) job;
   b. for those looking for experience;
   c. as a first step to permanent employment;
   d. for furthering the employability of the employee.
3. **society as a whole** – private initiative has added value: namely in the fostering of 'social integration' – latterly together with public employment agencies – of long-term unemployed, often of non or less qualified workers.

Questions

Given these developments, and especially the growing role of private employment agencies, should one not go a step further and allow private agencies to become fully fledged manpower agents providing, eventually on a permanent basis, enterprise-users with the manpower they need, taking care of selection, training, administration, paying of wages, of taxes and social security contributions, and concluding collective agreements? This would be a sort of leasing of personnel, eventually on a permanent basis, to users which pay for the service. This would establish dual employers in the agency and the user, in the sense that the user would have to take care of payments and other obligations, if the agency failed to do so.

Let us bear in mind that the proposed EU directive on temporary work allows agencies to employ workers on a permanent contract, meaning also that employees could be put at the disposal of one or many users, eventually for a longer, perhaps permanent period of time.

I would also like to indicate in this context that a Belgian law of 12 August 2000 allows a permanent provision of employees by any company to a user without restriction as to the tasks involved, assignments or their length.

A second question is: what wage and working conditions should agency workers enjoy? Let's say that the European Union, regarding health and safety for temporary workers, has propounded from the outset (1991) equal treatment with the comparable employee of the user firm. The same approach was followed under the directives on fixed-term and part-time workers' contracts: equal treatment with workers who are full-time and/or engaged for an indefinite period.

The proposed EU directive on the working conditions of temporary agency workers goes in the same direction: equal treatment with comparable workers of the user company unless:

- the temporary worker has a permanent contract and continues to be paid between assignments;
- there is a collective agreement covering the temporary agency, which provides adequate social protection; or
- the assignment does not exceed six weeks.

Most employers, and some member states (including Germany, UK and Denmark) contest this equal treatment rule as it would result in certain workers, especially those previously paid less than comparable workers, not being hired since the cost of doing so would be too high for the user.

So, two matters require further consideration:

1. the role of private employment agencies as fully integrated manpower providers; and
2. the wage and working conditions of workers put at the disposal of users, under equal treatment or another adequate social protection system.

Solutions to these matters merit great attention as they will determine the way our labour markets – at national, European and international level – will function for years to come.

This volume contains reports given at the International Conference on Temporary Agency Work and the Information Society, held in Brussels, 28–29 April 2003.

Finally, a word of thanks to our good colleagues for their outstanding contributions and to Mr Ronnie Graham, who was more than helpful in assisting in the editing of this volume.

General Reports

2. Challenges for Temporary Agency Work in the Information Society

Jan Denys

I. INTRODUCTION

Temporary agency work is booming business. In Belgium, which has the eighth biggest market in the world, the number of temporary agency workers increased from 50,000 in 1985 to 316,000, not including students, in 2001 (Upedi, 2002). In Denmark, Spain, Italy and Sweden the industry has increased five-fold in terms of number of workers in the 1990s. Temporary agency work is now a global business phenomenon.

The largest temporary work agency business, Adecco, operates in 60 countries on five continents. Manpower, number two in the business, is also worldwide with a presence in 50 countries. The next top players, Vedior and Randstad, operate in 25 and 15 countries respectively. Although temporary agency work does exist on all five continents, the United States, Europe, Japan and Australia have more than 95 per cent of the global turnover. Almost half of all temporary agency workers are found in the United States. Europe is second with almost 40 per cent.

Although the recent recession had an impact on the industry's performance, it is clear that its potential is still enormous. In this article we will first give some facts and figures on the industry, which are sometimes not directly comparable because of variations in the quality of available data. The importance of the industry is often underestimated because experts often focus too much attention on penetration rates of temporary workers in overall employment and not enough on the potential for their use. We will then suggest why the industry has been so successful. To conclude, some recent trends and future challenges are considered.

II. SOME FACTS AND FIGURES

Table 1 gives an overview of the penetration rates of temporary agency work in the most important countries.[1] The penetration rate is the number of temporary agency workers on a daily basis compared with total employment.

Although the penetration rate is the most popular indicator of the importance of the industry, it gives only a partial view of its impact. Some experts and trade union officials are using these figures to 'prove' that the industry still has a marginal role in the labour market. However the penetration rate is a stock figure. The real impact of the industry is better viewed with flow data. Unfortunately, such data is harder to come by and more difficult to collect. The proportion of temporary agency

1. The quality of the data varies per country. In addition, the research methodology can also differ.

R. Blanpain & R. Graham (eds.), Temporary Agency Work and the Information Society, 9–18

Table 1. Penetration rate in the year 2000/2001

Country	*Value in %*
Austria	1.0
Belgium	1.9
Denmark	0.8
Finland	0.7
France	2.7
Germany	0.8
Ireland	0.6
Italy	0.7
Japan	0.7
Luxembourg	3.5
The Netherlands	3.6
Portugal	1.1
Spain	0.9
Sweden	0.8
United Kingdom	3.8
EU	1.5
United States	2.4

Sources: CIETT (2000), Randstad (2003).

workers in the national workforce at least triples or quadruples each year in most countries. If we calculate the extent to which temporary agency work acts as a recruitment channel then the figures are also much more significant. In Belgium, 10 per cent of all workers are recruited via temporary agency work (Delmotte *et al.*, 2001). In the Netherlands this proportion is even higher, at 17 per cent. In such cases, after fulfilling a temporary assignment the worker is offered temporary or permanent employment by the user company. This data can only be obtained by comprehensive research. Generally, data on how vacancies are filled does not exist. Until now research in this area has taken place only in Belgium and the Netherlands.

Another interesting observation is that in Belgium 26 per cent of the working population have worked at some time as a temporary agency worker (Federgon, 2002). That figure rises each year because of the substantial growth of the sector in the last decades. This means that younger workers have worked as a temporary agency worker more commonly than older workers. A further statistic indicates the impact that agency work has had in the industrial sector. In Belgium more than 50 per cent of all blue collar workers in the industrial sector are recruited via temporary agency work (Delagrange, 2001).

III. THE SUCCESS OF TEMPORARY AGENCY WORK EXPLAINED

The success of temporary agency work can be explained by the fact that it creates added value for the worker, the employer, the labour market and society as a whole.

The Worker

Clearly, workers join temporary work agencies out of choice. In all developed countries there are many alternatives for finding suitable work (through public employment services, advertisements, internet providers, personal contacts etc.). In 2000 more than 7 million agency workers were working worldwide on a daily basis and between 20 and 25 million on a yearly basis.[2] Furthermore many more people were candidates for temporary agency work but were not offered work.[3] These statistics simply indicate the added value of temporary agency work for many workers in developed economies.

Some still consider the industry as a modern form of slave labour, arguing that those who register with these agencies are vulnerable, low-skilled and desperate for work. Those who take such a view should step inside a temporary work agency; they would meet a majority of self-confident individuals comparing the services of different agencies and looking for the best deal.

There are three main reasons why people register with temporary work agencies. The majority of people use temporary agency work as a stepping stone to permanent employment. There are three ways in which taking an agency assignment might lead to permanent employment (Heather *et al.*, 1996). The most important is the internal direct route. More and more employers are using temporary work as a screening opportunity. In this case temporary agency work is used as a recruitment channel and not as a way to fulfil the company's flexible labour needs.

The internal indirect route is a second way of entering permanent employment. Most jobs are not advertised on the external labour market, but are filled either internally by vertical or horizontal transfer or by someone who is recommended by a member of staff or a client of the firm. Temporary agency workers have automatic access to this kind of insider information in the user firm.

Finally there is an external route which also leads to permanent employment. By doing temporary agency work the individual is gaining work experience, technical and social skills, and an improved work ethic. The simple fact that someone is employed enhances his attractiveness for other employers. There is sufficient empirical evidence that temporary agency work is indeed functioning as a stepping stone to permanent employment. Although on specifics figures differ between countries they are generally very consistent. Many temporary agency workers find permanent employment. The most recent figures for Belgium indicate that 57 per cent of all temporary agency workers found permanent employment after finishing their last temporary job (Federgon, 2003). This is a very good result if we compare it with other national statistics.[4]

Less well-known is that many temporary agency workers already have a permanent job. They carry out temporary agency work as a means of additional income. This is the second largest incentive to do temporary work. In Belgium, 8 per cent of all temporary agency workers (not including students) carry out temporary work for this reason. A closer look reveals that this category is notably heterogeneous. Some workers combine permanent employment during the week with agency work at the weekend. Others work part-time and take agency work from time to time. There are also self-employed or free-lancers combining their work with agency work.

---

2. This indicates that they worked at least one day as an agency worker in the whole year.
3. A Belgian research project revealed that 37 per cent of the Belgian labour force was at least once registered with a temporary work agency, and 26 per cent had worked at least one day as a temporary agency worker. The other 11 per cent were never offered work.
4. International figures range from 29 per cent (Germany) and 53 per cent (The Netherlands) (CIETT, 2000). Comparisons between countries are problematic however because of different methodologies used in the research concerned.

A new category is retired people occasionally supplementing their pension with agency work.

Finally there are workers who carry out temporary agency work because, for various reasons, they do not want permanent employment, at least not for the time being. They differ, however, from the former category in that they do not have a permanent position in the labour market. This category is again heterogeneous (those between two permanent positions, students, people with a good earning partner, women with children who want to balance work with other activities, amongst others). A special sub-category are workers (mostly school leavers entering the labour market) who take agency work because they want experience with a range of employers and/or jobs. Approximately 10–15 per cent of all agency workers in Belgium are in this category (Delagrange, 2001). The same result is found in the Netherlands, France and Germany (Ecorys-Nei, 2002).

The Employer

Why do employers use temporary work agencies? As stated above, employees have alternatives for finding suitable jobs. The same is true for employers. In Belgium more than 50 per cent of private firms with more than 100 employees are making use of temporary agency workers (Delarue *et al.*, 2003). There are again three main reasons for employers to use the services of a temporary work agency.

The first and most well-established is the need for (external) flexibility. Employers need flexibility to minimize costs and/or maximize profits, particularly in a global economy where competition is not only over prices but also over quality, delivery time and so on. The need for flexibility can be divided into many subcategories. The replacement of absent employees is perhaps the most traditional reason for hiring agency workers. Later on, the use of agency workers became a strategic element in adjusting the company labour force to changes and fluctuations in market demand. These changes may be cyclical, seasonal or sporadic (Ecorys-Nei, 2002). In another development, firms are using temporary agency workers to act as a buffer to manage increased economic uncertainty. In such cases, the use of agency work is permanent and pre-planned. Almost twenty years ago, Atkinson described a model distinguishing between core and periphery workers within the firm (Atkinson, 1984). The periphery workers consist partly of agency workers. The model became popular with academics and business strategists but until now empirical evidence supporting its use was not very convincing. Although the presence of core and periphery workers is clear in many enterprises, the suggestion that there is a strict distinction between these two categories (in terms of pay, training etc.) was not convincingly substantiated, and there is much evidence of mobility from periphery to core.

This brings us to the second motivation for hiring temporary workers, namely as a means of recruiting. Recently, more and more employers have been using temporary agency work to recruit permanent employees. The assignment is seen as a screening period for both employer and worker without long-term commitment on either side. In Belgium, use of temporary work for this reason became more significant between 1995 and 2000 (Delmotte *et al.*, 2001). With the current recession we assume that its importance is decreasing again but there is no doubt that temporary work agencies have become an important recruitment channel for employers. Moreover, they are now much more significant than traditional recruitment and selection firms.[5] In Belgium, temporary work agencies are filling 10 per cent of all vacancies in the private sector.[6] The traditional recruitment and selection firms fill only 3 per cent (Delmotte *et al.*, 2001). In this regard, the entire private staffing industry (which includes both temporary work agencies and recruitment and selection firms) is almost as important as the public employment service (15 per cent) in Belgium.[7] The impact of the private staffing industry is even bigger in the Netherlands, where it fills 17 per cent of vacancies. Since the use of temporary work for recruitment purposes is more recent, its regulation has not yet evolved in many countries.

The last reason for using temporary work has to do with outsourcing (or co-sourcing). As firms focus more and more on their core competences and outsource other activities, it is clear that many human resources activities are or will be outsourced.[8] When a firm recruits temporary workers, thus putting them on the payroll of the temporary work agency, this is not a case of recruitment and/or selection being outsourced but simply administration of the process. In the United States there is a complete industry built on this trend: the professional employer organizations are one of the biggest boomers in the industry in the last decade. Many temporary work agencies are also offering extra services: training, operational human resources advice or consultancy, IT-related systems (e.g. for time registration). In these ways, temporary work agencies effectively become a partner for the human resources departments. They transform from a temporary work agency to a human resources service provider by offering temporary agency work, recruitment and selection, outplacement, pay-rolling, training, and project work amongst other things (Denys, 1999). All international temporary work agencies are following this trend which is at least partly a reaction to the outsourcing strategies of user firms.

The Society

If workers and employers want to make use of the services of temporary work agencies then it should not come as a surprise that the labour market and society as a whole benefit from this. Temporary agency work has a positive effect on the functioning of labour markets. It facilitates the matching of labour supply and demand. It reduces frictional unemployment, which in part accounts for its positive impact on the employment rate and its negative impact on the unemployment rate. There is empirical evidence for this in the United States (Katz *et al.*, 1999) and in Europe (Neugart *et al.*, 2001). Other research suggests that temporary work has reduced illegal labour activities. As part of the same research, user firms were asked if the tasks for which agency workers were used would have been carried out if these workers had not been available (CIETT, 1999). Seventeen per cent replied that the tasks would not have been performed at all. It is also clear that an absence of temporary agency work promotes internal flexibility strategies such as extra hours for permanent employees.

5. Many researchers and also the International Labour Organization have not taken this development into account. In failing to do so, they are underestimating the role and impact of the entire private staffing industry on the labour market (Walwei, 1997; Phan Thuy *et al.*, 2001).
6. Agency work is not included in this figure.
7. Many companies provide both temporary work and recruitment and selection.
8. A recent study by Berenschot reveals that 88 per cent of firms with a HR-department in Belgium are outsourcing HR-activities. Training, recruitment and selection and administration are mostly outsourced (Berenschot, 2003).

In that case, extra work does not create extra jobs.[9] More jobs mean additional income and less expenditure for social security funds.[10]

There is also evidence that temporary agency work has a good impact on the integration of so-called risk groups. For low-skilled workers, long-term unemployed, and ethnic minorities, temporary agency work offers an opportunity for (re)integration. Research in Belgium suggests that for these groups the probability of finding permanent employment after temporary agency work is only slightly lower than in general (Idea Consult, 2000). The same was found to be the case in the Netherlands (Ecorys-Nei, 2002).

One can explain the growth of the temporary work sector by taking a longer-term perspective. Indeed, this overview makes clear that over time the sector is increasingly fulfilling the needs of employers and workers. Initially merely replacing absent workers, the industry now provides external flexibility for the workforce. In time, employers started to use agency work as an additional recruitment channel. Anticipating outsourcing trends in modern economies, the industry is now transforming itself into full-service human resources provision. At the same time the agency workforce has become more diversified as well. Originally, agency workers consisted largely of housewives (Finney, 1991). Subsequently, the main group of agency workers were young people starting their career. A decade ago, students became a very important category.[11] In the last decade, more and more segments have developed within the agency worker population. A significant part of the current workforce consists of workers changing jobs via temporary agency work (Federgon, 2003).[12] Another segment are workers who do temporary agency work as a means of additional income. A substantial part of the working population discovered temporary agency work as a means of transition in the labour market, and consequently temporary agency work plays a very important role in the transitional labour market.[13]

The fact that temporary agency work created win-win situations for both employer and worker is an important explanation for the structural growth of the

---

9. There are other positive influences which temporary agency work may have on the functioning of the labour market and on the economy as a whole. The availability of temporary agency work can be seen as a competitive advantage in a global economy. Even trade union professionals admit that without temporary agency work there is no future for industrial activities in Belgium. Another positive influence is the matching function. In addition to the speed with which matching is achieved (which has an influence on frictional unemployment), the quality of the matching is also significant. A better match is good for productivity, and a high level of productivity is essential in a high wage economy. The problem is that it is very difficult to prove empirically that temporary work currently influences the labour market.

10. The fact that the social security system is gaining from the activity of temporary agency work is a problem for unions. They often simply deny its positive influence on the number of jobs (Leurs, 2003).

11. This was the case in Belgium. In other countries such as the Netherlands, students had already been doing agency work for a long time.

12. Twenty-three per cent of all temporary agency workers had permanent employment before they started working on their last assignment.

13. The concept of the transitional labour market was originally described by Gunther Schmid, a well-known German sociologist, who distinguishes 5 human activities: learning, paid work, being unemployed, domestic and caring activities and retirement. In his model, he argues that it is important for workers to make transitions between these activities very easily. By creating a transitional labour market, it is easier to manage unemployment (Schmid 1995, 2000). It can be argued that temporary agency work plays a very important role in this transitional labour market (Denys, 2002).

sector. As the positive effects of temporary agency work at macro-level became clear, many European governments started to eliminate barriers hindering activities in the sector. This further explains the recent growth of temporary work agencies. Moreover some governments have started to use the temporary work industry to integrate unemployed people.[14] The idea that the industry plays a positive role in the labour market is also part of the background of the European Directive.

In this section we have explained why the industry has grown so much in the last decades. We have not explained why the sector grew more quickly in some countries than in others. Very often, regulation is seen as the major factor. Although it is clear that regulation plays an important role, it does not explain all differences which have arisen. Why is the industry more successful in the United Kingdom than in the United States? In both countries there is almost no regulation specifically designed for temporary work agencies, especially in comparison to most European nations. Why is temporary agency work in France more successful than in the United States, although regulation in France is much more restrictive? In addition to regulation of agency work, the regulation of permanent employment also plays a very important role. The more restrictive and regulated employment practices are in general, the more attractive temporary employment (agency and non-agency work) becomes.

IV. TRENDS, CHALLENGES AND OPPORTUNITIES

What are the main international trends, challenges and opportunities in the industry? Here are ten of the most important future trends.

1. The potential growth of the industry is still very high since many countries have a penetration rate of only 1 per cent or less. In Europe, the industry certainly has the potential to double.
2. In the industry, we detect consolidation between both large and independent firms and at the same time we still see many new entrants.[15] On the one hand, mergers and acquisitions are a current trend, although with the recession this activity has slowed down; on the other hand, the high number of new entrants is partially due to the removal of licensing systems and liberalization of the regulatory system. In the Netherlands this development has attracted hundreds of new entrants into the market.
3. A less encouraging development (at least from the point of view of the industry) is that costs are increasing. These rising costs are caused by scarcity of labour, new regulation and growing expectations of user companies. There is a fear that the new Directive (if adopted) and more specifically the introduction of the user pay system in the European Union will further increase costs. In addition, it is clear that marginal players in the industry will come under increasing pressure due to more intensive competition.
4. Strategies for countering rising costs and lower profit margins are twofold. All companies (and certainly those listed on the stock market) have had major cost-cutting programmes within the last years. Further, all

14. This is the case in the United Kingdom, the Netherlands, Belgium, France and recently Germany.
15. Even in a mature market such as in the Netherlands, the removal of the licensing system attracted hundreds of small companies into the business.

companies have put more emphasis on specialized services with higher profit margins. It is also clear that IT has a potentially major effect on the huge processing costs of the industry. The standardization of processing, which is essential for the industry to decrease its costs, is a major challenge for the industry.

5. One of the most important trends is the transformation of big temporary work agencies into human resources providers. Temporary agency work is only one (although by far still the most common) of the services they deliver. Outplacement, recruitment, selection and assessment, payrolling, training, and IT-services are now complementing the services on offer. Providing other services is partly a strategy to tackle overall decline in profit margins as mentioned above. However, the main impetus for the diversification in services offered comes from large users who want to reduce the number of staffing services they use. In future, global staffing will be divided into human resources providers on the one hand and niche players on the other (Denys, 1999). This transformation is progressing slowly due to the time required for the temporary agency industry to acquire the necessary skills and infrastructure.
6. Skill shortages will remain a problem for the industry (and for the whole labour market). The current recession is masking this problem but it will return immediately when the economic cycle inevitably moves into the expansion phase. A variety of strategies will be available for use in response: activation of the non-active working population, more training, more immigration, longer duration of contracts, loyalty programmes, amongst others.
7. The public sector remains a substantially untapped market for the industry. In most countries this sector is not (entirely) open to temporary agency work. In many countries the public sector accounts for between one-fifth and one-fourth of the working population. So the potential market is clear. The same goes for many 'social profit' sectors.
8. As well as being a client in the industry, the public authorities can play another key role. As already discussed, in some countries public authorities are making use of private temporary work agencies to integrate unemployed people or people on welfare benefits. In the future, public authorities could therefore use the industry for this additional purpose. If this model were to be implemented in most of the European countries, which is doubtful at present, it may have an important impact on the industry.
9. Another new client (besides private industry and public authorities) are households. In the near future, an important industry will emerge in supplying households with cleaning, gardening, babysitting and other services. At present, these services are delivered on the black market. Using substantial subsidies, the public authorities want to bring this sector into the normal economy. It is clear that the industry is in a good position to operate in this new market.
10. As already mentioned above, IT solutions will be important for the industry. First of all, IT applications make processing in the industry less labour intensive and less costly (e.g. mailing costs). Additionally, IT-related products (e.g. for time registration, information management etc.) will be further developed and sold. The fear that the internet would

render the industry redundant has proved unjustified, at least for the foreseeable future. It is clear that the involvement of the personal consultant will remain important in the temporary assistance industry. This is not to say that parts of the matching process cannot become electronic (e.g. registering, forms of testing etc.), but rather that there is an integral personal component which cannot be substituted electronically. But experience has shown that new developments are proceeding very slowly. Much trial and error should be allowed for in forecasting any rate of change.

BIBLIOGRAPHY

Atkinson, J.S. (1984), *Flexibility, Uncertainty and Manpower Management*, IMS report. No. 89, Brighton Institute of Manpower Studies

Berenschot (2003), *HRM in de praktijk*, Berenschot, Belgium

CIETT (2000), *Orchestrating the evolution of Private Employment Agencies towards a stronger society*, Brussels

Delagrange, H. (2001), *Uitzendarbeid in de Vlaamse Industrie: Inzet en Ontwikkelingen*, Brussel

Delarue, A., *et al.* (2003), *Panel Survey of Organisations in Flanders*, Katholieke Universiteit Leuven

Delmotte, J., *et al.* (2001), *Hoe werven Bedrijven in België in 2000*, Katholieke Universiteit Leuven

Denys, J. (1999), 'Public and Private Placement Services: An Appraisal', in Blainpain, R. (ed.), *Private Employment* Agencies, pp. 133–144, Kluwer, The Hague/London/Boston

Denys, J. (2003), *De Rol van Uitzendarbeid in de transitionele Arbeidsmarkt* (to be published)

Ecorys-Nei (2002), *Socio-economic Functions of Agency Work in the European Union*, Rotterdam

Finney, M., *et al.* (1991), *A Heritage of Service, the History of Temporary Help in America*, National Association of Temporary Services, Alexandria

Federgon (2002), *De Kwaliteit van Uitzendarbeid: Perceptie en Realiteit*, Brussel

Federgon (2003), *Uitzendarbeid in België: Profiel- en Tewerkstellingskenmerken*, Brussel

Katz, L.F. & Krueger, A.B. (1999), *The high-pressure U.S. Labor Market of the 1990's*, Brookings Papers on Economic Activity, Washington

Leurs, A. (2003), 'Europa als Promotor van Uitzendarbeid', in *Ons Recht*, p. 7, Januari

Neugart, M. & Storrie, D. (2001), *Temporary Agency Work and Equilibrium Unemployment*, Working paper, Department of Economics, Gëteborg University

Thuy, P. (2001), *The Public Employment Service in a changing Labour Market*, International Labour Office, Geneva

Randstad (2003), *Annual Report 2002*, Diemen

Schmid, G. (1995), 'Is Full Emploympent Still Possible? Transitional Labour Markets as a New Strategy of Labour Market Policy', in *Economic and Industrial Democracy*, 1995, 16(3), pp. 429–456

Schmid, G. (2000), 'Transitional Labour Markets. A New European Employment Strategy' in Marin, B., *et al.*, *Innovative Employment Initiatives*, Aldershot, Ashgate, pp. 223–254

Storrie, D. (2002) *Temporary Agency Work in the European Union*, Dublin European Foundation for the Improvement of Living and Working Conditions

3. Public and Private Employment Services: From Co-existence to Co-operation

Junko Nakayama and Alexander Samorodov[1]

Recent years have witnessed enormous changes affecting employment services throughout the world. An important element of these accelerating developments has been the growth of partnerships between public employment services and other stakeholders in the labour market such as local government, training and educational institutions, business and, most importantly, private employment agencies.

This article discusses general trends in the development of employment services in various groups of countries, the genesis of private employment agencies after a *de facto* ban on them was lifted, legal and practical issues in relation to public/private co-operation, and ILO international labour standards. The article then draws conclusions from the information presented, looking towards increased co-operation between public and private agencies.

The article is based on consultation with employment service staff, ministries of labour, the social partners in all countries, research institutes, training and educational establishments, international associations of public and private employment agencies, labour economists and others interested in labour market and human resources development issues. It aims, in particular, at stimulating debate on the issue of partnerships between public and private employment agencies.

Mr. Alexander Samorodov wrote the bulk of the paper while Ms. Junko Nakayama provided information on the legal framework regulating private employment agencies. She also contributed examples from practice in some industrialized countries.

Thanks are extended to Peter Auer, Ellen Hansen, Emily Sims and Guy Standing of the ILO for their valuable comments on an earlier version of the paper.

I. INTRODUCTION

The twenty-first century is going to be very different from its predecessor, both in qualitative and quantitative terms. The acceleration of human, scientific, societal and technological development affects all aspects of peoples' lives. In some countries, employment and production systems will undergo massive restructuring, and the world of work will acquire previously unknown features. In most of the world, the population continues to rise faster than the number of new job opportunities. There

1. The views expressed in the article are solely these of the authors and should in no way be interpreted as representing the official position of the International Labour Office of Geneva. The authors take responsibility for any errors.

R. Blanpain & R. Graham (eds.), Temporary Agency Work and the Information Society, 19–44

is an urgent need for efficient measures to counter unemployment. On the other hand, some countries have a declining workforce and labour shortages are in sight.

Technological change, turbulence in financial markets, the emergence of global markets for products and services, international competition, dramatic increases in foreign direct investment, new business strategies and management practices, innovative forms of business and work organization are among the most significant developments transforming the world of work. For, example, national economies need an ever growing number of experts in information technology.

In the 1990s, new practices were introduced in welfare systems in the OECD countries. The new approach represented a kind of contract between those receiving benefits and those supporting them (taxpayers, the state), comprising a balance between rights (the right to a job or to training, in particular) and duties (the duty to work or to undergo training in exchange for benefits). It was considered important to avoid resorting to workfare. These new practices have increased the workload of employment services entrusted with making people more employable, providing labour market information, organizing training and retraining, and offering job placement. Active labour market policies implemented by public employment services, activation, and welfare-to-work became popular in the developed industrialized countries while transition economies were struggling with open and hidden unemployment, and Third World countries had enormous poverty and development problems to overcome.

Although overall global employment currently looks more hopeful now than in the past, the tasks still remain formidable. In all major groups of countries, for example, the rates of unemployment in 2000 were higher than in 1990.[2] This has many implications, including greater responsibilities for employment services under public-private partnerships.

II. TRENDS IN EMPLOYMENT SERVICES DEVELOPMENT

The developments mentioned above have complicated the business environment in which employment services operate. As a result, policy makers have begun a drive for partnership between all actors in the market, especially local government, private providers of employment services, training institutions, and social and welfare institutions. Setting up active partnerships and diversifying organizational models have become key tasks for public employment services, along with using and developing modern technologies, notably the Internet.

Employment services (ES) help to make individuals employable but they also make workers aware of their rights, and of job opportunities. In this way, ES contribute to economic development, full and productive employment, and social inclusion. They also help individuals gain access to decent jobs which bring them out of poverty and a marginalized existence in a world where close to half of the population live on two dollars a day. ES are also an important gateway to lifelong learning for adults.

Employment services must adapt and be flexible in organizational and technological terms in order to be valuable to workers, employers and state bodies.

Pressure to reorganize employment services has been great and the last decade of the twentieth century saw an active search for ways to reform and modify, to make employment services more up-to-date, more responsive, flexible and accessible.

2. ILO, *World employment report 2001* (Geneva), January 2001, Table 1.1.

Employment services, particularly in developed countries, underwent greater change than ever before. Some preliminary conclusions can be drawn from recent experience.

The positive impact of new technologies on ES has been so great that some have predicted public employment services will disappear, at least in their present form. Information technology has the potential to bring job seekers into close contact with employers, thus bypassing ES, while unemployment benefits can be claimed over the telephone and automatically paid into the claimant's bank account.

Although new technology has certainly assisted the operation of ES, it is probably premature to predict the end of public employment services. Many job seekers need professional help in finding work; they require personal assistance, coaching and encouragement to participate in the labour market programmes provided by public employment services. Besides, not all countries have the most up-to-date information technology. The 'digital divide' applies to national employment services as much as elsewhere.

Despite the many recent changes, the core functions of public employment services remain the same and remain important. They are:

- job broking;
- labour market information (LMI);
- administration of labour market programmes (LMPs); and
- administration of unemployment benefits.

There have been many efforts to reform public employment services, but so far no developed country has abolished theirs. Moreover, the European Union countries have identified the public employment service as a key labour market institution.

Private employment agencies have grown spectacularly in recent years. They do not administer public labour market programmes or unemployment benefits, but their future is assured through the new interest in temporary work, and contract labour, migration for work abroad, and tailored services oriented to customer needs.

In the United States, for example, temporary workers and others who were not full-time employees, such as freelancers, consultants, independent contractors and the self-employed, made up as much as a third of the workforce at the end of the 1990s.[3] The number of temporary workers has increased significantly worldwide. Thus, in the European Union, over 50 per cent of the unemployed who found jobs in the middle of the 1990s took temporary positions.[4] The development of private employment agencies is supported by this trend.

Temporary jobs are concentrated among the young and are important in flow terms but much less so in their overall number. That is, many eventually translate into longer-term jobs. However, it is true that they represent an increasingly large part of the labour market and most people start work with a temporary job.[5]

One of the big problems in temporary work is the inequality between temporary workers' rights and those of the permanent staff. Temporary workers have now begun to defend their rights and in a number of cases they have won, against Microsoft for example (cf. Box 1). The press reports that in addition to inequalities inside the enterprise, temporary workers may suffer disproportionately in terms of income erosion and the provision of social benefits, while their labour market position is also more precarious.

---

3. Walkin, D.J., 'The permanent stopgap in staffing is still a temp', in *New York Times* (New York), 30 January 2001.
4. CIETT website http://www.ciett.org, 10 January 2001.
5. Auer, P., personal communication (Geneva, 23 November 2001).

Box 1: Temporary employees against Microsoft

Microsoft is to pay $97 million to settle a class action lawsuit from thousands of temporary workers who were denied stock options and other benefits awarded to permanent employees.

Source: *The Daily Telegraph,* December 14, 2000 (London).

Another noticeable trend in the industrialized market economies is the shift towards job broking over the internet. This activity was transformed in the 1970s with the introduction of self-service vacancy displays; several national ES have now placed their vacancy files on the internet, with in some cases job seeker files. 'Résumé builders' help job seekers prepare their CVs for posting on the internet along with the job titles that interest them.

Ideally, job seekers can now conduct their own independent job search from ES premises or libraries or from home if they have internet access. In the United States, for example, people can post their résumé on a website entitled America's Career InfoNet, though usually for a limited period.[6] Job seekers can express interest in a particular sector, industry or activity. Similar services are now being provided in many countries, including transition economies and developing nations.

With the proliferation of these cyber job banks, people have been able to make better informed and more rapid decisions on job opportunities. Employers, along with job seekers, can post job listings on national and international labour exchanges on the internet which are accessible to employers and workers, every day. This innovation has reduced the costs of job seeking and freed ES staff to perform other functions which are more difficult to run electronically, such as personal interviews with job seekers or the design of labour market programmes. Job seekers need individual consultation and customized services. Those who have special difficulties require special attention from individual 'case managers' at the ES.

Information and Communication Technology (ICT) has enabled a more active exchange of information between public and private employment agencies. Until now, however, at least in Europe, this has generally been one way, with private employment agencies advertising vacancies in public employment service offices.

With regard to labour market information, the main trend has been towards a sharper focus on the users (including individuals) and greater responsiveness to user needs. Other trends have been easier access to information through the use of modern technologies, links with more information resources and improved reliability of data with the same level of confidentiality. National ES in different countries are more unified on the basis of international labour standards regarding statistics. Consequently, more information of better quality and of more comprehensive coverage is theoretically available to the social partners who are responsible for employment policies and labour market programmes, and also to individual job seekers. However, in dozens of countries labour market information systems are in practice either underperforming or inadequate.

A number of industrialized countries have recently integrated (or are about to integrate) their public employment services and benefits administration into a single

6. America's Career InfoNet website http://www.acinet.org, 10 January 2001.

organization: New Zealand and Australia have fully integrated administrations; Germany has had a combined system for some time (available to most categories of unemployed workers); the Netherlands and the United Kingdom are planning to implement a new system. However, France and the United States continue to maintain relatively 'fragmented' systems.

Countries that are actively integrating benefit administration and employment services have also introduced, or are introducing, a single point of access ('one-stop-shops') for claimants: one-stop-shops can be found in New Zealand, Australia and the United Kingdom; the Netherlands introduced them in 2001.[7]

Integrating benefits administration with the public employment service is an important element in activation in which people must follow work or training programmes to receive benefits. In other systems, benefits administration is usually based on a welfare logic, while the public employment service is based on a work-integration logic.

The Government of the United Kingdom has coupled policy change with radical organizational reform. Most significantly, it has announced the creation of a new agency, combining the employment service and the unemployment benefits agency, with a clear focus on work. The new agency will deliver an integrated service to all working-age benefit claimants and employers.

In the 1990s, transition countries had to set up a modern public employment service capable of dealing with open unemployment and operating in a market economy. Private employment agencies did not exist under the central planning system in these countries. Hence, the issue of co-operation between public and private agencies was not on the agenda. In a number of transition countries during the 1990s, employment services either concentrated on passive programmes, such as paying unemployment benefits, or they scaled down their activities to one or two basic functions, such as registering job seekers and assisting them in seeking work, as in Georgia. At the same time, the development of private staffing agencies and temporary work agencies often proceeded in an uncontrolled manner. Licensing was the most common method of controlling these agencies. But even with licensing procedures in place, transition economies were often unable to report on the number of private employment agencies in their countries, or the outcome of their activities, such as placement figures. Again, there was no public-private co-operation.

Only in the middle or late 1990s did some transition countries achieve relative success in setting up modern public employment services while allowing for private labour market operators. At that time, the issue of public-private co-operation assumed a practical dimension. Still, the weakness of both public and private services together with an inadequate legal framework makes co-operation problematic in several transition economies.

Third World countries present a heterogeneous picture. In a number of these countries, public employment services are quite well-developed; in others, especially those torn by war and conflict, they are rudimentary or virtually non-existent. Common problems include general budget constraints, low levels of computerization and poor staff qualifications. A peculiar difficulty in developing countries is the size of the informal sector with huge numbers of own-account and family workers. This makes job broking particularly difficult. Very little is known about private employment agencies in these countries.

---

7. United Kingdom Department of Education and Skills, *International trends in employment and benefits service delivery* (London, March 2001), p. 1.

III. THE LEGAL FRAMEWORK FOR EMPLOYMENT SERVICES

A. International Labour Standards up to 1997

The public employment service (PES) began as a state job-broking organization in most countries, often with a monopoly on placement. Up until the Second World War, the main argument for this monopoly was the need to protect workers from exploitation. In addition, the PES wanted access to all data available on job vacancies. But even at that time private employment agencies were operating in a number of countries parallel to the PES.

International labour standards include three Conventions on employment services which are not public; the Fee-Charging Employment Agencies Convention, 1933 (No. 34)[8] which was superseded by the Fee-Charging Employment Agencies Convention (Revised), 1949 (No. 96)[9] and the Convention on Private Employment Agencies, 1997 (No. 181),[10] replacing Convention No. 96.

ILO Conventions Nos. 34 and 96 were adopted in the first half of the twentieth century, when the PES was introduced as the central agency offering employment services.[11] Countries which ratified Convention No. 34 were required to abolish for-profit employment agencies within three years, and for that reason the Convention was considered to be radical. Convention No. 96 was more flexible as it requested ratifying member States to accept either Part II of the Convention (i.e. the progressive abolition of fee-charging employment agencies managed with a view to profit and the regulation of other agencies), or else Part III (i.e. the regulation of fee-charging employment agencies including those managed with a view to profit).[12] Overall, these two Conventions were prohibitive with respect to the operation of private employment agencies (PREA) and vested the member States with the right of control over PREA activities.

After the Second World War, an ILO Convention on free public employment services was adopted, the Employment Services Convention, 1948 (No. 88). According to this international labour standard: 'Each Member of the International Labour Organization for which this Convention is in force shall maintain or ensure the maintenance of a free public employment service.' The essential duty of the employment service on the basis of Convention No. 88 is 'to ensure, in co-operation where necessary with other public and private bodies concerned, the best possible organization of the employment market as an integral part of the national programme for the achievement and maintenance of full employment and the development and use of productive resources'.[13]

Over the next four decades, PES maintained a strict monopoly on placement once ILO Convention No. 96, Fee-Charging Employment Agencies (Revised) was adopted in 1949.

---

8. This Convention was superseded by Convention No. 96 and is no longer open for ratification. Convention No. 34 is still in force in Bulgaria, Chile and Slovakia, but reports on its implementation in these three countries are no longer requested by the ILO Committee on Application of Conventions and Recommendations.
9. Convention No. 96 has been ratified by 42 countries, and remains in force in 32 countries as of August 2001.
10. There were 11 ratifications as of December 2001.
11. The Employment Service Convention (No. 88) was adopted a year before, i.e. in 1948, a year ahead of the adoption of Convention No. 96.
12. Article 2.1 of ILO Convention No. 96, ILOLEX (the ILO database on international labour standards (Geneva)).
13. ILO Employment Service Convention, 1948 (No. 88), Articles 1 and 2.

Although not all members of the ILO ratified the above instruments, the level of ratification has been impressive, especially for Convention No. 88. As of May 2003, Convention No. 88 has been ratified by 86 countries while Convention No. 96 has been ratified by 42 countries with 10 denunciations, six of which are due to ratification of Convention No. 181. Convention No. 181 has 13 ratifications so far.

B. The End of the PES Monopoly on Placement

Generally, the PES has always had to manage a large number of unemployed workers, some of whom it has had difficulty in placing. This partly explains its alleged ineffectiveness. Private employment agencies on the other hand often find jobs for easy-to-place workers (there are some exceptions, however, such as the Dutch 'start' agencies). The PES dilemma is as follows: either leave easy-to-place job seekers to the private agencies and face criticism for inefficiency and a bad image, or compete with private employment agencies for the same workers. The dilemma can only be solved through co-operation between public and private employment agencies.[14]

In the late 1980s and 1990s, more and more countries expressed dissatisfaction with the PES monopoly on placement. There were additional factors involved. First, the post-war era of full employment was long over. There were oil price shocks and adjustment measures in the industrialized countries but also in other parts of the world. Part-time and temporary work became more common, and neo-liberalism seemed to be gaining ground. More emphasis was placed on active labour market programmes and workfare approaches. PES had to deal with growing unemployment but the resources allocated were constrained by public-spending budgets. National PES could not provide narrowly customised services with the limited funds at their disposal, while PREAs were prepared to offer such services. Hence, the ban on PREAs became increasingly unjustifiable at least in the eyes of employers, who were ready to pay for private-sector labour market services. It is mainly the employers' position that prompted the change, but job seekers played a role too.

As unemployment in all segments of the labour market became too widespread for PES to cope with alone, PREAs were capable of alleviating the problem, together with PES. The number of temporary work businesses had been growing steadily in many OECD countries. Their activities became more visible from year to year; although the number of temporary workers in total employment still remained at around 10 per cent in the OECD area. More and more job seekers turned to temporary work as some preferred flexible working time while others could not find good permanent posts. Furthermore, economic globalization accelerated the growth of the PREA market. Several powerful worldwide temporary work businesses appeared such as Manpower, Adecco, and Kelly Services. They set up branches in transition economies and developing countries as well, where they continue to operate successfully.

The PES monopoly was formally removed in a large number of developed countries in the late 1980s and 1990s, and the number of PREAs grew rapidly.

Many OECD countries have taken steps to increase competition in areas that were dominated by public monopolies in the past. The goal has been to improve the production and delivery of public services. Several governments have introduced market signals to make the PES open to competition in order to improve its overall

14. Auer, P., personal communication (Geneva, 23 November 2001).

effectiveness. This has involved i) liberalizing the rules and regulations governing PREAs; ii) using market-type mechanisms such as contracting out; and iii) introducing organizational reforms such as separating purchasers and providers of job seeker services.

Deregulation of placement services is thus to some extent the result of a general trend, including a weakening of PES, though dissatisfaction with their performance has played a role too. Active labour market policies pursued by PES in the OECD area failed to bring down the high unemployment rates of the 1980s. The PES were blamed, it is argued here that the fault was not solely theirs. There were other reasons for labour market failures, but their discussion is beyond the scope of the present paper.

Individual job seekers were dissatisfied with PES, complaining of poor quality services in the absence of competitors. Clients wanted a choice. Such considerations gradually eroded the PES monopoly on placement.

In 1997, the PES monopoly on placement was brought to an end through the adoption of the Convention on Private Employment Agencies, 1997 (No. 181), 48 years after the adoption of Convention No. 96. Convention No. 181 was essential for countries with rapidly increasing PREAs, but also for workers who needed protection in their dealings with private employment agencies.

C. PREA Convention No. 181, 1997 and PREA Recommendation No. 188, 1997

At international level, attitudes towards the PES monopoly on placement changed in 1997 with the adoption of ILO Convention No. 181 Private Employment Agencies which recognized and legalized PREAs as providers of the following labour market services:

(a) services for matching offers of and applications for employment, without the private employment agency becoming a party to the employment relationships which may arise therefrom;

(b) services consisting of employing workers with a view to making them available to a third party, who may be a natural or legal person (referred to below as a 'user enterprise') which assigns their tasks and supervises the execution of these tasks;

(c) other services relating to job seeking, determined by the competent authority after consulting the most representative employers' and workers' organizations, such as the provision of information, that do not set out to match specific offers of and applications for employment.[15]

According to the provisions of Convention No. 181, PREAs are generally not allowed to charge directly or indirectly, in whole or in part, any fees or costs to workers.[16] However, exemptions are made for certain categories of workers, generally in higher paid professions, or for certain services provided. Any such exemptions are to be made in consultation with workers' and employers' representatives. Thus, the provision of basic, or core, labour market services to workers has to be free, regardless of whether such services are provided by public or private operators.

---

15. Convention on Private Employment Agencies (No. 181), Article 1, ILOLEX.
16. ILO Convention No. 181, *ibid.*, Article 7.1.

ILO Convention No. 181 has changed the prevailing paradigm of relying solely on a free PES and has a number of attractive new features which merit special discussion. In particular, this Convention:

- extends the scope of the previous ILO Convention No. 96 of 1949 on fee-charging employment agencies to include, in addition to intermediaries in placement, other emerging private agencies such as labour skill providers and suppliers of direct employment support services to respond to the new realities of the modern labour market;
- recognizes the fact that private employment agencies can contribute to the functioning of the labour market;
- sets general parameters for the regulation, placement and employment of workers engaged by private employment agencies. It provides, in particular, that national measures should be taken to ensure: (a) adequate protection for job seekers using the services of PREAs; (b) adequate protection of workers engaged by temporary work agencies; (c) adequate allocation of responsibilities between PREAs and user enterprises in relation to protection of workers engaged by temporary work agencies; and (d) that adequate machinery and procedures exist for the investigation of complaints, alleged abuses and fraudulent practices concerning the activities of PREAs; and most importantly,
- *promotes co-operation between the PES and PREAs for the best functioning of the labour market while the public authorities retain final authority for formulating labour market policy and utilizing or controlling the use of public funds earmarked for the implementation of that policy* (authors' emphasis).[17]

Convention No. 181 has thus created a radically new legal environment for employment services in the ratifying states. At the same time, it is a flexible legal instrument which provides the necessary freedom for governments to apply it to their own national context. It also contains provisions on co-operation between the PES and PREAs.

Importantly, the Convention sets minimum standards for the protection of temporary workers. Workers placed by temporary work agencies (TWAs) should receive decent treatment in terms of their conditions of work and the social protection extended to them. The minimum protection specified in the Convention includes: (a) freedom of association; (b) collective bargaining; (c) minimum wages; (d) working time and other working conditions; (e) statutory social security benefits; (f) access to training; (g) occupational safety and health; (h) compensation in case of occupational accidents or diseases; (i) compensation in case of insolvency and protection of workers' claims; (j) maternity protection and benefits, and parental protection and benefits. It is for the government to decide how to allocate responsibility for protection of these rights between the private employment agency and the enterprise.[18]

The protection of temporary workers is an important issue because more and more people are placed by temporary work agencies. In the United Kingdom, for example, 94 per cent of businesses use, or have used, a recruitment agency to meet staffing demand. Use of agencies across every commercial sector is widespread, with

---

17. Sims, E., ILO internal letter (Geneva, 3 August 2001).
18. ILO, ILOLEX (http://www.ilo.org), Convention on Private Employment Agencies, 1997 (No. 181), Articles 11 and 12 (Geneva).

many organizations using them as a central means of recruitment. Employers in some countries are increasingly dependent on the immediate availability of suitably experienced and skilled temporary staff.[19]

The adoption of ILO Convention No. 181 has thus been a milestone in the history of employment services, representing a legal response to an important global trend in employment services. The particular significance of this instrument is that it institutionalizes co-operation between public and private employment services, and so puts the issue on the international agenda.

The Private Employment Agencies Recommendation, 1997 (No. 188), which relates to Convention No. 181, contains specific provisions to promote co-operation between public and private employment services. Measures to promote co-operation between the PES and PREAs could include:

(a) pooling of information and use of common terminology so as to improve the transparency of labour market functioning;
(b) exchanging vacancy notices;
(c) launching joint projects, for example in training;
(d) concluding agreements between the PES and PREAs regarding the execution of certain activities, such as projects for the integration of the long-term unemployed;
(e) training of staff;
(f) consulting regularly with a view to improving professional practices.[20]

D. National Regulations on PREAs

National regulations on PREAs are diverse, falling into three main groups: countries with relatively liberal regulations on PREAs; countries which require PREAs to be licensed; and countries which ban PREAs.

A few countries have liberalized regulations on PREAs and impose no specific obligations on them. For example, in Finland[21] and the Netherlands,[22] no ministerial authorization is required to begin PREA activities. Most countries with operational PREAs, however, require that these agencies obtain a government licence before they commence business operations. Some examples of national regulations on PREA licensing are given below.

Ethiopia

'Any person who wishes to operate a private employment agency shall have to obtain a licence from the following authorities; 1) (. . .) from the Regional Authority responsible for the implementation of labour laws, if the employment service is confined within that region; 2) from the Ministry if the employment service is to be rendered in two or more regions; 3) from the Ministry if the employment service is

19. Recruitment and Employment Confederation of the United Kingdom: 'Mori research reveals flaws in DTI recruitment industry proposals', http://www.rec.uk.com (London, 28 November 2001).
20. ILO, ILOLEX, Recommendation on Private Employment Agencies, 1997 (No. 181), Article 17.
21. Act Respecting Manpower Services, No. 1005 of 26 November 1993 (Työvoimapalvelulaki), Helsinki.
22. Flexibility and Security Act No. 300, 14 May 1998 (Wet van 14 mei 1998, houdende wijzigingen van het Burgerlijk Wetboek, het Buitengewoon Besluit Arbeidsverhoudingen 1945 en van enige andere wetten, Flexibiliteit en zekerheid).

to hire and send abroad an Ethiopian worker to a third party' (Article 4, Private Employment Agency Proclamation, No. 104 of 1998).

Ireland

'A person shall not carry on the business of an employment agency except under and in accordance with a licence under this Act' (Article 2, Employment Agency Act, 1971).

Japan

The temporary work business (TWB) in Japan is regulated by the Law on securing the proper operation of worker dispatching undertakings and improved working conditions for dispatched workers (Law No. 88 of 5 July 1985, Tokyo). TWBs in Japan are divided into 2 categories: one is a general temporary work business and the other is a specified temporary work business. A general TWB[23] needs to be licensed for its activities by the Minister of Health, Labour and Wealth (Article 2 (4)). As temporary workers are not hired at all times their status can be unstable. Having given consideration to protection of those temporary workers who are employed by general TWBs, it has been decided that such TWBs should be reviewed before they start their operations. On the other hand, a specified TWB[24] is not required to obtain a licence for its activities (Article 2(5) of the above Law) as its temporary workers are regularly employed, and therefore such TWB is only requested to submit a notification of its activities before the commencement of business operations.

Malaysia

'No person shall carry on the business of a private employment agency except under the authority of a valid licence issued by the Director General' (Article 7(1), Private Employment Agencies Act 1981 (Act 246); Akta Agensi Pekerjaan Swasta 1981).

South Africa

'Any person who wishes to provide employment services for gain must apply for registration to the Director-General (of Labour) in the prescribed manner' (Article 24(1), Skills Development Act, 1998).

PREAs are still prohibited in many Arab states and some African countries.

IV. PRIVATIZATION AND DECENTRALIZATION OF EMPLOYMENT SERVICES

In the 1990s, a number of countries experimented with placing greater reliance on private operators in the labour market. Faced with the dilemma of higher efficiency

23. Article 2(4) of the Worker Dispatching Law states that 'a general temporary work business means a temporary work business other than a specific temporary work business'.
24. Article 2(5) states that 'a specific temporary work business means a temporary work business in which temporary workers (restricted to those whom a TWB regards as a business target) are composed exclusively of regularly employed workers'.

and cost-effectiveness on the one hand, and on the other the need to preserve a good image with tax payers to whom the PES is accountable, governments considered a new approach. Decisions, however, depended heavily on a number of factors, including the political situation, party politics and the state of the national economy.

Separating purchasers and providers is an important precursor to opening public services to competition. For example, if the PES provides training and also purchases it on the open market, it may deal with only one segment of the training market. This would make it difficult to compare theperformance of the PES with that of other training providers, and thus to say whether it was providing the most cost-effective service. Separating purchasers and providers is also a pre-requisite for the introduction of market-type mechanisms such as contracting out. Many OECD countries do contract out various active labour market programmes (ALMPs). But there are few robust studies determining the extent of cost savings achieved through contracting out and indicating whether they persist over the longer term. Studies of contracting out in other areas of the public service reveal fairly substantial cost savings: more studies are needed on the contracting out of PES services.[25]

Privatization of placement services covers the following activities: 1) privatizing the PES but maintaining its public funding; 2) shrinking the PES by reducing public funding and leaving a larger part of job placement to the private market; 3) shrinking the PES by forcing it to outsource implementation of some (or even all) of its activities to private companies. At the heart of privatization has been a concern for the interests of the individual job seeker. In many PES this concern was linked to a growing use of private organizations and voluntary associations to provide labour market delivery mechanisms.[26]

In Australia, considered by many as a classic example of PES privatization, the employment service is now supplied by private sector providers. More administrative decentralization is encouraged, using the service to ensure success in local labour market programmes.[27]

Recent labour market reforms in Australia included the formation of Centrelink as the initial contact point for job seekers. Centrelink provides for the initial registration, classification, referral to employment services and payment of job seekers. In addition, self-help facilities (job vacancy touch screens, personal computers, printers, photocopiers, facsimile machines, telephones and relevant newspapers) are provided in Centrelink offices as the first tier of job search support for job seekers. Profiling and classification of job seekers ensures that the appropriate interventions can be focused on those who are at highest risk of becoming or remaining long-term unemployed. The provision of a contestable employment services market is effected through the Job Network. Job Network services comprise: job matching, job search training, intensive assistance, the new enterprise incentive scheme (NEIS), and project contracting. In addition to the services provided under Job Network, the Department of Employment, Workplace Relations and Small Business of Australia supports efficient job matching by providing electronic services, including Australian Job Search.[28]

---

25. Fay, R.G., *Labour market and social policy* (Paris, OECD, Occasional Paper No. 25, document OECD/GD/(97)172, 1997), p. 3.
26. de Koning, J. *et al., Deregulation in placement services: A comparative study for eight EU countries* (Brussels, European Commission, Directorate-General for Employment, Industrial Relations and Social Affairs, January 1999), p. 7.
27. 'IT and the transformation of job seeking', in *Financial Times* (London), 8 February 2001.
28. Department of Employment, Workplace Relations and Small Business, Australia: *Australia for OECD: Labour market review of Australia*, Background paper (Canberra, August 2000), p. 39.

These have been the prominent organizational features of the Australian 'PES privatization' experiment. Most importantly, the PES outsources to private operators the provision of employment services to the long-term unemployed and other target groups such as youth. There are incentives for private operators to place as many unemployed persons as possible. Payments in respect of the unemployed who are referred to a private operator are conditional on successful placement and adequate job retention. Payment is made in instalments and only the first is unconditional. Thus, private operators have an interest in taking on the long-term unemployed and in placing them in jobs which they will keep for a reasonable period. In a classical public employment service the situation may be different. The financial incentive is a key difference in the privatized system.

In the EU countries the general tendency has been towards privatization of government services but also liberalization (for which a misnomer 'deregulation' has been sometimes used), by which one understands in the European context the removal of legal restrictions on private placement services. Liberalization may go hand-in-hand with privatization, but this is not necessarily the case. Liberalization need not be far-reaching. It may simply mean the removal of a ban on private placement, while a completely state-subsidized PES is maintained at the same time. In that situation private agencies would be more or less forced to concentrate on new forms of placement services which were not offered by the PES at all. Liberalization would then lead to an increase in the total supply of placement services instead of a substitution of public services by private providers.[29]

As a result of the above developments, particularly in Europe, the respective roles of the main public and private service providers have changed. Until recently private employment services, especially placement and recruitment, focused primarily on highly skilled or better educated employees, while public employment services concentrated on blue-collar occupations. This distinction now seems to be diminishing. Some PES have broadened their work profile to include special services for highly skilled job seekers. They also offer selection services and hiring-out activities for employers. Conversely, in some countries, PREAs have started to provide services for hard-to-place job seekers.[30]

V. TYPES OF PES-PREA RELATIONSHIPS

The main change in PES-PREA relationships is the move from co-existence to co-operation. The first and simplest form of relationship implies shared ordinary working contacts. Regular contacts have not been common except in the United Kingdom and in Germany, where they have been formally endorsed by the Government.

The European Commission[31] has identified three possible types of relationship: first, co-operation in the fields of information and basic matching services and in active brokage and adjustment; second, complementarity in particular labour

29. de Koning, J. *et al.*, 1999, *op. cit.*
30. Employment Services and Readaptation – EURES (European Employment Service), *Relationship between private and public employment services* (Brussels, document HC/MRO/evh- EMPL/1058/00-EN, 13 April 2000), p. 1.
31. European Commission, *PES-PREAs relationship in a European framework*, Issue paper submitted to the Meeting of Heads of Public Employment Services within the EEA (Baden, Austria, 16 November 1998), Section II, p. 4.

market segments or in particular kinds of service; third, competition in providing services to employers with the possibility of fee-charging by PES.

All three approaches are being adopted. Co-operation or partnership is illustrated by the arrangements that have been made in France and the United Kingdom which allow the PES, for example, to fill PREA vacancies. The same arrangement is evident in joint ventures such as in the Netherlands between the PES and two major temporary work agencies to deliver a wide range of services to employers. Co-operation can also take the form of contracting with PREAs to deliver services for government, such as in St. Gallen, Switzerland, where PREAs were commissioned to assist unemployed people.[32] These partnerships aim at improving the services rendered to firms, increasing both the flexibility of the labour market and the employability of workers and job seekers.

The idea of complementarity is illustrated in Mexico, where 32 state employment systems have been set up to foster the exchange of information on openings and job seekers. In general, however, the PES may well decide to leave the professional and executive market largely to the private sector because it lacks the resources to provide a credible service. Competition exists naturally where the PES and PREAs are operating in similar segments of the market and this can be healthy in encouraging sensitivity to customer needs. However, PREAs complains of unfair competition where PES services are free or subsidized.[33]

The International Confederation of Temporary Work Businesses (CIETT), which is the most representative international association of PREAs for temporary work and which is financially supported by its members, agrees that areas of potential co-operation between PES and PREA include:

- pooling labour market information, including exchange of vacancies;
- subcontracting certain projects by PES to PREAs;
- training the staff;
- participating in committees or councils;
- training workers.[34]

With regard to the data on vacancies, in most countries PES serve notice to PREAs as to other employers and notifying vacancies is voluntary, with rare exceptions. The vacancies, however, should be properly described.

Formal relationships between PES and PREAs can be more effectively promoted through the creation of co-operation councils or steering committees with representatives from both sides. This seems to be a feasible and efficient way of maintaining a permanent dialogue on issues of interest to both parties. However, it should be kept in mind that the public employment services themselves in many countries are managed, or assisted, by advisory committees set up at different levels upon ILO recommendation (Box 2). The same type of management is not applied to PREA. PES participation in co-operation councils may require consultation with the social partners, which could be time-consuming. On the other hand, endorsement by the social partners guarantees that decisions represent their vested interest in specific types and modes of delivery of labour market services.

32. OECD, 'To prevent "creaming", PREAs are compensated on time-budget basis', in *Labour market policies in Switzerland* (Paris, OECD, 1996).
33. Phan Tuy *et al.*, *Public employment services in a changing labour market* (Geneva, ILO, 2001), Ch. 9, p. 154.
34. CIETT, *Overview of examples of co-operation between the public and private employment services* (Brussels, 2001), p. 4, http://www.ciett.org

Box 2: The Employment Service Convention, 1948 (No. 88)

Article 4

1. Suitable arrangements shall be made through advisory committees for the co-operation of representatives of employers and workers in the organization and operation of the employment service and in the development of employment service policy.
2. These arrangements shall provide for one or more national advisory committees and where necessary for regional and local committees.
3. The representatives of employers and workers on these committees shall be appointed in equal numbers after consultation with representative organizations of employers and workers, where such organization exists.

The organizational and financial aspects of co-operation give rise to a variety of relationships between PES and PREAs. Outsourcing and contracting out are among them. Countries are striving to identify the best ways of arranging organizational and financial co-operation between the public and private sectors. A certain degree of trial and error is involved but when positive results are achieved they represent the optimal relationship. This is especially important because no international recommendations on the subject exist as yet, although some progress has been made at regional or country level. It should be added that the characteristics of the national labour market, particularly the distribution of active and passive labour market measures, can affect the type of PES-PREA relations in a given country. For example, the need to deal more effectively with long-term unemployment facilitated the introduction of the Australian model of PES privatization, while a desire to promote labour mobility has given rise to some forms of private-public partnership in Belgium.

Most recently, public employment services in the European Union have been working towards a broader strategy of active partnership with all actors in the labour market, i.e. the social partners, business chambers/associations, institutions of basic and further training, vocational guidance, local governments, social and welfare authorities, and private providers of employment services. This strategy is designed to facilitate and provide a comprehensive range of services for job seekers. Networking is a key factor in achieving employment policy goals, and establishing partnerships at all levels is integral to an efficient PES. By co-operating with third parties, the PES can bring together several complementary capabilities, thus widening the range of services which may be delivered locally. This makes PES an important element of local economic development too.[35]

For some countries in other parts of the world the issues look much more problematic. In certain developing and transition economies where the PES is weak or even non-existent, attempts have been made to rely solely on private labour market operators, shifting responsibility for the provision of labour market services on to them. While private employment agencies operate in an uncertain legal environment in many of these countries, their number and basic data on them and their operations are likely to be unavailable to the authorities. Furthermore, PREAs do not always have a national representative body to engage in dialogue with the government. This situation deserves

35. EU/EEA, *The future of the public employment service*, Joint Mission Statement of PES in Europe, High Level Group of the PES (Paris, December 2000), p. 7.

special attention, and intervention by national policy makers and international organizations. The best approach is to promote a sound national PES as well as PREAs on the basis of ILO Conventions Nos. 88 and 181 respectively, and then to establish practical co-operation arrangements between the two.

In other countries there are examples of the 'self-regulation' of PREAs (the staffing sector), which may influence the modalities of PES-PREA co-operation. This could serve as an alternative to state regulation. In Denmark for instance, the Association of Danish Temporary Work Agencies stipulated that TWAs may not take fees from job seekers and that temporary workers should enjoy working conditions equivalent to those laid down in the prevailing labour market agreements. Self-regulation can also play a complementary role. For example, state regulation might deal with reliability and solvency criteria and leave the suitability criteria for self-regulation. State regulation and self-regulation can also have mutual effects. Government authorities can borrow from the texts of self-regulation documents and incorporate the same provisions in the state regulations. They can even support self-regulation of the different types of PREA. In the Netherlands, for instance, the authorities are delegating responsibility for regulation more and more to the social partners and to the sector. However, self-regulation does not function as an alternative to state regulation at the moment. Countries with the best developed self-regulation (like the Netherlands) still have highly developed state regulation as well.[36] Self-regulation can also take place in an international context. For instance, the International Confederation of Temporary Work Businesses (CIETT) has its own Code of Ethics (http://www.ciett.org).

A. National Practices

National practices have produced various types of co-operation arrangements between public and private employment agencies. A number of factors encourage collaboration. First, there are common points of interest: success in placing job seekers and sharing labour market information are important mutual interests. Second, the PES needs to ensure that its operations are cost-effective, given the limited nature of public funds at its disposal. That is why it outsources the implementation of some of its programmes to private operators. Third, private operators as a rule are better at providing specialized services, such as head-hunting, temporary work and placements abroad, which PES may not offer at all. Fourth, parallel and complementary operations in various segments of the labour market may contribute to smoother functioning of labour markets overall, with other positive outcomes such as employment growth.

Box 3 gives some idea of the basic functions performed by public and private employment agencies. The best chances for co-operation exist in respect of those functions which are carried out by both PES and PREAs, and where both have gained experience. Entrusting the private sector with new and unfamiliar functions will require capacity building for PREA staff, as well as organizational backstopping measures.

In addition to the difference in their basic functions, research has shown that public and private employment services still largely operate in different market segments, particularly in Europe. The results from employer surveys in Western Europe provide some background material on this point. Concerning occupational groups (but also sectors and qualification levels), PREAs and PES obviously work

36. de Koning, J. *et al.*, 1999, *op cit.*, pp. 29–30.

Box 3: Unique and common PES and PREA functions

Unique PES functions
- Administration of public active labour market programmes (all)
- Administration of unemployment benefits

Functions common to PES and PREA
- Job broking and placement
- Labour market training
- Labour market information (LMI)

Unique PREA function
- Temporary work (rental services)[37]

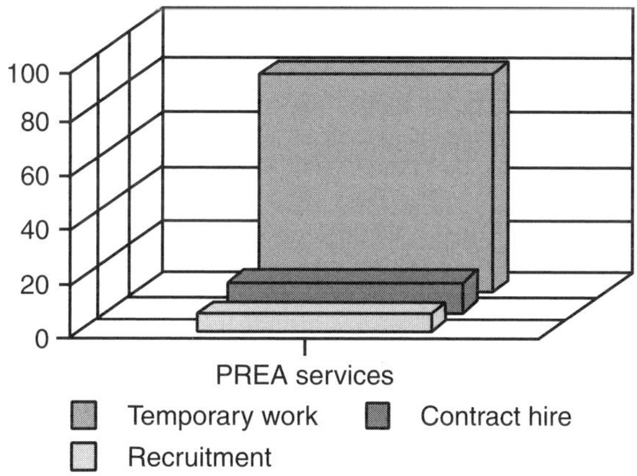

Figure 1. PREA services
Source: Swedish National Labour Market Board *(AMS), Relations of the public employment service with temporary work businesses and staffing services*, 1999, p. 3 (Stockholm).

in different market segments. But this complementarity function is only valid for intermediating agencies. If one includes, however, information on temporary work agencies used as a recruitment channel (at least for Belgium and the Netherlands where such information is available) the relationship seems to be more competitive. The importance of TWAs (as a recruitment channel) in certain labour market segments is similar to that of the PES.[38]

Much depends on national practices. In Sweden, for example, the bulk of services offered by private operators relate to temporary work, followed by relatively marginal contract hire and recruitment services (*see* Figure 1). That is probably why the Swedish PES co-operates with temporary work businesses and staffing agencies and gives them a service equivalent to that received by other employers recruiting personnel. The PES informs job seekers of the possibility of looking for work through manpower service mechanisms.[39]

37. In very few countries the PES runs temporary work branches.
38. de Koning, J. *et al.*, 1999, *op cit.*, p. 54.
39. Arbetsmarknadsstyrelesen, *Sweden's public employment service: Organization and activities* (Stockholm, document Icen 2001:8, March 2001), p. 11.

Some countries which are developing a one-stop model for PES are also creating a competitive market for employment services in which purchasers are separated from providers. Under such a system, job seekers and the unemployed receive streamlined services from the agencies concerned, while the agencies have additional incentives to place people in the labour market. This is particularly important in the case of disadvantaged groups such as the long-term unemployed. The incentives framework aims to reward employers providing labour market assistance by placing job seekers in employment.[40] It should be noted, however, that these innovative approaches have not yet been evaluated at international level.

PES-PREA co-operation can be greatly facilitated by administrative acts. In Germany, for example, the Federal Ministry of Labour adopted a circular in July 2000 entitled *Main directives for public employment service co-operation with temporary work agencies*. At that time, there were some 11,000 temporary work agencies and around 300,000 employers using temporary labour in Germany.[41] As stated, the Directives aim to promote and enhance PES-PREA co-operation as an official policy.

In the United Kingdom, public and private employment services are both delivering the New Deal nationwide programme to promote employment. More specific examples of the modalities of PES-PREA co-operation are given below.

Working Links[42] *(UK)*

The employment service in the United Kingdom is trying to expand co-operation between staffing agencies and Job Centres and has developed a good practice guide jointly with the Recruitment and Employment Confederation (REC), which is the main industry body.

The United Kingdom also has a public/private partnership company called Working Links to bring unemployed people back to work. Working Links is an example of advanced public-private co-operation, being formed by the following agencies: the Public Employment Service,[43] Management and IT consulting firm, Cap Gemini Ernst and Young,[44] and Manpower.[45] It targets the long-term unemployed but also extends its services to employers and job seekers. It offers job seekers training opportunities for acquiring new skills as well as financial assistance. Working Links adopts a differentiated approach to job seekers, taking into account their specific characteristics such as age, linguistic skills, place of residence and personal background; it develops a personalized style in dealing with each candidate.

---

40. OECD, *Labour market review of Australia*, Background paper (Paris, 2000), Section 6.2, p. 43.
41. German Federal Ministry of Labour, Circular No. La3 – 5160.2(41)A/5400 (Berlin, 14 July 2000).
42. http://www.workinglinks.co.uk
43. The new Department for Work and Pensions (DWP) was formed on 8 June 2001, to deal with employment, equality, benefits, pensions and child support. The activities of the Department for Education and Employment (DfEE) concerning employment policy and the Employment Service were transferred to DWP, while activities concerning education and skills development were transferred to another new Department for Education and Skills (DfES). The Employment Service is the executive agency within DWP (http://www.employmentservice.gov.uk).
44. http://www.cgey.com
45. http://www.manpower.co.uk

Services to special groups in the labour market and government-owned temporary work agencies (Belgium)

Belgium has a number of programmes for PES-PREA co-operation but the Walloon Region Pasarelle Interim was the first agreement within the framework of ILO Convention No. 181 (1997) providing for public/private-sector co-operation on the reintegration of hard-to-place workers.[46]

T-intérim is a temporary work agency run by the Belgian PES. This public agency was created in 1980 with the official title T Service Intérim and it remained the only public temporary work agency for a long time. In accordance with the policy of decentralizing PES T Service Intérim as such was dismantled and its units were introduced into every public employment service, that is, FOREM,[47] ORBEM[48] and VDAB.[49] T Service Intérim changed its official name and became t-intérim as of January 1998. The objectives of establishing this government-owned temporary work agency include the integration of job seekers into the labour market and the provision of more and better job opportunities for them. T-intérim aims, in particular, at assisting job seekers who are looking for a permanent job after employment on a temporary basis.

Co-operation between PES and organizations for temporary work[50] *(France)*

ANPE (Agence Nationale Pour l'Emploi, the French public employment service), PROMATT (Syndicat des Professionals du Travail Temporaire) and UNETT (Union Nationale des Enterprises de Travail Temporaire) have agreed to co-ordinate their work to attain their common objectives. Their particular aims are to improve the services rendered to firms, to increase the flexibility of the labour market, and to prevent long-term unemployment by improving job seekers' chances for labour market integration. Temporary employment agencies and local public employment offices are expected to exchange information on the labour market situation and employment measures in order to adjust their services according to the needs of job seekers. Within this framework, ANPE wishes to develop an active partnership at the local level with TWBs, to increase the range of labour market solutions offered to job seekers and to widen the range of reintegration opportunities for them. ANPE has introduced website links to some private employment agencies on its own website accompanied by brief explanations of each website. This has made it possible for job seekers to learn about more job opportunities and to save time by visiting only one website.

46. CIETT, 2001, *op. cit.*

47. Office Communautaire et Régional de la Formation Professionnelle et de l'Emploi (Community and Regional Vocational Training and Employment Office) http://www.hotjob.be

48. Office Régional Bruxellois de l'Emploi (Public Employment Service for Brussels) http://www.orbem.be

49. Vlaamse Dienst voor Arbeidsbemiddeling en Beroepsopleiding (VDAB, Public Employment Service for Flanders) http://www.vdab.be. The VDAB website contains links within the private temporary work agencies of its partners, and this offers job seekers the possibility of looking into more job opportunities as they also have access to other PREAs through PES.

50. European Employment Observatory Mutual Information System on Employment Policies (MISEP), *Policies* (Berlin, European Commission), 1995, No. 51, Autumn.

LMI through the Internet in Japan (Shigoto Joho Net)[51]

The public employment service in Japan offers Internet job-search facilities for clients.[52] The website displays vacancies and business information from the PES and from private service providers, including temporary work agencies. The aim is to promote the active use of labour market information by job seekers.

More in-depth co-operation between PES and PREA in using the Internet for the job broking/labour exchange function has been noted in the United States.

Public/private partnership in the United States

The US Department of Labor has forged a partnership between its electronic job exchange, America's Job Bank (AJB), and the private Internet company Monster.com. AJB is the largest government electronic job bank and Monster.com is the largest private electronic job bank. The purpose of the agreement is to establish mutually beneficial collaboration and to specify the responsibilities of the parties. On the basis of the agreement, Monster.com will adopt, use, and promote (as a standard) the Standard Occupational Classification (SOC) taxonomy, which is the government's occupational classification system. Monster.com plans to deploy SOC internationally in its web-based products. Where appropriate, Monster.com may recommend formal changes to the SOC through the SOC Policy Committee. The two will adopt, use and exchange information on job vacancies. The Department of Labor and Monster will cross-reference each other's job listings, exponentially increasing the opportunities for job seekers. It is believed that the combination of these two very large data sources will generate invaluable real time labour market information.[53]

Other concrete examples of PES-PREA co-operation at country level are described in a recent overview prepared by the International Confederation of Temporary Work Businesses (CIETT).[54]

Transition countries have endorsed the replication of best experiences in public-private employment service partnerships despite the fact that private labour market operators appeared in these countries only recently and are not yet as developed and mature as elsewhere. The first International Congress held in Kiev in September 2000 'Eurasia: Employment in the XXIst Century' recommended expanding co-operation between public and private employment agencies in the transition countries of that region.[55]

---

51. This system was originally entitled 'Kan min renkei shita koyo joho system' and was launched on 8 August 2001. Since March 2002, this system became accessible by calling from a mobile phone.
52. Hellowork Internet Service: In March 1999 the Tokyo Public Employment Security Offices started providing job-search services through its Internet homepage http://www.hellowork.go.jp and in April 2000 provision of the same services was launched nationwide, mostly in large cities. Job seekers are now able to search job vacancies from home with their computers. This service is relatively popular and more and more job seekers are visiting this website as they may access it at any time without visiting the employment service to look for vacancies. This service allows more people to visit the same site simultaneously, which was not possible before. People do not need screen pages of those files, and it has been observed that the office is now quieter. Company names and addresses are not displayed in order to prevent possible abuse of such information.
53. 'AJB forms partnership with monster.com', 4 September 2001, http://www.icesa.org
54. CIETT, 2001, *op. cit.*
55. ILO, *The first international congress Eurasia: Employment in the 21st century*, Russian language text (Moscow, ISBN 92 9 412533 6), pp. 182–183.

It is worth mentioning that the European Commission has adopted its own general recommendation on PES-PREA partnerships, particularly with regard to exploiting synergies between public employment services and other relevant actors in the labour market. This entails developing good relations with the expanding sector of private employment services. Partnerships with self-help institutions for the unemployed can also improve service delivery.[56]

B. Temporary Work Negotiations between Social Partners

No universal guidelines on PES-PREA partnerships have yet been elaborated, although it is generally agreed that any recommendations should incorporate the provisions of the relevant international labour standards. The countries which have ratified the ILO Conventions on employment services, both public and private, are obliged to comply with their provisions.

Although little has been achieved at global level, more progress has been made at regional level, particularly in Europe. The Union of Industrial and Employers' Confederations of Europe (UNICE) and the European Trade Union Confederation (ETUC) reached an agreement on part-time work in June 1996 and another agreement on fixed-term work in March 1999.

The next step in the negotiating process included talks on temporary work, but these were less successful, and no agreement has yet been reached. The chief difficulty is the question of putting temporary agency workers on the same footing as other categories of workers for the purposes of equal treatment and adequate protection.

EURO-CIETT, representing temporary work business in Europe, announced in October 2001 that it reached agreement with the social partners on a Joint Declaration on the Objectives of the Future Directive on Private Agency Work.

The Joint Declaration, agreed within the framework of the Social Dialogue at the sectoral level, calls on the Commission to ensure that the future Directive:

1. Recognizes the use of agency employment as a means to enhance job opportunities and integration in the labour market in particular for special and/or disadvantaged groups.
2. Establishes the principle of equal treatment, at two levels:
   a) The equal treatment obligations which arise from the employment relationship between an employer and the worker, being the agency and the agency worker.
   b) The equal treatment obligations which arise from the fact that agency workers are assigned to work for and under the control of a user-enterprise.
3. Asks Member States to periodically identify and review obstacles which may prevent agency work from playing a positive role on the labour market and eliminate them if appropriate.[57]

On 29 March 2002, the European Commission issued a proposal for a European Parliament and Council Directive on working conditions for temporary agency workers. This proposal aimed to ensure equal treatment between temporary

56. European Commission, *The modernization of public employment service in Europe: Three key documents* (1999, Luxembourg, Directorate-General for Employment, Industrial Relations and Social Affairs, Unit V/A), p. 19.
57. http://www.ciett.org

agency workers and comparable workers in the user company on a range of basic working conditions, including pay, working time, breaks and holidays.[58]

Euro-CIETT, however, expressed its disappointment with the content of the proposal and its possible impact on job creation. In particular, Euro-CIETT did not support the Commission's choice to establish as a rule that the comparable worker is a worker of the user enterprise, regardless of the proposed exceptions, as no other European legislation allegedly attempted to achieve non-discrimination by comparing the working conditions of workers employed by different employers.[59]

In 2003, the Euro-CIETT urged the European Council to maintain the notion that user comparability should only apply to minimum pay provided that the agency worker is fully integrated in the user enterprise; through reinstating the concept of an integration period of the agency worker in the user enterprise before user comparability applies; and to extend the period originally proposed by the Commission to 12 months. The draft directive is to recognize temporary work agencies as employers. As employers, temporary work agencies have:

a) the right to determine the working conditions of their employees, the agency workers,
b) a legal obligation not to discriminate between their employees, the agency workers.[60]

C. Gains and Problems in Co-operation

The Employment Service Convention, 1948 (No. 88) provides that the staff of a free public employment service is to be composed of *public* (authors' emphasis) officials whose status and conditions of service are such that they are independent of changes of government and of improper external influences and, subject to the needs of the service, are assured of stability of employment.[61] When the public employment service outsources its functions to private operators whose employees work under different rules as compared to government service, they fulfil the above functions *in lieu* of PES public civil servants.

Problems in co-operation between public and private employment agencies are not common, but certain difficulties could arise. Most notable among them is the tendency of private agencies to consider the labour market information at their disposal as their own property, including data on 'hot' vacancies and lucrative placements such as top managerial positions or uniquely skilled workers in high demand with employers. The International Confederation of Temporary Work Businesses stated recently:

> on the specific principle of Article 13 of ILO Convention 181 of providing information to the public employment services, CIETT points out that some of the information that may be requested by the competent authority on the structure and activities of private employment agencies may be market sensitive and if made public would seriously undermine the competitiveness of the companies affected.[62]

58. EIRO On-line, http://www.eiro.eurofound/2002/04/Feature/EU0204205F.html, 23 May 2002.
59. Euro-CIETT, 'Commission Directive Agency Work. Euro-CIETT disappointed with its content and impact on job creation', 22 March 2002, http://www.ciett.org (Brussels).
60. http://www.ciett.org/euro_ciett/0,000002,en,21,1,euro_position.htm, 20 May 2003.
61. ILO Convention on Employment Service (1948), Article 9.1, ILOLEX.
62. CIETT, 2001, *op. cit.*

Compensation issues have been raised in some countries by the public employment service in its dealings with PREAs. For example, the Netherlands Public Labour Offices ('Arbeidsvoorziening') wanted varying amounts of compensation in respect of information needed for the PREAs to place candidates, while the regional PES offices 'felt out of their element' with the new co-operation/partner agreements. Besides, the CVs of job seekers were not systematically provided to the PREAs by the Arbeidsvoorziening.[63]

The majority of PREAs are in the temporary work business. There have been criticisms in the press and on the part of a few trade unions as well that some part-time and temporary jobs are very badly paid and involve poor working conditions with limited career prospects.[64] If temporary positions are going to be filled as a result of co-operation between public and private employment services, they will share responsibility for addressing such criticisms. This underscores the importance of applying the same principles and rules in job placement, which respect international labour standards. Temporary work is relatively important in the services sector in the OECD area, with an employment share amounting to 12.4 per cent (0.84 per cent overall).[65]

The situation is highly country-specific and although private placement may be authorized, legal restrictions may still exist. The private partners need to enjoy a legal status which does not hinder co-operation with the public service.

Not an obstacle to PES-PREA partnership in a direct sense is the fact that the PES in many countries, unlike PREAs, officially promotes social equity in the provision of labour market services for vulnerable groups such as persons with disabilities, older workers and youth. Being disadvantaged, these people bear the brunt of negative labour market developments such as open unemployment and discrimination. PES uses public money to invest in these groups, but private agencies may not do this unless they receive some financial compensation from the PES. Employers may not be willing to incur extra hiring costs in respect of vulnerable groups, knowing that PES will subsidize them, or to assist otherwise in finding employment for members of special groups. Private agencies, on the other hand, do not have access to public funds and need incentives such as 'purchaser' (PES) – 'provider' (PREA) agreements which provide financial guarantees.

PES retains a dual role in that it provides labour market services and purchases them at the same time. It is PES that decides, for example, which of the unemployed to train or to have trained at the provider's facilities. Drawing on experience in the OECD countries, the advantages and disadvantages of purchaser/provider agreements for the efficiency of operations of PES are presented in Box 4.

Some countries relying on the privatization model officially report savings and increased effectiveness resulting from outsourcing the provision of labour market services to private operators.

Experience in Australia demonstrates some of the challenges of providing services efficiently and effectively with public funds. In 12 months, around 269,800 job seekers participated in the Intensive Assistance (IA) Programme in Australia in 1999–2000. IA typically provides up to 12 months of personalized assistance to disadvantaged job seekers. Providers are paid an up-front fee and an outcome fee for

---

63. CIETT, 2001, *op. cit.*
64. OECD, *Employment outlook* (Paris), June 2001, p. 91.
65. OECD, *Employment outlook* (Paris), June 2001, Table 3.B.2.

Box 4: Advantages and disadvantages of purchase/provider arrangements between public and private employment agencies in terms of efficiency of operations

Advantages

These arrangements can:

- improve working relationship and clarify responsibilities
- minimize conflicts of interest
- facilitate contestability and competition
- enhance accountability
- increase managerial autonomy
- improve client responsiveness
- reduce client 'capture'
- assist managers to prioritize activities

Disadvantages

These arrangements can:

- reduce communication and co-ordination
- heighten the focus on inputs rather than outputs
- be based on inappropriate contacts (e.g. too general or, alternatively, too flexible)
- produce high transaction and compliance costs
- result in loss of in-house expertise
- blur lines of accountability
- disrupt staff

Source: OECD, 1997. Making the public employment service more effective through the introduction of market signals, Box 1 (Paris).

participants who find and keep suitable employment. An evaluation study has found that IA:

- participants are substantially more likely to leave income support than similar job seekers who have not recently participated in the programme: the prospects of leaving income support are some 47 per cent higher – that is, IA off-benefit outcomes averaged over 31 per cent compared with a little over 21 per cent for the control group, yielding a net impact of 10 percentage points;
- compares with the suite of previous labour market programmes operating in the mid-1990s (under Working Nation), in terms of off-benefit net impacts (which averaged 10 per cent, although individual programmes varied widely);
- is relatively cost effective at around US$22,000 per net impact outcome compared with a Working Nation average of US$35,100 for the programmes IA replaced; and
- was associated with a compliance effect (of around 3 percentage points), through job seekers leaving benefits between referral and commencement of the programme – the inclusion of impacts associated with compliance effects reduces the cost per additional off-benefit outcome substantially to US$16,500.[66]

66. Department of Employment, Workplace Relations and Small Business (DEWRSB), Australia, *Job Network: A net impact Study*, EPPB report (Canberra, April 2001), p. 2.

The performance of Australian Job Network may also be assessed in terms of cost-efficiency. The cost-per-participant (unit cost) is US$200, US$425 and US$2260 for Job Matching, Job Search Training and Intensive Assistance respectively. Costs-per-employment outcome are US$290 for Job Matching, US$1130 for Job Search Training, and US$6200 for Intensive Assistance. Comparing the estimates for Job Search Training and Intensive Assistance to costs applying under the programmes replaced by Job Network shows that:

- Job Search Training is delivered at about half the cost-per-job of Job Clubs (which offered a similar type of assistance).
- The cost-per-job for Intensive Assistance is, in real terms, more than US$5000 lower than the average of the major labour market programmes operating in 1995–1996 that it replaced.[67]

At the same time there were other, more pessimistic evaluations of the Australian model relying on private service delivery in partnership with the public employment service, especially in respect of the long-term unemployed whom the model targeted specifically. For example: 'On the grounds of value for money – if the more-difficult-to-place job seekers were to receive only minimal assistance, the government has paid a substantial fee but received little in return'.[68] Certainly, further research and investigation is required on the new modes of PES-PREA co-operation, particularly their cost-effectiveness and the equity issues that arise.

One cannot exclude certain local rivalries between the public employment service and private agencies, should the PES expand its services to the spheres where PREAs are active, such as improved services for employers or individualized labour market services.

Some tentative conclusions can be drawn from the above discussion.

- As co-operation always begins with contacts, working contacts between responsible representatives of public and private employment agencies are to be encouraged at all levels, that is, local, regional, national and international. Preparation of guidelines on co-operation between PES and PREAs by international experts can play a considerable facilitating role in respect of the above partnerships at country level.
- There seems to be consensus among those concerned that ILO Convention No. 181 (1997) provides for a general and flexible framework of co-operation between public and private employment agencies.
- Establishing co-operation councils between PES and PREAs can serve as a useful institutional measure promoting co-operation between the two. PES and PREAs have their own segments of the labour market while PES also is a public provider.
- At advanced stages of co-operation, should the private sector be entrusted to deliver labour market policies, the PES is ultimately responsible for providing support to job seekers and for implementing public employment policies and labour market programmes as a statutory duty.

---

67. Department of Employment, Workplace Relations and Small Business (DEWRSB), Australia, *Job Network Evaluation: Stage two – Progress report* (Canberra, February 2001), p. 6.
68. Department of Employment, Workplace Relations and Small Business (DEWRSB), Australia, *Job Network Evaluation: Stage one – Implementation and market development* (Canberra, February 2000), p. 89.

- As the public is always concerned by possible abuse, particularly in the private sector, a verification mechanism can be created to monitor organizational, managerial, and financial aspects of co-operation between public and private employment agencies. Such co-operation should be made transparent in respect of both process and outcomes, possibly on the basis of existing structures.
- Co-operation between public and private employment agencies in the future will be affected by the allocations made for labour market policies at national level, notably the balance between active and passive measures, the capacity to deliver of each partner and their credibility with clients.
- Co-operation between public and private actors can also be affected by the chosen national model: should public employment services be carried out by government agencies or should implementation be outsourced to private companies? In the latter case private providers become 'arms' of the public employment service and public/private co-operation assumes a different, more integrated approach.
- Conducting joint activities such as job fairs, workshops on labour market developments, labour market information projects, etc., always contributes significantly to PES-PREA co-operation.
- The fact that PES and PREAs in many countries operate in largely different segments of the labour market reduces tension between them and facilitates co-operation through complementarity of activities and synergy effects. Studying positive examples of PES–PREA co-operation can be advantageous to other countries.
- The potential of public-private co-operation in employment services is enormous, and promoting it would benefit the social partners and the general economic and social development of nations.

National Reports

4A. Belgium – A General Overview

Frank Hendrickx

I. GENERAL INTRODUCTION

In essence, temporary jobs have long been a feature of the labour market in Belgium. Since the existence of modern labour law, employers have been able to hire employees for the performance of a temporary task or for a fixed period of time. However, more recent is the use of 'temporary work'. This concept refers to the business of temporary work agencies, whereby the agency puts employees at the disposal of users. Here, the employer's authority is 'delegated' to the user, but the temporary work agency remains the legal employer of the worker. This concept has expanded in meaning with the growth of a sector which was initially regulated by some collective agreements and a *provisional* law of 28 June 1976. The provisional law nominally covered a period of only four years, or a maximum five years. When it expired, the legal gaps it left were filled by several collective agreements. These were concluded in the National Labour Council, meaning that they became legally binding for all employers and employees of the private sector in Belgium. The drive for greater flexibility extended the use of temporary work and, eventually, in 1987 a permanent law was passed. It is entitled the Law on Temporary Work of 24 July 1987.[1] Since 1993, a specific Joint Committee has functioned on behalf of the temporary work sector (Joint Committee No. 322).

During the eighties there have been important constitutional reforms in Belgium. Belgium became a federal state, with three Regions (Brussels, Flanders, Wallonia) and three Communities (Flemish, French, German) each having competences conferred upon them by the federal constitution. Although labour law and social security have remained national matters, employment policies have been transferred to the regions, including employment services. The competence to regulate the recognition of temporary work agencies is now exercised by the regions, resulting in a number of regional decrees mostly in the eighties and nineties. These regional laws will be discussed below.

In legal terms, temporary work, governed by the Law of 24 July 1987 on Temporary Work, is an activity performed under *an employment contract* to carry out one of the following tasks:

- To replace a permanent employee;
- To respond to a temporary increase in workload; and
- To perform exceptional work.[2]

1. *Belgian State Gazette*, 20 August 1987.
2. Article 1, §1 Law on Temporary Work.

R. Blanpain & R. Graham (eds.), Temporary Agency Work and the Information Society, 47–62

Temporary work can be provided by a direct relationship between employer and employee or by a trilateral relationship, i.e. whereby an employer calls on a temporary work agency which provides a temporary worker. This article will mainly concentrate on temporary work in the framework of a trilateral relationship, meaning that the concept will be used in terms of temporary agency work. For some aspects reference will be made to other kinds of temporary work.

The following statistics on temporary work in the Belgian labour market for 2001 are worth mentioning.[3] In that year, approximately 133.8 million hours were worked in the temporary work sector. With regard to the proportionate regional use of temporary work, Flanders represented 62.44 per cent, Wallonia 25.80 per cent and Brussels 11.76 per cent of the overall amount. As far as the structure of the temporary work sector is concerned, there were about 986 temporary work agencies in operation in 2001, with 315,763 temporary workers, and on average 68,183 temporary workers per day, and temporary work represented 1.98 per cent of overall employment.

II. TEMPORARY WORK

§1. Notion

As explained above, the concept of temporary work is defined in the Law of 24 July 1987 on Temporary Work. Temporary work is activity performed under an employment contract to replace a permanent employee; to respond to a temporary increase in workload; or to perform an exceptional work. These are the only reasons for which temporary work can be used.

§2. Cases in which Temporary Work is Allowed

A. Replacement of a permanent employee

The replacement of a permanent employee is possible in the following instances:[4]

- For the temporary replacement of a permanent employee whose employment contract has been suspended. Such replacement is not possible if the employment contract of the permanent employee has been suspended for reasons of lack of work for economic reasons or bad weather.[5] An employment contract for temporary work is legally permitted, however, in case of sickness, pregnancy leave, etc.
- The temporary replacement of an employee whose employment contract was ended.
- The temporary replacement of a civil servant who does not hold his office either wholly or partly.
- The replacement of an employee who has temporarily diminished his working time in accordance with the legal provisions regarding reduction of professional working.

3. Latest available numbers (2001) obtained from Federgon, federation of temporary work agencies: www.federgon.be
4. Article 1, §2 Law on Temporary Work.
5. *See also* the collective agreement concluded in the Joint Committee on Temporary Work on 14 May 1997.

Except for the replacement of an employee whose employment contract was ended, the length of the replacement is not limited in time. No prior permission is required either.

In the case of an employee whose employment contract was ended, the procedures and duration of temporary work are further determined by collective agreement, concluded in the National Labour Council.[6] A distinction can be made between temporary work without intermediation of temporary work agencies and temporary work provided by a temporary work agency.

1. Temporary work without intermediation of a temporary work agency

a. Procedure

The temporary replacement of an employee whose employment contract has been terminated with a *term of notice* or because of dismissal for *serious cause*, can only take place when specific conditions and procedures are followed.[7] The temporary replacement of an employee whose employment contract has been terminated otherwise, is not subject to the specific conditions or modalities, but prolongation of the replacement is subject to the specific conditions and procedures.

Replacement can only take place with the *prior permission of the trade union delegation* of the enterprise where the employee is replaced. Within a period of three working days after the permission has been received, the employer must inform the local labour inspectorate. In the event that no trade union exists, the employer needs to obtain the permission of the *trade union organizations* that are represented on the Joint Committee which is applicable to the enterprise. If there is no such Joint Committee, or if there is no active Joint Committee, then such permission should be obtained from the unions represented on the *National Labour Council*.

Where permission is received, or if there is no decision within a period of seven days following the employer's request, the employer may replace the employee concerned, on condition that the employer *informs the competent local labour inspectorate* within a period of three days from receipt of the permission, or from expiry of the aforementioned seven day-period.

If there is no agreement among the trade union organizations, the employer may request the local labour inspectorate to reconcile the viewpoints. If the reconciliation fails, the employer must request a decision from the public servant, who will give a binding opinion on the matter.

In the event that no trade union exists, and the employment contract is terminated because of the death of the employee, agreement of the parties, or dismissal for serious cause, the employer may provisionally replace the employee with a temporary worker for a maximum period of fifteen days, from when the request was made to the trade union organizations.

6. Collective Agreement No. 58, concluded in the National Labour Council on 7 July 1994, extended by Royal Decree of 23 September 1994, *Belgian State Gazette*, 18 October 1994; amended by Collective Agreement No. 58*bis*, concluded in the National Labour Council on 25 June 1997, extended by Royal Decree of 14 September 1997, *Belgian State Gazette*, 15 November 1997.
7. Article 3 C.B.A. No. 58.

b. Duration

The duration of the replacement of the permanent employee is limited.[8] In case of replacement of a permanent employee whose employment contract has been terminated, the duration of the replacement is limited:

- To a period of three months, starting from the moment of termination, in case of termination with a term of notice;
- To a period of six months, starting from the moment of termination, in case of termination for serious cause;
- To a period of three months, starting from the moment of termination, in case of other forms of termination. In this case, there is a possibility of prolongation for a *total* duration of three months.

2. *Temporary work provided by a temporary work agency*

a. Procedure

1. The temporary replacement, via a temporary work agency, of an employee whose employment contract has been terminated with a *term of notice*, or for *serious cause*, can only take place following specific modalities and procedures mentioned below. The same applies to *prolongation* of a replacement. In the event of temporary replacement due to other forms of termination of the employment contract, there are no such specific modalities and procedures, except for the *prolongation* of the replacement.
2. Where there is a trade union delegation in the enterprise, the same procedure must be followed as explained above for the situation in which temporary work is not performed via a temporary work agency. If there is no trade union delegation, the temporary work agency must inform the *Social Fund for Temporary Workers* of the name and address of the user as well as of the number of the applicable Joint Committee. This communication should take place at the latest on the twentieth day of the month following the temporary employment of the temporary worker of the user firm. The user must communicate the same information if it is provided in the written agreement with the temporary work agency. The user must also provide the name of the temporary work agency.

b. Duration

Also in these cases, the duration of the replacement of the permanent employee is limited.[9]

The replacement of a permanent employee whose employment contract has been terminated, is limited:

- To a period of six months – with the possibility of extension for another six months – starting from the moment of termination, in case of termination with a term of notice;

8. Article 6 C.B.A. No. 58.
9. Article 5 C.B.A. No. 58.

- To a period of six months – with the possibility of extension for another six months – starting from the moment of termination, in case of termination for serious cause;
- To a period of six months – with the possibility of extension to a total maximum duration of six months – starting from the moment of termination, in case of other forms of termination.

B. Temporary increase in workload

Temporary work is permitted in cases of a *temporary increase in workload*. In the original version of Law of 24 July 1987, temporary work was permitted in order to cope with *an extraordinary increase* in the workload. This notion of 'extraordinary' increase in workload is also used in the 1971 Labour Act. According to the 1971 Act, overtime is permitted in order to respond to an extraordinary increase in workload.[10] The Law of 26 July 1996 modified the Law of 1987. It replaced the notion of 'extraordinary increase' by the much broader notion of 'temporary increase'.[11] It gave, in other words, greater possibilities to make use of temporary work.

Procedures and duration of temporary work are determined by Collective Agreement No. 58, concluded in the National Labour Council on 7 July 1994.[12]

1. Temporary work without intermediation of a temporary work agency

In the event of a temporary increase in work, temporary work is permitted, provided the trade union delegation or, in the absence of a union delegation, the trade union organizations agree in advance. The employer must inform the labour inspector that such agreement has been given within three working days.

In his request, the employer must state the number of employees involved and the duration of the temporary work. The request can only be made for a maximum period of one calendar month, except in the case of employment abroad, but it is renewable.

If the trade unions do not reply within seven days following the request, the employer may proceed to employ temporary labour, provided he so informs the labour inspector. If within seven days following the request the trade unions inform the employer of their disagreement, the employer must inform the labour inspector within three working days and request him to reconcile the differing viewpoints. If the attempt at reconciliation fails, the employer shall ask the labour inspector to give his opinion, which will be binding on the parties involved. If no favourable opinion is given within seven days, the employer may not have recourse to temporary work.

In the absence of a union delegation, the employer may provisionally have recourse to temporary work for a maximum period of fifteen days, following the request for temporary work. During one calendar year however, this provision shall apply only to the *first request* made for the same technical production unit and the same occupational category of workers (e.g. blue-collar or white-collar). If the employer is not authorized to have recourse to temporary work, he shall immediately end this provisional engagement. The employee, however, will receive any remuneration that remains due to him up to the end of his employment contract.

10. Labour Act of 16 March 1971, Article 25.
11. Law of 26 July 1996, Article 47.
12. *Belgian State Gazette*, 18 October 1994.

2. Temporary work provided by a temporary work firm

The procedure is alike but the renewable period of temporary work can be longer than one month. In his request, the employer must state the number of employees involved and the duration of the temporary work. The trade union delegation has to agree both to the number of employees involved and to the duration of the employment.

If there is no trade union delegation, temporary work is possible for a maximum period of six months, renewable for a second period of maximum six months. The procedure is the same as for the temporary replacement of an employee whose employment contract was ended. If the employer wants temporary work for a period longer than six or twelve months or longer than the shortened period in accordance with the above mentioned procedure, he has to follow the same procedure as for temporary work for a temporary increase in work without intermediation of a temporary work agency.

C. Exceptional work

Temporary work is also permitted in order to carry out 'exceptional work'. The concept is defined in Collective Agreement No. 36, concluded in the National Labour Council on 27 November 1981,[13] as follows.

In so far as it does not relate to the usual activities of the user undertaking, the following activities are considered to constitute exceptional work:

- work regarding the preparation, running and winding up of trade fairs, congresses, workshops, seminars, public events, parades, exhibitions, receptions, market research, inquiries, elections, special promotions, interpretations, removals;
- unloading of lorries, provided the union delegation of the user agrees in advance;
- secretarial work for businessmen staying temporarily in Belgium;
- work for embassies, consulates and international bodies, provided the Belgian representative trade unions have agreed in advance;
- performance of short and specialized tasks which require special professional qualifications. In this case the user shall inform the labour inspector 24 hours beforehand and must have the agreement of the union delegation or, in the absence of a union delegation, of the trade unions. If the unions disagree, agreement can be obtained by the competent joint committee;
- carrying out of new activities, when the employer has not yet been able to engage permanent employees, after having made an appeal to the director of the Regional Employment Service;
- work in urgent cases (e.g. in the event of accident or imminent accident, repairing machines or material, circumstances beyond control);
- to take stock, to draw up the balance sheet. The duration of such work shall not exceed seven days per calendar year.

§3. Cases in which Temporary Work is Prohibited

Even when the conditions to allow temporary work as explained above are met, the use of temporary workers provided by a temporary work agency may still be

13. Extended by Royal Decree of 9 December 1981, *Belgian State Gazette*, 6 January 1982.

prohibited in some cases. The most important exception is the prohibition on using temporary workers in cases of strike at the user enterprise. Collective Agreement No. 58 of 7 July 1994 concerning the procedure and duration of temporary work, concluded in the National Labour Council, implements this provision.[14]

In order to avoid abuses, temporary work has traditionally been prohibited in some particular sectors of industry and for some categories of workers, such as in the construction industry and removal companies (in relation to blue-collar workers).[15] As far as the construction industry is concerned, a recent decision of the Flemish Government modified the Decision of 8 June 2000 in order to permit temporary work in this sector.

III. THE TEMPORARY WORKER

§1. The Relationship between Worker and Agency

There is a legal presumption that the temporary worker is an employee of the temporary work agency. This is a presumption *juris et de jure*, which means that it cannot be refuted. Article 7, 3° of the Law of 1987 provides that 'the temporary employee is an employee who enters into a contract of employment with a temporary work agency to perform, for remuneration, work as permitted by this Law to the benefit of one or more users'.

A. Object and nature of the employment contract

The object of the contract is the performance of legally permitted forms of temporary work (outlined above). As regards its nature, the contract can be concluded for a fixed duration, for specific work, or for the replacement of a permanent worker. Therefore, the contract is in principle not a contract for an indefinite period. However, according to some authors, the conclusion of a contract for an indefinite period is not excluded either.[16] It is also possible for the temporary worker and the temporary work agency to conclude successive fixed-term contracts.

B. Form of the employment contract

The Law of 1987 stipulates that parties must conclude two separate contracts. The first of these contracts will indicate that the parties intend to conclude an employment contract for temporary work. This contract must be in writing, and must be concluded before the commencement of the first assignment under the temporary work agency. However, it does not have to be renewed every time the temporary employee accepts a new assignment from the same employer.

14. Extended by Royal Decree of 23 September 1994, *Belgian State Gazette*, 18 October 1994. *See* Article 8 of the Collective Agreement.
15. Law of 24 July 1987, Article 23 and Collective Agreement No. 36, concluded in the National Labour Council on 27 November 1981, extended by Royal Decree of 9 December 1981, *Belgian State Gazette*, 6 January 1982, Article 18. *See also* the Collective Agreement concluded in the Joint Committee for Temporary Work on 14 May 1997, Reg. No.: 44282/cob/322, *Belgian State Gazette*, 11 July 1997.
16. R. Blanpain, *Arbeidsmarktrecht*, Brugge, die Keure, 2001, pp. 86–87.

The second contract, which must also be in writing, is the actual employment contract for temporary work. This contract must be agreed at the latest within two working days of commencement of the first assignment.

If there are no such written contracts, the rules governing employment contracts for an indefinite period shall be applicable. However, in such a case, the employee may still terminate the contract without notice or payment in lieu of notice, until seven days after the first two days of initial employment.

C. *Trial clause*

Unless otherwise stated, the first three working days constitute a trial period, during which each party may terminate the contract without notice or compensation. When a temporary employee works with consecutive employment contracts for a definite period for the same user in the same position, consecutive trial periods are not allowed.[17]

D. *Contents of the employment contract*

The employment contract for temporary work must contain the following items:[18]

- the name of the user;
- the reason for the contract and, where applicable, the duration of the contract;
- the reason for the replacement;
- the occupational qualifications of the temporary employee;
- the place of employment;
- working hours; and
- the agreed remuneration and the benefits to which the employee is entitled.

The absence of one of the required items renders the temporary work contract null and void and consequently the employee is considered to be the employee of the temporary work firm, engaged on the basis of an employment contract for an indefinite period of time.

The temporary employee will also receive a document relating to the contract between the temporary work agency and the user.

§2. Remuneration, Seniority and Social Advantages

Remuneration of the temporary employee may not be lower than that to which he would have been entitled if he had been hired directly by the user as a permanent worker under the same conditions.[19] Departure from this stipulation is permissible, however, if equivalent benefits are granted by a collective agreement concluded in the joint committee for temporary work and extended by Royal Decree.

Seniority is usually only acquired on the basis of employment with the same employer, without interruptions. So normally a temporary employee will lose his seniority if he works for another temporary work agency, or when he has a period of

17. Collective Agreement concluded in the Joint Committee on Temporary Work on 30 June 1995, extended by Royal Decree of 6 June 1997, *Belgian State Gazette*, 28 November 1997.
18. Article 9 Law on Temporary Work.
19. Article 10 Law on Temporary Work.

inactivity between two assignments for the same temporary work agency. The Law of 1987 has tried in part to remedy this situation, and sets out specific rules for calculation of the seniority of the temporary employee.[20] In order to determine the seniority of the temporary worker, the following periods will also be taken into account:

- periods in which performance of the employment contract was suspended and during which the temporary employee was covered by the social security system, in so far as he has not been employed by another employer;
- a period of inactivity of one week or less (e.g. between two assignments with the same temporary work firm).

It should be noted that the periods of temporary work carried out for a user do not count towards calculation of seniority in the user firm in the event that the temporary worker becomes employed by the user.[21]

§3. Termination of the Contract

In principle, the general rules which govern termination of an individual labour contract also apply in cases of temporary work. In principle, a contract for a *fixed term* ends at the expiry of the period which was provided for; a contract for *specific work* ends when the work is finished; a *contract for replacement* ends when the replaced (permanent) employee returns to his job.

When a contract is for a fixed term or for specific work, the party that terminates the contract before expiry of its term, and without serious cause, is required to pay to the other party compensation equal to the amount of the remuneration due up to the expiry date, provided that this amount shall not exceed twice the amount of the remuneration corresponding to the period of notice that would have governed the contract had it been one of indefinite duration.[22] This compensation is not due where the underlying service agreement is terminated by the user, if the temporary work agency, for the remaining period, provides another job to the temporary worker which entitles him/her to the same remuneration and working conditions of an equal value.

If the employment contract was concluded as a contract for replacement of a permanent employee for a non-specified period, premature termination (i.e. before the end of the period of replacement) will give rise to compensation of three months' pay. This compensation is not due if the user is responsible for the premature termination and the employee receives comparable work from the temporary work agency for a period of three months.[23] If the employment contract was concluded as a contract for replacement of a permanent employee for a non-specified period, the temporary worker can terminate the contract with a term of notice of seven days where he/she has found other employment.[24]

§4. Employment with the User

Temporary workers and users are always free to alter their relationship and to conclude an employment contract. According to the Law of 1987, contractual

20. Article 13 Law on Temporary Work.
21. Labour Tribunal Brussels 4 March 1982, J.T.T. 1982, 233.
22. Article 14 Law on Temporary Work.
23. Article 15 Law on Temporary Work.
24. Article 15 Law on Temporary Work.

clauses prohibiting the hiring of a temporary worker by the user are considered to be null and void.[25]

IV. THE TEMPORARY WORK AGENCY

Temporary work agencies can only supply temporary workers as defined in the Law of 24 July 1987. If these businesses operate outside the scope of the law, they may lose their recognition and incur criminal sanctions. Furthermore, in order to operate as a temporary work agency, a governmental permit is required. The Flemish, the Walloon, or the Brussels' regional government provide the permit on fulfilment of certain conditions.

§1. Official Recognition

In order to have the maximum guarantee that the firm will respect its obligations to its temporary employees, as well as to the users, the law provides that temporary work firms can only operate in Belgium when they are recognized. Under the federalized Belgian State, this competence lies with the Regions.

A. Flemish Region

In Flanders, the rules regarding recognition are laid down in a Decree of 13 April 1999 concerning private employment services.[26] This decree covers not only temporary work, but also various other forms of private employment services. The decree also covers recruitment and selection businesses, headhunters, outplacement businesses, sports agents, etc. The Flemish government found its inspiration in the new ILO Convention 181. The Flemish regulation is only applicable in the Flemish Region, which excludes the Walloon and Brussels Regions, where there is still a general prohibition with regard to the operation of private employment services. The Decree of 13 April 1999 has been further implemented in a Decision of 8 June 2000.[27]

The operation of a private employment service as regulated by the 1999 Decree is subject to prior recognition by the (Flemish) Government. This formal licence must be obtained prior to operation or publicity regarding the business or its services. The governmental permit is issued by the Flemish Minister of Employment upon the advice of the so-called 'Advisory Commission'. This is a governmental body, established by law under the framework of the Social Economic Council of Flanders, in which the most representative trade unions and employers' organizations are represented. Each application for recognition as a private employment service will be considered by this Advisory Commission, which holds hearings at which cases can be presented and defended. In principle, a licence is given for an indefinite period and stays valid until governmental withdrawal. Furthermore, there are various conditions to be met, such as:

- to be properly formed as a commercial company with by-laws stating the nature of the activities;

25. Article 13 Law on Temporary Work.
26. *Belgian State Gazette*, 5 June 1999.
27. *Belgian State Gazette*, 11 November 2000.

- to be neither in a state of bankruptcy, nor the subject of bankruptcy proceedings, nor having requested or received a judicial agreement;
- the managers, business managers or persons having the authority to commit or to represent the company
  - may not have been prohibited to perform these duties, under the Royal Decree No. 22 of 24 October 1934 which prohibits certain condemned and bankrupt persons to perform particular duties;
  - may not have been held liable for the obligations or debts of a bankrupt company, during the period of five years preceding the request for recognition or renewal of recognition, under Article 35, 6°, 63*ter*, 123, p. 2, 7° or 133*bis* of the co-ordinated laws respecting commercial companies;
  - may not have been repeatedly or seriously in breach of the law respecting tax duties, social duties or the performance of the activity of a private employment service;
  - may not have lost their civil or political rights.
- fulfilling all duties with regard to taxes and social security;
- having no employment contrary to public order or contrary to social or tax legislation;
- considering all employees in an objective, respectful and non-discriminatory manner; not drafting or publishing personnel advertisements that may give rise to discriminatory treatment;
- respecting the privacy of employees;
- imposing no fee on the employee for any services;

The recognition is granted for an indefinite period. In some cases, the Government can withdraw the recognition, such as in cases of violation of the provisions of the 1999 Decree, after hearing the advice of the Advisory Commission.

B. Walloon Region

For the Walloon Region, the rules are laid down in the Decree of 27 June 1991[28] and the Decision of the Walloon Executive of 6 September 1991[29] and of 9 September 1993[30] concerning the recognition of temporary work agencies. The conditions required to obtain recognition are similar to those required in the Flemish Region. Moreover, the agency is obliged:

- to undertake to furnish the advisory committee with all the documents and information requested by this committee;
- to undertake not to send temporary employees, or to keep them working, in the case of a strike or lock-out in the enterprise of the user;
- to undertake to keep, for five years after the expiry of the contracts, a copy of each labour contract for temporary work and of the contract between the temporary work firm and the user;

---

28. *Belgian State Gazette*, 13 September 1991. Amended by decree of 28 April 1994 (*Belgian State Gazette*, 25 May 1994).
29. *Belgian State Gazette*, 30 October 1991.
30. *Belgian State Gazette*, 11 November 1993. Amended by the decision of the Walloon Executive of 21 September 1995, *Belgian State Gazette*, 14 October 1995.

- to undertake not to provide temporary employees, or to keep them working, in the case of a user who is in breach of the legislation respecting temporary work.

The recognition can be withdrawn when the firm:
- no longer complies with the conditions for recognition;
- is in breach of the social legislation and the legislation regarding temporary work. Before withdrawal of recognition, the temporary work agency must be heard or at least offered a hearing.

C. Brussels Region

For the Brussels Region, the rules are laid down in the Royal Decree of 3 December 1981[31] and the Ministerial Decision of 9 June 1982[32] concerning the recognition of temporary work agencies in the Brussels Region. The conditions required to obtain recognition from the Regional Secretary for employment are:
- to be properly formed as a commercial company, with temporary work as an exclusive activity according to the by-laws;
- to have a fully-deposited registered capital of 1,250,000 Belgian Francs (or 30,986.69 Euros);
- to undertake not to provide temporary employees, or to keep them working, in the case of a strike or lock-out in the enterprise of the user;
- to have joined a recognized social secretariat for employers, when the company is not based in Belgium.

The recognition can be suspended or withdrawn, after consultation with the National Labour Council, when the firm:
- no longer complies with the conditions for recognition;
- does not live up to the obligations required by social legislation or collective agreements;
- fails to respect the undertaking not to provide temporary employees, or to withdraw them, in the case of a strike or lock-out in the enterprise of the user.

The recognition cannot be suspended or withdrawn unless the temporary work agency has been heard, or has at least been offered a hearing.

§2. The Agency as an Employer

The temporary work agency is the employer of the temporary worker. This status entails the duty to comply with all obligations arising from normal labour and employment law as well as social security law. As indicated above, according to the Law of 1987, there is a legal assumption that the contract between the agency and the worker is a contract of employment.

---

31. *Belgian State Gazette*, 12 December 1981. Amended by the Decision of the Brussels Regional Government of 21 March 1996, *Belgian State Gazette*, 7 May 1996.
32. *Belgian State Gazette*, 29 June 1982. Amended by the Decision of the Brussels Regional Government of 21 March 1996, *Belgian State Gazette*, 7 May 1996.

V. THE USER

§1. The User – Temporary Work Agency Relationship

The relationship between the user and the temporary work agency is based on a contract. It consists of a service contract whereby the temporary work agency agrees to put a temporary worker at the disposal of the user for the performance of temporary work and whereby the employer's authority is delegated to the user. In case law, this service agreement is often labelled as a contract *sui generis*.[33] The relationship is strictly regulated by the Law on Temporary Work of 24 July 1987.

The contract entered into between the temporary work agency and the user must be established in writing at the latest within seven working days of the commencement of performance by the temporary worker.[34]

The contract must include the following items:

- the temporary work agency's recognition number;
- the registration number under which the temporary work agency is registered with the National Social Security Service;
- the designation of the joint committee or the joint sub-committee applicable to the user;
- the reasons for employing the temporary employee;
- the place and duration of the employment;
- working-time regulations in the user undertaking;
- the professional qualifications of the temporary employee;
- remuneration of a permanent employee with the same qualifications in the user undertaking;
- the manner in which the remuneration is to be paid;
- specific characteristics of the assigned workplace.[35]

Within at least two working days after the date of commencement of his/her performance, the temporary worker must receive a written communication containing the items which have to be included in the contract between temporary work agency and user.[36]

§2. The User – Temporary Worker Relationship

The user is not the employer of the temporary worker, but is delegated exercise of an employer's authority by the temporary work agency.

For the period during which the temporary employee is at the disposal of the user, the user is responsible for the observance of the provisions of labour regulation and protection that apply to the workplace.

These cover:

- working hours;
- public holidays;
- Sunday rest;

33. Cf. Court of Appeal, Ghent, 23 December 1998, T.G.R. 1999, 74.
34. Article 17 Law on Temporary Work.
35. Article 17, §1 Law on Temporary Work.
36. Article 17, §2 Law on Temporary Work.

- employment of women;
- employment of young people;
- night work;
- work rules;
- health and safety of employees;
- the salubriousness of the work and the workplace.

In this respect, mention should be made of a Royal Decree of 19 February 1997.[37] This Royal Decree indicates the respective duties of the user and the temporary work agency with regard to health and safety. The user, the temporary work agency and the temporary worker have to exchange information on the risks of the job and the precautions that have to be taken. According to the Royal Decree, the user must supply working clothes and personal protective equipment. The medical services of the user and of the temporary work agency are jointly responsible for the medical care of the temporary worker. Centralized medical files are to be kept. A Royal Decree of 4 December 1997[38] establishes a centralized prevention of risk service for temporary work agencies.

The relationship between user and temporary worker may change. The temporary worker and the user are always free to alter their relationship and to conclude an employment contract. As indicated above, according to the Law of 1987, contractual clauses prohibiting the hiring of a temporary worker by the user are considered to be null and void.[39]

It may also be that the user will be held to be (or to have become) the employer of the temporary worker. This is provided as a form of sanction by the law of 1987.[40] The user and the temporary employee are considered to be bound by a contract of employment for an indefinite period if:

- the user continues to employ a temporary worker even though the temporary work agency has informed the user of its decision to withdraw the employee;
- the user employs temporary workers in breach of the 1987 Law.

It may also be that the relationship between user and temporary worker has to be addressed for the proper application of labour laws that come into operation only for businesses that employ a certain number of employees, e.g. 50 for the obligatory establishment of a committee for prevention of risk and protection at work or 100 for a works council. In these instances, the temporary employees are counted as employees of the user. An exception is made when temporary workers replace permanent employees whose contract is suspended. All this is without prejudice to the application of legislation under which the same temporary workers have to be included in computing the workforce of the temporary work agency. A similar rule exists with regard to union delegation thresholds.[41]

---

37. *Belgian State Gazette*, 18 December 1997.
38. *Ibid.*
39. Article 13 Law on Temporary Work.
40. Article 20 Law on Temporary Work.
41. Collective Agreement No. 58, concluded in the National Labour Council on 7 July 1994 concerning the procedure and the duration of temporary work, extended by Royal Decree of 23 September 1994, *Belgian State Gazette*, 18 October 1994, Article 10. This collective agreement was amended by Collective Agreement No. 58*bis*, concluded in the National Labour Council on 25 June 1997, extended by Royal Decree of 14 September 1997, *Belgian State Gazette*, 15 November 1997.

VI. COLLECTIVE LABOUR RELATIONS ASPECTS

The Law of 24 July 1987 provides that a specific Joint Committee will be established for temporary work,[42] namely Joint Committee No. 322, which was established by Royal Decree of 8 April 1988. The Joint Committee is competent to act for temporary work agencies and temporary workers. Like other joint committees established at sector-level, it is competent to establish wages and working conditions for temporary workers by way of collective agreements concluded between the representative employers' associations and the unions represented on the committee. If such an agreement is extended by Royal Decree, it binds all temporary work agencies, and can be enforced with criminal sanctions. Many collective agreements have been concluded within Joint Committee No. 322.

In addition to its general competence, the 1987 Law specifically provides that the joint committee has the task of setting up a Livelihood Guarantee Fund for temporary workers. This Fund was set up by collective agreement No. 36*bis*, concluded in the National Labour Council on 27 November 1981.[43] In the event that a temporary work agency fails to meet its financial obligations *vis-à-vis* temporary workers, the Fund, financed by contributions from temporary work agencies, guarantees to the affected workers payment of:

- remuneration payable under individual contracts of employment or collective agreements;
- allowances and benefits payable by law or under collective agreements.

VII. THE ROLE OF THE GOVERNMENT

As indicated above, the operation of a temporary work agency requires prior governmental recognition, which is the responsibility of the regional governments (Flanders, Wallonia, Brussels) in Belgium. If the temporary work agency does not live up to its duties under social legislation, the recognition may be withdrawn.

As well as social inspection competences, the Law of 24 July 1987 provides for civil and criminal sanctions in case of violation of one or more provisions of the law.

On the basis of the Collective Agreement of 8 July 1993, a Commission of Good Services was established. The Commission is competent to deal with any problem with regard to the application of legal and regulatory provisions by which temporary work agencies are bound. The Commission is composed of an equal number of representatives of the employers' and workers' organizations that have a seat on the sectoral Fund mentioned above.

---

42. Article 27 of the Law on Temporary Work.
43. Extended by Royal Decree of 9 December 1981, *Belgian State Gazette*, 6 January 1982. Here, the National Labour Council acted as a joint committee. At that time the Joint Committee for Temporary Work was not yet established. According to Article 7 of the Act of 5 December 1968 in respect of collective agreements and joint committees, an agreement may be concluded in the National Labour Council for a branch of activity in which there is no joint committee. The collective agreement was amended several times, most recently by the collective agreement concluded in the Joint Committee on Temporary Work on 15 May 1997.

4B. Belgium – Putting Workers at the Disposal of a User

Chris Engels

I. INTRODUCTION

The present paper will focus on the limits within which workers can be put at the disposal of another employer, namely the user company. The emphasis is on leasing of personnel or putting workers at the disposal of users. The discussion does not concern temporary work agencies. The concept of worker in the present paper refers to a person who is delivering services, either as a subordinate worker, or as a self-employed person.

A company receives orders from clients to provide them with certain services, such as the development of specific software programs or the implementation of an internal company network. The company will then look for a specialist, either within its workforce, or within the pool of independent contractors it normally contracts with. The person who is chosen to perform the services will often carry them out on the premises of the client. Any such projects can continue over an extended period of time (often more than one year). The performer of the services may be more or less integrated within the organizational framework of both the hiring-out company, and/or the client.

When the company with whom the worker contracts is not itself developing any of the activities in the area in which the worker is active, and is merely bringing together 'client' and 'worker', the activity is one of match-making rather than subcontracting of services. In this case, one is basically dealing with the activity of *placing* self-employed service providers. Placement seems to be the main activity of agencies involved in 'interim management'. Interim management agencies differentiate themselves from temporary work agencies as regulated under Belgian Law,[1] in that they do not deal with subordinate employees, but with self-employed workers. For example, interim managers are placed with companies that need to fill a vacancy at management level which is not filled with a contract of employment with the company. Instead, a self-employed manager, selected by an interim management agency, will perform the requested services.

In this context, questions arise as to the legality of activities performed in this manner. Where the services could be rendered by subordinate personnel in the user company, questions may be raised as to the legality of the circumstances under which such a worker is put at the disposal of a user.

---

1. Act of 24 July 1987 on temporary employment work through temporary work agencies and putting workers at the disposal of users, Official Gazette, 20 August 1987, subsequently amended several times [hereinafter referred to as 1987 Act on Temporary Employment].

R. Blanpain & R. Graham (eds.), Temporary Agency Work and the Information Society, 63–78

In the event that such activities are performed by self-employed workers, it is unclear whether the company which placed the workers is an employment agency or an agency specialized in placement of the self-employed.

The first questions which arise deal with the legal nature of the relationship between the worker on the one hand, and the user company on the other:

– Is the relationship one with an independent contractor?
– Is there any risk that the relationship will be re-labelled as a contract of employment?
– Can a contract with the independent worker be re-labelled as an employment contract, and under what conditions? If the answer to this question is positive, all issues concerning the leasing of personnel and its restrictions must be revised.

II. THE RELATIONSHIP BETWEEN THE WORKER AND THE USER PARTY

Principles

The nature of this relationship is important, since it will determine whether or not the protective labour law provisions will be applicable. Belgian labour law will become applicable whenever a person is performing services in exchange for remuneration and under the authority of another (legal or physical) person. It is performance of the work outwith such a person's authority that differentiates the independent contractor from the employee.[2]

Whether a contract of employment exists does not depend on a written agreement between the parties. The fact that an agreement for the independent delivery of services has been formally concluded between the parties does not prevent a re-labelling of the contract as a contract of employment.[3] The actual manner in which the contract is performed will be the determining factor. This means that the existence of a subordinate relationship between the worker and the company may be determined merely by relying on the facts of the individual case.

In order to determine whether a person is an employee or is self-employed, the courts consider it important to know whether the person concerned:

– receives instructions;
– needs to conform to a working time schedule applicable to other (subordinate) workers within the same company;
– receives a fixed salary or a guaranteed minimum income;
– in any way participates in the economic risks run by the company;
– uses the infrastructure of the company;

2. *See* C. Engels, *The relationship of subordination in Belgian labour and employment law* [*Het ondergeschikt verband naar Belgisch arbeidsrecht*], Brugge, Die Keure, 1989, 644. *See also* C. Engels, 'Subordinate employees or self-employed workers? An analysis of the employment situation of managers of management companies as an illustration', in *Comparative Labour Law & Policy Journal* 21, 1999, 47–76.

3. *See* C. Engels, 'Management companies and social law, Update after the Leekens case', ['De management-vennootschap en het sociale recht, Update naar aanleiding van het geval Leekens'], in *Orientatie*, 1995, p. 192, 203–204.
See also Supreme Court, 7 September 1992, *Soc. Kron*, 1993, 13, note; Supreme Court, 13 April 1992, *Soc. Kron*, 1992, 320 and *R.W.* 1992–93, 460.

- is on the telephone directory of the company;
- has an exclusive relationship with the company (the existence of other contracting parties);
- is controlled or supervised as regards performance;
- has certain reporting duties to the company;
- has a duty to be present at working meetings;

The risk of re-labelling is significantly *reduced* in the event that the performer of the services is allowed to perform the task with the help of workers chosen and remunerated by him/herself. This would show that the agreement concluded clearly focuses on the work to be performed (result-oriented) instead of the person who will actually deliver the services (which is typical for a contract of employment).[4]

In this respect, it should be mentioned that the independent worker is capable of incorporation. A legal entity cannot under Belgian law be considered an employee. However, the interposition of a legal entity does not prevent a re-labelling of the agreement as a contract of employment. It will merely be one factor that is taken into account by the courts, among the host of other factors equally considered.[5]

The risk of re-labelling *increases*, however, if the agreement for the independent delivery of services is concluded between parties that were previously bound by a contract of employment. In such circumstances, there will be a factual presumption that the subordinate employment relationship continues to exist.[6]

It should be stressed in this context that the existence of an employment relationship does *not require* the employer to *actively exercise its authority*. The right to exercise authority over the worker suffices, even when the employer does not activate its rights under the employment contract.[7]

Quite often, when dealing with highly qualified personnel, employers refrain from directly intervening in the way the services are delivered. In these circumstances, the courts may decide upon the existence of a relationship of authority, on the basis of what is often referred to as 'secondary indicia' of authority.

Consequently, a relationship of subordination is derived from the worker's participation in an organization not controlled by him/herself. Reference is then made to factors such as:

- general working hours;
- place of actual performance of the services;
- equipment with which the work is being performed;

---

4. *See* Supreme Court, 16 January 1978, *Arr. Cass.*, 1978, 577 and *Pas.*, 1978, 551; Supreme Court, 23 October 1978, *Arr. Cass.*, 1978–79, 203 and *Pas.*, 1979, 219.
   See also C. Engels, *Het ondergeschikt verband naar Belgisch Arbeidsrecht*, Brugge, Die Keure, 1989, 165–182.
5. *See* C. Engels, 'Het sociaal statuut van de manager in de managementvennootschap', in *Soc. Kron.*, 1992, 353–362; C. Engels 'De managementvennootschap en het sociale recht, Update naar aanleiding van het geval Leekens', in *Orientatie*, 1995, 92–210.
6. *See* C. Engels, 'De managementvennootschap en het sociale recht, Update naar aanleiding van het geval Leekens', in *Orientatie*, 1995, 192–204.
7. *See* Supreme Court, 15 February 1962, *T.S.R.*, 1962, 357 and *Pas.*, 1962, 680; Supreme Court, 30 June 1966, *R.W.*, 1966–67, 1523 and *Pas.*, 1966, 1398; Supreme Court, 14 March 1969, *Arr. Cass.*, 1969, 652 and *Pas.*, 1969, 620; Supreme Court, 27 February 1970, *Arr. Cass.*, 1970, 604 and *Pas.*, 1970, 565; Supreme Court, 18 May 1981, *Arr. Cass.*, 1980–81, 1080.

- assisting personnel (e.g. personnel of the client);
- administrative organization.[8]

Every case is decided on its merits, taking into account individual circumstances and peculiarities.

While the criteria of actual or potential control and instructions with respect to the way the job is being performed go to the heart of the matter, the courts have taken into account several other factual indicia such as the full-time nature of the performance, the economic dependence of the individual on the user company, the existence of a guaranteed level of income, the premises on which the work is performed and any support staff used for the work. However, in a very recent case (23 December 2002) the Belgian Supreme Court made it clear that certain of these criteria should not be seen as an indication of subordinate employment status.

The Supreme Court has always held that economic dependency does not in itself signify the subordination required for the existence of an employment contract. The 23 December 2002 ruling concurs by stating that the fact that a worker works 8 or 9 hours a day for the same contracting party – and thus in practice has no time to perform tasks for anybody else – is not an indication of subordinate status. The same position was stated with respect to the absence of any business risk (economic and financial) as well as non-possession of equipment to perform the tasks. The Supreme Court clearly stated that the indicia mentioned above do not signify subordinate status, either individually or together.

Attention should be drawn, however, to a recent legislative proposal. The Belgian Ministry of employment intends to change the law on employment contracts by introducing a presumption that a worker carrying out tasks for a user firm is presumed to be an employee if a number of factual criteria are satisfied. The draft Royal Decree mentions twelve criteria. If 7 or more of these criteria are satisfied, the worker will be presumed to be an employee. An employer would be allowed to rebut the presumption. However, given that the twelve criteria are all considered to point to the existence of a subordinate employment status, it may become hard to do so.

The criteria mentioned are the following:

- absence of substantial participation in profits or losses of the company;
- absence of personal and substantial investments;
- absence of the power to decide on the financial strategy to keep the company profitable;
- guaranteed period payment of wages;
- primarily working for one user firm;
- absence of employer status and free selection of own employees;
- not being able to decide freely on work and working time;
- otherwise acting as an enterprise;
- working on premises and with materials owned by the user firm or made available by the user firm;
- subject to internal control and potential sanctions;
- not being able to decide on the pricing policies of the company; and
- lacking competence to purchase on behalf of the company.

8. *See* C. Engels, 'De Juridische duiding van de overeenkomst tussen ziekenhuis en ziekenhuisgeneesheer, Arbeidsovereenkomst of overeenkomst tot zelfstandige samenwerking', in O. Vanachter (ed.), *Arbeidsrecht, een confrontatie tussen theorie en praktijk*, Antwerpen – Apeldoorn, Maklu Uitgevers, 1993, 31.

It is clear that if this proposed modification became law, a number of workers will be presumed to be working in an employment relationship for the first time. Overcoming the burden of proof may then become extremely difficult.

In practice it is important to determine whether so called *independent contractors are actually performing the task in a manner distinct from the subordinate employees*. In the event that the independent contractor operates in exactly the same way as the subordinate worker, there will be at least a *de facto* presumption that the independent contractor should be considered an employee even without the legislative modification. The burden of proof would then be on the employer to prove, for example, that the independent contractor can refuse to perform certain services, and actually did so in the past; that there is no way the alleged employer would be able to require the consultant to justify the use of time (except for example, billing purposes); that the contractor performs tasks at the same time and/or consecutively for several other contractual parties; or that he/she is not economically dependent on the user firm.

III. PUTTING WORKERS AT THE DISPOSAL OF CLIENTS/USERS

A. Principles

The Parliamentary Act of 24 July 1987 on temporary work, work provided by temporary work agencies and putting workers at the disposal of users, regulates this matter in a very stringent way.[9] Article 31 and following of the Parliamentary Act of 24 July 1987 deal with the issue of putting workers at the disposal of users outside the context of temporary work and work provided by temporary work agencies. The Act in principle severely limits the activity of a physical person or legal entity that puts employees at the disposal of third parties who exercises the authority of an employer over them.[10]

The prohibition is restricted in its scope to subordinate workers. This means that a company can contract with an *independent* consultant or specialist, for the latter to perform certain jobs at the premises of a third party (who is the client) or user. In the event that a company does not exercise any authority over the consultant, obviously it cannot delegate any authority to the user. In the event that the user exercises authority over the consultant, it does so on its own account.

The 1987 Act only *prohibits putting subordinate workers at the disposal of users* when such leasing of personnel is accompanied by delegation of some part of the employer's authority. It should be noted that neither all nor even a major part of the employer's authority need be transferred for the prohibition to apply. A delegation of *some* authority is sufficient. However, an amendment to the Act in 2000 severely reduces the scope of the prohibition. The amended Act now leaves quite some room for putting employees at the disposal of another employer.

Severe sanctions apply in case of violation of the provisions of the Act. A limited number of exceptions within the scope of the Act itself are provided.

The Act foresees only a limited number of situations in which it would be permissible to delegate authority from one employer to another. Even in those circumstances additional limitations come into play.

9. Act on Temporary Employment. *See* C. Engels, *Overdracht van Onderneming en Outsourcing*, Larcier, Brussels, 2000, 127–154.
10. Article 31, §1 Act of 24 July 1987.

B. Exceptions to the Prohibition

1. *Putting a worker at the disposal of a user without any delegation of authority – implicit exception for subcontracting, falling outside the scope of the Act*

a. Situation prior to the Law of 12 August 2000[11] *(currently applicable)*
The 1987 Act only prohibits workers being put at the disposal of a user company with a transfer of authority from the original employer to the user. *A contrario*, one could state that putting a worker at the disposal of a user is allowed when it is not accompanied by any delegation of authority.[12]

In order to fall within the scope of the prohibition it is not required that the original employer transfers its entire authority. It will suffice that part of the authority is transferred to the user. The user must therefore exercise no authority over the workers to avoid the restrictions applying. In order to determine whether the user is exercising any form of authority over the consultants, the same indicia are taken into account as those used in order to determine whether an employment relationship exists.

It is important to stress here that *Belgian labour courts* are *liberal* in their interpretation of the existence of employment contracts. The courts are willing to accept the existence of an employment relationship in circumstances where the alleged employer's actual or potential exercise of authority over the alleged employee is not so apparent. Often the employer's authority is derived from secondary instead of primary indicia of subordination. Primary indications would be the fact that the (alleged) employer gives the worker mandatory instructions in respect of where, when, and on what to work. The same is true when the employer effectively controls the way the worker is performing tasks.[13]

While a sub-contractor (performing tasks under a relationship other than a contract of employment) may also receive instructions and guidelines, these are of a different nature. The Belgian Supreme Court accepted, in line with the independent status of the subcontractor, that a subcontractor's user firm may give instructions, provided these are general.[14] Furthermore, an independent contractor can agree to deliver certain services at a pre-determined time and place, as ruled by the highest court.[15]

Given the fact that highly skilled workers are often granted considerable freedom in the performance of their tasks (e.g. as far as time and place of performance is concerned), the labour courts looked for other indications that would allow them to make the distinction between the subordinate and self-employed worker. The courts therefore started to look more and more at the external circumstances within which a task is being performed for an indication of the existence of an employment relationship.

The external, material organization within which the work is being performed is increasingly relied on to establish the existence of an employment relationship.

---

11. Article 181, Act 12 August 2000, *Official Gazette*, 31 August 2000.
12. *See* Brussels, 7 September 1994, J.T.T., 1996, 81; Labour Tribunal Brussels, AR. n. 33.539/93, re: *Eltzroth c. Morgan Lewis & Bockius*.
13. *See* C. Engels, 'De Juridische duiding van de overeenkomst tussen ziekenhuis en ziekenhuis geneesheer, Arbeidsovereenkomst of overeenkomst tot zelfstandige samenwerking', in O. Vanachter (ed.), *Arbeidsrecht, een confrontatie tussen theorie en praktijk*, Antwerpen – Apeldoorn, Maklu Uitgevers, 1993, 31, 56–63.
14. Supreme Court, 13 October 1957, *Arr. Cass.*, 1958, 48.
15. Supreme Court, 11 September 1978, *Arr. Cass.*, 1978–79, 32.

This tendency has been commonplace in examining the performance of tasks by medical doctors in hospitals. The question arose whether such medical doctors could be considered employees of the hospital or not, given that they have complete operational independence. The courts started to look at factors such as the location where the medical acts were performed, the equipment that was used for it, and the team the doctor could or had to rely on, among other things. In other words, the courts assessed whether the medical doctor was working within an organization managed by someone or some entity other than him or herself.[16]

The courts are thus willing to find that one party exercises authority over the other, within the work relationship, on the basis of criteria that relate merely to the external circumstances, rather than to the manner, in which the tasks are performed.

The above should make it evident that only in the clearest circumstances of sub-contracting are workers put at the disposal of the user firm without transferring even part of the normal employer's authority. Here attention should be drawn to the recent Supreme Court ruling of 23 December 2002 mentioned above, in which the Court decided that a number of the indicative criteria should not be taken into account for deciding whether or not an employment contract exists.

b. Situation since the Act of 12 August 2000 – extending the possibilities for putting a worker at the disposal of a user

The Act of 12 August 2000 does not remove the prohibition on putting employees at the disposal of another employer. However, by adding a new paragraph to Article 31 of the Act of 24 July 1987, it renders the prohibition rather meaningless, at least when dealing with employers who formalize their relationships with user firms in which their employees will perform services. The new paragraph introduced in the Act of 24 July 1987 reads as follows:

> 'The observation by the third party [read: user] of the obligations that rest on it with respect to well-being at work, as well as the instructions the third party gives in furtherance of the agreement it reached with the employer, both with regard to working time and rest time, as well as with regard to the execution of the agreed work, will not be considered as an exercise of authority in the sense of this article.'

When a third party user instructs the employees of the employer with respect to health and safety matters, it is clear that this should not be seen as an exercise of authority over the worker concerned.[17] Also the Act on well-being at work foresees itself that certain health and safety measures, precautions and obligations need to be respected outside the context of an employer/employee relationship.[18]

Equally so, giving instructions with respect to working time and time-off is not an indication of the employer's authority being exercised. It is explained as a practical necessity for co-ordinating the work of one's own employees with the work of those performing services in the company.

16. C. Engels 'Belgium', in B. Brooks and C. Engels (eds.), *Employed or Self-employed*, Bulletin of Comparative Labour Relations 24, 1992, 29es, especially 31–32.
17. C. Engels *Het ondergeschikt verband naar Belgisch Arbeidsrecht*, Brugge, Die Keure, 1989, 75.
18. Article 8, e.s., Act of 4 August 1996 with respect to the Well-Being of Workers in the Execution of their Work, *Official Gazette*, 18 September 1996, modified thereafter.

More surprising is the reference in the new paragraph to 'instructions with respect to the work to be performed'. It is surprising that the Act now states that such instructions are not to be seen as an expression of the employer's authority over the workers concerned. This exception seems to be very broad and would include putting workers at the disposal of a user firm, at least if the employer and the user enter into an ordinary service agreement in which they describe the work to be performed. All instructions that the user gives with respect to the work to be performed will not be seen as an expression of an employer's authority within the meaning of the Act of 24 July 1987.

In the event that the courts give a broad interpretation of 'instructions with respect to the work to be performed', the prohibition on putting workers at the disposal of a user will become an empty shell, at least in comparison to the situation prior to the year 2000 amendment of the Act. The question then arises as to which instructions a user would not be able to give to the workers, without violating the prohibition contained in the Act of 24 July 1987. These are likely to include instructions with respect to disciplinary sanctions, decisions on wage increases, evaluations and promotions.[19]

As a result of the new paragraph in Article 31, the service agreement between the employer and the user now has to define clearly the work that needs to be performed for the user. All instructions the user gives to workers performing the task will not lead to a violation of the Act of 24 July 1987.

2. *Putting workers at the disposal of a user with delegation of authority*

An employer can exceptionally put some of its regular workers at the disposal of another employer and thereby delegate some of its normal authority over the worker concerned. However, as a general rule, *a government authorization* is required. In order to obtain this authorization, the consent of the trade union delegation within the user company is equally required.

However, *neither* the trade union delegation's *consent, nor* the government *authorization will be required* if a worker – whose original contract of employment is preserved – is exceptionally put at the disposal of the user:

1. within the framework of a collaboration between employers of the same economic and financial entity; or
2. in light of the *short-term performance of specialized tasks* that require special professional qualifications.

However, in either of these cases the government needs to be *notified* 24 hours before the worker is put at the disposal of the user. A written document must be drafted and signed by the three parties involved (the (normal) employer, the user and the worker concerned) prior to actually putting the employee at the disposal of the user.

The contract of employment between the original employer and the worker remains in existence. However, the original employer and the user become jointly liable for the payment of all wages, indemnities, benefits and social security contributions.

19. *See* C. Engels, *Overdracht van onderneming en Outsourcing*, Brussels, Larcier, 2000, 133.

The 1987 Act furthermore states that a worker who is put at a user's disposal should not be treated in a less favourable way than the regular workers of the user, performing the same kind of job. Consequently the conditions of employment (including wages and all kinds of benefits) of the worker put at the user's disposal should certainly not be inferior to the wages of the user's employees with the same job description.[20] Self-evidently, this provision does not apply when dealing with a form of subcontracting that falls outside the scope of the Act of 24 July 1987. If the latter Act is not applicable and a third party comes to do work at the user's premises, there is no obligation for the third party to pay its workers at the same level of remuneration and benefits as a similar worker of the user doing the same or similar work.

A few provisions of the 1987 Act that deal with temporary work agencies are equally applicable to the situation of workers put at the disposal of a user. For the period during which a worker is at the disposal of a user, the latter shall be answerable to the observance of provisions of labour regulation and protection that are applicable in the workplace.[21] The Act itself specifies those provisions as those relating to:

- working time;
- public holidays;
- Sunday rest;
- female labour;
- work by young people;
- night work;
- internal company working rules;
- control on work of certain part-time workers; and
- health and safety of workers and salubriousness of work and the workplace.

The exception allowing a worker to be put at the disposal of a user with a delegation of authority 'in light of the short term performance of specialized tasks that require special professional qualifications' was of extreme importance prior to the year 2000 amendment of the Act of 24 July 1987. This exception was among other things meant to cover situations where *computer specialists* are provided to other companies. Another example, from case law, is the leasing of a crane with trained crane operators accompanying it in order to handle the crane for a specific task.[22]

The year 2000 amendment of the Act of 24 July 1987 grants the National Labour Council the competence to define the concepts of 'short term performance' and 'the requirement of special professional qualification'. Up to now, no collective agreement on these matters has been concluded. It is clear that it will be very hard, if not impossible, to come up with acceptable definitions at national level, across the various industries.

Putting a worker at the disposal of another employer *has to remain exceptional*, the Act stated prior to its amendment on 13 February 1998. While it was not clear what 'exceptional' meant in this context, it seemed to exclude the idea of permanently putting workers of one company at the disposal of another. A very broad interpretation of the Act and of this particular concept was proffered by some commentators, who implied that the restrictions would not survive. This lenient

20. Article 32, §4, Act on Temporary Employment.
21. Article 19, §1, Act on Temporary Employment.
22. Court of Appeals Liège, 12 March 1983, *J.L.M.B.*, 1994, 126.

reading, however, made a distinction between the normal activity which the employer is ordinarily engaged in, and the activity of putting workers at the disposal of another employer. Some authors then defended the position that the Parliamentary Act provided for – concurring with the limits of the two exceptions mentioned above, and with permitting putting workers at the disposal of another employer so long as this does not become the normal or regular activity of the employer.[23]

Since the amendment of the Act of 24 July 1987 on 13 February 1998, it is clear that the circumstances in which it is permissible to put normal workers at the disposal of users need to be not only restricted in time. The amended version of the 1987 Act states that 'the employer, contrary to the general prohibition (stated in Article 31 of the same Act) is allowed to put its permanent employees at the disposal of a user if a number of conditions are together satisfied', namely:

- the workers can be put at the user's disposal only for a limited period of time; and
- putting workers at the user's disposal can be done by the employer only alongside the employer's ordinary or normal activities.

The Parliamentary discussion highlighted that putting workers at the disposal of a user should not be a part of the employer's normal activities. The employer should engage in such an activity only occasionally. It was stressed that in the event that such activity becomes the employer's normal activity, the employer becomes a temporary work agency. Both the occasional nature (as compared to the employer's normal activities) and the limited duration of being put at the user's disposal are therefore stressed in the current versions of the legal text.[24]

The civil servant should be able to determine whether or not putting workers at the disposal of users belongs to a company's normal activities. The relative importance of the activities an employer is engaged in must be weighed against one another.

How should one determine what the employer's ordinary activities are? Should one look at its main activities? Does an employer have to be engaged mainly in putting workers at the disposal of users before one can state that this is part of the employer's ordinary activities? Or should one consider an activity which the employer has engaged in over a longer period of time as (part of) the company's ordinary activity, regardless of the fact that this activity represents only a minor part of the employer's business? Taking into account that the modified text of the 24 July 1987 Act explicitly refers to the employer's ordinary activities, in the plural, the latter interpretation seems to be the correct one.

Furthermore, the Act presently expressly states that it is possible to put permanent workers at the user's disposal only for a limited period of time ('beperkte duur'/'durée limitée'). The year 2000 amendment of the Act states that a Collective Agreement concluded with the National Labour Council can define the concept of 'limited period of time'. Neither the preparatory works leading to the adoption of the Act, nor the Parliamentary Act itself give any indication of what the concept implies. No definition has yet been given within the National Labour Council either. The civil

23. *See* in general F. Tilleman, *Tijdelijk Arbeid uitzendarbeid en ter beschikkingstelling van werknemers*, Kluwer Rechtswetenschappen, 1982, 151–152; V. Peting, 'Detacheringen ter beschikkingstelling: een gespleten identiteit', in *Orientatie*, 1993, 195, 198–199; J.F. Gérard, 'La mise de travailleurs à la disposition d'utilisateurs' in *Orientations*, 1992, 14, 21–22.

24. Chamber of Representatives, 1997–98, 16 December 1997, Amendment No. 15, Document No. 1269/3-97/98 p. 6.

servants that will have to grant or refuse the requests for approval are left without any (official) guidance as to the limits of the duration of leasing personnel which the law requires. It is striking here that the Parliamentary Act uses the term limited duration and not the term fixed duration. The civil servants will have to judge whether the worker is put at the user's disposal for a duration of time which is justified by the particular circumstances of the case.

C. Sanctions for Violation of the Act

Both criminal and civil sanctions can be imposed for violation of the provisions of the Act of 24 July 1987.

The prohibition on putting workers at the disposal of users, contained in Article 31 of the Act of 24 July 1987 does not come into play:

1. if the subordinate workers are put at the disposal of the users without any delegation of authority;
2. a. when the subordinate workers are put at the disposal of users for a limited period of time;
   b. when putting workers at the disposal of users is not part of the employer's normal activities;
   c. when governmental (and trade union delegation) approval has been given or governmental notification has been made (with a few exceptions for the latter requirement);
3. when dealing with self-employed performers.

The courts' liberal construction of the concept of authority under Belgian Law, and the stress on the worker's integration in the firm of the alleged employer in order to determine the existence of an employment relationship, made it difficult to lease personnel to a user without delegation of any of the authority normally exercised by the employer. But the amendment of the Act that was passed in the year 2000 'neutralized' a number of indicia that were previously looked on as signifying the exercise of authority normally belonging to the employer.

When leasing takes place over an extended period of time, it may still be contrary to the provisions of the Act of 24 July 1987, if:

- not all governmental notifications and approvals have been made or obtained,
- when the leasing is not for a limited period of time, or
- when leasing of personnel belongs to the regular or normal activities of the employer.

1. Civil sanctions

a. Presumption of a contract of employment for an indefinite period of time with the user

The Act explicitly states that if any form of prohibited employment of this kind takes place, a contract of employment for an indefinite period of time is presumed to exist between the worker and the user. This presumption cannot be rebutted.[25] Termination of such a contract will have to follow the rules set out above. The original intention

25. Article 31, §3, al. 1, Act on Temporary Employment.

to lease the personnel only for a fixed period of time will not have any effect in practice.

b. Termination of a contract of employment for an indefinite period of time, by the employee, and without notice

A worker put at the disposal of a user in violation of the 1987 Act can terminate his/her contract of employment with the user immediately, without respecting any term of notice, with lasting effect until the end of the service period agreed between the original employer and the user firm.[26]

In the event that the worker was specifically hired to be put at the disposal of a user and the activity was carried out in violation of the 1987 Act, the original employment contract is null and void.[27]

c. Joint liability of the (original) employer and the user

Both the original employer and the user will be liable (jointly) for payments of all indemnities, wages, benefits and all social security contributions. This joint liability includes liability for the termination indemnities.[28] The latter rule could be particularly severe where the original contract of employment (now considered void, on the grounds that the conditions for acceptable leasing of personnel have not been satisfied) was a contract for a specific period of time.

Since the contract is to be replaced with a contract of employment for an indefinite period of time, evidently the contract will not automatically come to an end at the date foreseen in the original agreement. Where the work for which the worker was leased has been completed, the contract will have to be terminated in accordance with the rules dealing with terminations of contracts of employment for an indefinite period of time. Both the original employer and the user will be jointly liable for the termination indemnity.

2. Criminal sanctions

The 1987 Act provides criminal sanctions at the following levels:

- eight days to 1 month imprisonment for an employer or its agents who violate provisions of the Act and/or
- a fine of between 26 and 500 Euro (to be multiplied by 5 in accordance with inflation). This sanction can be applied as many times as there are workers who are employed in violation of the Act, up to a maximum of 50,000 Euro (equally to be multiplied by 5 for inflation purposes).
- A court can take mitigating circumstances into account when determining the level of the criminal sanctions. However, the criminal fine cannot be set below 40 per cent of the minimum amount mentioned above.[29]
- In case of repetition within the year, the sanction may, at the maximum, be doubled.[30]
- If the authorities decide not to enforce criminal charges, administrative fines may be imposed by the Ministry of Labour. The fines may run from

26. Article 31, §3, al. 2, Act on Temporary Employment.
27. Article 31, §2, Act on Temporary Employment.
28. F. Tilleman, 'Het sluipend gewoon van de terbeschikkingstelling', in *Orientatie*, 1997, 121, 123.
29. Article 43, §2, Act on Temporary Employment, 24 July 1987, as amended.
30. Article 41, Act on Temporary Employment, 24 July 1987, as amended.

50 Euro up to 1,250 Euro and are multiplied by the number of employees that are illegally employed in violation of the 1987 Act. The absolute maximum of the administrative fine is 20,000 Euro. Mitigating circumstances can be taken into account. However, the fine can never be below 40 per cent of the minimum provided.[31]

IV. INTERIM MANAGEMENT

Interim management companies deliver managers (of all kinds) to companies that have (temporary) vacancies. In the event that the interim management company attempts to provide the user company with *subordinate employees*, it will fall squarely within the scope of the basic prohibition on putting workers at the disposal of users. Doubts would not only arise over whether the provision of services was only an occasional activity of the interim management company. Were the company to be putting workers at the disposal of users as part of its ordinary activity, this would be contrary to the mandatory provisions prohibiting an employer from leasing out personnel as part of its normal activities. The above of course applies only when there is at least a partial delegation of the employer's normal authority. Where there is no delegation of authority, the approach whereby the interim management firm leases out its subordinate manager (who is its employee) seems to be perfectly valid, even when this is done over an extended period of time. That situation qualifies as sub-contracting, since the sub-contractor (the interim management firm) is performing the requested services with its own personnel.

In the event that there is a delegation of the employer's authority to the user, the services can only be legally delivered within the framework of temporary work, through a temporary work agency.

The above applies to interim managers that work as subordinate employees, as part of the workforce of the interim management company. It is therefore of the utmost importance to determine the nature of the relationship between the interim manager and the interim management company. As already expressed above, the label given to the relationship by the two parties is not determinative.

Most interim management firms, however, claim to provide *independent contractors* rather than subordinate employees. The basic activities the interim management firm performs are very similar to the activities performed by temporary work agencies in the sense they are defined by the Act of 24 July 1987. The Act itself defines a temporary work agency as an undertaking whose business consists of engaging temporary staff and making them available to users for the purpose of performing temporary work, as defined by the Act itself.[32] The temporary worker and the agency enter into an agreement whereby the temporary worker undertakes to perform temporary work, as defined by the Act.[33] The contract is presumed to be a contract of employment and that presumption cannot be rebutted.[34] Temporary employment is defined as work performed in furtherance of an employment contract

31. Article 1ter Act on administrative fines, 30 June 1971, as amended by the Parliamentary Act of 13 February, 1998, *Official Gazette*, 19 February 1998.
32. Article 7,1 Act on Temporary Employment.
33. Article 7,2 Act on Temporary Employment.
34. Article 8,1 Act on Temporary Employment.

with the aim of replacing a permanent worker, to respond to a temporary increase in workload or to perform a clearly defined task.[35]

Evidently, assignments are offered to interim management firms for similar reasons. Arguments have been advanced that the interim management firms are therefore actually temporary work agencies and that the contracts they conclude with the managers, are irrefutably presumed to be contracts of employment.[36]

Such an interpretation of the Act is not sound. It would create long-standing relationships between contractors and sub-contractors whenever they enter into a framework agreement that contains the basic principles for collaboration when and if sub-contracting jobs arise. Whenever such a job comes up, contractor and sub-contractor enter into a specific agreement outlining the details of the work to be performed. Where the framework agreement is devoid of references to an exercise or potential exercise of authority, and is not contradicted by actual practice, the relationship between the contractor and the sub-contractor cannot be considered an employment relationship.

Here the presumption contained in Article 8 of the Act of 24 July 1987 should not come into play at all. The presumption aims to confirm that the temporary work agency should be considered the employer of the subordinate worker. The agency retains general authority over the worker concerned, while the worker is performing at the user's premises where direct instruction is received.[37]

Where one is dealing with a framework agreement between an interim management firm and an interim manager through which the 'agency' cannot or does not retain even general authority over the worker, the provision on temporary work agencies (including the irrebuttable presumption of the existence of a contract of employment) should not be considered.

Given that there is no relationship of authority between the interim management firm and the interim worker, the firm does no more than match supply and demand with regard to independently delivered services. This service is more comparable to placement of self-employed workers (with a fee) than to the work of temporary work agencies. In this context, the crucial question of course is whether or not the allegedly independent manager is truly independent. If he/she is not truly independent, then all restrictive rules dealing with temporary work agencies and the leasing of personnel will come into play.

V. CONCLUSION

Truly independent contractors, acting as sub-contractors, perform a pre-determined service at a given time and place, as previously agreed. They are not subject to the user's authority, though. They may receive some general instructions with regard to the work to be performed.

When subordinate workers are leased out to other companies, outside the context of the strictly regulated temporary work agencies, a general prohibition applies. Leasing of ordinary personnel cannot validly be part of an employer's

35. Article 1, §1, Act on Temporary Employment.
36. *See* F. Tilleman, 'Het sluipend gevaar van de terbeschikkingstelling', in *Orientatie*, 1997, 121, 128.
37. *See* R. Blanpain, 'Uitzendarbeid', in R. Blanpain (ed.), *Arbeidsrecht*, Brugge, Die Keune, o.d., 37, No. 60 referring to the Parliamentary preparatory work of the Act that preceded the 1987 Act.

normal activities, nor can the leasing last for a long period of time. This is so, at least, when the normal employer delegates some of its normal authority over the worker to a user.

Leasing out subordinate workers to an employer without delegation of any authority, is in practice difficult, at least when dealing with activities that have to be integrated into the operation of the user company.

Furthermore Belgian labour courts have given a broad interpretation to the notion of authority that needs to be present for a contract of employment to be found to exist. Consequently the courts are willing to find an employment relationship wherever they might reasonably do so, and often base their assessment on factors that relate to the external circumstances in which the work is performed.

Against this background it is likely that the leasing of personnel would go hand in hand with at least some delegation of the employer's normal authority.

For companies ordinarily engaging in services that require performance at user enterprises, for an extended period of time, the above implies that they are likely to be carrying out activities that are subject to criminal sanctions under Belgian Law. Evidently, that situation was hardly compatible with the development of the network society in modern businesses where 'companies' consist of independent entities performing services for each other and at each other's premises. Companies outsource activities which are no longer part of the core of their business. For example, canteen and cleaning services are transferred or outsourced to independently operating businesses. The services have to be delivered, however, on the premises of the user company. It may be hard to avoid *any* indication of the user exercising authority over the workers.

That, however, was the situation under Belgian Law prior to the amendment of the Act of 24 July 1987 on 12 August 2000. The amendment stated that a number of indicia, that would normally be looked upon as indicating that the user exercised authority over the employees of the third party company, are no longer considered as such under the Act of 24 July 1987. To its advantage, the user can now give all instructions with respect to the execution of the agreement it concluded with the third party company. The amendment was necessary from a business point of view. It decriminalized a number of current business practices. But clearly abolition of the general prohibition on the leasing of personnel would have provided greater coherence.

4C. Belgium – Temporary Work Agencies and the Role of the Social Partners[1]

Willy van Eeckhoutte

I. TEMPORARY WORK IN BELGIUM: INTRODUCTION

A. In General

In the seventies and following its evolution in the United States, the phenomenon of 'interim work', sometimes also described as temporary work, became more and more popular. In brief, a temporary work agency lends out one or more employees to a person that has a temporary need for workers, but does not wish to recruit the employees himself.

Originally, temporary workers were not considered as employees, at least not in the event that they provided mainly non-manual labour. It was assumed that no sufficiently strong link of authority existed between the temporary workers and the temporary work agency. As a consequence, these workers were considered as self-employed. The lack of social protection that followed, however, led to various legal disputes before the labour courts. Increasingly, these courts were of the opinion that temporary workers had to be regarded as employees of the temporary work agency. Following this evolution, in 1970 the legislator brought temporary workers under the social security legislative scheme for employees.

The activities of temporary work agencies were in these days regarded with suspicion, because their activity was sometimes considered as contrary to the internationally accepted principle that job-seeking was in principle a task of the authorities that could not be profit-oriented. It should be noted, however, that temporary work in the narrow sense of the word could not be regarded as job-seeking, since the temporary work agency and the person to whom it provides a job are bound by an employment relationship. For that reason, the legislator decided to regulate temporary work provisionally, under a provisional act. The results of that Act would be evaluated subsequently with a view to definitively prohibiting or permitting temporary work under certain conditions.

Accordingly, the Act of 28 June 1976 concerned the provisional regulation of temporary work, interim work and the lending out of personnel to users. That Act was valid for four years.

---

1. Text prepared by Mrs. Elisabeth Matthys and Mr. Pieter Spinnewijn, both assistants at the University of Ghent, the former being also a member of the Brussels bar.

R. Blanpain & R. Graham (eds.), Temporary Agency Work and the Information Society, 79–100

On expiry of the operational term of the Act, the legislator failed to establish a new regulation. As a consequence, Collective Agreement No. 36 of the National Labour Council, of 27 November 1981, concerning temporary measures with regard to temporary work, interim work and the lending out of personnel to employees was enacted.

The Temporary Work Act of 24 July 1987 finally established permanent regulation of temporary work. Alongside that Act and in anticipation of the enactment of executive decrees, the stipulations of Collective Agreements Nos. 36 to 36 *sexies* remain applicable.

In the meantime, public opinion on employment services has changed drastically. Nowadays, the International Labour Organisation starts from the premise that private employment services play a considerable role in a well-functioning labour market. The new ILO Treaty of 3 June 1997 in principle permits profit-oriented employment services. ILO Treaty No. 181 was implemented in the Flemish region by a decree of 13 April 1999 with regard to private employment services in the Flemish region. Under Article 4 of the latter decree, advertising or promoting private employment services for business purposes is permitted in certain circumstances.

At European level a proposal for a directive of the European Parliament and the Council on working conditions for temporary workers has been presented by the European Commission, in the light of the employment strategy adopted by the European Council in Lisbon in March 2000 to make the Union the most competitive and dynamic knowledge-based economy in the world. In the eyes of the European Commission, temporary work is seen as an important instrument to reconcile flexibility and job security and create more and better jobs.

B. Statistics

On a yearly basis, the temporary work sector employs 350,000 workers of which 100,000 are students. On a daily basis, a full time equivalent of approximately 70,000 workers was employed in 2001 by 1,000 temporary work agencies.Temporary workers accounted for 1.6 per cent of the working population in 1999. This number is lower than in the Netherlands, the UK, France and Luxembourg, but is higher than in Germany, Austria, Scandinavia and the countries around the Mediterranean Sea. In the fourth quarter of 2002 the temporary work sector showed a slight decrease of 0.7 per cent in relation to the third quarter of 2002, even though there was at the same time a serious increase of 10.5 per cent in the amount of temporary work done by students. Thirty-one per cent of all students working in July, August and September are employed by a temporary work contract.

Proportions of temporary workers by category of employees (2001)

	Men (%)	*Women (%)*	*Total (%)*
Blue-collar	46.4	15.2	61.6
White-collar	14.4	24.0	38.4
Total	60.8	39.2	100.0

Division of temporary workers by category of age (2001)

0–21 years old	13.3%
21–25 years old	33.7%
26–30 years old	19.3%
31–45 years old	26.9%
46+ years old	6.8%

A recent study by Federgon, the Belgian federation for partners for work, shows that employees often use temporary work as a means of transition by which important steps can be taken in the development of their professional career. It appears that more than 30 per cent of all temporary workers were unemployed before their last temporary work assignment. Of this group, seven out of ten persons remained employed after their temporary job and only three out of ten persons became unemployed. It can thus be said that temporary work plays an important role in reintegration, transition and career reorientation.

C. Legal Sources and Legal Evolution

The regulation of temporary work and of interim work is rather complicated in Belgium. Not only are there rules at federal level as well as at regional level, but regulation is essentially a combination of legislative and agreement-based provisions. Codes of conduct, made by the regional executives, play a minor role in the regulation of temporary work (contrary to Sweden, for example).

1. The regulatory competences of the federal state and the regions

Belgium is a federal state, in which competences are divided between the federal level, the three regions and the three communities. According to Article 6, §1 VI 12° of the Special Act Reforming the Institutions, the federal state is competent for labour law and social security law. As a consequence, the greater part of employment legislation is federal.

The 'three-way relationship' between a user undertaking, an employee and a temporary work agency, as well as the basic principles concerning temporary work and leasing out of personnel, are governed by the Act of the National Parliament of 24 July 1987 concerning temporary work, interim work and the leasing out of personnel to users (*Official Gazette*, 20 August 1987) (hereafter referred to as the 'Temporary Work Act').

The regional legislator and the regional executive, however, have certain important competences concerning employment legislation, more precisely in the field of employment policy. The Belgian Constitution provides in Article 39 that the regions can enact decrees concerning the topics described in Article 6 of the Special Act Reforming the Institutions. Provision of employment services (including the recognition of temporary work agencies) is a regional competence, giving rise for example, to Flemish regulations on the recognition of temporary work agencies, and equivalent regulations for the Walloon area of Belgium and for Brussels. An agency that wants to operate throughout Belgium needs three recognitions: recognition for Brussels, one for Flanders and one for the Walloon region.

2. *The combination of legislative and agreement-based provisions*

The Temporary Work Act is the basic Act concerning temporary work. However, some very important issues are not dealt with in this Act, due to the fact that it was impossible to reach a political agreement on all issues related to temporary work. The most debated issue was whether a user may replace striking workers with temporary workers. The discussion on this matter between the social partners and the legislator lasted more than five years, and produced no concrete results. As a consequence, the provision on strikes was deleted from the draft legislation and the problem was transferred to the social partners to deal with. The Temporary Work Act simply states in Article 1, §5 that the strike issue will be dealt with by a collective agreement concluded in the National Labour Council. The Temporary Work Act has thus created a framework for temporary work and leasing out personnel.

Implementing the Temporary Work Act, on 18 December 1990 the National Labour Council concluded Collective Agreement No. 47 concerning the procedure that must be respected and the possible duration of temporary work and interim assignment in the event of an exceptional increase of the workload, a strike or lock-out and the replacement of an employee whose employment contract was terminated (now replaced by Collective Agreement No. 58).

Collective Agreements, dealing with issues that were not addressed by the national legislator are agreed upon in the joint committee No. 322 for temporary work and in other joint committees at sector-level.

II. REGULATION OF TEMPORARY WORK IN BELGIUM: BASIC PRINCIPLES

In Belgium the conditions governing both employment of temporary and of interim workers and the posting of workers by an employer to a user company are *strictly regulated*.

A. Legal Restrictions on the Use of Temporary Work Contracts

Under Belgian Labour law the basic principle is that employment contracts are agreed upon for an indefinite period of time, in order to give job security and income stability to the employees. However, due to the limited flexibility this type of contract allows the employer, he will look for alternatives to this standard employment contract when faced with a need for temporary labour. However, atypical contracts are subject to legal restrictions and can only be agreed upon under specific conditions.

First of all, an employer can hire employees under a fixed-term contract or contract solely for a clearly determined job. Further, he can agree upon a contract for the replacement of an employee whose employment contract has been suspended. All these atypical forms of employment contract are laid down in the Act of 3 July 1978 concerning employment contracts (hereafter referred to as the 'Employment Contracts Act').

In addition to these atypical forms of contracts allowing a degree of flexibility, the Belgian legislator created the temporary work contract under the Temporary Work Act. According to Article 1, temporary work is defined as the activity performed on the basis of an employment contract with the goal of replacing a permanent employee, responding to a temporary increase in workload, or performing an exceptional task.

A temporary work contract can be agreed upon either directly between the employer and the temporary worker, or indirectly by the intermediation of a temporary work agency that puts its employee at the disposal of a user company (interim employment contract). In the latter case, the employer enters into a contractual relationship with the temporary work agency rather than with the temporary worker. The temporary worker is bound by a temporary employment contract with the temporary work agency. Under certain restricted circumstances, an employer can also request from another company to provide an employee for a temporary assignment. Usually, such a worker is a permanent employee of the company leasing out its personnel, but in theory, temporary workers can also be leased out by an employer (*see*, *infra*, Section II.B).

According to Article 2 of the Temporary Work Act, the temporary work contract can only take the form of one of the above mentioned atypical contracts: a fixed-term contract, a contract for clearly determined work or with a view to replace a permanent employee. It is widely accepted that the contract cannot be for an indefinite period of time (contrary to the situation in Sweden and Germany). During the parliamentary discussions on the Temporary Work Act, the Minister stated explicitly that an indefinite employment relationship with a temporary employee is contrary to the philosophy of the Temporary Work Act.

Increasingly, however, it is thought that this should be possible under the present legislation. One argument is that the Temporary Work Act seeks to protect temporary employees as much as possible and that there is no greater protection than a contract for an indefinite period of time, which places the economic risk on the temporary work agency and not on the temporary employee. Furthermore, the exclusion of an indefinite employment relationship cannot be justified as protecting the permanent workers of the user company because this is already guaranteed by the fact that the use of temporary workers is only permissible in very limited situations. Another argument for allowing indefinite contracts for temporary workers is that the civil sanction for not having a written employment contract with the temporary worker in accordance with the Temporary Work Act is the application of legal provisions governing indefinite contracts. Clearly, the Temporary Work Act is not completely strange to the idea of having indefinite employment relations with temporary workers. That is confirmed by a recent law which created the possibility for temporary work agencies to employ long-term unemployed persons for an indefinite period of time with a view to facilitating their re-employment.

In any case, the use of atypical employment contracts within the scope of the Temporary Work Act is more flexible than under the Employment Contracts Act. It must be stressed though that the employer can always use traditional employment contracts under the Employment Contracts Act in the event that a temporary shortage of labour. The following is an overview of the main 'advantages' for the employer if the conditions for temporary work are fulfilled.

1. Replacement of a permanent worker

Replacement under the Employment Contracts Act cannot exceed a period of two years and is only possible when the employment contract of an employee is suspended, except in cases of strike and suspension for economic reasons. In cases of suspension, replacement under the Temporary Work Act is possible for an indefinite period of time, without requiring any further condition to be fulfilled. Moreover, the prohibition on replacement in cases of strike only applies to temporary work agencies.

Replacement under the Temporary Work Act is also, under certain conditions, permitted when the employment contract of a permanent employee is terminated. The maximum duration of the temporary work assignment and the procedures to be followed when seeking temporary work are determined by a collective agreement concluded in the National Labour Council. The maximum duration and the procedure depend on how the employment contract is terminated (whether with notice, for a just cause, or for another reason) and on whether or not a temporary work agency is involved. The maximum duration is longer and the procedure less strict when notice is not required for termination and when the temporary contract is not concluded with a temporary work agency.

The maximum duration for a replacement assignment is relatively short. It varies from three months to six months. In most cases, the parties can renew the temporary work contract for the same period. In principle, the approval of the trade union delegation is needed, both for the initial contract and for renewal. A trade union delegation represents the unionized workforce within the company. It is not clear whether all members of the trade union delegation or only a majority have to agree. If no approval is given, the employer may not have recourse to temporary work. When no trade union delegation exists in the company, the employer has to ask the authorization of the trade unions, which are represented in the Joint Committee to which the employer belongs. When these trade unions inform the employer of their disagreement, the employer shall inform the Labour Inspector within three working days and request him to reconcile the differing viewpoints. If the attempt at reconciliation fails, the employer shall ask the Labour Inspector to give his opinion, which will be binding on the parties involved. If no favourable opinion is given within seven days, the employer may not have recourse to temporary work.

2. *Temporary increase of work and exceptional work*

Unlike fixed-term contracts or contracts for clearly determined work under the Employment Contracts Act, temporary contracts for the same work and with the same employer may be made repeatedly, according to Article 3 of the Temporary Work Act. The temporary work contract is thus of particular use for employers who cannot predict exactly the duration and the extent of labour shortage. But the use of temporary work is only possible in the event of a temporary increase in workload or in cases of exceptional work. The procedure and duration of temporary work are determined by the previously mentioned collective agreements.

In the event of a temporary increase in the workload, temporary work is permitted provided the trade union delegation agrees in advance. In the absence of a trade union delegation, the trade unions within the Joint Committee have to give their approval. In case of disagreement between the trade unions in this committee, the procedure outlined above must be followed. The request can only be made for a maximum period of one calendar month, except in case of employment abroad, but permission relating to the length of the assignment is renewable.

When the temporary worker is provided by a temporary work agency, the temporary work contract can exceed one month, but the approval of the trade union delegation still has to be sought. If there is no trade union delegation, temporary work is possible for a maximum period of six or twelve months, renewable for a second period of up to six months, on condition that certain information obligations are fulfilled. If the employer however wants the temporary worker for a period longer than eighteen months, he must follow the same procedure as in cases of temporary work required for a temporary increase of work without the intermediation of a temporary work agency.

Temporary work is also possible when required for exceptional work. Exceptional work, according to Article 1, §4 of the Act on Temporary Work, is to be defined by the Executive or the National Labour Council. As long as the executive has not enacted a Royal Decree in this regard, Article 2, §5 of Collective Agreement No. 36, concluded in the National Labour Council on 27 November 1981, remains applicable.

Under that provision, exceptional work is not part of the ordinary activities of the undertaking, and may be, for example, work regarding the preparation, running and winding-up of trade fairs, congresses, workshops, seminars, public events, parades, exhibitions, receptions, market research, inquiries, elections, special promotions, interpretations, removals; all of which must demand the performing of short and specialized tasks which require special professional qualifications. The concept of exceptional work is extended in as far as the exceptional work is to be performed by temporary workers within a clearly defined assignment which falls within the frame of training projects through which temporary workers can integrate themselves into the labour market, or which is part of a project with the aim of helping employees recently subject to a collective dismissal or a business closure to find a new job.

The maximum duration of activities that may be performed as exceptional work is three months. A longer period is provided for some forms of exceptional work. In some cases the user has to fulfil obligations concerning the giving of information or to obtain the approval of the trade union delegation.

B. Legal Restrictions on Putting Employees at the Disposal of Third Parties

The greater part of temporary work is provided by temporary work agencies, even though, given a need for temporary labour, an employer can also choose to use the services of employees that are engaged by another employer. The second employer then puts these workers at the disposal of the first employer, the 'user', and delegates some or no authority over the employees. The Temporary Work Act, however, limits the possibilities of putting workers at the disposal of another employer, due to the fact that the legislator wanted to provide greater incentive for hiring workers. Putting workers at a user's disposal is only allowed within the framework of the authorized activity of temporary work agencies and in very exceptional cases.

Putting employees at the disposal of a user is moreover prohibited when the user exercises some of the authority which normally belongs to the employer. Therefore this activity is only permissible when done without any delegation of authority to the user (i.e. subcontracting). In 2000, an amendment to the Temporary Work Act enlarged the scope of the exceptions in a considerable way. Article 31, §1 of the Temporary Work Act stipulates that the user's respect of obligations concerning well-being at work, as well as his giving instructions concerning working time, rest time and performance of the employment contract are not considered as an exercise of authority by the user. As a consequence one could say that putting workers at the disposal of a user has evolved from being generally prohibited with exceptions to being generally permitted with exceptions.

1. Putting employees at the disposal of a user without any delegation of authority

In this case, putting employees at the disposal of a user constitutes subcontracting. There is, however, no clear-cut definition of sub-contracting. It has been described as a procedure used by companies to sub-let certain parts of their operation to subcontractors, rather than having the company's own employees performing the work. The rationale of this type of subcontracting or outsourcing is that in this way the work can often be done more efficiently and with fewer expenses to the company. It should however be stressed that subcontracting is not necessarily limited to temporary work, since it can be of a permanent nature, such as the allocation of certain tasks, for example the cleaning of buildings.

The key element which makes subcontracting lawful is that there is no delegation of authority from the employer to the user. This means that the work done by the employees for the user is performed under the sole direction or control of the employer. According to Belgian labour legislation, where the employee receives orders from the user or from his representatives, the subcontracting will become illegal. Again, it should be mentioned that the Act of 12 August 2000 has stipulated that the giving of instructions is in certain cases not considered as the exercise of authority.

There are not the same legal restrictions on subcontracting as there are on temporary work and on putting employees at the disposal of a user. However, it should be mentioned that the contractor as well as the subcontractor have special duties and responsibilities concerning the health and safety of the employees of both the contractor and the subcontractor.

2. Putting employees at the disposal of a user with delegation of authority

a. In exceptional cases

An employer can according to Article 32 of the Temporary Work Act exceptionally put some of his permanent employees at the disposal of another employer if the following conditions are fulfilled:

- Permission is obtained from the Labour Inspectorate:
  This permission is not required when a permanent employee, who remains employed by his (original) employer following his labour contract, is put at the disposal of a user: (i) within the framework of co-operation between enterprises belonging to the same economic or financial entity; (ii) with a view to the short execution of specialized tasks that require special professional experience.
- Agreement is obtained in advance from the employees' representatives:
  In case the employee representatives do not agree, the agreement can be obtained from the joint committee.

The terms and the period in which the worker is to be put at the user's disposal are laid down in a written document signed by the employer, the user and the employee. The contract must be drawn up before the start of the work. The salary and working conditions may in any case not be less than the salary of employees with the same function in the user company.

It should be noted that during the assignment, the actual employer remains the employer and has to respect all obligations that are imposed on him, such as paying the salary. The user is, however, together with the employer, responsible for payment of social security contributions, the salary and indemnifications.

b. Temporary work agencies

Temporary work agencies can only employ temporary employees as defined in the Temporary Work Act. If they operate outside the scope of the Act, they may lose their recognition and be subject to penalties. A temporary work agency may not operate without having obtained an official permission to do so. As indicated above, the Flemish, Walloon, or Brussels' regional government gives permission where certain conditions concerning the financial stability of the agency, capital requirements, etc. are fulfilled.

Under the Temporary Work Act, the temporary work agency is the employer of the temporary employee, with all the obligations under Belgian labour law and social security that this entails. Temporary work, provided by temporary work agencies, has to be performed by its employees. Temporary work agencies cannot contract 'independent' workers to perform temporary work. The Temporary Work Act stipulates very clearly that no evidence is admissible to prove that the contract is made with a self-employed worker, rather than being an employment contract (Article 8 of the Temporary Work Act).

When a temporary work agency puts a temporary employee at the disposal of a user contrary to the stipulations of the Temporary Work Act, the user will be considered as the employer of the temporary employee. Nevertheless, the temporary work agency remains responsible, together with the user, for the payment of the salary and the indemnifications to which the temporary employee is entitled, as well as for the payment of social security contributions.

3. The recognition of the temporary work agency

In order to have the maximum guarantee that the temporary work agency will respect its obligations towards its temporary employees, as well as to users, Belgian legislation provides that temporary work agencies can only operate in Belgium if recognized before starting their activities. As stated above this competence lies with the regional authorities.

a. Conditions required for recognition

(1) Flemish region

The person or company that wants to establish an employment service in the Flemish region or wants to advertise or make publicity in this regard needs to obtain recognition before starting to operate. For the Flemish Region, the rules are laid down in the Decree of 13 April 1999 concerning private employment services in the Flemish region and in the Decree of 8 June 2000 implementing the latter decree. A distinction should be made between the general recognition conditions for all offices that are engaged in employment service in the Flemish region and the specific recognition conditions for temporary work agencies operating in the Flemish region.

A temporary work agency with a registered office in the Flemish Region and wanting to engage temporary employees in order to put them at the disposal of users must fulfil the following conditions: (i) the agency has to be properly established as a commercial company; (ii) it needs to have a fully-deposited registered capital of

30,986.69 Euro; and (iii) the agency should also not have any arrears in payment of taxes, social security contributions or contributions to the livelihood guarantee fund.

As well as these specific conditions for temporary work agencies, certain general conditions have to be fulfilled by all offices operating in the sector of employment services. The conditions relate to (a) respecting the rights of the person looking for a job, (b) the quality of the service and (c) the *bona fide* character of the service.

(a) Rights of the person looking for a job. The privacy of the person looking for a job must be respected by the temporary work agency, by only using personal information for professional purposes and afterwards returning the acquired information to the employee. The person looking for a job must be treated in a non-discriminatory way and can never be required to pay for employment services. He must be properly informed about the activities of the service. The service may not start any search for employment which is contrary to public policy or when it can clearly determine that its activities are contrary to social and fiscal legislation.

Concerning employees of foreign nationality, the service can only intermediate if the legislation concerning the employment of foreign employees is respected. The service may not provide employees in cases of strike or lock-out.

The service has to subscribe to and respect a code of conduct. It cannot intervene in the creation of employment policy of the employer.

(b) Quality of the service. In order to guarantee the quality of the service, the managers in the service should have the necessary experience or education. Personal surveys and psychological tests also have to be done by or under the supervision of a psychologist.

(c) Quality of the service and bona fide character of the service. In order to assure the quality of the service and in order to guarantee its *bona fide* character, it must be properly established as a commercial company where the service is established as a legal person. Where it is established as a natural person, that person has to hold all civil and political rights.

The following further conditions are also imposed in this regard:

- the service should be neither in a state of bankruptcy, nor be the subject of bankruptcy proceedings, nor having requested or received a judicial agreement;
- the managers, business managers, or persons having the authority to commit or represent the company may not have been prohibited to perform duties under the Royal Decree No. 22 of 24 October 1934 which prohibits certain condemned and bankrupt persons to perform particular duties; the managers, business managers, or persons having the authority to commit or to represent the company may not have been held liable for the obligations or debts of a bankrupt company, during the five years preceding the request for recognition or renewal of recognition, under Article 35, 6, 63*ter*, 123, part 2, 7° or 133*bis* of the co-ordinated laws on commercial companies;
- the managers, business managers, or persons having the authority to commit or to represent the company may not have been repeatedly or seriously in breach of the tax legislation, the social legislation or of the legislation concerning the operation of an employment service.

In addition to these general service quality conditions, there are certain conditions that aim to guarantee the quality of specific activities in the service. In the Flemish region there's also a code of conduct that must be respected by employment services. Amongst other things the company must send an annual report of its activities to the Flemish Minister of Employment and to the advisory committee for the recognition of temporary work agencies.

A temporary work agency with a registered office in the Brussels or Walloon Region, or in a Member State of the European Community must meet the equivalent conditions imposed in its own region or country in order to obtain recognition by the Flemish authorities. If those conditions have no equivalence with the Flemish ones, the Flemish Minister for Employment can ask temporary work agencies to meet the conditions described above.

A temporary work agency with a registered office outside the European Union must meet the conditions mentioned above. Moreover, it needs to prove that it is active as a temporary work agency in the country of origin and that it is observing social and tax legislation there. It must also join a recognized social secretariat for employers in Belgium. The temporary work agency shall report the name of the person(s), and their home or address in Belgium, having the authority to act as an agent for and to represent the temporary work agency.

Moreover, a temporary work agency with a registered office outside the Flemish Region shall hand over the following documents: a copy of every employment contract for temporary work, a copy of every contract between the temporary work agency and a user, evidence of the posting of temporary employees or other employees under the EC regulations concerning social security and evidence of payment of contributions to the livelihood guarantee fund for temporary employees.

(2) Walloon Region

For the Walloon Region, the rules concerning recognition are laid down in the Decree of 13 March 2003 concerning the recognition of temporary works agencies. The conditions required to obtain recognition are almost the same as those required in the Flemish Region. Moreover, the following conditions have to be fulfilled: (i) the temporary work agency has to give the advisory committee all the documents and information requested by this committee; (ii) the temporary work agency is also obliged not to provide a user with any temporary employees in cases of strike or lock-out; (iii) the agency has to keep a copy of each employment contract for temporary work and of the contract between the temporary work agency and the user company for five years after the contracts expire. The recognition cannot be refused when the temporary work agency meets the equivalent conditions in its region or country.

A temporary work agency with a registered office outside the European Union and active in the Walloon region has to meet the conditions mentioned above. It is sufficient to prove however that is has met the equivalent conditions in the country of origin. Moreover, it must meet the following conditions: (i) it has to appoint a person domiciled in Belgium who has the authority to act as an agent for and to represent the temporary work agency; (ii) it must be active as a temporary work agency in the country of origin; (iii) it has to join a recognized social secretariat for employers in Belgium; (iv) the agency also must comply with Belgian social security legislation, unless an international convention states otherwise.

(3) Brussels Region

The rules are laid down in the Royal Decree of 3 December 1981 and in the Ministerial Decision of 9 June 1982 concerning the recognition of temporary work agencies in the Brussels Region. The conditions required to obtain recognition from the Regional Secretary for Employment are the following: (i) to be properly formed as a commercial company, with temporary work as an exclusive activity according to the bylaws; (ii) to have a fully-deposited registered capital of 30,986.69 Euro; (iii) not to provide a user with temporary employees, or to keep them working, in cases of strike or lock-out; (iv) to have joined a recognized social secretariat for employers, when the company is not based in Belgium.

b. Length of the recognition

(1) Flemish Region

In the Flemish Region, recognition is given for an indefinite period of time. It is however possible to withdraw recognition in the event that the legal obligations have not been fulfilled (e.g. the submission of a yearly activities report). An ongoing recognition for an indefinite period of time can also be transformed into recognition for a limited period of time.

(2) Walloon Region

The recognition is granted for a period of two years. It is renewable for a second period of two years or for an indefinite period. After the expiry of the second period of two years, the recognition can be renewed for an indefinite period or it can be refused.

(3) Brussels Region

The recognition is granted for up to one year, for as long as Royal Decree of 3 December 1981 concerning the recognition of temporary work agencies in the Brussels Region remains in force. The recognition is renewable.

III. OBLIGATIONS AND RIGHTS OF TEMPORARY WORK AGENCIES

A. Towards the User of Temporary Workers

1. Division of authority

Although the temporary work agency is the actual employer of the temporary employee, the temporary assignment is performed for the benefit of the user, to whom the temporary work agency delegates a part of the employer's authority, or more precisely the power necessary to direct and to control the job to be done at the user's undertaking. For the period during which the temporary employee is at the disposal of the user, the latter is responsible for the observance of those provisions of labour regulation and protection that apply to the workplace. These provisions relate amongst other things to: working time, public holidays, Sunday rest, work done by women, work by young people, night work, work rules, health and safety of employees, salubriousness at work and of the workplace.

The user and the temporary employee shall be considered to be bound by an employment contract for an indefinite period of time if: (1) the user continues to employ a temporary employee even though the temporary work agency has informed the user of its decision to withdraw the employee; (2) the user employs temporary employees in breach of the Temporary Work Act.

2. *The contract between the temporary work agency and the user*

The contract agreed upon between the temporary work agency and the user must be made in writing within seven working days of the date on which the employment of the temporary employee begins and must include at least the following stipulations:

- where recognition is required, the temporary work agency's recognition number;
- the registration number of the temporary work agency with the National Social Security Service;
- the designation of the Joint Committee or the Joint Sub-committee that the user falls under;
- the reasons for employing the temporary employee;
- the place and duration of the employment;
- working time rules in the user's undertaking;
- the professional qualifications of the temporary employee;
- the remuneration of a permanent employee with the same qualifications in the user undertaking;
- the way in which the remuneration is paid;
- specific characteristics of the assigned workplace;
- the registered office of the temporary work agency and the establishment where the temporary employee is working;
- the name of the vacation fund and the registration number;
- the insurance company providing cover against occupational accidents and the number of the insurance policy;
- the family allowance scheme and the registration number;
- if possible, the social secretariat for employers;
- the name of the undertaking's medical service;
- the gross remuneration not including holiday allowance; possibly the net remuneration;
- where appropriate, the date of the prior agreement or favourable advice;
- if the employee is a student, the fact that the contract has also been entered into within the framework of Title VI of the Employment Contracts Act;
- the post or qualifications of the temporary employee must be mentioned, under a designation used in the user undertaking, in such a way that the remuneration of the temporary employee can be determined in the easiest possible manner.

Any stipulation agreed upon between the temporary work agency and the user to the effect that the salary shall be paid to the temporary work agency in the event of a temporary employee being recruited by the user shall be null and void.

3. *Prohibition of temporary work agencies*

The employment of temporary workers through a temporary work agency is prohibited in some industrial sectors and for some categories of workers (e.g. blue-collar workers in removal companies).

No employment of temporary workers is possible in the event of a strike or lockout. The National Labour Council has implemented this provision. According to

Collective Agreement No. 58 of 7 July 1994 concerning the procedure and duration of temporary work, temporary work cannot be undertaken in cases of strike or lock-out at the user enterprise.

4. Calculation of the number of employees employed by the user

The temporary employees also have to be included in counting the number of the user's employees, for purposes of applying collective bargaining, except where they replace permanent employees whose contract is suspended.

To apply certain labour legislation which only enters into force where the company employs a certain number of employees (e.g. 50 for the mandatory establishment of a committee for preventing risks and protection in the workplace, or 100 for a works council) the temporary employees are considered as being employed by the user. Again, an exception is made where temporary employees replace permanent employees whose contract is suspended. This general rule is of course without prejudice to the application of the legislation under which the same temporary employees have to be included in counting the workforce of the temporary work firm.

B. Towards the Temporary Worker

1. The employment contract for temporary work

The temporary employee is an employee, *juris et de jure*, of the temporary work agency, under a contract for temporary work. No proof is allowed to counter the presumption that this is an employment contract. Article 7.3 of the Temporary Work Act indicates that: 'the temporary employee is an employee who enters into a contract of employment with a temporary work agency to work as permitted by the Temporary Work Act, to the benefit of one or more users for remuneration'.

The employment contract will be either a contract for blue-collar or for white-collar work, depending on whether the employee performs manual or intellectual work. The temporary employee will enjoy the same rights as permanent employees in the agency regarding social security (pension, sickness benefits, unemployment, family allowances, annual paid vacation). The normal rules in case of work accidents and professional illnesses apply. The employee also has access to the social services in the user undertaking.

The object of the contract is the performance of legally permitted temporary work. The contract can be concluded, as far as its nature is concerned, for a definite period, for precisely indicated work, or for the replacement of a permanent worker.

The Temporary Work Act stipulates that the parties have to agree upon two separate contracts: the first indicates that the parties intend to agree upon an employment contract for temporary work. This contract has to be in written form and has to be agreed upon before the start of the first assignment by the temporary work agency. It should be mentioned however that this contract does not have to be renewed every time the temporary employee accepts a new Assignment. The second contract also has to be in written form and constitutes the actual employment contract for temporary work. This contract shall be confirmed in writing at the latest within two working days following the actual start of service.

Article 8 of the Employment Contracts Act stipulates that in the absence of written contracts, the only rules applicable to the contract shall be those for employment contracts of an indefinite period of time. In that case, however, the employee may terminate the contract without notice or compensation up to seven days after expiry of the period of two days following the start of employment.

It should be stressed that any clause in the employment contract under which a temporary employee is forbidden to enter into the service of a user company on a permanent basis is null and void.

2. *Trial period*

Unless stipulated otherwise, the first three working days of employment constitute a trial period during which each party may end the contract without having to give either a term of notice or a termination indemnity. In the event a temporary employee works under consecutive employment contracts for a definite period of time for the same user in the same function, consecutive trial periods are not allowed.

3. *Content of the employment contract*

The employment contract for temporary work must contain the stipulations given above. A model contract that can be used by a temporary work agency has been designed under a collective agreement. The absence of one of the required items renders the temporary work contract null and void and the employee and the agency will then be considered to be bound by an employment contract for an indefinite period of time. The temporary employee must also receive, as indicated above, a copy of the document relating to the contract agreed upon between the temporary work agency and the user.

4. *Remuneration and seniority of the temporary employee*

The remuneration of the temporary employee cannot be lower than that to which he would have been entitled if he had been taken on directly by the user as a permanent worker under the same conditions. This means that a temporary worker, being sent for the first time to a user company, is not entitled to the salary of the employee he is replacing, but has to be paid according to the applicable wage-scale in the company, taking into account his age, qualifications and skills, function in the company and seniority.

Contrary to the proposal for a Directive on working conditions for temporary workers, the legal text does not speak explicitly about other working conditions. The method of comparison under the proposed Directive is also slightly different. The point of comparison is a comparable worker, which is a worker in the user undertaking occupying an *identical or similar* post to that occupied by the worker posted by the temporary agency, taking into account seniority, qualifications and skills.

It is also noteworthy that under the Temporary Work Act employees of hiring-out companies, aside from temporary work agencies, are only entitled to the remuneration of a permanent worker with *identical* functions. If no employee with identical functions exists, this equal treatment provision does not apply.

The Temporary Work Act does not specify what is meant by salary, though it is widely accepted that a broad interpretation of the term must be given. This means that all sorts of premiums must be paid to temporary employees, so that the conditions for acquiring temporary workers are fulfilled. It is less sure whether under the Temporary Work Act the temporary worker is also entitled to the communal facilities and services of the company (collective transport, day care centre for children, personal car).

Derogations from the equal treatment principle for temporary workers employed by temporary work agencies are authorized if equivalent benefits are granted by a collective agreement concluded in the Joint Committee for Temporary Work and extended by Royal Decree. The same derogation is possible regarding payment of remuneration in the event of suspended performance of the contract (e.g. due to sickness), provided the collective agreement makes equal pay the responsibility of the livelihood guarantee fund for temporary employees.

Normally a temporary employee would lose his seniority if he worked for another temporary work agency, or when there's a period of inactivity between two assignments for the same temporary work agency. The Temporary Work Act tries to remedy this situation and sets out special rules for the calculation of the seniority of the temporary employee. Also taken into account for the calculation of seniority are: (i) periods of suspension of the employment contract during which the temporary employee continued to fall under the social security system in as far he was not employed by another employer; (ii) periods of inactivity of one week or less between two assignments.

5. *The termination of the employment contract*

In principle, the general rules that apply to the termination of an individual employment contract apply in cases of temporary work. This implies that the employment contract agreed upon for an indefinite period of time will come to an end by giving notice. The contract for a definite period will end when the stipulated period expires. The contract for a precisely indicated task ends when the work is finished. The contract for replacement ends when the replaced employee returns to his job, though whether notice must be given depends on the terms of the contract.

When a contract is agreed upon for a definite period of time or for clearly defined work, an employer who terminates the contract before the expiry of its term and without reasons showing dismissal for just cause is required to pay to the other party an indemnity equal to the amount of remuneration until the last working day, provided that this amount shall not exceed twice the amount of remuneration corresponding to the period of notice that should have been respected where the contract was for an indefinite period of time.

The temporary work agency will, however, not be obliged to pay this indemnity when the user is responsible for early termination of the contract and provides the temporary employee with a comparable job (in terms of conditions and remuneration) for the remaining period. In the event of replacement of a permanent worker for an indefinite period, the indemnity is equal to three months, unless the user is responsible and the employee receives comparable work for a period of three months.

IV. THE ROLE OF THE SOCIAL PARTNERS

The representative employers' associations (the central employers' association, namely the Federation of Belgian Industries (FEB-VBO), the representative employers' association for temporary work agencies (FEDERGON)) and the trade unions are closely associated with the preparation, implementation and application of legislation concerning temporary work. The most important role of the social partners is in negotiating collective agreements on temporary work in all its forms. In Belgium, collective agreements are agreed at inter-industry level, in the National Labour Council, at industry level in the Joint Committees and at enterprise level.

A special joint committee has been established in which negotiations take place, dealing exclusively with issues concerning the employment relationship between temporary workers and temporary work agencies, of which most are members of FEDERGON. It should be underlined that hiring-out companies, aside from temporary work agencies, who lease out their personnel in accordance with the Temporary Work Act, are not bound by the collective agreements agreed upon by this committee.

Collective agreements negotiated within the National Labour Council or industrial Joint Committees bind employers who are members of one of the employer's associations represented in the Joint Committee, and all their employees, whether unionized or not. Employers who do not belong to an employer's association are only bound by collective agreements negotiated within a Joint Committee in as far as the individual labour contract does not contain conflicting provisions, unless these collective agreements are declared to have a generally binding effect by Royal Decree.

A. The Preparation of the Temporary Work Act

When temporary work started to gain popularity in the labour market in the early seventies, it had no legal framework. In those days, the activities of the temporary work agencies were considered with suspicion. An ideological debate arose between the social partners. The socialist trade union considered the principle of hiring out employees for profit as violating ILO Convention No. 96 of 1949. In their opinion employment services in the broad sense of the term were in principle to be supplied by the authorities, and could not be profit-oriented.

Given the ideological opposition, the conclusion of collective agreements in the National Labour Council in this area was very unlikely. As a consequence, the government took the initiative to propose an Act based on the majority opinion in the National Labour Council. A provisional Act concerning the provisional regulation of temporary work, interim work and the leasing out of personnel was adopted on 28 June 1976. That Act was valid for four years and expired on 30 November 1981 without replacement or extension by new legislation.

In anticipation of a definitive regulation concerning temporary work, provisional measures were taken by means of Collective Agreement No. 36, concluded in the National Labour Council. The content of this collective agreement did not differ substantially from the 1976 Act. In the following years the social partners in the National Labour Council made proposals for new legislation. The social partners negotiated various collective agreements concerning many aspects of temporary work.

The Act of 24 July 1987 finally provided permanent regulation of temporary work. The Temporary Work Act is the result of discussions between the social partners in the National Labour Council, rather than of deliberation in the Belgian parliament. In fact, the National Labour Council carried out the preparatory work required.

B. Supplementary Regulation on Recourse to Temporary Work

The Temporary Work Act constitutes the legal framework regulating the use of temporary work. A number of issues in this area were too contentious to be dealt with by legislation and were addressed instead by collective agreements at national, inter-industry level or by Royal decrees based on the proposal or advice of the social partners. In some industries the social partners agreed additional restrictions on the use of temporary work.

1. Collective agreements in the National Labour Council

Collective Agreements No. 36 of 27 November 1981 and No. 58 of 7 July 1994, both concluded in the National Labour Council and extended by Royal Decree, contain important provisions on the regulation of temporary work in addition to the Temporary Work Act.

a) Provisions on the procedure and duration of temporary work
The social partners in the National Labour Council defined the meaning of exceptional work. They also established the procedure to be followed in cases of replacement of a permanent employee whose employment contract was terminated and in cases of a temporary increase in workload. Finally they determined the maximum duration of temporary work in cases of replacement, temporary increase in workload and in cases of exceptional work.

b) Provision on temporary work in case of strike and lock-out
In the original draft of the Temporary Work Act, temporary work was prohibited in cases of strike and lock-out. It was impossible to reach agreement on this provision among the political parties represented in government (Christian democrats and liberals). The prohibition was not new. It was taken from the provisional Temporary Work Act of 1976. The trade unions as well as the employers' associations agreed upon the same stipulation in Collective Agreement No. 36 of 27 November 1981 and in the advice of the National Labour Council in preparation of the 1987 Act. The political discussion lasted more than 5 years. The only possibility of breaking the political deadlock was to delete the prohibition in the draft. Due to the lack of agreement in parliament, the social partners in the National Labour Council were asked to deal with the problem in a collective agreement. The social partners did so in 1990 by prohibiting temporary work in cases of strike and lock-out. This prohibition, however, only applies to temporary work agencies. There's no similar provision for employers who hire out their permanent employees to other employers.

2. Royal decrees based on the advice or proposal of the social partners

a) In the Joint Committee on Temporary Work

In accordance with the Act of 5 December 1968 on collective agreements and joint committees, a Joint Committee for temporary work has been established. This joint committee is composed of representatives of the employers' association (the users), the temporary work agencies as well as the trade unions. A Royal Decree of 8 April 1988 was enacted concerning the establishment and determination of the name and competences of the Joint Committee for Temporary Work.

Under the Temporary Work Act, the Joint Committee on Temporary Work has to give its advice to the Executive on Royal Decrees regulating (amongst other things): the respective obligations of the temporary work agencies and the user company concerning health and safety in the workplace, the obligations of temporary work agencies to give information to the National Labour Council and the maximum fee to be paid by the user company to the temporary work agency.

b) In the Joint Committee of user companies

Under the Temporary Work Act, other joint committees can intervene and make proposals to the Executive to limit the number of temporary employees to a certain percentage of the permanent workers employed by the user or to forbid the employment of temporary employees in certain sectors of industry or in certain professions.

As long as no Royal Decree has been enacted to implement these provisions, Article 18 of Collective Agreement No. 36 of 27 November 1981 remains applicable. Consequently, temporary work shall not be authorized in case of manual workers in undertakings whose business relates to removals, furniture warehousing and related activities falling within the competence of the Joint Committee for the Transport Industry. Until recently, the Collective Agreement No. 36 also prohibited temporary work in the construction industry. Since the modification under Collective Agreement No. 36 *quaterdecies* of 19 December 2001, temporary work provided by temporary work agencies is now authorized with a view to replace incapacitated employees and in cases of a temporary increase in workload under the specific conditions provided for by the collective agreement concluded within the Joint Committee for the Construction Industry.

3. Collective agreements within Joint Committees of user companies

Although Joint Committees at sector level only have advisory competence under the Temporary Work Act and have no explicit competences to regulate recourse to temporary work, many collective agreements on this issue are negotiated at industry level, especially in the Joint Committees, which are only competent for blue-collar workers. In some cases, social partners in the Joint Committee only reiterate the existing legal provisions on temporary work. In other cases, recourse to temporary work is more strictly regulated. Social partners sometimes agree upon a maximum percentage of the workforce that can perform temporary work in the company, upon restrictions in length of assignments or upon additional procedural obligations. In some rare cases, temporary work provided by temporary work agencies is prohibited for certain activities (e.g. in printing).

It should be underlined that collective agreements concluded in a Joint Committee of user companies are not binding on temporary work agencies and their employees because they only fall within the competence of the specific Joint Committee for temporary work. If a temporary work agency puts his personnel at the disposal of a user company in violation of a collective agreement applicable to the industry to which the user belongs, only the user can be held responsible. Furthermore, a potential issue of future debate is whether very tight restrictions on temporary work provided by temporary work agencies in a sector can be legally upheld in the light of (European) competition law, the possible European Directive on Temporary Work, and the growing acceptance of temporary work as a normal form of employment.

C. Supplementary Regulation on Salary and Working Conditions of Temporary Employees

1. The Joint Committee on Temporary Work

The Joint Committee on Temporary Work, like the other joint committees at sector level, is competent to establish salaries and working conditions for temporary employees employed by temporary work agencies. It may do so by way of collective agreements concluded between the representative employers' associations and the trade unions, which are represented on the committee. If Royal Decree extends such an agreement, all temporary work agencies are legally bound by it, and the related sanctions are criminal.

During the seventies and the eighties, the National Labour Council has fulfilled the tasks of the Joint Committee on Temporary Work and concluded a number of Collective Agreements concerning working conditions of temporary workers employed by temporary work agencies. It has continued this process until the members of that joint committee were nominated by Royal Decree of 3 May 1993. It seems accepted that the Joint Committee on Temporary Work modifies the collective agreements concluded within the National Labour Council before 1993, although the latter hold a higher status than the former.

One of the main objectives of the trade unions, which represent temporary workers employed by temporary agencies, is to obtain equal treatment for temporary workers as to working conditions in comparison with the permanent employees of the user company.

In this respect, it is important to recall that the Temporary Work Act does not contain a general anti-discrimination provision concerning all working conditions, but only provides that the remuneration of the temporary worker employed by a temporary work agency cannot be lower than that to which he would have been entitled if he had been taken on directly by the user as a permanent worker under the same conditions.

As mentioned above, derogation from the equal treatment principle for temporary workers employed by temporary work agencies is authorized if equivalent benefits are granted by a collective agreement concluded in the Joint Committee for Temporary Work and extended by Royal Decree. Here we can refer to Collective Agreement No. 36*decies*, agreed upon in the National Labour Council on 4 March 1986, concerning the end-of-year premium for temporary employees. The livelihood guarantee fund for temporary employees is charged with paying them an end-of-year bonus.

As well as collective agreements concerning wages, the Joint Committee on Temporary Work has also negotiated on prevention of risk and protection in the workplace, the establishment of trade union delegations in temporary work agencies and on working time. Very often the result of negotiations on a specific aspect of working conditions is that the temporary work agencies are bound to apply rules which are applicable in the user company (e.g. protective clothes, reduction of working time).

It is worth noting that collective agreements concluded in the Joint Committee for Temporary Work only bind the temporary work agency and not the user companies. This substantially limits the scope of negotiation for trade unions willing to defend the interests of temporary workers. That's why legal provisions or collective agreements at inter-industry level are often more effective.

In addition to this general competence, the Temporary Work Act specifically foresees that the joint committee has the task of setting up a livelihood guarantee fund for temporary workers. This fund was set up by Collective Agreement No. 36*bis*, concluded in the National Labour Council on 27 November 1981. In the event that a temporary work agency fails to meet its financial obligations towards temporary employees, the fund is responsible for paying to the temporary employees involved:

- the remuneration owed under individual employment contracts or collective agreements;
- the allowances and benefits payable under legislation or under collective agreements.

Temporary work agencies must comply with decisions taken in the Joint Committee for Temporary Work and the agreements concluded therein, even before they recruit employees, and from the moment they are recognized.

2. *The Joint Committee of the user companies*

There are few collective agreements concluded within Joint Committees, other than the Joint Committee on Temporary Work, which govern the working conditions of temporary workers employed by temporary work agencies because these provisions cannot be binding, in principle, on temporary work agencies and their employees.

However, in some rare cases, collective agreements provide that temporary employees have to be treated as favourably as permanent employees by the user company. Also exceptionally they oblige user companies having recourse to temporary employees for a time exceeding a fixed maximum period, to conclude an employment contract for an indefinite period of time with these employees. The judicial consequences for the temporary employee of the user violating such provisions are currently a subject of discussion. One can easily argue that the temporary employee is entitled to claim damages in case of violation if the provisions can be considered stipulations in favour of a third party according to Article 1121 of the Civil Code. But the provisions could also be considered merely contractual obligations of the user company towards the social partners.

D. The Recognition of the Temporary Work Agency

Since the special Act of 8 August 1980 concerning the reform of the Institutions, the recognition of temporary work firms is a competence of the Regions. In the three regions, the social partners play an active role in the recognition of temporary work agencies.

In the Social Economic Council of Flanders (SERV), an advisory commission concerning private employment services has been established, in which the employers' representatives and the employees' representatives participate. The commission gives advice concerning the recognition and withdrawal of recognition of temporary work agencies. Equivalent advisory commissions have been established for the Walloon and the Brussels Regions.

E. The Role of the Works Council and Trade Union Delegation in the User Company

On a yearly basis information has to be given by the user to its works council concerning the number of temporary workers hired, the reasons for their employment, the average length of their employment and the section of the enterprise in which they work.

As mentioned above, the trade union delegation has a critical role within the company with regard to temporary work. In principle, the approval of the trade union is needed in order to be able to use temporary work.

5. England

Gillian Morris

I. APPROACHES TOWARDS TEMPORARY WORK

Traditionally, English law has placed no substantive restrictions on the circumstances in, which, or duration for which, employers may use temporary workers, regardless of whether those workers are employed directly by the employer or supplied by a temporary work agency. The use of temporary labour employed directly is now subject to the Fixed-Term Employees (Prevention of Less Favourable Treatment) Regulations 2002,[1] designed to implement Directive 99/70 EC. However, there remain no general restrictions on employers' use of agency labour. Similarly, unlike some other European countries, the supply of labour by private organizations for profit has never been restricted.

Many employment agencies in the UK operate both as temporary work agencies and as recruitment agencies that place workers directly with employers.[2] The conduct of both these functions is subject to statutory regulation, and individuals may be barred from carrying on or being concerned with the carrying on of an employment agency if judged unsuitable to do so. The statutory standards are currently laid down in the Employment Agencies Act 1973[3] and the Conduct of Employment Agencies and Employment Businesses Regulations 1976 (henceforth 'the 1976 Regulations').[4] However, the 1976 Regulations are due to be replaced by regulations that, *inter alia*, afford greater protection to agency workers (for example, by making it unlawful to withhold payment from a worker because of non-receipt of payment, or documentary evidence that he or she has worked, from the user) and require users who wish to employ an agency worker as a permanent member of their staff to have the option of extending the hiring for a specified period rather than paying the agency a 'transfer fee'.[5] At the time of writing no date has

1. SI 2002/2034.
2. Known respectively as 'employment businesses' and 'employment agencies'; *see further* Section III below. A survey conducted for the DTI in 1999 suggested that some 63 per cent of agencies provide both temporary and permanent job-finding services: U. Hotopp, *Recruitment Agencies in the UK*, DTI, 2001.
3. As amended by the Deregulation and Contracting Out Act 1994, Section 35 and Schedule 10.
4. SI 1976/715.
5. Workers may not be charged fees by temporary work agencies, other than in exceptional cases, for which see the Employment Agencies Act 1973 (Charging Fees to Workers) Regulations 1976, SI 1976/714; Employment Agencies Act 1973 (Charging Fees to *Au Pairs*) Regulations 1981 SI 1981/1481. To date the fees charged to users have been unregulated, and, indeed, the Employment Agencies Act 1973 Section 5(1) originally prohibited such regulation. This prohibition was removed by the Employment Relations Act 1999, Section 31, Schedule 7, paragraph 2.

R. Blanpain & R. Graham (eds.), Temporary Agency Work and the Information Society, 101–114

been given as to when the new regulations will come into force. This paper is based on the existing law, but indicates where material amendments that are likely to be made.

As far as general labour law is concerned, agency workers are commonly denied access to protective legislation such as that relating to dismissal and leave for family reasons. This is because many statutory rights apply only to employees, and, to date, agency workers have generally been found by the courts not to be employees of either the agency or the user. Some measures, such as the anti-discrimination, minimum wage and working time legislation, make special provision for agency workers. This is unusual, however. There are no collective agreements at national or sectoral level relating to agency workers, and the Trades Union Congress reports that there is only limited collective bargaining covering this group.[6] The UK has not ratified ILO Convention No. 181 of 1997.

Estimates of the number of temporary agency workers vary widely, but all surveys reveal a substantial increase in their numbers over the past ten years or so.[7] The Department of Trade and Industry (DTI) estimates that about 600,000 people are working as temporary agency workers at any particular time in the UK.[8] The Labour Force Survey (LFS) of Spring 2002 asked more detailed questions about the characteristics of temporary agency workers, although because the total number reported by the survey to fall within this category (275,000) is regarded by the DTI as being unduly low these statistics should be treated with some caution. The LFS found that there are relatively high percentages of temporary agency workers in manufacturing, and in real estate and business activities (22.9 per cent and 21.1 per cent respectively). Health and social work and transport (where the percentages were 10.8 and 9.1) also rely heavily on agency staff.[9] Twenty one per cent of temporary agency workers were reported to work in the public sector.[10] In terms of occupational categories, the administrative and secretarial, elementary occupations and plant operative categories contain high proportions of temporary agency workers.[11] According to the LFS, 54 per cent of temporary agency workers choose to work as such, 45 per cent do so because they cannot not get a permanent job.[12]

As in the case of agency workers, estimates of the total number of employment agencies vary; the Government's Annual Business Enquiry suggested that there were 13,685 in August 2002;[13] the DTI suggests that the figure may be between 17,000 and 20,000.[14] The industry is highly fragmented; it is thought that the largest ten firms are unlikely to control more than 15 per cent of the market.[15] In the financial

6. Trades Union Congress, *Agencies for Change*, 2002, p. 27.
7. The Labour Force Survey indicates a 253 per cent increase between 1992 and 2001: DTI, *Discussion Document on Employment Status in Relation to Statutory Employment Rights*, July 2002, URN 02/1058, p. 31.
8. DTI, *Proposal for a Directive of the European Parliament and of the Council on Working Conditions for Temporary Agency Workers – Regulatory Impact Assessment*, p. 7. This figure contrasts with the figures of 275,000 given in the Labour Force Survey, and 1,336,699 given by the Recruitment and Employment Confederation, both of which are regarded by the DTI as unreliable for reasons explained in the Assessment. *See also* Hotopp, above, note 2.
9. DTI, above note 8, pp. 10–11.
10. DTI, above, p. 24.
11. As above, p. 12.
12. As above, p. 13.
13. Recruitment and Employment Confederation, *Annual Recruitment Industry Survey,* 2001/2, p. 8.
14. As above, note 42, p. 32.
15. As above, note 13.

year 2001/02, turnover in the recruitment industry as a whole (covering temporary work and direct placement) was estimated to be £23,387 million.[16]

At one time trade unions sought the abolition of all fee-charging employment services, but a State monopoly was rejected by successive governments on the grounds that this would be both costly and ineffective.[17] The contemporary trade union movement does not oppose the phenomenon of agency work as such, but is against the exploitation of agency workers and their use instead of permanent or directly-employed temporary staff to avoid employment rights. Some unions have set targets for the recruitment of temporary workers and implemented special measures such as portable membership schemes.[18]

The proposed Directive on working conditions for temporary agency workers, if accepted, would make a radical difference to the UK system. Currently there is no requirement that the 'basic working and employment conditions' of temporary workers should be at least those that would apply if they had been recruited directly by the user enterprise to occupy that job.[19] However, it has been suggested that this requirement may not affect some smaller users because 'basic working and employment conditions' are defined as 'working and employment conditions laid down by legislation, regulations, administrative provisions, collective agreements and/or other general provisions'. Smaller users are less likely to have formal pay scales, collective agreements or other forms of generally applicable provisions relating to these areas, and thus, it is argued, may be required only to adhere to legislative standards that apply to them already in the context of pay and working time.[20] The provisions relating to protection of pregnant women and nursing mothers, and equal treatment, may entail amendments to domestic legislation. The provisions on access to amenities and collective services have no equivalent in current law. Domestic law currently forbids a contractor placing on workers any prohibition or restriction that is calculated to deter them from taking up direct employment with a user. At present, there is no legal obligation for standing representative bodies to be formed at temporary work agencies or any other employers. Domestic legislation on European Works Councils would need to be amended so that all agency workers count towards thresholds when calculating if a European Works Council needs to be established. Finally, as discussed in Section V, it is by no means clear at present that temporary work agencies are recognized as 'employers' in English law, such recognition being identified as one of the purposes of the Directive.

The proposed Directive is very controversial in the UK. It is welcomed by the Trades Union Congress, although it considers that the principle of non-discrimination

16. As above, p. 6, quoting the Office of National Statistics Quarterly Turnover Inquiry.
17. B. Hepple, 'United Kingdom' in *Private Employment Agencies*, Bulletin of Comparative Labour Relations 36, Kluwer, 1999, p. 380.
18. Above, note 6, p. 2.
19. At the time of writing the question whether Article 141 EC enables an agency worker, in this case a female college lecturer, to compare herself for the purposes of claiming equal pay with a male lecturer employed directly by the College, even though they have different employers, on the ground that they work in the same establishment or service has been referred to the European Court of Justice: *Allonby* v. *Accrington and Rossendale College* [2001] EWCA Civ 529, [2001] IRLR 364. On 2 April 2003 Advocate General Geelhoed suggested that Article 141 could not be relied upon because the pay differences cannot be attributed to a single source and there is therefore no entity that can be held responsible for that difference and its elimination: Case C-256/01. *See further* Section IV.
20. DTI, above note 8, pp. 28–29.

should apply to all terms, including pay, from day one.[21] By contrast, employers' organizations are strongly against the proposals, arguing that they will reduce job opportunities and restrict labour market flexibility, impose onerous bureaucratic burdens on employers, and require employers to share information about pay and other conditions they may regard as confidential. Amendments proposed include a choice between 'agency' and 'user' comparisons for the purposes of equal treatment, or, if user comparisons are to be maintained, the option not to require them for up to 18 months.[22] The Recruitment and Employment Confederation, which claims to represent more than 50 per cent of the recruitment industry, considers that a minimum one-year threshold should apply.[23] The UK Government has concluded that the overall effect of the proposed Directive on the labour market for agency workers cannot be reliably predicted. On the one hand, it may improve the pay and working conditions for agency workers, so encouraging more people to work as such.[24] On the other, it may decrease demand for agency workers if higher fees are charged to user enterprises, although demand in those enterprises that choose to use agency workers primarily to maintain workplace flexibility may be unaffected.[25] To date, the Government has pressed for the non-discrimination principle to apply only after a year of employment. It has also reserved its position as to whether 'pay' can be included in a Directive based on Article 137 EC in the light of Article 137(6).

II. TEMPORARY WORK: DEFINITIONS AND POSSIBLE CHANNELS

> Temporary jobs can take a variety of forms. These have in common the fact that the jobs are held by someone who has been recruited to do them for a finite period of time (although this may be up to several years). They include seasonal work, casual work, non-permanent jobs obtained through a temporary employment agency ... and jobs carried out under a fixed-term contract.[26]

Since 1 October 2002, work carried out under a fixed-term contract is now subject to the Fixed-Term Employees (Prevention of Less Favourable Treatment) Regulations 2002,[27] designed to implement Directive 99/70 EC. These Regulations

21. Above, note 6, pp. 28–29.
22. Confederation of British Industry, *Parliamentary Brief on the Directive*, May 2002. *See also* DTI, *Summary of Responses to the Public Consultation on the Proposed Directive on Temporary (Agency) Work*.
23. Recruitment and Employment Confederation, *Response of the Recruitment and Employment Confederation to the Department of Trade and Industry's Consultation on the Proposed Agency Workers Directive*, 11 October 2002.
24. The DTI estimates that 54 per cent of agency workers could derive a pay benefit from the implementation of the Directive, assuming that the Directive does not include occupational pensions and occupational sick pay in the definition of 'pay': above, note 8, p. 18.
25. The Workplace Employee Relations Survey 1998 found that the most commonly cited reasons for workplaces to use temporary agency workers were short-term cover (59 per cent) and adjusting the labour force in line with demand (40 per cent): M. Cully S. Woodland, A. O'Reilly and G. Dix, *Britain at Work*, Routledge, 1999, p. 37.
26. F. Sly and D. Stillwell, 'Temporary Workers in Great Britain', in *Labour Market Trends*, September 1997, p. 347 at 348.
27. SI 2002/2034.

give fixed-term employees the right not to be treated less favourably than permanent employees of the same employer doing the same or broadly similar work, having regard, where relevant, to whether they have a similar level of qualification and skills. The right applies where the less favourable treatment is on the ground that the employee is fixed-term and is not justified on objective grounds. Less favourable treatment as regards any term of the contract is regarded as justified on objective grounds if the terms of the fixed-term employee's contract of employment, taken as a whole, are at least as favourable as the terms of the comparable permanent employee's contract of employment. Where a fixed-term employee who has been continuously employed on fixed-term contracts for four years or more is re-engaged on a fixed-term contract the new contract has effect as a permanent contract unless the renewal on a fixed-term basis was objectively justified (subject to any collective or workforce agreement modifying the four-year period or otherwise preventing abuse arising from successive fixed-term contracts). For the purposes of the Regulations, a 'fixed-term contract' in this context means a contract that will terminate on the expiry of a specific term, on the completion of a particular task, or on the occurrence or non-occurrence of any other specific event other than the attainment by the employee of any normal and *bona fide* retiring age in the establishment for an employee holding the position held by him. Agency workers are expressly excluded from the Regulations. There is no concept of 'emergency help' in English law. There is no restriction on subcontracting, that is independent contractors undertaking specific tasks using their own employees.

Temporary work as organized by employment agencies is discussed in the sections that follow.

III. THE TEMPORARY WORK ORGANIZATIONS

In the Employment Agencies Act 1973 the technical term for a temporary work agency is an 'employment business'. This is the term used to describe 'the business (whether or not carried on with a view to profit and whether or not carried on in conjunction with any other business) of supplying persons in the employment of the person carrying on the business, to act for, and under the control of, other persons in any capacity'.[28] This definition is not limited to organizations that supply labour on a temporary basis, but in practice this is what employment businesses do. 'Employment' extends to 'employment by way of a professional engagement or otherwise under a contract for services' and 'the reception in a private household of a person under an arrangement whereby that person is to assist in the domestic work of the household in consideration of receiving hospitality and pocket money or hospitality only' (so-called *au pair* arrangements). 'Contract for services' is not defined in the Act, but is commonly used to describe the arrangement whereby services are rendered by the self-employed.[29] The term 'employment business' is not, therefore, confined to bodies that have an employer/employee relationship with temporary workers (and, as described in Section V, temporary workers are not generally regarded as employees of the employment business).

28. Employment Agencies Act 1973, Section 13(1), (3). This corresponds to the definition of 'private employment agency' in Article 1(1)(b) of ILO Convention No. 181 (1997).
29. Some 'self-employed' persons may fall within the statutory category of 'workers', defined below.

The 1973 Act uses the term 'employment agency' for bodies that provide 'services (whether by the provision of information or otherwise) for the purpose of finding workers employment with employers or of supplying employers with workers for employment by them'.[30] It refers, therefore, to recruitment agencies that place workers directly with employers, usually (although not necessarily) on a permanent basis. Confusingly, however, the term 'employment agency' is commonly used in other contexts (including the case law on the employment status of agency workers) to describe organizations that would be classified under statute as 'employment businesses'. In this paper I use the term 'temporary work agency' synonymously with 'employment business'. In practice, as indicated in Section I, most bodies operate both as employment businesses and as employment agencies.

Originally the 1973 Act required employment businesses and agencies to be licensed. In 1995, however, this was replaced by a power for the Secretary of State to seek a prohibition order against a particular person, which an employment tribunal has power to grant. Such an order may prohibit a person from engaging in an activity altogether, or from doing so otherwise in accordance with specified conditions, for a specified period of up to ten years. An employment tribunal may not grant a prohibition order 'unless it is satisfied that ... [that person] ... is, on account of his misconduct or for any other sufficient reason, unsuitable to do what the order prohibits'. Failure to comply with a prohibition order is a criminal offence, punishable by a fine of up to £5,000.[31] It is also a criminal offence to breach the regulations relating to the conduct of employment agencies, again punishable by a maximum fine of £5,000.[32] Between the financial years 1994/1995 and 2001/2002, 85 prosecutions were brought (23 during the financial year 2001/2002); up to 2000/2001, a total of 26 prohibition orders had been granted.[33]

There is no requirement for an employment business (or agency) to take any particular legal form. The Recruitment and Employment Confederation has some 8,000 individual members and 6,000 corporate members.[34]

IV. THE USER OF TEMPORARY EMPLOYEES

There are no restrictions on the situations in which employers may use the services of temporary workers through a temporary work agency. However, employment businesses may not supply workers to a user as direct replacements of employees who are in industrial dispute with that user to perform the same duties as those

30. *Ibid.*, Sections 13(1), (2). This corresponds to the definition of 'private employment agency' in Article 1(1)(a) of ILO Convention No. 181 (1997). There are specified exceptions to the definitions of 'employment business' and 'employment agency', including services provided by any organization of employers or of workers for its members: Section 13(7).
31. Employment Agencies Act 1973, Sections 3A, 3B, inserted by the Deregulation and Contracting Out Act, 1994.
32. As above, Section 5(2).
33. Figures supplied by Employment Agency Standards Office at the DTI. Financial years commence on 6 April. Figures for 2001/2002 go only to February 2002. The DTI's Employment Agency Standards Inspectorate seeks to ensure compliance with the legislation wherever possible and few investigations lead to action in a court or tribunal: DTI, *Revision of the Regulations Covering the Private Recruitment Industry – Regulatory Impact Assessment*, paragraph 58.
34. There is no indication of the number of employment businesses and employment agencies that operate as partnerships.

normally performed by those employees.[35] A proposed amendment will remove this restriction where the industrial action is unofficial,[36] or where the employment business has no reasonable grounds for knowing that the worker to be replaced is taking part in industrial action. However, it will widen the prohibition on supply to cover performance of duties normally performed by a worker assigned by the user to substitute for those taking part in industrial action.

The relationship between the temporary work agency and the user of temporary labour will be governed by contract.[37] It is improbable that an agency worker will have any form of contractual relationship with the user.[38] In one recent case a court held, despite the fact that the user had not entered into a contract with the worker, he was nevertheless the user's employee given that in practice the user had exercised the same degree of control over him as it exercised over full-time 'direct' employees for the two years he had worked there.[39] However, this finding is unusual. Moreover, the court in this case was not required to consider the more commonly-raised alternative argument that the worker had a contract of employment with the agency. Had it been so required, and had it found that he did have such a contract, it would have been difficult to see how the worker could also have a contract of employment, in respect of the work in question, with the user.[40] In general users are unlikely to be regarded as the employers of agency workers. This does not mean that they owe no legal obligations to agency workers, however, although these obligations are derived from separate pieces of legislation rather than a single source.

The first group of obligations is in the area of health and safety. The Health and Safety at Work etc. Act 1974 Section 3 provides that every employer has a duty to conduct his undertaking 'in such a way as to ensure, so far as is reasonably practicable, that persons not in his employment who may be affected thereby are not thereby exposed to risks to their health and safety'. This is sufficiently wide to cover the relationship between the user and workers supplied by a temporary work agency. A worker who is injured while working for the user may also be able to sue for damages at common law in respect of negligence or breach of statutory duty by the user.[41]

Secondly, users owe agency workers specific duties in relation to sex, race and disability discrimination. The user, described here as the 'principal', must not discriminate on these grounds against 'contract workers'. A 'principal' is one who makes work available for doing by individuals who are employed by another person, who supplies them under a contract with the principal; a 'contract worker' is

---

35. Regulation 9(11) of the 1976 Regulations.
36. Within the meaning of the Trade Union and Labour Relations (Consolidation) Act 1992, Section 237. *See further* S. Deakin and G.S. Morris, *Labour Law,* 3rd edition, Butterworths, 2001, pp. 989–990.
37. The 1976 Regulations specify the information to be given to the user before the contract of supply is entered: Reg. 9.
38. *O'Sullivan* v. *Thompson-Coon* (1972) 14 KIR 108; *Hewlett Packard Ltd* v. *O'Murphy* [2002] IRLR 4.
39. *Motorola* v. *Davidson* [2001] IRLR 4. *See also Franks Ltd* v. *Reuters Ltd* [2003] EWCA Civ 417, where the Court of Appeal held that where an individual had worked for the same client of the agency for five years this was capable of generating an implied contractual relationship, and the employment tribunal should have considered whether there was such a relationship before determining whether he was an employee.
40. Deakin and Morris, above note 36, p. 176.
41. Hepple, above note 17, p. 386.

an individual supplied to the principal under such a contract.[42] The Court of Appeal has held that this provision is not limited to discrimination between the contract workers supplied to a particular employer, but also extends to discrimination between a contract worker and the principal's own employees.[43] However, the court emphasized the need to show that the alleged discrimination is *by the principal* rather than the agency. Thus, complaints about contractual matters are likely to lie against the agency rather than the principal, although it has been suggested that it may be necessary to inquire whether the principal would only allow the worker to do the work if the agency stipulated a specific condition in the contract.[44] The question whether Article 141 EC enables a contract worker, in this case a female college lecturer, to compare herself for the purposes of claiming equal pay with a male lecturer employed directly by the College, even though they have different employers, on the ground that they work in the same establishment or service has been referred to the European Court of Justice.[45]

In addition to these specific liabilities, there are three further areas where users may have statutory obligations to agency workers, depending on how the relationship between worker and agency, on the one hand, and worker and user, on the other, is constructed. In all three cases the statutory right in question applies to 'workers'. The definition of a 'worker' is not confined to employees, but extends to any individual who works under (or, where the employment has ceased, worked under) a contract whereby he or she undertakes to do or perform personally any work or services for another party to the contract whose status is not by virtue of the contract that of a client or customer of any profession or business undertaking carried on by that individual.[46] First, both agency and user are regarded as employers for the purposes of the statutory right to be accompanied by a companion at a disciplinary or grievance hearing where the agency worker does not have a 'worker's contract' with either party relating to that work.[47] As explained above, an agency worker is unlikely to have a contract of any kind with the user; whether he or she has a worker's contract with the agency is open to doubt, as discussed in Section V below. If he or she does have a worker's contract with the agency, the right may be exercised against the agency in the normal way; failing that, the right will be exercisable against both agency and user. Thus, this provision ensures that the worker's statutory right to be accompanied is protected even if there is no 'worker's contract' with either party. Secondly, users may be accorded the duties imposed upon employers to ensure that obligations relation to payment of the national minimum

42. Sex Discrimination Act 1975, Section 9; Race Relations Act 1976, Section 7; Disability Discrimination Act 1995, Section 12. In *Abbey Life Assurance Ltd* v. *Tansell* [2000] IRLR 387, the Court of Appeal held that the definition of 'principal' does not require a direct contract between the person making the work available and the employer of the individual supplied to do that work. The legislation applied, therefore, to a case where the supply of the employee was made by his company to the principal through a temporary work agency rather than direct to the principal.
43. *Allonby* v. *Accrington and Rossendale College* [2001] EWCA Civ 529, [2001] IRLR 364.
44. As above, Ward LJ at 376.
45. As above, note 19.
46. *See*, for example, Employment Rights Act 1996, Section 230(3). The definition varies somewhat between individual statutes (for example, under the Trade Union and Labour Relations (Consolidation) Act 1992 clients or customers of business undertakings are not excluded), but the requirement for personal service is common to all the basic definitions.
47. Employment Relations Act 1999, Section 13.

wage and working time and annual leave are met, although once again, this is only if there is no 'worker's contract' with either party relating to the work.[48] In these contexts, the employer's obligations fall on one party only; whichever of the agency or user is responsible for paying the agency worker in respect of the work or, if neither is responsible, whichever of them in practice pays the worker.[49] This is likely to be the agency rather than the user. (Under proposed amendments, it will be mandatory for a temporary work agency to undertake to pay the worker, irrespective of whether it is paid by the user for that work.) Finally, agency workers are accorded specific protection against detriment, including dismissal, for making a disclosure covered by the terms of the 'whistleblowing' legislation.[50] For these purposes a 'worker' is said to include a person who 'works or worked for a person in circumstances in which (i) he or she was introduced or supplied to do that work by a third person, and (ii) the terms on which he is or was engaged to do the work are or were in practice substantially determined not by him but by the person for whom he works or worked, by the third person or by both of them'. The 'employer', in relation to such a worker, includes 'the person who substantially determines or determined the terms on which he is or was engaged'.[51] It will need to be decided on the facts, therefore, whether the user or the agency substantially determined the terms of engagement in order to establish which of them has the liability of an 'employer' under the 'whistleblowing' provisions.

V. THE TEMPORARY WORKER

Social security law and *tax law* treat temporary agency workers as if they are the employees of the agency for the purposes of determining liability for income tax and national insurance contributions, provided that they are subject to, or to the right of, supervision, direction and control as to the manner in which services are rendered.[52] This means that the agency is required to deduct tax and national insurance contributions from workers' pay at source, rather than the worker himself or herself being responsible for making payment to the Inland Revenue or Department for Work and Pensions, as appropriate. The classification of agency workers as 'employed earners', rather than as self-employed, for social security purposes means that the agency, as well as the worker, is liable to pay 'Class 1' national insurance contributions in respect of the worker's earnings. Class 1 contributions entitle agency workers to the benefits available to 'employees', provided that any additional generally-applicable qualifying conditions are met.

Labour law, by contrast to social security and tax law, is silent on the legal status of agency workers. The 1976 Regulations require the employment agency to issue temporary workers with a written statement containing full details of the terms

48. National Minimum Wage Act ('NMWA') 1998, Section 34; Working Time Regulations ('WTR') 1998 SI 1998/1833, Reg. 36.
49. This provision does not apply where the agency worker is a party to a contract under which he or she undertakes to do the work for a client or customer of any profession or business undertaking that he or she carries on.
50. Employment Rights Act 1996, Sections 43A-L, 47B.
51. As above, Section 43K.
52. Income and Corporation Taxes Act 1988, Section 134; Social Security (Categorization of Earners) Regulations SI 1978/1689.

and conditions of employment of the worker, which must indicate whether the agency regards them as its employees or as self-employed.[53] However, they do not stipulate what the nature of that relationship should be, and this remains a matter for the courts to decide on the facts of the individual case. Thus, no clear answer can be given to the question of how English labour law treats agency workers. The 'label' that the agency puts on the relationship in the written statement is not decisive; even in cases where temporary workers have been designated as employees the courts have sometimes disregarded this and found them to be self-employed,[54] and vice versa.[55]

In practice it will usually be difficult to establish the existence of a contract of employment, required for access to the majority of employment protection rights, between the temporary work agency and the worker. This is because two of the tests applied by the courts to determine whether an individual works under a contract of employment may be hard for agency workers to satisfy. The first test is that of 'mutuality of obligation', which requires there to be mutual commitments to maintain the employment relationship in being over a period of time. On this basis, agency workers have been denied employee status on the basis that the agency for which they worked was not required to find them work, nor were they required to accept assignments offered by the agency.[56] This approach has not been uniformly applied; in 1997 the Court of Appeal held that the relevant question was the nature of the relationship while the worker was engaged on a particular assignment rather than the establishment of a 'global' contract.[57] This reasoning means that an agency worker who undertook a series of discrete jobs could be regarded as working under a separate contract of employment with the agency for each job he or she undertook, or, indeed, his or her legal status could vary from one hiring to the next, depending on the terms that governed it. However, while a more attractive approach than one that focuses on the 'global' relationship with the agency, it is not reflected in the general body of case law in this area. The second test that may debar agency workers from being classified as employees is that of 'control', which in its contemporary form 'includes the power of deciding the thing to be done, the means to be employed in doing it, the time when and the place where it shall be done'.[58] Lack of day-to-day supervision by the agency over the worker has been fatal in some cases,[59] despite the fact that the residual control the agency exercises may be no less than that of an employer over its permanent staff who work outside the employer's premises. In other cases, however, the courts have been prepared to find that the agency has sufficient powers over the worker for a contract of employment to exist.[60]

53. Regulation 9(6)(a) of the 1976 Regulations. The statement should also include details of the kind of work the worker may be supplied to do, the minimum rates of pay applicable to such work, and details of any expenses payable. The amending Regulations replace the term 'self-employed' with 'contract for services'.
54. *Wickens* v. *Champion Employment* [1984] ICR 365.
55. *McMeechan* v. *Secretary of State for Employment* [1997] IRLR 353; *Dacas* v. *Brook Street Bureau (UK) Ltd* [2003] IRLR 190.
56. *Montgomery* v. *Johnson Underwood Ltd* [2001] EWCA Civ 318,[2001] IRLR 269.
57. *McMeechan* v. *Secretary of State for Employment*, above, note 55; *Dacas* v. *Brook Street Bureau (UK) Ltd* above, note 55.
58. *Ready Mixed Concrete (South East) Ltd* v. *Minister for Pensions and National Insurance* [1968] 2 QB 497, 515.
59. *Montgomery* v. *Johnson Underwood Ltd*, above, note 56.
60. Above, note 55.

If a temporary worker is found to be an employee of the temporary work agency, he or she is potentially able to enjoy the rights available to those who are employees of any other employer, although their pattern of work may disbar them from those rights, such as protection against unfair dismissal and redundancy, that require a minimum continuous period of service.

Some employment rights, such as those relating to a minimum wage, working time, four weeks' annual leave, whistleblowing, and the right to be accompanied at disciplinary and grievance hearings, are granted to those categorized as 'workers' a category that, as explained in Section IV, extends beyond that of 'employees'. The precise definition of a worker varies as between individual statutes, but essentially it applies not only to those who have a contract of employment, but also those who have entered into or work under 'any other contract ... whereby the individual undertakes to do or perform personally any work or services for another party to the contract whose status is not ... that of a client or customer of any profession or business undertaking carried on by the individual'.[61] There is no reported case where it has been found that agency workers who are not employees are 'workers' according to this definition, and there is a difficulty that the definition requires an undertaking to render personally work or services 'for another party to the contract' rather than to a third party. In addition, recent case law suggests that some form of 'umbrella' contract may be required for an individual to constitute a 'worker'[62] if it is, then this may create the same difficulties for agency workers as the 'mutuality of obligation' test that must be satisfied for classification as an 'employee'. In two cases workers hired out by an agency for use by a third party were held to have a *sui generis* status, working neither under a contract of employment nor a contract for services.[63]

Some legislation makes special provision for agency workers, even if they do not fall within the category of 'employee' or 'worker'. Temporary work agencies are specifically required not to discriminate against agency workers on grounds of sex or race,[64] and they may, as a matter of construction, have duties under the Disability Discrimination Act 1995.[65] In addition, as explained in Section IV, they may have obligations under legislative provisions designed to ensure that agency workers are not left without a remedy against anyone. Agencies may have obligations relating to working time, annual leave and the national minimum wage on the basis that they are responsible for paying, or in practice pay, the worker; liability under the 'whistle-blowing' procedure if they substantially determine the worker's terms of engagement; and liability, together with the user, for the purposes of the right to be accompanied by a companion at a disciplinary or grievance hearing where the agency worker does not have a 'worker's contract' with either party relating to that work.

Agency workers do not belong to the community of permanent workers within the user enterprise for the purposes of collective representation. Trade unions

---

61. Above, note 46.
62. *Voteforce Associates Ltd* v. *Quinn* EAT/1186/00; *see also Byrne Brothers (Formwork) Ltd* v. *Baird* [2002] IRLR 96.
63. *Construction Industry Training Board* v. *Labour Force Ltd* [1970] 3 All ER 220; *Ironmonger* v. *Movefield Ltd t/a Deering Appointments* [1988] IRLR 461.
64. Sex Discrimination Act 1975, Section 15; Race Relations Act 1976, Section 14.
65. In the anti-discrimination statutes, 'employment' includes employment personally do to any work; it does not require that the work be for another party to the contract: *see Burton* v. *Higham t/a Ace Appointments* [2003] IRLR 257.

may apply for mandatory recognition in respect of a specified bargaining unit where an employer employs a minimum of 21 workers, but because the user is not (generally) the employer of an agency worker, he or she would not be counted as a member of a bargaining unit in respect of which recognition may be sought at the user enterprise.[66] There is currently no statutory system of works councils in the UK.

In the event of a strike of permanent employees at the workplace, a union or other dispute organizer that induced agency workers to participate in the strike would have no protection against the liability in civil law for inducing breach of contract that would arise if those workers owed a contractual obligation to the agency to work on the day in question (and assuming, as is generally the case, that the user is not the agency worker's employer).[67] The statutory protection against liability requires the dispute organizer to act 'in contemplation or furtherance of a trade dispute', but excludes secondary industrial action from protection, even if it furthers the dispute.[68] Secondary action occurs when a person induces another to break a contract of employment or interferes or induces another to interfere with its performance (or threatens such activities) and the employer under the contract of employment is not the employer party to the dispute.[69] Inducing agency workers to walk out in sympathy with permanent staff is likely, therefore, to be unlawful.[70] However, as described in Section IV, temporary work agencies may not supply workers to a user as direct replacements of employees who are industrial dispute with that user to perform the same duties as those normally performed by those employees. Proposed modifications to this restriction are also described in Section IV.

VI. THE ROLE OF THE SOCIAL PARTNERS

As indicated in Section I, employers regard temporary agency workers as an important source of flexible labour. Trade unions do not oppose the phenomenon of agency work as such, but oppose the exploitation of agency workers and their use instead of permanent or directly-employed temporary staff to avoid employment rights. There are no agreements at national or sectoral level covering agency workers, and only limited collective bargaining covering this group.

The social partners have no formal involvement in the administration of the legal system governing temporary work agencies.

VII. THE ROLE OF THE GOVERNMENT

There are no official temporary work agencies as such, although there is a national network of Government offices ('Jobcentres') that arrange placements for direct employment and give advice to employers and job seekers. As described above, the

66. Trade Union and Labour Relations (Consolidation) Act 1992, Schedule A1.
67. On English law relating to industrial action, *see* generally Deakin and Morris, above, note 36, Chapter 11.
68. TULRCA 1992, Sections 219, 224.
69. 'Contract of employment' in this context includes any contract under which one person personally does work or performs services for another: TULRCA 1992, Section 224(6).
70. Agency staff could not be made party to the 'primary' trade dispute because a 'trade dispute' is confined to a dispute between workers and their own employer: TULRCA 1992, Section 244(1)(5).

conduct of private temporary work agencies is subject to statutory regulations, and the DTI can seek a prohibition order against any individual deemed unsuitable to operate or work in an employment agency (*see* Section III). It is a criminal offence to breach a prohibition order.

VIII. CONCLUSIONS

Temporary agency work is well established in the UK, and has increased significantly in recent years. The future regulation of agency work is intimately connected with the fate of the proposed Directive. If the current proposals are accepted, their impact upon the use of temporary agency work is difficult to predict. For those employers that regard agency workers as a cheap alternative to permanent or other directly-employed staff, they may act as a disincentive to their use. However, employers resort to agency labour for a variety of reasons. At the present time, the future scale of agency work in the UK remains in the realm of speculation.

SELECT BIBLIOGRAPHY

Department of Trade and Industry, *Proposal for a Directive of the European Parliament and of the Council on Working Conditions for Temporary Agency Workers – Regulatory Impact Assessment*, 2002

Deakin, S. and Morris, G.S., *Labour Law*, 3rd edition, Butterworths, 2001

Hepple, B., 'United Kingdom' in *Private Employment Agencies*, Bulletin of Comparative Labour Relations 36, Kluwer, 1999

Hotopp, U., *Recruitment Agencies in the UK*, corrected version, November 2001, DTI

Recruitment and Employment Confederation, *Annual Recruitment Industry Survey* 2001–2002

6. France

Sabine Smith-Vidal

INTRODUCTION

The essential feature of temporary work is the existence of a three-way relationship between user-company, temporary worker and temporary work agency. Whether or not national legislation qualifies the temporary agency as employer and the temporary worker as employee, one is faced with the difficulty that the temporary worker is effectively employed by an enterprise other than the one with which he/she has a contractual relation and by which he/she is paid.

Temporary work activities are very strictly regulated under French Law, in order to protect the employees concerned, who are, by nature, less protected than employees under an indefinite-term employment contract. Furthermore, the purpose of the legislation concerned was to regulate the operations of many agencies which were bordering on the illegal.

As a consequence, a Law dated 1 January 1972 regulated the possibility for an employer to hire immediately the services of employees from another employer through a temporary work agency. Only a temporary work agency duly recognized by the French administration is allowed to act for profit as an intermediary between an employer and hired-out employees. Any other form of leasing employees for profit is prohibited and sanctioned by severe criminal penalties.

A national Collective Agreement was agreed on 24 March 1990 between the employers' representatives and three of the main trade unions: the CFDT, the CFTC and the CGC. This agreement was the inspiration for a new law, passed on 12 July 1990 'to favour stability of employment by adapting the regime of unstable contracts'. The Ministry of Labour has published two Circulars relating to the application of the Law, on 30 October 1990 and on 29 August 1992. Furthermore, on 2 April 1999, a new Circular required labour inspectors to take action against the abuse of temporary workers by employers.

However, in order to take into account the circumstances of certain professionals (artists, models, and others) or to develop opportunities for some categories of job seeker, the Law authorized exceptions to these strict regulations.

It must also be pointed out that under a decree of 1848, the French legislator's concern was to prohibit any form of leasing employees that could procure profits for its leasor. Consequently, an employer is prohibited from leasing its employees for profit. Therefore, the difficult distinction between a contract for the provision of services which is authorized and the leasing of employees for profit must be made. It must be added that not-for-profit leasing of employees is allowed under certain conditions (of duration for example).

R. Blanpain & R. Graham (eds.), Temporary Agency Work and the Information Society, 115–126

On 20 March 2002, the European Parliament and the Council proposed a directive on working conditions for temporary workers[1]. This draft Directive should be taken into account as it could modify the French principles in some respects.

Temporary work has grown significantly in France and appears, especially for younger persons, mothers and less qualified employees, as a way either to enter the job market or to pursue flexible working. On the other hand, for many employers, a temporary work contract is considered as a kind of 'trial period' before possibly hiring the employee concerned on an indefinite term employment contract.

According to the most recent statistics, 11.4 per cent of the working population consists of temporary workers. It should be noted that around 60 per cent of the blue-collar employees are temporary workers and 13 per cent of temporary workers are found in the car industry, 10.6 per cent in the semi-finished goods sector, 9.8 per cent in construction and 8.8 per cent in machine manufacturing.

The purpose of a temporary employment contract must not be to fill on a permanent basis a position related to the normal, continuous activity of the user undertaking. Consequently, a temporary assignment can be concluded, under a Law dated 12 June 1990, only in the following circumstances:

- To replace an employee in the event of absence, suspension of contract, permanent leave preceding termination of contract which has been approved either by the Works Council or any personnel delegates, or pending the actual arrival of an employee hired under an indefinite term employment contract who is to replace a former employee;
- To respond to a temporary increase in enterprise activity, for example in the event of an exceptionally large order from a customer. In such a case, prior to the hiring of temporary workers, the employer must consult the works council or any personnel delegates;
- To carry out urgent work in order to prevent accidents on the business premises;
- To perform well-defined occasional tasks which are unrelated to the user's regular operations, for example, an audit or a training program;
- To undertake seasonal employment or employment for which, in certain areas defined by decree or by an extended collective agreement, it is common practice not to use an employment contract for an indefinite term due to the nature of the activity or the temporary nature of the employment.
  - Seasonal work is found in, for example, agriculture, tourism, and teaching. However, it should be pointed out that the annual conclusion of a temporary work contract with the same employee can often lead to considering the actual relationship between user and temporary worker, *de facto*, as one of an indefinite term.
- As regards employment for which it is common practice not to use an employment contract for an indefinite term, the areas concerned are:
  - forestry;
  - ship repair;
  - removal services;
  - hotels and restaurants;

---

1. 'Proposal for a Directive of the European Parliament and the Council on Working Conditions for Temporary Workers, presented by the European Commission, of 20 march 2002, 2002/0072 (COD (COM 2002, 149)', amended on 28 November 2002, COM (2002), 0701.

- theatre, cultural activities and audio-visual shows;
- information;
- movie production;
- teaching;
- polling activities;
- phonographic publishing;
- leisure and holiday centres;
- meat storage;
- professional sport;
- building and civil engineering on foreign sites, co-operation and technical assistance, engineering and research activities in a foreign country;
- intermediary associations for labour supply activities and for placement services; and
- scientific research realized within the scope of an international agreement or international administration agreement or by foreign researchers working temporarily in France.

It should be pointed out that within the above-mentioned areas, only the positions that are by nature temporary can be filled by temporary workers. For example, in the hotel and restaurant sector, only supplementary waiters who may be hired for a weekend or a party can work under a temporary employment contract.

I. TEMPORARY WORK AGENCIES: RIGHTS AND OBLIGATIONS

1.1 The Recognition of a Temporary Work Agency

A temporary work agency is defined by the French Labour Code as a person or corporation whose exclusive purpose is to provide users with the temporary services of employees. The agency recruits and remunerates the temporary workers in line with established qualification levels.

The exclusivity of purpose is strictly interpreted by the courts which do not permit management of a temporary work agency together with another activity (especially where the secondary activity could be considered as complementary to management of a temporary work activity).

However, this exclusivity rule does not prohibit the managers of a temporary work agency from involvement in a different business as long as the other business is carried out by a separate company under its own finances. In the event that there is seen to be an overlap between the two activities, the managers may face severe sanctions of an administrative and even criminal sort.

Furthermore, the French Labour Code requires that persons or corporations intending to provide temporary workers as their business respect the relevant administrative formalities and provide a financial guarantee. The administrative formalities essentially consist of a declaration to the Labour Authorities before commencing operations to obtain their authorization. The declaration must indicate:

1. a description of the kind of business envisaged (such as the setting up of an agency or of a branch, or relocation of premises);
2. the exact date on which operations will be commenced;
3. the name, address and nationality of the manager(s);

4. the social security identification number of the business and the address of the social security centre responsible for the business;
5. the geographical and professional scope of the activities; and
6. the number of permanent employees.

Within fifteen days of sending the declaration to the Labour Authorities by registered mail, the Labour Authorities are required to confirm their authorization. These conditions are considered as matters of public policy. Failing to comply with any of them is a criminal offence.

These conditions must be fulfilled even by foreign temporary work agencies that work in France, whether established in an EU state or not. In order to respect the rules of fair competition, foreign temporary work agencies have the same constraints and obligations as French ones and must offer the same protection to temporary workers (Criminal High Court, 21 September 1999).

The agency must make its official declaration before commencing operations, and any opening or closing of an office of the agency must also be declared to the Labour Authorities. Each month, the temporary work agency must inform the Labour Authorities of all contracts entered into or terminated during the month. It must also justify the payment of social security charges.

The financial guarantee must take the form of a security granted by a bank, an insurance company or a financial establishment. It cannot be less than 8 per cent of the previous financial year's turnover before taxes. The guarantee covers the payment of salaries and social security contributions. The French High Court has considered that since financial guarantee is an important condition for the operation of a temporary work agency, in the absence of such a guarantee, the temporary work agency has no right to be remunerated by the user. Consequently, contracts concluded prior to a loss of the financial guarantee must be terminated while those concluded after such a loss are null and void (Criminal High Court, 22 February 2000).

If a temporary work agency does not respect the administrative formalities or the financial guarantee requirement, this can lead to severe criminal sanctions, including the closing of the agency and a prohibition on its managers to carry out this type of business for a 10-year period.

In conclusion, temporary work agencies are controlled by regular submission to the Administrative Authorities of the documents mentioned above and on a less frequent basis by visits and inquiries of the labour inspector and the social security authorities.

Where an agency fails to obtain correct registration or fails to provide a financial guarantee, the Civil Court ('*Tribunal de Grande Instance*') can order the closing of the temporary work agency for a maximum of two months. Furthermore, a prohibition on carrying out this type of business could be ordered against the temporary work agency for a period of two to ten years in the event of a serious violation of the regulations on temporary work (such as making false declarations).

1.2 The Temporary Work Agency as an Employer

The temporary work agency is the employer of the temporary worker, with all the obligations of labour law and social security law this implies. The temporary work agency also hires its own permanent employees who have the same rights and obligations as any employee. They are subject to a specific collective bargaining agreement.

The contractual relationship between the temporary worker and the temporary work agency contains rules relating to specific elements as follows.

- Trial period: if the temporary worker is assigned to a user during his/her trial period, the duration of that trial period cannot exceed two days for an assignment no longer than one month, three days for an assignment lasting between one and two months and five days for an assignment of greater length. The remuneration of the temporary worker during the trial period must be the same as that fixed for the whole assignment;
- Remuneration: the Labour Code obliges the temporary work agency (and consequently the user) to guarantee the temporary worker payment of the national minimum wage (SMIC);
- Temporary work agencies must pay to a complementary insurance fund 0.3 per cent of the salaries of temporary workers to cover the risk of work-related accidents ('*accord de prévoyance*');
- The number of employees of the temporary work agency is equal to the number of permanent employees and also consistent with the overall number of days worked by temporary workers under temporary employment contracts. The overall number of days worked is used to determine the application of the rules regarding individual training programs and the right to benefit from profit-sharing schemes.
- The right to benefit from occupational health services must be organized by the temporary work agency when the employee first goes on the agency's books and must be re-organized once a year, after a long period of illness and after maternity leave. The work doctor has a right of access to the user undertaking to check the working conditions of temporary workers.
- The temporary worker can participate in elections of the works council and/or personnel delegates after completing three months of service in the temporary work agency and can be elected after six months of service. Six months of service are completed as soon as the temporary worker has worked for 1014 hours during the 18-month period prior to the election. The purpose of this rule is to offer temporary workers working conditions as close as possible to those of a 'standard' employee. However, the mandates of employee representatives require a degree of availability that cannot easily be satisfied while the temporary worker is working for a user.
- The temporary worker is simultaneously considered part of the user's workforce (based on a *pro rata* calculation) for the twelve-month period prior to its calculation, even if the temporary worker does not work for the user anymore.
- The trade union representatives can go to court on behalf of temporary workers as long as they have informed the temporary workers of their action and the temporary workers do not require them not to sue the user. The temporary worker can require the trade union to cease the litigation at any point.
- The user works council must receive information relating to temporary workers on a regular basis. It must be informed and consulted prior to any decision concerning the hiring of temporary workers required by:
  - The replacement of an employee in the event of absence, suspension of employment contract, permanent leave preceding the termination of the work position;

- Temporary increase in the enterprise's activity, for example, in the event of an exceptionally large order from a customer;
- Temporary increase in activity where in relation to the position being hired out, a dismissal has been made for economic reasons in the past six months.

The user works council must also be informed and consulted prior to any decision concerning the evolution of the workforce especially where the number of temporary employment contracts has increased during the past three to six months. In each case, the employer should give information on the number of temporary workers and the reasons why it hired them.

II. THE USER: RIGHTS AND OBLIGATIONS

As indicated above, it is not possible to hire a temporary worker for a permanent job position in a company. It is only possible to hire temporary workers for one of the tasks, and under the conditions, mentioned by law.

2.1 The Contract Between the User and the Temporary Work Agency

2.1.1 A service contract must be entered into in writing between the user and the temporary work agency at the latest within two days of the provision of the temporary worker's services

For each employee concerned, the contract must:

- State the purpose for which a temporary worker is to be used and give the precise reasons therefore, including where appropriate the name and qualification of the employee being replaced or to be replaced;
- State the period that the assignment is to run;
- Include, where applicable, a clause making provision for a possible modification of the period of assignment;
- State the particular characteristics of the position to be filled, the occupational skills required, the place of the assignment and the working hours;
- State the amount of remuneration that an employee of equivalent qualification occupying the same position would receive after his/her trial period; and
- State the nature of individual protection measures that the employer is required to use, if any, and specify if this is to be provided by the temporary work agency.

It must be noted that any clause purporting to prohibit the hiring of the temporary worker by the user at the end of the assignment is null and void.

2.1.2 The sharing of liabilities between the user and the temporary work agency

In the event that the financial guarantee does not cover the salaries and social security charges of the temporary work agency, the user (instead of the temporary work agency) is required to pay the salaries, impermanent employment allowance[2] and the social security charges. Such payment must be made within ten days of the discovery of the temporary work agency's failure to pay. Once the user has paid, it is subrogated in all the rights and claims of the temporary worker and social security authorities against the temporary work agency.

These actions, the purpose of which is to protect temporary workers could become long-lasting and costly for the user. Consequently, in order to avoid or at least limit the risks involved, the user can require the temporary work agency to provide it with documentation from the social security authorities confirming the agency's position in these matters.

2.2 The Obligations of the User Towards the Temporary Worker

Throughout the assignment, the user is responsible for working conditions as established by measures provided in legislation, regulations and collective agreements. Working conditions comprise matters related to working hours, night work, weekly time-off and public holidays, health and security, and employment of pregnant women and young persons.

With respect to obligations concerning medical care at work, these are, in principle, the responsibility of the temporary work agency. However, should an activity be performed by the temporary worker which requires special medical supervision within the meaning of the industrial medical care regulations, the relevant obligations are incumbent upon the user undertaking.

Temporary workers have access to the transport services, catering and facilities available to the employees of the user under the same conditions as its employees.

If the user continues to employ the temporary worker after the end of the assignment without concluding an employment contract or without a new service contract, the employee is deemed to be working for the user under an indefinite-term employment contract. In such a case, the length of service of the worker is computed from the first day of the assignment with the user. Further, the length of the assignment must be deducted from any trial period involved. Moreover, when a user has recourse to the services of an employee of a temporary work agency in violation of the regulations, the worker is entitled to claim the rights attached to an indefinite-term employment contract with effect from the first day of the assignment.

As indicated above, the purpose of a temporary assignment cannot be to fill a post related to the normal, continuous activity of the user. Moreover, it is prohibited for the user to have recourse to the employees of a temporary agency to replace employees on strike, or for certain tasks that are subject to special medical supervision within the meaning of the industrial medical care regulations, and that appear on a list drawn up by orders issued by either the Minister responsible for employment or the Minister responsible for agriculture.

2. The impermanent employment allowance is the indemnity paid at the end of the contract by the employer to compensate the temporary worker for the loss of employment.

2.3 The Employment Contract for Temporary Work

The temporary employment contract between the agency and a temporary worker must be drawn up in writing and communicated to the employee at the latest two working days following the provision of services. The contract must include:

- the provisions and information mentioned above;
- the qualifications of the worker;
- details of the remuneration payable to the employee including those of the impermanent employment allowance. The allowance is currently equal to 10 per cent of all remuneration paid to the worker during the assignment;
- any particulars of a trial period;
- a clause to cover the repatriation of the employee at the expense of the temporary work agency if the assignment is located outside metropolitan France (such a clause would be void in the event of termination of the employment by the temporary worker);
- the name and address of the complementary pension fund and of the welfare fund to which the agency is affiliated.

In addition, the contract must state that the engagement of the employee by the user undertaking at the end of the temporary assignment is not prohibited.

In the event that an employee of a temporary work agency is in a regulated medical or paramedical profession, the temporary work agency must verify that the employee is duly authorized to exercise the profession.

The temporary work assignment must, from the moment of conclusion of the service contract, include a defined time limit as indicated above. The contract's total duration, including any renewal, cannot exceed eighteen months. The maximum duration is reduced to nine months where the temporary work takes place pending the arrival of an employee hired under an employment contract for an indefinite term or when the purpose of the contract is the performance of urgent work necessary under safety measures.

It is increased to twenty-four months when the assignment is performed abroad or, in the event of an employee leaving prior to completion of his work, on receipt by the enterprise (whether the principal or the sub-contractor) of an exceptional purchase order from abroad, where the size of the order requires work exorbitant in quality and quantity compared to that usually carried out by the company. In the last case, the duration may not be below six months.

However, when the contract is entered into either in order to replace an employee who is absent or one whose employment contract is suspended; or pending the arrival of an employee hired under an employment contract for an indefinite term, or on a contract which is by nature of a fixed term, the contract may not include a precise maximum limit but only a minimum duration, the time limit being the end of the purpose for which it has been concluded.

2.4 Termination of the Employment Contract

At the end of the temporary work contract, the temporary worker is entitled to an allowance to compensate for paid holiday, equal to at least one-tenth of the total remuneration payable during the assignment. The allowance is paid at the end of the assignment.

For the purpose of calculating the employee's entitlement, the assignment is to include any period during which the contract is suspended for maternity or adoption, or during which the contract was suspended on grounds of industrial accident or occupational disease, so long as the period did not exceed one year.

Furthermore, the temporary worker is entitled to an impermanent employment allowance that is additional to the rate of pay. The allowance, which depends among other things on the length of the assignment and on the remuneration of the temporary worker, may not be less than a minimum fixed by collective agreements or failing such by decree. The amount is generally equal to 10 per cent of the total remuneration.

III. THE DRAFT DIRECTIVE

The amended draft Directive primarily seeks to ensure that temporary workers are treated in the same way as if they had been recruited directly by the user company for the position. In order to achieve this, the draft Directive regulates the basic working and employment conditions to be agreed upon with temporary workers. It also tries to regulate the activities of temporary work agencies.

One of the aims of the draft Directive is to provide temporary work agencies with 'a consistent and flexible framework which is conducive to their activities without imposing any administrative, financial or legal constraints which would impede the creation and development of small and medium-sized undertakings' (recital 12). Furthermore, the draft Directive 'shall be implemented in compliance with the Treaty, specifically with regard to freedom to provide services and freedom of establishment' (recital 13).

The definition given by the draft Directive of a temporary work agency is therefore flexible, comprising 'any natural or legal person who, in compliance with national law, concludes contracts of employment or employment relationships with temporary workers in order to post them to user undertakings to work there temporarily under their supervision'.

This definition is not in direct contradiction with French law. However, it is likely that the aim of the draft Directive, as defined in recitals 12 and 13, may oblige French legislators to ease the administrative and financial constraints imposed on temporary work agencies. The purpose of the French constraints was to impose order on a market which was not regulated at all and where abuses were frequent in 1960s. However, these constraints impede or at least limit the creation of small or medium-sized temporary work agencies. Currently, the market is dominated by a few agencies which are often part of larger international groups.

Consequently, it is likely that French legislators will have to modify and ease the regulations imposed on temporary work agencies to comply with the Directive and to offer the French agencies the same growth opportunities as their main European competitors.

However, the revised November 2002 draft Directive does not require the same flexibility as the first version. In contrast to the recitals, Article 4 of the revised draft Directive is closer to the French principles:

> 'Prohibitions and restrictions on the use of temporary work are justified only on grounds of general interest relating in particular to the protection of

> temporary workers, the requirements of health and safety at work and the need to ensure that the labour market functions properly and abuses are prevented. The Member States, after consulting the social partners (…) shall review any restrictions or prohibitions mentioned above in order to verify whether they are justified on the grounds given in paragraph 1. (…) If not the member States shall discontinue them. (…) Paragraphs 1 and 2 are without prejudice to national requirements with regards to registration, licensing, certification, financial guarantees or monitoring of temporary agencies'.

It is very likely that the amendment of articles of the draft Directive will be followed by consequential amendments to the recitals before the end of the negotiation process. The new text of Article 4 is no longer at odds with French labour law. However, it is still difficult to envisage the juxtaposition of the current French constraints with the principles of freedom of establishment and service provision.

> 'The basic working and employment conditions applicable to temporary workers should be at least those which would apply to such workers if they were recruited by the user undertaking to occupy the same job' (recital 15).

This statement seems perfectly in accordance with French labour law. The purpose of the draft Directive is protection of the temporary worker. For years now, employers and their representatives have argued for more flexibility in this area. In particular, they have argued against the proposition that a temporary worker must be offered exactly the same terms and conditions as those offered to a permanent employee, since the overall cost of a temporary worker is higher than the overall cost of a permanent employee.

However, the text of the most recent draft of the Directive contains a new approach to the issue. Article 5, paragraph 1 of that version provides a general rule on non-discrimination which is that:

> 'The basic working and employment conditions of temporary workers shall be, for the duration of their posting at a user undertaking, at least those that would apply if they had been recruited directly by that enterprise to occupy the same job.
>
> When applying the above paragraph, the rules in force in the user undertaking on:
>
> i) protection of pregnant women and nursing mothers and protection of children and young people and
> ii) equal treatment for men and women and any action to combat any discrimination based on sex, race or ethnic origin, religion, beliefs, disabilities, age or sexual orientation must be complied with as established by legislation, regulations, administrative provisions, collective agreements and/or any other general provision.'

The draft Directive gives three exceptions to this rule, in Article 5, paragraphs 2, 3 and 4:

> 'As regards pay, Member States may, after consulting the social partners, provide that an exemption be made to the principle established in paragraph 1

> when temporary workers who have a permanent contract of employment with a temporary agency continue to be paid in the time between postings'.
>
> 'Member States may, after consulting the social partners at the appropriate level, give them the option of upholding or concluding collective agreements which derogate from the principle established in paragraph 1 as long as an adequate level of protection is provided for temporary workers'.
>
> 'Without prejudice to the provisions of paragraphs 2 and 3 above, Member States may, with regard to pay, provide that paragraph 1 shall not apply where a temporary worker works on an assignment or series of assignments with the same user enterprise in a post which, due to its duration or nature, can be accomplished in a period not exceeding six weeks'.

The wording of Article 5.1 of the amended draft Directive as set out above is different from the original wording of the draft Directive. The original draft Directive proposed equal treatment with comparable workers within the user company; the amended draft Directive establishes equal treatment with the hypothetical situation that the temporary worker was recruited directly by the user company for the same job. In the event that the draft Directive is implemented in its latest version, this will lead to a modification of French Law and more crucially to a change in the approach of the Labour Authorities towards temporary work.

In France, the indefinite-term employment contract is considered as the 'standard' form of employment. The fixed-term employment contract and the temporary work contract are therefore considered as 'atypical', and as an exception to the general rule. Consequently, labour legislation in this area primarily aims at limiting the development of these flexible forms of employment. The draft Directive appears to share this aim only in part.

Article 5(4) is very clearly in contradiction with the French principles. It seems to create the possibility of different treatment between temporary workers and permanent workers and will make it more advantageous for user companies to hire temporary workers for short periods. It should be noted that the amendment proposed by the European Parliament to delete this exemption was not accepted by the Commission. One can imagine a situation in which a position could be filled by a series of different temporary workers, each of them hired for less than 6 weeks. It is likely that French courts would try and avoid such a situation. However, European courts may decide to accept this situation in the interests of flexibility.

In conclusion, it should be stated that the current draft of the Directive is in some respects contradictory to French law. If the draft Directive is adopted largely in its current form, it is likely to require reform in the approach to temporary work in France, and in particular, moves towards greater flexibility in its provision. The necessity to reform the rules applicable to temporary work in France seems obvious, though the willingness of politicians to do so is less clear.

7. Germany

Manfred Weiss

I. INTRODUCTION

Temporary work is presently one of the most heavily debated issues in German labour law. A recent amendment of December 2002 has dramatically changed the legal framework governing this type of work. The driving force behind this amendment was the idea of developing a tool to decrease the still frightening level of unemployment. In order to understand the nature of the change it will be necessary to describe the legal situation as it was before and to contrast it with the new regulatory scheme. This new structure has to be analysed in detail in order to speculate, at the very least, on its impact on the labour market.

It is useless to discuss temporary work in isolation. Its function can only be properly assessed if it is related to other elements of labour regulation. The most important of these elements is the fact that in Germany each employee in an establishment with more than five employees (apprentices excluded) enjoys significant protection against dismissals after an initial 6-month period. Beyond that period dismissal is only possible if it is justified by specific reasons. And it has to be added that the labour courts by interpreting and further developing this element of law have significantly increased its complexity. The resulting opaqueness has, for employers and – in particular for small and medium-sized enterprises – led to a fear of running into difficulties in cases of dismissal. Therefore employers try to avoid disputes over dismissals by hesitating to employ at all. In this context the employer may have recourse to temporary workers to sidestep the issue of dismissal: disposing of a temporary worker does not require dismissal. Therefore, the respective protective rules do not apply.

Theoretically there might be a possibility to avoid disputes over dismissal in other ways such as through use of fixed term contracts or subcontracting. However, these too may be problematic. Fixed term contracts in Germany are only possible for a maximum of two years for newly hired employees if there is no specific justification. The standards for such a justification are high and scrutinized by the labour courts. The initial two years in which fixed term contracts are allowed without precondition may be split into three fixed term periods, but without intervals in between. However, there is another restriction which has to be observed: if the new employee was employed in the same company at previous a fixed term contract cannot be concluded without precondition. In that case justification is required. A further consideration is that, under the principle of equal treatment, fixed term employees are to be treated equally in all respects compared to permanent employees. As employees of the company they are covered by the same protective laws, by the same works agreements and by the same collective agreements. At least

R. Blanpain & R. Graham (eds.), Temporary Agency Work and the Information Society, 127–142

until now, temporary workers have been in a very different situation: their working conditions have been significantly lower than those of regular employees in the user companies. The wage level of temporary work employees on average has been much lower than the wage level of other employees. It amounts to little more than 60 per cent of the average wage of comparable regular employees. It has to be stressed that no matter what their skills, temporary workers always on average earn less than the reference group with the same qualifications (unskilled workers about 40 per cent less, skilled workers lower than 30 per cent less). These gaps are not decreasing but increasing.

Subcontracting might be considered another alternative to temporary work. However, it has to be understood that the demarcation line between subcontracting and employment in Germany is not at all clear. In particular the title of the employment relationship is not determinative. For a relationship to qualify on subcontracting, the following characteristics are required: the subcontractor himself must carry out operations necessary to complete the task, following his own working strategy; the subcontractor must specify the nature of the work and how it should be divided; most importantly, the person requiring the work to be carried out has no right to instruct the subcontractor's employees. This last characteristic in particular is often seen as unsatisfactory by the employer. If they infringe on these essential characteristics of the subcontracting relationship, employers can easily be caught out. The courts make every effort to prevent deviation from the subcontracting rulesby assuming that there is an employment relationship if there is any doubt.

It is in this context that temporary work in Germany is to be seen. In view of this legal framework governing dismissals, fixed term contracts and subcontracting, temporary work at first glance looks an attractive alternative for an employer. Nevertheless the figures tell a different story. Temporary workers in Germany still amount to only 1.24 per cent of the workforce. However, it should be stressed that the amount of temporary work today is four times as much as it was in 1980: despite significant fluctuation, there has been a steady increase. From 1980 to 2001 the number of temporary work relationships lasting longer than three months has increased from 16.7 per cent to 42.7 per cent. However only 20 per cent of all temporary work relationships last longer than six months, only 10 per cent longer than one year and only 1 per cent longer than three years. In short: temporary work up to now still is a marginal phenomenon and mainly a relationship of short duration in Germany. However, there are at least two promising signs. Two thirds of temporary work employees were previously unemployed, meaning that a temporary jobs offer important opportunities of entering or re-entering the job market. One third of temporary work employees have subsequently become regular employees, indicating that temporary work is functioning as a bridge to permanent employment.

Temporary work in Germany is male-dominated. In West Germany only one fifth and in East Germany one tenth of temporary workers are women. Foreigners from other EU countries are over-represented: in West Germany they amount to about 20 per cent.

The number of unskilled among temporary employees is increasing. It presently amounts to about 25 per cent. In addition many temporary employees work in areas where the necessary skills can be acquired quickly and easily. It should be mentioned, however, that all skill-levels are represented among temporary workers. It is important to stress that in Germany a large majority of temporary work still takes place in manufacturing and not in services.

II. THE ACT ON TEMPORARY WORK UNTIL THE RECENT AMENDMENT

1. The Genesis and the Development

In Germany temporary work refers to employees who have a normal contractual relationship with an enterprise whose role it is to hire-out (hirer-out) employees temporarily to a third party (user) where the employees perform work. Originally hiring-out was considered to be incompatible with the Federal Employment Office's monopoly on labour exchange. Therefore temporary work was banned. In 1967 the Federal Constitutional Court, however, ruled that temporary work has nothing to do with labour exchange if an indefinite employment relationship between the temporary employee and the hiring-out enterprise is established. In that case, at least, the ban was considered to be unconstitutional. The 1972 Act on Temporary Work does no more than enact this decision of the Constitutional Court. At the same time, EC law has seen the monopoly of the Federal Employment Office on labour exchange brought to an end. Therefore, today there is no longer a need under constitutional law to distinguish temporary work and labour exchange. That allows the legislative greater leeway in deciding how to regulate temporary work. The relevant framework in the future will be the intended EC-Directive if it is adopted.

The Act on Temporary Work has been amended several times. However, its basic structure has remained intact until the recent amendment mentioned above. The Act intended to provide minimum protection for employees engaging in temporary work. In the building industry, which is a very important sector of the economy, temporary work has been banned since 1982 for blue-collar workers. The ban was a reaction by the legislative to the ever-increasing abuses temporary work in the industry. Administrative control of the abuses turned out to be ineffective. However, in 1994 the ban for the building industry was significantly weakened. Construction companies covered by the same collective agreements were allowed to hire-out blue-collar workers amongst themselves.

Until recently, trade unions were striving for an extension to all other sectors of the original ban in the building industry. This merely defensive position turned out to be politically futile, and could not have been easily reconciled with the Constitution. On the contrary there was a tendency to facilitate temporary work in order to increase flexibility. The first step in this direction was the Act on Improvement of Employment Opportunities of 1985. In 1994, in 1997 and in particular in 2001 the Act on Temporary Work has been further amended to increase opportunities in this type work, without changing the basic structure. The change in paradigm only happened very recently and will be discussed later.

2. The Hiring-out Enterprise

By law, the hiring-out enterprise needs a licence, for which an application must be made. Applicants can be persons, legal entities under public law (i.e. churches or a municipality) and legal entities under private law (i.e. joint-stock companies) and groups of persons. The licence is bound to the person or legal entity to who or which it is issued.

In principle the applicant is entitled to a licence if none of the statutory reasons for refusal apply. Several reasons for refusal are exclusively laid down in a specific Section of the Act so that the issuing authority is not entitled to refuse a licence for other reasons. If any one reason applies, the issuing authority is obliged to refuse the application for a licence. Prior to the most recent amendment, the Act stipulated that a licence should not be issued or extended if there was reason to believe (a) that the applicant did not have the reliability required for performance of the activities of a temporary work business, in particular because he failed to comply with provisions of social insurance legislation, provisions concerning deduction and transfer of wage tax, provisions concerning placement, recruitment abroad or work permits or provisions of industrial safety legislation or failed to fulfil his obligations under labour law; (b) that the applicant aw, according to the managing body of the establishment, incapable of properly fulfilling the usual employers' obligations; (c) that the application concluded with temporary workers employment contracts of limited duration unless the limitation was justified and was made with reference to an employment contract which follows immediately after a previous one with the same employee; (d) that the application concluded unlimited employment contracts with temporary workers, dismissed and re-engaged them within three months of the termination of the employment relationship; (e) that the application repeatedly limited the duration of the employment relationship to the period of the first assignment, unless the temporary work employee engaged in an employment relationship with the user enterprise immediately following the assignment where the Federal Employment Office had recognized the employee as belonging to a group with specific difficulties in entering the labour market; (f) that the applicant hires out a temporary worker to a user for all or part of a total period longer than twenty-four consecutive months in which the worker has been assigned to the same user, including any time in which the worker was hired out to the user by a different temporary employment business.

Furthermore the issuing authority has to refuse to issue or to extend a licence if the establishment, branch of the establishment or subsidiary establishment providing the temporary worker is not situated in a Member State of the EU. Applicants from EC Member States can obtain licences under the same conditions as German nationals. The burden of proof rests on the issuing authority to prove the existence of facts justifying the assumption that reasons for refusal apply. The crucial moment to challenge whether a statutory reason for refusal applies is once the authority's decision is made. Licences may be issued subject to conditions and requirements in order to provide for circumstances which would justify their withdrawal.

Licences are issued for a maximum of one year. An application for extension of a licence has to be made no later than three months before the end of the year. A licence is extended for a further year unless the issuing authority refuses to extend it before the end of the year. If the issuing authority refuses to extend a licence, its validity continues for no more than six months in order to permit the termination of contracts lawfully concluded. Only if a temporary work organization has been operating lawfully for three consecutive years may licences be issued for an indefinite period.

The hirer-out has a legal duty to inform the administrative authority of all the relevant facts relating to the preconditions of the licence. In addition every six months the hirer-out has to deliver to the administrative authority a report containing the number of temporary employees, their citizenship, their occupation before becoming a temporary worker, the occupation performed as temporary worker, the number of assignments of temporary workers, the number of users, the number and length of employment relationships etc.

According to the Act, a licence which does not comply with the law may be withdrawn with effect from the date of its withdrawal. Since most licences are of limited duration the most common reason for expiry of licences is simply termination of the period of validity.

The hiring-out enterprise is the temporary worker's employer. In principle, the employment relationship between the hiring-out enterprise and the temporary work employee is to be an indefinite one. The legislator's idea was to establish a stable relationship. In particular, it wanted to prevent limitation of the period of employment to the period for which the temporary employee works for a specific user (the prohibition on synchronization). Otherwise the hiring-out enterprise would be no more than a labour exchange undertaking. While the Federal Employment Office monopolized labour exchange, that had to be avoided in this field, had to be excluded. Since the abolishment of the labour exchange monopoly there has been a tendency to weaken the prohibition on synchronization. The amendment to the Act, other than the most recent one, allowed the conclusion of a contract for a definite period as a one-off. Repeated conclusion of such a contract was still prohibited. Even that, however, was exceptionally permitted if a specific justification could be given. Exactly what may constitute such a justification is of course a matter of interpretation.

It should be stressed that the prohibition on synchronization has become extremely controversial. It was considered by the hiring-out industry to be the most significant obstacle to using temporary work to decrease unemployment. And as already indicated above it has not succeeded in fulfilling its purpose, namely to guarantee long-term employment relationships for temporary work employees.

3. The User Enterprise

The user enterprise has a contractual relationship only with the hiring-out enterprise. This contract has to be written and must fulfil certain conditions. No contractual relationship between the temporary employee and the user exists. If, however, the hiring-out enterprise has no licence or loses its licence the law treats the user as if an employment contract existed between the user enterprise and the temporary work employee to protect the worker.

The maximum period for which a temporary employee can be hired-out to a user has been extended several times: originally three months, it has now reached months as stated above. According to the amendment of 2001, temporary work employees had to be treated the same way as permanent employees in the user enterprise from the thirteenth month onwards which – as is clear in light of the statistics given above – affected few. The number of temporary workers fell significantly after the amendment was introduced since employers tried to evade it with assignments less than thirteen months.

Though no contractual employment relationship exists between temporary work employee and user enterprise, it has to be stressed that the user nevertheless has certain rights and duties towards the temporary employee. The contract between user and hirer-out leads to a sharing of the function of employer between hirer-out and user. In particular, the user holds all rights in relation to performance of the work, specifying the contractual obligations by giving orders and instructions to the temporary employee. This of course implies duties: the duty to give assistance and to respect all the protective regulations concerning the temporary employee's integration in the user enterprise. The user has to make especially sure that the health and safety rules are observed. But of course many of the rights and risks of an employer remain with the hiring-out enterprise.

4. The Temporary Work Employee

The hiring-out enterprise is the only contractual partner of the temporary work employee. All the worker's contractual claims (wage, benefits, annual vacation etc.) can only be made against the hiring-out enterprise. And of course the hiring-out enterprise has to pay the employer's share of social security contributions.

Prior to transposition into German law of the Directive requiring an employer to inform employees of the conditions applicable to the contract of employment, the Act on Temporary Work stipulated that specific working conditions are to be contained in a written document given to the temporary worker. The compulsory content of this document in the meantime has been extended in line with the Directive's requirements. It has to be stressed, however, that this document is to be given to the temporary employee before performance of the work agreed is commenced. In the event that the hiring-out enterprise does not fulfil this duty the contract does not become void; instead, the Act provides for a fine.

One of the basic problems for temporary work employees is whether and how far they are integrated into and covered by the works council system in the user enterprise. They of course can elect a works council in the hiring-out enterprise and become members thereof. The problem, however, is that there is only a very distant relationship between the temporary work employees of a hiring-out enterprise due to the fact that they all work elsewhere. Therefore, a works council in a hiring-out enterprise is rather the exception. Where one does exist it is of little assistance: the works council's rights are focusing on the establishment where the worker is integrated in order to work there.

The more interesting question relates to the relationship between the temporary employee and the works council in the user enterprise. Until recently the temporary employee had neither voting rights nor the right to be elected to such a works council. An amendment to the Works Constitution Act of 2001 has changed their position, so that they now have the right to vote in the works council if they work at the user enterprise for a period longer than three months. Controversy has arisen over this threshold. Whether a works council is to be elected and what size it should be depends on the number of employees in the establishment. The question now is whether temporary work employees enjoying the right to vote in the works council are to be taken into account for those purposes. The Federal Labour Court has not yet resolved this question. The majority of the judgements of lower courts are in favour of not taking into account temporary workers. Regardless of the frequency of those judgements, the Federal Labour Court is instead likely to decide the matter on the basis of the arguments put before it, until which time it will remain a matter for debate.

The works council of the user enterprise has at least a basic obligation to take care of temporary work employees: it has to be available for consultation during its office hours and give assistance in cases of complaint. Temporary work employees have a right to participate in works meetings. While these aspects of the relationship between temporary worker and the user enterprise works council are expressly spelt out in the Act, the case law of the Labour Courts goes considerably further.

The works council's codetermination rights in social matters also cover temporary workers in as far as these matters have an impact on their integration into the user enterprise. In particular, the works council has the right to monitor whether unjustified discrimination of temporary work employees is prevented.

Importantly, the works council of the user enterprise has a right to be informed and consulted before the start of every assignment of a temporary work employee. In this regard the user has to present a written declaration by the hiring-out enterprise confirming that it has a licence. Under certain conditions enumerated in the Act on Works Constitution, the works council is entitled to refuse to consent to the hiring of temporary workers. It has to be admitted, however, that this is usually only possible if the user violates legal provisions referring to the employment of temporary workers. Therefore the works council's role in this matter may be described in large part monitoring legal compliance. But it should be stressed that the works council's capability to prevent the hiring of temporary workers could go further. One of the reasons for allowing the refusal to consent consists in the fact that due to the hiring of a temporary worker 'there is a likelihood that employees of the respective establishment are to be dismissed or to suffer other disadvantages'. If such a link can be demonstrated the works council can refuse its consent in order to protect the existing employees of the respective establishment. In actual practice, though, proving such a link is very difficult.

Finally, it is at least theoretically possible to extend the monitoring capacities of the works council by work agreements. However, the user cannot be forced to sign such an agreement. Since the employer, for reasons which have to do with the works council's power concerning its co-determination rights, is very eager to remain on good terms with the works council, there is an indirect pressure on the employer to agree which should not be underestimated. Of course such pressure is only brought to bear if the works council is interested in monitoring the use of temporary work. Normally the works council's interests tend to exclude temporary work. Therefore this instrument is unlikely to be used to facilitate temporary work in the user company. However, as will be shown below new developments have occurred affecting this matter with the most recent amendment of the Act on Temporary Work.

Even if the law establishes some sort of relationship between the temporary work employee and the works council in the user enterprise, it is clear that in their dealings with one another the temporary workers remain outsiders. The works council of course is inclined to focus on its electorate, and this will not necessarily include temporary workers even if they participated in the previous election due to the fact that they had stayed longer than a period of three months. Only workers who will vote at the next election are likely to be of specific interest to the works council.

A temporary work employee is not obliged to work for a user directly affected by a strike or lock-out. In such a case the hiring-out enterprise has to inform the temporary work employee of his or her right to refuse performance of the work.

5. The Role of Social Partners

Until recently trade unions tried to do everything to oppose temporary work. They refused – at least in principle – to conclude collective agreements in this area. Very few collective agreements exist and mostly relate to certain skilled groups. The practical problems obstructing the regulation, by collective agreements of working conditions for temporary employees should not be overlooked. A collective agreement with the user enterprise or its employers' association is not possible since temporary workers have no employment relationship with them. The lack of collective agreements with hiring-out enterprises or their employers' associations is explained by the difficulty in unionizing temporary workers. This problem has become a burning issue since the recent amendment, and is examined below.

In some areas at least (*sui generis*) agreements were concluded. They were not collective agreements in a strict sense, but established merely a normal contractual obligation. For example in the mining industry an agreement was made whereby users agreed to apply to temporary workers the rules of the collective agreement covering their employees. That agreement did not of course relate to matters for which the hiring-out company is exclusively responsible (wages etc.).

In the absence of collective agreements, the Federal Association for Temporary Work (BZA), which is the leading association of hiring-out enterprises, has taken steps to improve the image of temporary work as lacking in worker protection. The Association developed a self-binding declaration laying down minimum standards, which are not yet guaranteed by the statutory protection from which temporary employees benefit. To give two examples from the catalogue contained in this declaration, which serves as a code of conduct: bonus payments are guaranteed to a certain extent; temporary workers may not be hired during a strike in the user enterprise. The declaration of course has no binding effect and data on how far it has actually been applied are not available.

The principal problem relating to temporary work in Germany is that abuses can only be controlled to a very limited extent. The extent of illegal supply of temporary work (hiring-out without a licence and not observing the minimum standards of labour law) is estimated to be very high. Some experts suggest that the ratio of (instances of) legal hiring-out to (instances of) illegal hiring-out is about one to ten. Even when hiring-out enterprises operate with a licence, it is difficult to eliminate abuses.

III. THE RECENT AMENDMENT: THE CHANGE OF PARADIGM

1. The Hartz Commission

In order to develop a consistent and comprehensive approach to fighting unemployment, the Federal Government established a commission on 'modern services in the labour market' on 22 February 2002. This commission consisted of fifteen members representing all relevant groups of society, including trade unions and employers' associations. It was chaired by Peter Hartz who is responsible for social affairs on the executive board of Volkswagen. On 16 August 2002 – little more than a month before the Federal election – the commission presented its report of almost 350 pages. It contained thirteen innovative programmes, ranging from improvements in the labour exchange services to proposals for encouraging and subsidizing self-employment. One element of this set of proposals related to temporary work, and put forward three strategies: (a) significant deregulation of the Act on Temporary Work (including abolition of the prohibition on synchronization, abolition of the special prohibition on fixed term contracts for temporary work employees, abolition of the prohibition on temporary work in the construction industries, abolition of the maximum duration of an assignment and abolition of several administrative requirements applying to the hiring-out enterprise as well as the user enterprise); (b) establishment of a new institution handling temporary work (the so-called Personnel Service Agencies); and (c) a significant shift of regulatory responsibility from the legislator to parties concluding collective agreements. The report, which was unanimously adopted by the commission, was accepted by the existing and re-elected Federal Government and proclaimed as the basis for reforms in employment policy. Its basic philosophy was shared by all relevant political parties and groups of society, even if there remained controversies over some important details.

The impact of the Hartz report can barely be overestimated. In all the years before the commission was established, deregulating temporary work was an unthinkable concept for the trade unions. However, the fact that they were represented in the commission made it difficult for them to ignore the consensus reached, not only in relation to temporary work but also to many other matters contained in the report. Other groups, likewise previously opposed to the resolutions made by the commission on other matters, lacked grounds to object for the same reason. Deregulation of temporary work and promotion of temporary work as a legitimate type of work was no longer a taboo. Fundamentalist approaches could no longer be maintained. In short, the Hartz commission paved the way for a fruitful political discussion.

2. The Genesis of the Amendment

The Federal Government's promise to transpose the Hartz proposals into legislation without modification was clearly impractical; compromises were inevitable. Trade union leaders as well as left-leaning politicians could only convince their supporters of the need for deregulation if they could offer something in return.

In the meantime the first two statutes on 'modern services in the labour market' were passed by the Federal Parliament on 23 December 2002. These transposed only a small part of the Hartz proposals – and of course in modified form. Therefore, many more statutory changes will follow. Some are already fully prepared.

The provisions relating to temporary work and to the so-called Personnel Service Agencies (PSAs) are contained in the first statute on 'modern services in the labour market'. It was presented to the Federal Parliament on 7 November 2002 and quickly passed, on 15 November 2002. However, the Federal Council representing the interests of the Länder brought the Statute before the conciliation committee responsible for resolving conflicts between the two legislative bodies. Minor modifications were made. The new statute was confirmed by the Federal Parliament and has been in force since 1 January 2003. However, regarding the new provisions which relate to temporary work the situation is much more complicated. They are normally to be applied only onto temporary work relationships concluded from 1 January 2004. However, the situation is different if a collective agreement of a certain form, specified for the first time in the statute and explained below, has been concluded. Where such an agreement has been made after 15 November 2002 the new provisions apply immediately.

3. The Main Content of the Amendment

The amendment has abolished the prohibition on synchronization, the special rules on fixed term contracts for temporary work employees and the maximum amount of time they may work in the user enterprise. Consequently, the chances of a hiring-out enterprise obtaining a licence and its ability to operate more flexibly have increased significantly. The amendment has significantly facilitated temporary work in the construction industry, even though the ban on such work has not been entirely lifted. In particular, hiring-out is now permitted between construction companies and hiring-out enterprises if permitted by collective agreements, which cover the hiring-out enterprises and if these collective agreements are declared to be generally binding. (A difficulty arises here, which will be explained below.) Hiring-out between construction companies has been further facilitated, not least in view of the number of construction companies established in other EU Member States who hire out temporary work employees to German construction companies. In addition hiring-out enterprises as well as the user-enterprises have been relieved of some administrative requirements. Taken together, the legislation in essence loyally transposed the Hartz proposals.

As already indicated there had to be a trade-off in order to win the support of the trade unions, namely ensuring that the equal treatment of temporary work employees be enforced as comprehensively and as early as possible. According to the relevant section of the statute, the temporary work employee is entitled 'for the time of his or her stay in the user enterprise to the same essential working conditions, including remuneration, of comparable employees in the user enterprise'. Firstly, this does not apply for the first six weeks 'if the temporary work employee was previously unemployed and is paid by the hiring-out enterprise a net remuneration at least the amount he or she had received as unemployment benefit'. This exception does not apply if at any previous time there has been an employment relationship between this temporary work employee and the hiring-out enterprise. A second exception is much more important: the equal treatment principle does not apply if a collective agreement allows for different treatment. This shifts the responsibility for the final scheme of equal treatment to the trade unions and the employers associations and/or the individual employers. It should be recalled that normative clauses contained in collective agreements in Germany only apply to employees who are unionized and whose employer is either party to, or a member of the employer's association which is party to the collective agreement. All others are not bound. However, under the amendment, employers and temporary work employees who are not bound by such a collective agreement can bind themselves to its content in their individual employment contract.

If the hiring-out enterprise is not fulfilling its duties regarding the essential working conditions the temporary work employee is entitled to claim fulfilment from the user. In addition to the written information which must be given, the hiring-out enterprise has to provide written documentation on 'the kind and amount of remuneration and other working conditions for periods in which the temporary work employee is not working in a user enterprise'. The user is obliged to include, in the written contract with the hiring-out enterprise, information on the essential working conditions, including remuneration of comparable employees in the user enterprise. Finally, the temporary work employee is entitled to claim this very same information from the user.

The introduction of the principle of equal treatment in the user company has led to much controversy. It is seen by many in the employers' camp as a mechanism to destroy the intentions of the Hartz proposals. Much will depend in the end on the collective agreements to be concluded in this area. Throughout the legislative process outlined above, the proposal for a Directive on temporary work has played a big role as an argument for establishing the principle of equal treatment in the user company.

4. Problems of Implementation

Though the amendment has only recently been passed, there is already a significant amount of literature dealing with problems of interpretation and implementation of its new provisions.

One of the questions is how to combine the principle of equal treatment in the user enterprise with the original aim of the law, namely stabilizing the employment relationship of the temporary work employee. Even though the prohibition on synchronization and the specific rules on fixed term contracts for temporary work were abolished, the general rules for fixed term contracts describe above still apply. This means – as already indicated – that a fixed term contract without preconditions can only be concluded three times within a maximum of two years. Further, if the respective temporary work employee was employed by the hiring-out enterprise at any previous time, a fixed-term contract without precondition is not permitted. Consequently, a hiring-out enterprise will in many cases still have no choice but to hire out the temporary work employee for an indefinite period. By implication, the temporary work employee will remain on the pay roll of the hiring-out enterprise in periods in which no user needs him or her. This forces the hiring-out enterprise to calculate the fees charged to the user enterprise in such a way that these periods are also covered. In light of such a development, it may well be that the strict application of the principle of equal treatment in the user enterprise overburdens the hiring-out enterprise as well as the user enterprise and so decreases the attraction of using temporary workers rather than increasing it. Therefore, it is of utmost importance that a reasonable scheme for ensuring equal treatment is designed by collective agreement.

Difficulties are likely to arise over the amendment's terminology. There is for example much debate over the meaning of 'essential working conditions, including remuneration'. Does this include all types of fringe benefits; does it include, for example, services in kind and pension schemes? In some automobile companies the employees are entitled to buy cars at reduced price; does this fringe benefit also apply to temporary work employees? Essential working conditions may differ in meaning depending on context; their definition is fairly unclear. It is even more difficult to determine 'comparable employees' in the user enterprise. In general terms they may be defined as employees with an identical or similar position and/or qualification. On a case-by-case basis, however, that will be difficult to specify. In this regard, the works council in the hiring-out company could have an important monitoring task. The works council has the right to monitor each classification or reclassification of an employee, including the integration of a temporary work employee. However, there are practical limits to the monitoring possible. The works council in the hiring-out enterprise would certainly not be familiar with the conditions in the user enterprise. Therefore, it is doubtful whether it can properly fulfil the monitoring task. In addition it should be recalled that until now a works council in hiring-out companies is rather the exception than the rule. Often there might not be a comparable employee because the temporary work employee performs a function completely absent in the enterprise. In such a case, what is the point of comparison? Employees of an identical or similar position and/or qualification in other enterprises? What if they are paid differently? Should the higher or the lower wage apply or is it necessary to take an average? Several unresolved questions arise.

5. The New Role of the Social Partners

Due to the legislative amendment the focus is now on collective bargaining. Employers are interested in reaching a collective agreement, and so enjoying the deregulatory aspects of the amendment as soon as possible. They would otherwise have to wait until 1 January 2004. They also expect that it will be possible to specify and thereby limit the meaning of essential working conditions and to agree a level of remuneration below the amount that would ensure strict equal treatment with comparable employees in the user enterprise. The trade unions also are interested to reach such an agreement. For them it is important to obtain minimum standards for essential working conditions, including remuneration, which are significantly above the level granted so far. In addition both sides are under great public pressure: they are expected to give a form to temporary work which will help to reduce unemployment.

Therefore, negotiations are presently taking place. On one side are the two employers' associations representing the hiring-out enterprises, the Federal Association of Temporary Work (BZA) and the Society representing the Interests of Temporary Work (IGZ). The hiring-out companies represented by the BZA employ 37 per cent of temporary workers and those represented by the IGZ 5 per cent, a total of 42 per cent. On the other side, all eight trade unions of the German Trade Union Confederation (DGB) have joined forces to combine efforts to reach an agreement.

The collective agreement is not expected to be finalized before the end of May. But already in February a consensus was reached on some basic elements. According to this consensus, the regular basic wage for unskilled temporary work employees is supposed to be 8.40 Euro per hour, and for skilled temporary work employees 10.60 Euro per hour. However for skilled temporary work employees two more wage levels above the existing one are to be established; the parties could not yet agree on the exact amount. The regular basic wage is to be paid to the employee whether he or she is needed in a user enterprise or not. For specific groups of the labour market in which it is particularly difficult to find employment, the basic wage can be lowered for a short period (still to be fixed), to 6.85 Euro for unskilled workers and to an amount yet to be fixed for skilled workers. It also is still unclear how these groups are to be defined.

When a temporary work employee works in a user enterprise he or she is entitled to a supplementary payment. These supplementary payments will be different for each sector. There will also be different classifications of skilled and unskilled workers. Negotiations are presently focusing on these supplementary payments. The object is to establish classifications which can easily be applied in practice, to make the search for comparable employees in the user enterprise obsolete. The amount of these supplementary payments is of course a very controversial issue: the employers want to keep the payment as low as possible whereas the trade unions attempt to ensure equal treatment.

In addition, the collective agreement is supposed to contain rules on working time. There is already agreement on an average weekly working time of 35 hours for full timers. Since in some sectors the working time is still longer, means of compensation, with periods in which the temporary work employee cannot be hired out to a user, are provided for.

Whatever the content of the final collective agreement will be, a significant issue will remain to be resolved. As already indicated, normative clauses of collective agreements only apply to unionized employees whose employer belongs to the employers' association which has concluded the collective agreement. Since many hiring-out enterprises do not belong to the two employers' associations and since only very few temporary work employees are unionized, the majority of employment relationships in the temporary work sector will not be bound by the prospective collective agreement. Theoretically this problem could be resolved by a mechanism of declaring the agreement generally binding. By using such an instrument at the request of either the trade unions or the employers' associations or both the Federal Minister of Economics and Labour can extend the scope of the collective agreement to outsiders, namely non-unionized employees and employers not belonging to the employers' association. However, there is a precondition which is not met here. A declaration that the collective agreement is generally binding is only possible if members of the employers' associations who are parties to the agreement employ at least 50 per cent of employees in the region and in the sector for which it is concluded. As indicated above, this figure only amounts to 42 per cent. Therefore, a declaration that the collective agreement is generally binding would only be possible if before concluding the collective agreement the employers' associations succeed in significantly increasing their membership. This, however, is rather unlikely.

In view of these difficulties the trade unions will have no choice but to pursue another strategy: first to integrate into the collective agreement a clause whereby members of the employers associations are obliged to transfer the content of the collective agreement into the individual employment contracts of non-unionized employees; and secondly to conclude with each hiring-out enterprise which is not a member of one of the two employers' associations a collective agreement of the same content. The question again is how to bring this about. It would be unrealistic to think of using strikes; no sector would strike for working conditions in the temporary work business. Nevertheless, optimism is justified; not only the trade unions but also the hiring-out enterprises have an interest in these collective agreements. Therefore, in the end there will be almost full coverage. Though, this will take some time.

6. Supporting Strategies by Works Councils

Even if the trade unions in principle welcome the promotion of temporary work as a tool to decrease the amount of unemployment, they are still afraid that employers could be tempted to replace regular employees with temporary work employees. In order to prevent such a development some trade unions are trying to convince works councils in their sectors to conclude works-agreements with the employers. In order to facilitate this task for the works councils they have drafted model works agreements to be adapted to the specific circumstances of each enterprise. The main purpose of these works agreements is to extend works council's rights in the user enterprises. As indicated above, the Works Constitution Act allows the works council to refuse both the hiring and the integration of temporary workers under certain conditions.

To take an example, the model works agreement drafted by the metalworkers' trade union stresses the fact that temporary work should only be permitted if the work cannot be executed by the regular employees and if it is of a temporary nature. If the requirement can be met by transferring employees within the enterprise, by fixed-term contracts, by altered working-time arrangements or by other personnel policy measures, the use of temporary work employees should be excluded. The use of temporary work employees should be included in the dialogue on personnel planning which is compulsory under the Works Constitution Act. These principles do not exactly change the regulatory scheme but are rather non-binding guidelines for the employer.

Of greater importance is the extension of works councils' rights. According to the metalworkers' trade union model workers agreement, the works council should be entitled to refuse the integration of temporary work employees into the user enterprise, if their conditions of work do not meet the standards fixed in the collective agreement, concluded with the associations of hiring-out enterprises, discussed above. This is an indirect strategy to extend the scope of application of that collective agreement. A hiring-out enterprise which does not abide by the collective agreement would be unable to find a user for its temporary work employees. Consequently, the works councils would indirectly become supervisors of the extension of the collective agreement to cover non-unionized temporary work employees.

So far it is totally unclear whether such works agreements will actually be concluded. After all, the works council has no means by which to force the employer to sign such an agreement, and it is worth recalling that the effect of such an agreement would evidently be an increase in the works council's monitoring power. Nevertheless, it is very difficult to give a prognosis. First it has to be re-emphasized that the user company also has an interest in enforcing the more favourable conditions implied by the collective agreement. And secondly it has to be kept in mind that employers tend to avoid conflicts with their works councils since they are frequently dependent on them.

7. The Personnel Service Agencies (PSA)

According to the new law, at least one so-called Personnel Service Agency is to be established (in each local employment office). The purpose of a PSA is to provide a means by which the unemployed, mainly those with specific handicaps and problems in the labour market, can be reintegrated into permanent employment. The PSA not only has to find a user enterprise for the unemployed person but also to provide training to increase skills. The law provides the PSA's function is 'hiring-out in order to transfer the unemployed into employment and to train and qualify the person in periods where he or she cannot be hired-out'. The local employment office is supposed to find – by way of a tender – a private enterprise serving as PSA. The enterprise has to fulfil all requirements of a hiring- out enterprise and also needs a licence. The only important difference is that this enterprise is subsidized by the local employment office. The idea is very simple: instead of paying unemployment benefits it is more beneficial to pay for integration into employment. If the local employment office does not succeed in finding a private enterprise it is supposed to run a PSA itself. The terms and conditions for employment in a PSA and for hiring-out in a user enterprise are to be fixed in a collective agreement. Here again negotiations are going on presently. Until the end of 2003, the collective agreement is a precondition of the contract between the local employment office and the PSA. After that date the equal treatment principle would in any event apply so long as it has not been abrogated by a collective agreement.

In large part, the PSA will be a tool for the reintegration of persons with severe problems entering or re-entering the labour market. It is not at all clear how far they will compete with the normal hiring-out enterprises. Since they are subsidized, significant competition could be problematic. However, it is much too early to make an assessment. Currently, the PSAs, yet to become a reality, exist only in law.

IV. CONCLUSION

Until now temporary work in Germany has remained a marginal phenomenon, though its growth is evident. Only recently has it been discovered as a means of tackling unemployment. In the wake of the Hartz commission, the reluctance of the trade unions to accept that temporary work should be encouraged was to some extent overcome. The philosophy underlying the metalworkers' union draft works' agreement for replication in user companies, shows that there still is a tendency to exclude temporary work as much as possible, and to accept it only as a last resort. On the other hand the present negotiations for a collective agreement demonstrate the willingness of trade unions to contribute to a fashioning of temporary work as an instrument used to decrease unemployment.

In states where the principle of equal treatment in the user enterprise is already established, there is no indefinite relationship with the hiring-out company and the hiring-out company resembles a labour exchange. As outlined above, the German legislator is still abiding by the notion that there should be a permanent relationship between the hiring-out enterprise and the temporary work employee and even so has established the principle of equal treatment in the user company. It may be doubted whether the combination will be attractive enough to fulfil the goal of reducing unemployment. However, it has to be taken into account that the legal scheme of establishing a stable relationship between temporary work employee and hiring-out-enterprise has never really worked in reality. Further due to the forthcoming collective agreement, the impact of the principle of equal treatment in the user company will be significantly less.

Whatever the form of the collective agreement, the regulation of temporary work will still be much too bureaucratic and too complicated. The recent amendment is no more than a step towards a new perception of this type of work. At the very least it has challenged the responsibility of all actors involved to reflect on a fair balance of flexibility and protection and, particularly, on reducing unemployment.

SELECTED BIBLIOGRAPHY

Bauer, J.H., 'Gesetze für moderne Dienstleistungen am Arbeitsmarkt', in *Neue Juristische Wochenschrift*, 2003, pp. 537–545.

Hartz, P., *et al.*, 'Moderne Dienstleistungen am Arbeitsmarkt', in *Bericht der Kommission*, 2002.

Lembke, M., 'Die "Hartz-Reform" des Arbeitnehmerüberlassungsgesetzes', in *Arbeits- und Sozialrecht*, pp. 98–104.

Rieble, V. and Klebeck, U., 'Lohngleichheit für Leiharbeit', in *Neue Zeitschrift für Arbeitsrecht*, 2002, pp. 23–29.

Ulber, J., 'Personal-Service-Agenturen und Neuregelung der Arbeitnehmerüberlassung', in *Arbeit und Recht*, 2003, pp. 7–15.

Walwei, U., 'Leiharbeit: Bedeutung für Wirtschaft und Beschäftigung', in *EuroAS*, 2002, pp. 149–166.

Wank, R., 'Der Richtlinienvorschlag der EG-Kommission zur Leiharbeit und das "Erste Gesetz für moderne Dienstleistungen am Arbeitsmarkt"', in *Neue Zeitschrift für Arbeitsrecht*, 2002, pp. 14–23.

Wank, R., 'Neuere Entwicklungen im Arbeitnehmerüberlassungsrecht', in *Recht der Arbeit*, 2003, pp. 1–11.

Weiss, M. and Schmidt, M., 'Germany', in Blanpain, R. (ed.), *Temporary Work and Labour Law of the European Community and Member States*, Kluwer 1993, pp. 121–161.

Weiss, M., 'Germany', in Blanpain, R. (ed.), *Private Employment Agencies*, Bulletin of Comparative Labour Relations, Vol. 36, 1999, pp. 255–265.

8. Italy

Michele Colucci

INTRODUCTION

Unlike other European countries, Italy has traditionally prohibited temporary work. The supply of workers by temporary work agencies was outlawed as a form of serious exploitation of labour and so their regulation has always been very strict.[1] However, significant changes have been made in the last decade by introducing flexibility in this field through tripartite negotiations between government, employers and trade unions. From the 1990s onwards, the objective has been to guard against any undermining by employers of workers' rights and job protection measures, won by previous trade union campaigns.[2] That objective has been pursued by introducing collective bargaining at all levels.

Law 196/1997,[3] known as the 'Treu Package', finally lifted the prohibition on temporary work. Complete deregulation in this field has, however, only been achieved by the adoption of the Biagi Law in February 2003.[4]

This paper will first focus on the genesis of the legal framework governing temporary work in Italy and its content. It will then analyse the principles and rationale behind the introduction of greater flexibility into the Italian labour market. Finally, it will examine the main provisions concerning the status of temporary worker, temporary agency and user enterprise.

To place the legal framework in context, some facts and figures should first be provided. According to a survey conducted by the European Foundation, there are at present 50 temporary work agencies registered with the Ministry of Labour and licensed to operate in Italy.[5] A total of 470,000 temporary agency workers are hired out in Italy, with 55 per cent working in the industrial sector and 23 per cent in the services sector.

Further, according to Istat (the Italian statistics body), in 2002 the total labour force of 15.9 million dependent workers was divided as follows: 84 per cent permanent full-time; 6 per cent permanent part-time; 3 per cent temporary part-time; and 7 per cent temporary full-time. Only 3.2 per cent of men are self-employed on a part-time basis, while this proportion reaches 17.7 per cent among women. Part-time

---

1. T. Treu, *Labour Law and Industrial Relations in Italy*, Kluwer Law International, 1998, p. 42.
2. *See* M.A. Agostino and S. Leonardi, *The Social Dialogue in Italy: A Recent Evaluation.*
3. Law No.196 of 24 June 1997 on 'Provisions in the field of employment', in *Gazzetta Ufficiale* No. 154 of 4 July 1997.
4. Law No. 30 of 14 February 2003 on 'Employment and Labour Market', in *Gazzetta Ufficiale* No. 47 of 26 February 2003.
5. European Foundation for the Improvement of Living and Working Conditions, *Temporary Work in Italy*, Dublin 2002.

R. Blanpain & R. Graham (eds.), Temporary Agency Work and the Information Society, 143–158

work is most common in the sectors of agriculture (17.7 per cent of employees) and in services (11.3 per cent), while it is less frequent in industry (4.5 per cent).[6]

1. THE LEGAL FRAMEWORK

1.1 The legislation before the 'Treu Package'

In Italy, the intermediary role played by a temporary work agency was prohibited in any form by Law No. 264 of 1949, which entrusted the placement of workers exclusively to the public employment services.[7] Law No. 264 was complemented by Law No. 1369 of 23 October 1960, which prohibited so-called fraudulent interruption of employment or sub-contracting of labour, i.e., the hiring of a worker by a person other than his or her employer. At the same time, Law No. 230 of 1962 set precise guidelines for direct fixed-term hiring either on a seasonal basis or in substitution of permanent workers.[8]

The trilateral 'social pact' signed by government, employers' associations and trade unions on 23 July 1993 was to provide 'social legitimacy' for temporary agency work. But in the following years, the government and Parliament failed to legislate on this matter. The political will to remove obstacles preventing lawful recourse to temporary agency work was reaffirmed in the tripartite agreement of 24 September 1996. This time, the government followed up the agreement by drafting legislation which was approved by Parliament as Law No. 196 of 24 June 1997.

1.2 The Treu Package (1997)

Law 196/1997 was important and innovative in that it gave temporary agency work a legal status in Italian law for the first time. But its regulatory scheme, which will be analysed in detail in the second part of this paper, remained strict due to the traditional Italian diffidence towards this type of labour.

1.3 The White Paper on the Italian Labour Market (2001)

In October 2001, the Italian government published a White Paper on the Italian labour market (*Libro bianco sul mercato del lavoro in Italia*). This work was co-authored by a group of five experts in labour law and economics including Professor Marco Biagi.

The main objectives of the White Paper were 'to guarantee a substantial increase in the employment rate, to improve the quality of work and to obtain greater social cohesion'. The White Paper is based on the view that the Italian labour market is still afflicted by crippling worker protection which stifles the entrepreneurial spirit of companies and employees alike. In discussing each labour institution, reference is made to best practice in EU states with the most deregulated systems – in particular to the UK and Dutch models. On this matter, the White Paper

6. Istat, *Labour Force Survey*, October 2002.
7. T. Treu, *Labour Law and Industrial Relations in Italy*, Kluwer Law International, 1998, p. 42.
8. T. Treu and L. Pero, *Legal and Contractual Limitations to Working Time in the European Union*, 2nd edition (R. Blanpain (ed.)), Peeters, 1997.

also refers substantially to relevant EU directives. The measures proposed include new forms of employment contracts and a reform of collective bargaining to encourage the setting of wages at local level.

The document is divided into two parts, the first containing an analysis of the labour market and the second a series of proposals. The analysis is centred on both the performance and characteristics of the Italian labour market. It assesses the impact of EU guidelines on current passive and active labour policies, focussing particular attention on the 'social shock absorbers' which cushion the effects of redundancies and restructuring, on employment incentives and on the training system.

The second part of the White Paper sets out its objectives and the means available to achieve them. The objectives are given as: increased employment and labour quality (more and better jobs); greater flexibility and security; equal opportunities; and social inclusion. The means available to achieve these objectives are: 'social dialogue' based on the EU model; development of the current 'federalist' decentralization of labour market regulation to the regions; the use of 'soft' law; and legislative interventions.

The White Paper also highlights demographic and generational problems. Young people have difficulty with the transitions from school to work and from training to work. Older people struggle to ensure their vocational skills satisfy current requirements and to adapt to new forms of flexible work. Further, women find it difficult to enter and to remain in the labour market.

Mediocre job quality is common in 'non-regular' work. Non-regularity of work is the major employment incentive for 14.7 per cent of the employed population. The current system of incentives and 'social shock absorbers' is regarded as inadequate and inefficient, as are the public employment services, which are unable to provide workfare services.

The White paper underlines the need to free the labour market from the economic and regulatory mechanisms which are considered obstacles to its development. The government intends to overcome these obstacles by:

1. modernizing and liberalizing public employment services;
2. improved public intervention in the school-work-training transitions; ongoing training will be supported by greater public intervention. Apprenticeship will be promoted as a training tool while the work/training contract will be used as a means of recruitment; and
3. reforming 'social shock absorbers' in order that they act as employment incentives. People benefiting from the social shock absorbers must be 'actively seeking employment'. The methods of job-seeking must be agreed with the public employment services.

Within the proposed framework, all types of employment contracts currently in force will have to be adapted, and flexible contracts will have to be altered, so as to remove any regulatory obstacles.

The authors of the White Paper wanted to facilitate the provision of private employment services, and the integration of public and private employment services into a single national system. In this regard, private operators are to receive, on approval of their application, authorization to supply job placement services. Temporary work agencies will be classified as providers of private employment services, since the present stringent legislation limiting their activity to the supply of temporary labour is to be abolished.

1.4 The Pact for Italy (2002)

In 2002, the so-called Pact for Italy was agreed between the government and the relevant social parties. It contained a series of provisions on new forms of work and it laid down guidelines for drawing up legislation to reform the Italian labour market and the tax system. With particular regard to reform of the labour market, the agreement aimed to promote higher incomes, placement services and opportunities in training, employment and self-employment by:

a) reorganizing job placement services by improving co-operation with workers' local employment offices;
b) increasing awareness of the availability of employment services, including those operating in the 'Third sector' (voluntary and non-profit organizations);
c) improving co-ordination of labour supply and demand, training needs, personnel selection and job placement.

1.5 The Biagi Law (2003)

The Biagi Law was passed in February 2003, and included amendments originating in the Pact for Italy. The amendments related to job placement services, new forms of employment contract and part-time work, amongst other matters. The Italian government will now have to issue several decrees in order to implement the provisions contained in the law. It has committed itself to completing that legislative process by June 2003, so that the new rules will be in force by the end of summer 2003. Hereafter we briefly examine the law's main innovative provisions, which – it is important to stress – will apply only in the private sector.

1.5.1 The end of the monopoly on job placement by public employment services

The Biagi Law repeals Law No. 1369 of 23 October 1960 which outlawed intermediation in the hiring of labour and which banned labour-only subcontracting. Under the Treu package, Law No. 1369 continued to apply to any organization which was supplied with temporary agency workers either by agencies not in possession of the required authorization or in situations which it did not expressly permit. At last, the monopoly on job placement by public employment services in Italy has been brought to an end. Employment consultants, temporary work agencies, universities and joint bodies established by the social partners will be allowed to provide placement services in future. Reform in this area will also allow for the creation of a 'continuous labour exchange' (*Borsa continua del lavoro*), namely an employment service in which public and private bodies will continuously update information on labour supply and demand.

1.5.2 New forms of employment contract

The Law introduces new forms of employment contract governing

a) 'On call Jobs' (*Lavoro intermittente*), whereby employees are available to work on a discontinuous or intermittent basis. Workers are able to choose whether or not they will have to accept a call to work from their employer. If they elect that acceptance will be obligatory, the employer is obliged to pay them an allowance;

b) 'Job-sharing' (*Lavoro ripartito*), whereby two workers share the same position. This form of work has been simplified and given a legal basis. Workers are able to organize job-sharing between themselves without constraints being imposed by the company; and

c) 'Additional Work' (*Lavoro accessorio*) – contracts in this area have been simplified and are to be tried out for jobs involving personal care.

1.5.3 Work organization and social protection measures

Companies will be able to outsource units to a greater extent, but only if the units are already established and working autonomously. Staff leasing will be allowed by companies which hire out workers on a regular basis and which post them on open-ended contracts to other companies.

Social security and labour inspection activities, which are at present entrusted to the Ministry of Labour and the National Social Security Institute (*Istituto Nazionale Previdenza Sociale*, Inps), will be reviewed and decentralized.

Flexible forms of part-time work will be introduced, and part-time employment will be allowed in the agricultural sector. Greater flexibility in part-time work will be achieved by new rules on working extra hours (i.e. for work exceeding normal part-time hours but less than full-time hours), while there will be greater opportunities for workers to switch from part-time to full-time work and vice versa.

2. THE REGULATION ON TEMPORARY WORK

2.1 Notion of Temporary Work

Law No. 196/1997 defines and regulates contracts for temporary work arranged by a temporary work agency. It thereby introduces a derogation from Law No. 1369/1960 which permitted derogation only under specified conditions.

According to Law 196/1997, temporary work entails a trilateral relationship between the agency (which is the employer), the temporary employee, and the enterprise using the services of the employee, as in other states. Only two contracts govern this trilateral relationship. Firstly a contract for the supply of temporary agency labour exists between the agency and the client, i.e., the user enterprise. Secondly a contract for the supply of temporary employment services exists between the worker and the agency.

2.2 Form and Content of the Contracts

2.2.1 Contract for the supply of temporary labour

Under Article 1 of Law No. 196/1997, a 'contract for the supply of temporary labour' is defined as a:

> Contract whereby an enterprise supplying temporary labour ('supplier enterprise'), registered as required (i.e. under Article 2, registered with the

Ministry of Labour, and granted the relevant licence), places one or more workers ('temporary workers') employed by itself under a contract of employment as required (i.e. under Article 3, either a fixed-term or open-ended contract) at the disposal of another enterprise which makes use of their labour ('user enterprise') to meet specified needs of a 'temporary nature'.

The contract for the supply of temporary agency workers must be in written form and must indicate:

a) the number of workers requested;
b) the tasks involved and the relevant job classification;
c) the location, working hours, as well as financial and regulatory terms and conditions for the labour envisaged;
d) an express undertaking of the obligation to pay the worker directly on the part of the supplier enterprise or, in the event of its default, on the part of the user enterprise; and
e) the starting and finishing dates of the contract; and the essential particulars of the licence issued to the supplier enterprise.

In the absence of a written contract for the supply of temporary agency labour, a worker who provides labour to the user enterprise is deemed to have been employed under an open-ended employment contract.

Any clause intended to limit, even indirectly, the right of the user enterprise to employ the worker at the end of the contract for temporary work is null and void. Further, a copy of the contract for the supply of temporary agency workers must be sent by the supplying agency to the Provincial Labour office responsible for the territory within ten days of its being signed.

2.2.2 Contract of employment

A contract of employment for the performance of temporary work which is concluded between the worker and the supplier enterprise must state, in writing:

a) the reasons for use of temporary labour;
b) the name of the supplier enterprise and its official registration and reference;
c) the name of the user enterprise;
d) the tasks concerned and the worker's job classification level;
e) whether there is a probationary period, and if so its duration;
f) the location, working hours, as well as financial and regulatory terms and conditions involved;
g) the starting and finishing dates of the work assignment in question;
h) any safety measures necessary for the type of work that is to be done.

In the absence of a written contract or of any indication as to the starting and finishing dates of employment at the client organization, a temporary employment contract converts into an employment contract binding the agency for an open-ended period. However, where the period of the assignment is specified, it may be extended by a written agreement, with the consent of the worker, and for the duration allowed by the national collective agreement applicable to the sector.

If an assignment continues beyond its specified duration, the worker is subsequently deemed to have been employed on an open-ended contract by the user enterprise. Thus if an assignment continues beyond the term initially specified or is extended, the worker has the right to an increase in daily pay of 20 per cent for each day that the employment relationship continues, for the following 10 days. That increase is to be met by the agency so long as continuation of the work has been agreed.

2.3 Cases in Which Temporary Work is Allowed

Under Article 1, paragraph 2 of Law No. 196/1997, the use of temporary agency workers is allowed:

a) in circumstances foreseen by national collective agreements covering the sector to which the user enterprise belongs. (The use of temporary work consequently depends considerably on the practice of collective bargaining);
b) in circumstances requiring the temporary use of skills not available within the structure of the undertaking which seeks to use them;
c) to replace absent workers.

In the agricultural and construction sectors, temporary agency work has been permitted only on an experimental basis subject to an agreement between trade unions and employers.

The Decree implementing Act No. 59/1997, which concerns employment relationships in the public sector, explicitly permits public sector employees to carry out temporary work.

Finally, following the Framework Agreement of 23 May 2000 concluded between the unions and ARAN, which conducts collective bargaining on behalf of employers in the public sector, public authorities may now employ temporary agency workers, though they may not compose more than 7 per cent of their total workforce.

2.4 Cases in Which Temporary Work is Prohibited

The supply of temporary labour is prohibited:

a) where the work in question requires little occupational skill. This prohibition is scarcely justified. Its scope is determined by collective agreement or, in the absence of a consensus, by Ministerial Decree. It confirms the principle, established by the law of 1984 on part-time and fixed-term work that the regulation of 'atypical' employment relationships in Italy shall generally be negotiated by social partners;
b) where the labour in question is sought to replace employees who are on strike;
c) where an undertaking has, in the previous twelve months, carried out collective dismissals or introduced part-time work in the area of operation in which it now seeks to use temporary labour;

d) where the work in question is of a particularly dangerous nature, or is carried out by undertakings which have not complied with the law on health and safety in the workplace.[9]

A number of amendments to the regulation of temporary agency work were introduced by Law No. 488 of December 1999. The amendments are based on suggestions made under the social partners' agreement of 22 November 1999, and are the product of the concerted follow-up required by Law No. 196/1997 (at Article 11) two years after its entry into force.

The main changes have been introduced by way of the Finance Act for 2000. First, the restriction originally imposed on the use of temporary labour in the agricultural and construction sectors has been removed. Secondly, the prohibition on the use of temporary agency work for work requiring little occupational skill has been abolished. The equivalent prohibition regarding certain tasks, specified by collective agreement, 'whose performance may present some considerable danger to the safety of the worker or of third parties' has had considerably less impact and has been maintained.

3. THE LEGAL STATUS OF THE TEMPORARY WORKER: RIGHTS AND OBLIGATIONS

Temporary workers have principally the same rights as ordinary employees of the user undertaking. A temporary worker can be hired out by an agency for a fixed term, determined by the period of employment foreseen by the user undertaking, or for and indefinite period. Where hired out for an indefinite period, a temporary worker will be entitled to an indemnity determined by collective agreement (or by decree) in compensation for being 'on call' and at the disposal of the agency, in addition to remuneration for work carried out.[10]

3.1 Remuneration and Social Benefits

A temporary worker has the right to the same level of financial treatment, namely wages, benefits and contributions to social support schemes, as that enjoyed by an employee of the user enterprise. Responsibility for the equal financial treatment of the temporary worker lies with both the user enterprise and the temporary work agency. In the event that an employment relationship continues beyond the date of termination stated in the contract, the Law stipulates a 20 per cent increase in the daily rate of pay for the ten days following that date; after the ten day period, the agency worker is deemed to be employed by the user enterprise employed under an open-ended contract.

3.2 Health and Safety

A temporary agency worker has the right, and an employer the obligation, to be informed about health and safety issues, pursuant to the provisions of the Italian

9. Legislative Decree No. 626 of 19 September 1994, implementing Directives 89/391/EEC, 89/654/EEC, 89/655/EEC, 89/656/EEC, 90/269/EEC, 90/270/EEC, 90/394/EEC, 93/88/EEC, 97/42/EEC and 1999/38/EC on the improvement of the Health and safety of Workers, in *Gazzetta Ufficiale* of 12 November 1994, No. 265.

Civil Code and those of D.Lgs. No. 626/1994,[10] which introduced specific 'rights of information' and 'rights of negotiation' for workers. An employer is required to take any measure in order to ensure the health and safety of workers in all aspects of work under Article 2081 of the Italian Civil Code.

Article 9 of Act No. 300/1970 gives to workers, and their representatives, the right to make proposals on health and safety issues at work, and gives to workers' representatives the right to monitor the application of the relevant legislation.

Ensuring a higher degree of workers' safety by implementing preventative measures to guard against accidents at work and occupational diseases is the objective of D.Lgs. No. 626/1994, as modified by D.Lgs. No. 242/1996, and other legislative Acts which have implemented the EU Directive.[11] In particular, an employer must provide employees with all relevant information on the general and specific risks related to their jobs as well as to the measures adopted to avoid such risks (under Article 21 of D.Lgs No. 626/1994).

In each establishment, a workers' representative with specific responsibility for the health and safety of workers (*Rappresentante per la sicurezza*) must be informed by the employer of any measure which could substantially affect health and safety.

An employee has the right to be informed about matters relating to any occupational risk including the choice of work equipment and the fitting-out of workplaces, and about risks related to exposure to chemical, physical and biological agents at work.[12]

An employee also has the right to make provision for adequate protective and preventative services. On the other hand, an employer is obliged to record and draw up reports on occupational accidents. According to D.Lgs. No. 242/1996, no such obligation applies to undertakings with less than 10 employees.

For all activities likely to involve a specific risk of exposure to harmful agents, processes or working conditions, the employer shall assess the nature, degree and duration of exposure in order to:

- evaluate any risks to the health and safety of workers, and in particular to the health of pregnant workers and those who are nursing mothers;
- decide what measures should be taken.

---

10. Legislative Decree No. 626 of 19 September 1994, implementing Directives 89/391/EEC, 89/654/EEC, 89/655/EEC, 89/656/EEC, 90/269/EEC, 90/270/EEC, 90/394/EEC, 90/679/EEC, 93/88/EEC, 97/42/EC and 1999/38/EC on the improvement of the Health and safety of Workers, in *Gazzetta Ufficiale* No. 265 of 12 November 1994.
11. D.P.R. No. 459 of 24 July 1996, implementing EU Directives 89/392/EEC, 91/368/EEC, 93/44/EEC and 93/68/EEC on the approximation of the laws of the Members States relating to machinery, S.O. No. 146 of O.J. of 6 September 1996, No. 209;

    D.Lgs. No. 493 of 14 August 1996, implementing Directive 92/58/EEC on the minimum requirements for the provision of safety and/or health signs at work, S.O. No. 156 of O.J. of 23 September 1996, No. 223, p. 3;

    D.Lgs. No. 494 of 14 August 1996, implementing Directive 92/57/EEC on the implementation of minimum safety and health requirements at temporary or mobile construction sites, S.O. No. 156 of O.J. of 23 September 1996, No. 223, p. 24;

    D.Lgs No. 624 of 25 November 1996, implementing Directive 92/91/EEC concerning the minimum requirements for improving the safety and health protection of workers in the mineral-extracting industries through drilling, S.O. No. 219 of O.J. of 14 December 1996, No. 293, p. 5.
12. D.Lgs. No. 277 of 15 August 1991, implementing EU Directives on No. 80/1107/EEC, No. 82/605/EEC, No. 83/477/EEC, No. 86/188/EEC and No. 88/642/EEC, on the protection of workers from the risks related to exposure to chemical, physical and biological agents at work, S.O. No. 53 of O.J. of 27 August 1991, No. 200.

Finally, specific provisions contained in Article 22 of D.Lgs. No. 626/94 aim to ensure that each worker receives adequate health and safety training when hired out and throughout the whole period of employment. An employer who does not comply with the Legislation on Health and Safety at work may incur both civil and criminal liability.[13]

Despite the existence of the considerable legislation outlined above, it is in practice very difficult for temporary agencies to command any real control of training, health and safety and environmental hazards in all sectors. In addition, user enterprises are less inclined to provide training or ensure environmental safety for workers who are only temporarily in their employment.[14]

3.3 Vocational Training

A temporary work agency must arrange adequate training for the specific tasks which a temporary worker is required to carry out. However, it may pass this responsibility to the user enterprise under the contract for the supply of temporary labour.

Article 5 of the Treu Package, previously established a 'training fund', which was managed by the national Institute of Social Insurance (INPS), and financed by contributions paid by the agencies, at a rate of 5 per cent of the gross wage of each temporary worker. Recently, that provision has been rewritten. The new Article provides for the establishment of a Bilateral Fund, at the suggestion of the representative employers' organizations for temporary work agencies and the most representative unions. The range of undertakings that participate in the training scheme under the new Fund is greater than under the 'Fund for Vocational Training of Temporary Workers'.

These changes were brought about as a result of strong criticism expressed by both unions and temporary work agencies. The agencies, in particular, had voiced vigorous objections to the clause which required them to pay 5 per cent of the value of each temporary worker's wage towards employee training. The rate of that contribution has now been lowered to 4 per cent of the worker's wage.[15]

4. THE LEGAL STATUS OF THE TEMPORARY WORK AGENCY

Prior to the Biagi Law, only undertakings and not individuals could supply temporary labour under Italian law.[16]

4.1 Official Certification

A register of agencies which are certified to provide labour is currently being drawn up by the Ministry of Labour and Social Security. An agency is certified only if it

13. Article 612 and following of Italian Civil Procedure Code; Articles 437 and 451 of the Italian Criminal Code.
14. P. Andreoni (2000), 'Sicurezza e lavoro temporaneo', in Andreoni and Stanzani (eds.).
15. European Foundation for the Improvement of Living and Working Conditions, *Temporary Work in Italy*, Dublin, 2002.
16. M. Biagi, *Private Employment Agencies: Italy*, Bulletin of Comparative Labour Relations No. 36, Kluwer, 1999.

meets the following requirements, thereby guaranteeing its economic and organizational stability. Pursuant to Article 2, paragraph 2 of the Treu package, an agency must:

a) be a joint-stock company or co-operative;
b) carry on hiring-out of labour as its sole business activity;
c) include the words 'temporary work agency' in its company name;
d) possess paid-up capital of not less than one billion lire, and deposit a sum of 700 million Lire (350,000 euros)for the first two years with a credit institution as security for payments due to employees;
e) have either a branch or its registered office based in Italy;
f) have offices in at least four regions and possess appropriate professional competence; and
g) have no individuals among its top-level management who have ever been convicted of a criminal offence.

The requirement that agencies be economically and organizationally stable, which was imposed by the unions and associated parties, immediately placed the temporary work market in the hands of multinationals. Due to the scale on which they may supply temporary labour, multinationals dominate this sector throughout the EU, and in Italy they had lobbied tirelessly for the opening up of the temporary work market.

The stipulation that hiring-out must be the sole business activity prevents an agency from carrying out other activities, such as co-ordinating supply and demand of labour, and personnel search and selection for purposes other than the immediate supply of temporary work, as well as offering placement services to workers seeking to change employment. According to the White Paper, although co-ordinating supply and demand of temporary labour is restricted, labour supply undertakings are in fact performing this activity, and with great efficiency. The restriction has been disregarded in the face of setbacks in the operations of public employment services. Consequently, Article 1 of Act 30/2003 expressly provides that temporary work agencies are also entitled to co-ordinate supply and demand, to carry out personnel search and selection activities as well as offering placement services to workers seeking to change employment. Undertakings carrying out these activities, as well as agencies which only supply temporary labour, are no longer obliged to pursue a sole business activity. Therefore, all private agencies co-ordinating the supply and demand of labour now require certification under a single system.

4.2 The Agency as Employer: Rights and Obligations

The agency as employer must guarantee, in agreement with the user undertaking, a wage that is not lower than that paid to ordinary workers of the same level employed in the user undertaking. Workers must receive appropriate training for the job to be performed and appropriate information on health and safety in the workplace. Temporary work agencies have the following obligations towards their employees:

a) agencies must pay remuneration at least equivalent to that to which comparable employees of the user enterprise are entitled;
b) in the case of those employed under an open-ended contract, agencies must continue to pay employees during periods when they are not working;
c) agencies must pay the required insurance and social security contributions;

d) they must grant paid annual holidays;
e) they must pay the end-of-service allowance on termination of an open-ended employment contract; and
f) they must pay for employee insurance against accidents at work and occupational illness.

5. THE LEGAL STATUS OF THE USER ENTERPRISE

Article 1 of the Treu Package imposes a number of obligations on user undertakings, including:

a) implementing all safety measures, and providing agency workers with information on safety arrangements;
b) allowing agency workers the use of all social and welfare facilities;
c) compensating third parties who have suffered damage caused by agency workers;
d) notifying the temporary work agency in writing in the event that an agency worker is assigned tasks of a higher level than those originally envisaged (should it fail to notify the agency, the user enterprise becomes liable for any difference in pay arising from the new nature of the assignment); and
e) communicating any complaints about workers directly to the agency.

No limit may be imposed on the right of the user enterprise to hire a worker directly at the termination of an assignment.

6. COLLECTIVE LABOUR RELATIONS ASPECTS

At the outset, collective bargaining played a key role in introducing temporary agency work in Italy: the Treu package confirmed how crucial a tool it was in creating more flexibility in the Italian labour market. For instance, Article 1.2 stipulates that a contract for the supply of temporary agency work may be agreed not only in certain situations explicitly provided for in legislation but also in circumstances identified by national collective agreements agreed by unions which are 'comparatively representative' in the sector to which the user enterprise belongs. According to Professor Biagi, attention should be paid to the formula 'comparatively representative unions' which reflects the growing problem of several unions co-existing in the same industry, and each claiming to represent employees. This formula is designed to empower the government and local authorities to select unions which represent (though do not necessarily organize) comparatively more workers than others in a specific sector.[17]

The development of collective bargaining on behalf of temporary agency workers has increased since 1998, resulting in numerous agreements and draft agreements between social partners at different levels and in various sectors.

17. M. Biagi, *Private Employment Agencies: Italy*, Bulletin of Comparative Labour Relations No. 36, Kluwer, 1999.

Law No. 196/1997 identifies two kinds of collective agreements, namely those concluded by associations of user enterprises and those stipulated by associations of temporary work agencies. The first are deemed to be essential, the second to some extent optional. In both cases, social partners have been given a highly important role in regulating experimentation with this form of flexible work.

A collective agreement was made in January 1998 between the commercial sector unions (FILCAMS-CGIL, FISASCAT-CISL and UILTUCS-UIL) and associations of temporary work agency employers (Assointerim and Assilt, which subsequently merged with Assointerim). The agreement classifies workers who are directly employed by agencies in the commerce and services sector. As a result, two new professional categories have been defined (specialist in personnel selection or placement, and agency manager), and these are included in the agreement of January 1998.[18]

The framework agreement of 16 April 1998 between the three union confederations (CGIL, CISL and UIL) and Confindustria, in accordance with Law No. 196/1997, establishes core rules and conditions of employment for temporary agency work in Italy. It also delegates the laying down of sector-specific rules and conditions to the industries themselves, stipulating that they should be established by collective agreement.

Regarding the core rules and conditions, the maximum number of agency workers which an enterprise may employ is equivalent to 8 per cent of the total number of its permanent employees as averaged over a calendar quarter; reasons permitting their use are specified: to respond to high levels of business; for services or tasks which cannot be performed by company resources; and for unusual commissions which, because of the particular nature of a product or process, demand skills other than those available within the enterprise. The agreement also lists the type of low-skilled jobs which may not be performed by temporary workers under Law No. 196. It differentiates them from other professional categories which are graded at a skill-level lower than 'intermediate' but which have been defined in a national multi-industry agreement of 1995 on training contracts (relating, in practice, to the lowest two professional categories).[19]

Lastly, on 28 May 1998, the first national agreement relating specifically to temporary agency workers was concluded between Assointerim (the association of temporary work agency employers) and the new unions representing temporary agency workers (NIDIL-CGIL,ALAI-CISL and CPO-UIL). This is a genuine industry-wide agreement which is based on the earlier agreements and legislation, provides for rights to information and union rights, and defines professional categories and rules relating to illness or accident. It also introduces new arrangements for possible extensions of assignment, up to a maximum of four (over a maximum period of twenty-four months); for a stand-by allowance fixed at 700,000 Lire a month; for disciplinary rules; and for the establishment of the Bilateral Agency for training.

These are the three main collective agreements which have accompanied the introduction of temporary agency work in Italy as enacted in the Law of 1997. The subsequent agreements, in practice, implement the three main agreements in the various sectors and at different levels, although some contain innovative elements.

18. European Foundation for the Improvement of Living and Working Conditions, *Temporary Work in Italy*, Dublin, 2002.
19. European Foundation for the Improvement of Living and Working Conditions, *Ibidem*.

CONCLUSIONS

The introduction of temporary agency work in Italy was preceded by a heated debate in national politics and among trade unions. Differing standpoints, rooted in opposed ideologies, remained entrenched for many years. Meanwhile, on the ground, precursors to the temporary work agency were established to respond to the nascent demand for temporary work in Italy. Some of these undertakings have been operating legally providing contracting, subcontracting, collaborative and consulting services while others, including fake co-operatives and illegal work contractors (*Caporalato*), have carried on their business despite their prohibition. The 'Treu package', in providing for the operation of temporary work agencies, therefore marked an important turning point in the regulation of the labour market.

The requirement that agencies must be economically and organizationally stable, which was imposed by the unions and associated parties, has immediately placed the market in supplying temporary work in the hands of multinationals. The scale on which multinationals can supply temporary labour has allowed them to dominate the sector throughout Europe, and in addition they lobbied tirelessly to open up the Italian temporary labour market. The other most significant restraint imposed by the new legislation on the operation of temporary work agencies is the obligation to bargain collectively with regard to, firstly, establishing rules and conditions of work and, secondly, determining circumstances which limit the supply of temporary labour.

Adoption of the Biagi Law has been a significant step towards deregulation in the field of employment services and temporary work. Clearly some important matters remain at issue such as the obligation to provide temporary workers with adequate vocational training, and the obligation to give information on health and safety issues. At a fundamental level, however, the new law enlivens the long-stagnated Italian labour market, which is now more liberalized than ever before.

BIBLIOGRAPHY

Andreoni, P. (2000), 'Sicurezza e lavoro temporaneo', in Andreoni and Stanzani (eds.).

Assointerim, Alai-Cisl, Cgil-Nidil, Cpo-Uil (1999), *Contratto collettivo nazionale di lavoro per la categoria delle imprese fornitrici di lavoro temporaneo*, Editoriale Itaca, Roma, 28 maggio 1998.

European Foundation for the Improvement of Living and Working Conditions, (2002), *Temporary Work in Italy*, Dublin.

European Foundation for the Improvement of Living and Working Conditions (1999), *Flexible Employment Policies and Working Conditions*, Consolidated Report and National Reports, Dublin.

Istat (1999), *I principali risultati della rilevazione sulla flessibilità nel mercato del lavoro*, www.istat.it/novita/Fless.htm

Magnavita, N. (2000), 'Il lavoro temporaneo: un nuovo rischio professionale', in Andreoni and Stanzani (eds.).

Marocci, G. (2000), 'Lavoro organizzazione e stress', in Andreoni and Stanzani (eds.).

Mascini, M. (2000), 'I nuovi soggetti delle relazioni industriali: il NIDIL CGIL', in *Lavoro e Informazione*, No. 4.
Megale, A. and Leonardi, S., (2002) 'The Social Dialogue in Italy: a recent evaluation'.
Negrelli, S. (2000), 'Social Pacts in Italy and Europe', in Pochet, P., and Fajertag, G. (eds.), *Social Pacts in Europe. New Dynamics*, ETUI, Brussels.
Prestileo, C. (2000), 'Il profilo dei lavoratori temporanei', in *Lavoro e Informazione*, No. 3.
Treu, T., and Pero, L. (1997), *Legal and Contractual Limitations to Working Time in the European Union*, 2nd edition, (Blanpain R. (ed.)) Peeters.
Treu T., *Labour Law and Industrial Relations in Italy*, Kluwer Law international, 1998, p. 42.

9. Japan

Tadashi Hanami

I. APPROACHES TOWARDS TEMPORARY WORK: LEGAL SOURCES

1. National Proportion of Regular and Non-regular Workers

In Japan, non-regular workers include: (1) employees employed for a definite period (normally a short period such as one week, one month, or two months); (2) employees employed for an indefinite period who are distinguishable from regular workers also employed for an indefinite period but expected to work for a longer time (usually until the retirement age established by company rules); (3) part-time workers (called part-timers in Japanese); and (4) so-called dispatched workers (workers sent from man-power companies).

The Labor Force Survey of 2001 classified 87 per cent of Japanese workers as permanent workers with an indefinite contract (*Jo-yatoi*), and 13 per cent as workers with fixed-term contracts (Ministry of Public Management, Home Affairs, Posts and Telecommunications, *Rohdohryoku Chohsa* (Labor Force Survey), 2001). According to other statistics, some 72.3 per cent of the total workforce were regular employees, 20.5 per cent were part-time workers and 7.2 per cent temporary workers (Ministry of Public Management, Home Affairs, Posts and Telecommunications, *Rohdohryoku Tokubetu Chohsa* (Report on the Special Labor Force Survey), August 2001).

Such official statistics are largely misleading, especially for foreign readers. The gap between the two sets of statistics is caused by different definitions. In the former survey all workers except those employed for a fixed-term are classified as 'permanent workers'. And thus those workers employed under open-ended contracts or without explicit fixed-term contracts though without job security are counted as 'permanent workers'. There is no legal definition of a permanent worker; the individual companies responding to the survey were responsible for classifying their workers under this heading. It is more accurate to assume that the proportion of workers with permanent status and with job security in the ordinary sense is much smaller than indicated by the above statistics.

From a comparative point of view, the percentage of 'temporary workers' among the total employed workforce in different countries is probably more suggestive. According to the OECD *Labour Force Statistics*, the figure in Japan is inconspicuous, being roughly the global average (*see* Table I).

2. Growing Trend of Non-regular Workers

The number of non-regular workers has been growing in each sector in the past few years. The percentage of temporary workers (employed for a definite period or

R. Blanpain & R. Graham (eds.), Temporary Agency Work and the Information Society, 159–170

Table I. Percentage of temporary employment in total employed workforce (2000)

Country	*Value in %*
Japan	12.9
Canada	12.5
UK	6.8
Germany	12.7
France	15.0
Italy	10.0
The Netherlands	14.0
Belgium	9.0
Luxembourg	3.4
Denmark	10.2
Sweden	14.7
Spain	32.1
Australia	27.3

Source: OECD, Labour Force Statistics, Online Database.[1]

employed on a daily basis) in the total employed workforce increased from 10.2 per cent in 1985 to 12.9 per cent in 2000 (OECD, 'Labour Force Statistics', Online Database).

The ratio of part-time workers (those working less than 35 hours per week) among the total employed workforce also increased from 15.7 per cent in 1980 to 23.1 per cent in 2000 (*Ibid*.)

The total number of workers registered for hiring-out by temporary work agencies increased from 436,336 in 1993 to 1,113,521 in 2000. The increase in 2000 was particularly remarkable, one of 24.8 per cent from the previous year (Ministry of Health, Labor and Welfare, *Rohdohsha Haken Ziggyoh* (Reports on Worker-Dispatching Businesses) Tokyo, 2002, p. 9).

3. Legal Sources

(1) International

Japan has ratified ILO Convention No. 96, Fee-Charging Employment Agencies, of 1964 but has not yet ratified Convention No. 181, Private Employment Agencies, of 1997.

(2) Regional legal sources

There are no regional legal sources applicable to Japan since there is no regional organization regulating labour practices in Asia.

1. In OECD statistics, 'temporary employment comprises work under a fixed-term contract, in contrast to permanent work where there is no end-date. Employment under temporary contracts often entails a different set of legal obligations on behalf of employers: in particular, certain aspects of employment protection legislation do not apply to temporary contracts' (OECD, Glossary of Statistical Terms, OECD Online Database).

(3) National legal sources

The right to work is guaranteed as a basic human right under Article 27 of the Constitution, which provides a foundation for the legal regulation of terms and termination of employment. On the basis of this constitutional requirement, the Labour Standards Law established rules concerning dismissal, mainly regulating the period of notice and prohibition of dismissal in difficult personal circumstances, such as during leave of absence caused by an accident at work or maternity leave.

The Employment Security Law of 1947 (most recently amended in 2000) provides comprehensive regulations on employment exchange. However, as far as concerns hiring-out (known as 'worker-dispatching'), the Law for Securing the Proper Operation of Worker-Dispatching Undertakings and Improved Working Conditions for Dispatched Workers ('the Worker Dispatching Law') of 1985 regulates the hiring-out business so as to protect hired-out workers.

The Law for the Improvement of Management of Short-Term Workers (Short-Term Workers Law) of 1993 established policy measures for the part-time labour market aimed particularly at the 'short-term worker whose prescribed weekly working hours are relatively shorter than those of the workers ordinarily employed in the same business establishment' (Article 2).

II. TEMPORARY WORK: DEFINITIONS AND POSSIBLE CHANNELS

1. Temporary Workers

'Temporary workers' are comprized of different categories of workers as indicated above (Section I.1). From a legalistic point of view, it is rather confusing that there are two different types of contract for temporary work, namely one for a definite and another for an indefinite period. Regular workers and non-regular workers, which both work under an indefinite contract, are only distinguishable by an implicit understanding between employer and employees which is taken for granted by all parties. In many though not all cases, a written notice of employment (*Jirei*) issued by the employer is given to newly employed persons, but such a document is not usually given to non-regular employees.

Japanese law does not restrict short-term employment in the same way as do European countries, but allows employers considerable discretion in choosing between a definite and an indefinite employment contract. No particular circumstances are required to allow employers to employ workers for a period of one year or less. However, the following workers may only be employed for up to three years: (1) workers with the professional knowledge, skills and experience necessary for developing new products, services or technologies or for scientific research; (2) those with professional knowledge, skills or experience necessary to start up, convert, expand, downsize or close down an enterprise; and (3) workers aged sixty years or older (Article 14 of the Labour Standards Law).

2. Part-time Workers

'Part-time workers' are defined in the official statistics as 'workers whose actual working hours per week are shorter than 35 hours'. However, in practice they are often defined by their relatively short working hours, compared to the hours worked by regular full-time workers in the workplace in question. Thus the Short-Term Workers' Law, mentioned previously (Section I.2.(3)), is applied to workers whose hours are shorter than those of ordinary workers. Despite the legal definition, some 'part-time workers' work for the same or almost the same number of hours per week as regular full-time employees. They are often called 'quasi-part-time workers'(*Giji paato*)[2] since they do not have the same security of employment as regular employees.

3. Contract Work Arrangements

Under a contract work arrangement, workers perform specific tasks using the client company's facilities but without the user's supervision. They work under the supervision of the contracting company which employs them. If the client company supervises and directs such workers the arrangement is regarded as an illegal supply of labour which is prohibited by Article 44 of the Employment Security Law. A legitimate contract arrangement is distinguished from illegal labour supply by four elements: (1) the contractor takes all financial and legal responsibility for completion of the work; (2) the contractor himself directs and controls his workers who perform the work; (3) the contractor is the employer with respect to all obligations owed to his workers; and (4) the contractor provides the machinery, equipment, appliances or necessary materials, or, where the work to be performed is not simply physical labour, the professional technology or experience required to carry out the planning or work (Article 4 of the Enforcement Order of the Employment Security Law).

4. Dispatched Workers

'Worker-dispatching' is defined by the Worker Dispatching Law as 'causing a worker or workers employed by one person to be engaged in work for another person under the direction of the latter, while maintaining their employment relationship with the former, except in cases where the original employer agrees with the client that such a worker or workers shall be employed by the client' (Article 2, No. 1). Thus 'dispatched workers' are workers sent to a client company by companies engaged in worker-dispatching.[3] Such a business activity was traditionally prohibited by the Employment Security Law until the Worker-Dispatching Law was introduced in 1985 to legalize it in sixteen specified types of work.

Before the introduction of the Worker-Dispatching Law, the Employment Security Law prohibited worker-dispatching activities to protect job opportunities

2. Such quasi-part-time workers are estimated at 20 per cent of all part-time workers (Ministry of Labor, *Part Time Rohdohsha Sohgoh Chohsa* (General Survey on Part-Time Workers), Tokyo, 1995).
3. Sometimes the term 'temporary worker' is used to mean a worker provided by a 'temporary work agency' to other employers. In order to avoid confusion, in this Article the term 'temporary workers' is used to mean workers in 'temporary employment under a fixed-term contract, in contrast to permanent work where there is no end-date' (although 'employment under temporary contracts often entails a different set of legal obligations on behalf of employers' – OECD, Glossary of Statistical Terms, OECD Online Database, *see* note 1, *supra*.), while the term 'dispatched worker' is used to mean a worker provided by an agency.

for regular employees. The sixteen types of work for which dispatched workers could be used included those requiring professional knowledge, skills or experience such as computer programming, production of broadcast programmes, interpretation, translation and shorthand, and those requiring management of employees, such as cleaning buildings, and the operation and maintenance of building equipment. Despite their previous opposition, unions tolerated regulation of worker-dispatching under the pretext that dispatched workers with professional expertise are limited in number and are unlikely to seriously damage job opportunities for regular workers. They further reasoned that highly-skilled workers may not be so seriously exposed to the risks of exploitation that arise in short-term employment.

However, as a result of the growing demand for dispatched workers, the range of work in which it was permissible was gradually extended. In 1994, the general occupational restrictions on worker-dispatching were abolished for workers older than sixty years except in a few occupations (port transport services, construction, security guard services and production services). In 1996, the range of work in which dispatching was permitted was extended to cover ten additional types of work such as research and development, creating and editing of publications, designing goods and advertisements, hosting events, office automation instruction, telemarketing, sales engineering, television and radio installation. In 1999, the prohibition was abolished in principle except for port transport, construction, security guard services and other occupations designated by the Cabinet Order. In 1996, worker-dispatching to replace workers on leave for reasons of child or family care was also permitted for a maximum period of one year.

5. 'Farming-out' (*Shukko*)

'Farming-out' is the transferring of a worker to another company (host company) while the employment relationship with the original (transferring) company is maintained. The practice has been used effectively by Japanese companies for different purposes under the so-called life-time employment system in which regular employees are supposed to stay in the company by which they were originally employed upon graduation until retirement age.

The following observations are important to understand the role played by farming-out in Japan. (1) The practice was originally initiated by larger companies (often by parent companies) to send their employees to related companies including subsidiaries. The larger companies thus transferred technological know-how, thereby providing training and education to their employees and to those of host companies. (2) The subsidiaries also transferred their employees to parent companies to learn skills by working there. (3) Furthermore, this practice has been extended by the growing need to establish subsidiaries which assume certain operations previously carried out by the parent company. (4) Finally, particularly at the end of the recent rapid economic growth, the transfer of employees to other companies was carried out in order to cope with redundancy.

In the latter two instances of farming-out, the practice started to take on a different form. In such cases, employment of the farmed-out employees was sometimes removed from the original company and transferred to the host company (a practice called *Tenseki* in Japanese).

III. TEMPORARY WORK ORGANIZATIONS

1. Definition of a Temporary Work Agency

A temporary work agency is only permitted in Japan if it carries out 'worker-dispatching' as defined by the Worker-Dispatching Law (*see* Section II.4). The Law permits two types of dispatching: (1) regular employment, or specified, worker-dispatching, where a dispatched worker is employed on a permanent basis, which must be notified to the Ministry of Health, Labour and Welfare; and (2) registered, or general, worker-dispatching, for which the agency is required to obtain permission from the Ministry. The requirements for the two types of dispatching differ because of the unstable nature of the employment under general dispatching, where the worker is only employed when the agency received requests from the client company.

2. Conditions for Licensing

Notification or permission for carrying out worker-dispatching cannot be granted to the following persons; (1) any person sentenced to a penalty more severe than imprisonment, or to a fine under the provisions of the Workers-Dispatching Law, provisions of other laws prescribed by the Cabinet Order relating to labour, the provisions of the Law concerning the Prevention of Unjust Acts by Racketeers, or having committed an offence referred to in certain provisions of the Penal Code concerning violence, threat, breach of trust etc., or in the Law concerning Physical Violence, for whom five years have not elapsed from the date of completion or invalidation of the sentence; (2) any person sentenced to a fine under provisions concerning workers' health insurance and compensation for accidents, due to negligence of requirements concerning notice, reporting or payment of insurance fees by employers; (3) any person declared to be incompetent, quasi-incompetent or bankrupt and whose status has not been reinstated; (4) any person whose licence for registration worker-dispatching was revoked and for whom five years have not elapsed from the date of the revocation; (5) any minor who does not possess the same competence for conducting business as an adult and whose legal representative falls under any of the preceding categories; and (6) any legal person employing an executive who falls within any of the preceding categories (Articles 6 and 17 of the Worker Dispatching Law).

3. Their Legal Status

Both individual persons and persons with authority may run a worker-dispatching business unless they are disqualified under the above-mentioned Article 6 or 17 of the Worker-Dispatching Law.

IV. THE USER OF TEMPORARY EMPLOYEES

1. The Nature of the Worker-Dispatching Relationship

The nature of the worker-dispatching relationship is complicated, triangular and requires regulation to protect temporary employees. The employment relationship exists between the temporary employee on the one hand and the worker-dispatching agency on the other but not with the client company. Thus, as a principal employer, the dispatching agency is responsible for observance of the protective labour laws, including the Labour Standards Law. However, because of the triangular nature of the relationship, the Worker-Dispatching Law imposes certain duties on the client company which are normally those of the employer. This is because the client company is in a position to direct and control dispatched workers in the workplace.

2. Rights and Duties of the User of Dispatched Workers

As users of dispatched workers, client companies are responsible for matters such as guaranteeing the freedom of workers to exercise their civil rights, regulation of working hours, and regulations for women and children regarding hazardous work and mining work. Furthermore, after the 1999 Amendment of the Worker-Dispatching Law, certain provisions of the Equal Employment Opportunities Law concerning sexual harassment and protection for pregnant workers became applicable to client companies.

Both the dispatching agency and the client company share responsibility for other matters such as equal treatment, prohibition of forced labour or abuse of trainees under the Labour Standards Law, and health and safety regulations under the Industrial Safety and Health Law.

The 1999 Amendment also introduced provisions to protect personal and private information relating to dispatched workers. An agency carrying out registered dispatching must take proper measures to control personal information and to keep confidential information private (Article 7, paragraph 1, No. 3). Any dispatching agency is permitted to collect, keep and utilize personal information only to the extent necessary for its business activities (Article 24-3). Taking into consideration complaints about the unfair selection of dispatched workers on grounds unrelated to job performance, the Amendment also imposes an obligation on the client company to endeavour to refrain from requesting interviews or photos of workers prior to executing a contract with a dispatching agency (Article 26, paragraph 7). A duty to ensure the confidentiality of information concerning workers, which is obtained in the course of the performance of their assignment, is also imposed on a dispatching agency, its agent, representatives, and its workers including persons who have left employment with the agency (Article 24-4).

Violation of these obligations by dispatching agencies and client companies is criminally sanctioned with either imprisonment or a fine.

3. Regulation of the Length of an Assignment

Until its regulation in 1985, dispatching work was seriously opposed on the ground that it would displace regular employment and as a result eventually erode opportunities for regular employment. The restriction on the range of tasks for which dispatching was permitted was only gradually reduced. Furthermore, even after extension of the range of tasks, and abolition of the general prohibition in 1999, the duration of an assignment is still restricted except in the three following cases: (1) for the 26 tasks for which dispatching was permitted prior to the 1985 regulation;

(2) for starting, transporting, enlarging, reducing or dissolving a business which is scheduled to be completed within a specified period; and (3) for the replacement of a worker at the client company who is on maternity leave or child care leave (Article 40-2, paragraph 1, No. 3).

The restriction on the length of assignment is based on the assumption that an increase in worker-dispatching replaces regular employment and eventually damages the employment security of regular workers. On those grounds, administrative guidance given by the Health, Employment and Welfare Ministry discourages renewal of a year-long assignment more than three times, although further renewal is not prohibited by Law. Furthermore the Ministry can advise the client company to employ the dispatched worker if he or she so wishes, so that the restriction on length of assignment does not seriously damage the employment opportunities of dispatched workers (Article 49-2).

V. THE TEMPORARY WORKER

1. Protection of Temporary Workers

A dispatched worker is an employee of the dispatching agency and so is covered by the Labour Standards Law, the Workers' Accident Compensation Insurance Law, the Industrial Safety and Health Law, the Equal Employment Opportunities Law and all other protective statutes which are applied to all employees.

2. Social Security

The dispatching agencies are in principle responsible for compensation under the Workers' Accident Compensation Insurance Law. Thus all necessary insurance arrangements such as payment of insurance fees and administrative procedures are to be taken care of by the agencies. At the same time, client companies are also responsible for the safety of dispatched workers although there is no direct employment relationship between them. As for Health Insurance, Employment Insurance and Pension Insurance, the situation is straightforward for regular employment dispatching. On the other hand, for registered dispatching, certain requirements regarding insurance must be satisfied, because the workers concerned are not considered employed during periods in which they are not on assignments. Administrative guidance of the Ministry of Health, Employment and Welfare provides that 'repeatedly and continuously employed dispatched workers' should subscribe for all social insurance except if they are employed (1) only for a very limited number of days; (2) for few hours per day; (3) wishing to work only for a short period; (4) with the expectation that they will work only for a short period judging by the nature of the job or the available technology; or (5) as a second breadwinner. Table II shows the percentage of dispatched workers actually provided with social insurance for the two types of worker-dispatching.

The dispatching agencies are responsible for providing annual holiday pay guaranteed under the Labour Standards Law. In the case of registered dispatching, the amount of annual holidays given to individual workers is calculated on the basis of actual employment.

Table II. Percentage of dispatched workers actually subscribing for social insurance

	Total (%)	*Regular employment dispatching (%)*	*Registered dispatching (%)*
Employment Insurance			
Subscribing	78.7	83.9	74.9
Not subscribing	8.7	4.3	12.5
Health Insurance			
Subscribing	70.1	76.9	66.4
Not subscribing	12.8	6.9	15.8
Pension Insurance			
Subscribing	67.4	74.5	63.7
Not subscribing	13.7	7.0	17.3

Source: Ministry of Health, Employment and Welfare, *Rohdohsha Hakenzigyoh Zittai Chohsakekka Hohkokusyo* (Report of Worker-Dispatching Survey), 2001.

3. Collective Relations for Dispatched Workers

Theoretically speaking, dispatched workers are entitled to the right to organize, bargain and act collectively which Article 28 of the Constitution guarantees as a fundamental human right for all workers. However, collective labour relations in Japan are mostly conducted within the enterprise due to the hegemony of enterprise unionism. Thus dispatched workers have been excluded from collective labour relations, although in theory they should benefit from them as a fundamental human right. Most dispatched workers are not organized into unions. They are also excluded from works-councils since employee representatives on the works-councils are usually elected from enterprise unions whose members are exclusively regular employees. In the event that dispatched workers are organized, they are in principle entitled to bargain with the dispatching agencies and not with client companies.

Article 7, No. 2 of the Trade Union Law prohibits an employer from refusing 'to bargain with the representative of the workers employed by the employer without proper reason', classifying such a refusal as an unfair labour practice. Accordingly, the dispatching agencies but not the client companies are prohibited from refusing to bargain with the unions representing workers which they employ or which they have registered.

VI. THE ROLE OF THE SOCIAL PARTNERS

1. Opposition from the Social Partners

The majority of trade unions in Japan are enterprise-based, and organize mainly regular employees of the particular enterprise. Their interests are in working conditions and welfare in the particular enterprise. They do not organize non-regular workers such as temporary and dispatched workers even where they share the same employer. Unions, particularly at national levels, and industrial federations pretend to represent the interests of the working class in general and provide a lot of lip-service to the cause of non-regular workers. But in reality they are not seriously interested in promoting the interests of such workers and are strongly against the expansion of non-regular employment since this would erode traditional long-term employment. Enterprise unions and their national-level associations and federations naturally have a strong vested interest in long-term employment.

At the same time, employers are also interested in preserving long-term employment because of their pride in the traditional practice of lifelong employment. Thus the social partners in Japan are still inclined to approve of regular employment as the norm and to look down on non-regular employment as abnormal.

2. Recent Change

In the last decades, this simplistic view has been gradually changing as a result of the so-called 'liquidation of the labour market'. On the one hand, lifelong employment is declining due to the rapid growth of non-regular employment described above (Section I.2), and the dwindling use of lifelong employment on the other. This type of employment is used less as a result of (1) the continuing decrease in regular employment opportunities since the end of a period of rapid economic growth, and; (2) increased termination of regular employment as a means of restructuring in the last decades.

At the same time, the regulation of worker-dispatching and the gradual extension of its practice is only one element in the diversification of forms of work and employment patterns, which are a consequence of substantial change in the structure of industry and in lifestyles in the information society. Thus the opposition to worker-dispatching could not be sustained in the face of the demand for this type of work. Accordingly employers started to take advantage of this new form of employment as a convenient means of creating flexibility in employment. Employers slowly began to acknowledge the need for worker-dispatching, though their attitude remains one of acceptance rather than encouragement. In other words, employers in Japan still regard the traditional regular employment system as the most reliable and most important one, but they are ready to utilize different kinds of non-regular employment including worker-dispatching to good effect.

Unions are still sticking to the traditional notion of lifelong employment and their attitude remains opposed to non-regular employment. They take the view that the latter will erode the established interests of regular employment. In this respect it is interesting to observe that some of the unions and their leaders are more conservative than employers.

VII. THE ROLE OF THE GOVERNMENT

The Government is now determined to promote further deregulation in every area of economic activity including the labour market and it intends to increase acceptance of worker-dispatching. At the same time, the need for protection of dispatched workers is emphasized in government policy. The Government is in a position to regulate both dispatching agencies and client companies in order to protect the interests of workers by applying protective labour law as well as social security law.

Another important problem to be addressed by the Government is the maximum duration of an assignment for dispatched workers. As already mentioned, this limit intends to protect the interests of regular employees from possible replacement of regular employment by non-regular employment. However, it obviously harms longer-term employment opportunities for dispatched workers. Future policy must reconcile the interests of regular and non-regular workers, taking into consideration the inevitable trends of the labour market in a time of growing flexibility in business management and globalization.

An opinion survey on dispatched workers, their agencies and client companies shows that they are equally interested in an extension of the one-year limit. They are also interested in developing opportunities for improving knowledge and technical skills, as well as matching workers' abilities and job opportunities. They look for greater initiative from the government to meet such expectations (Health, Employment and Welfare Ministry, *Rohdohsha Hakenzigyoh Zittai Chohsakekka Hohkoku* (Report on Worker-Dispatching Survey), 2003).[4]

As already explained (Sections V and VI), the crucial point concerning the collective relations of dispatched workers is that the majority of unions in Japan do not organize them. Recently some unions have launched organizing campaigns but with limited success. It is worth considering what government initiatives could encourage unions to accept membership of dispatched workers. One possibility is the introduction of an American-style exclusive bargaining unit and imposition of an obligation of fair representation on the unions. Another is to require unions to admit the membership of dispatched workers by amendment of the Trade Union Law.

Furthermore, there is currently no statutory basis for consultation of workers in Japan. Works councils and various types of workers' consultation have been developed informally within individual enterprises at the initiative of enterprise unions and management. Non-regular workers have again been excluded from participating in this informal process. A further advance might be to introduce, as a governmental initiative, a workers' consultation system that involves non-regular workers.

Governmental initiatives are clearly not the ideal way to progress, from the standpoint of freedom of association and voluntary unionism, but they may be necessary if the Japanese unions continue to advocate for vested interests of regular workers only and to ignore the interests of non-regular workers.

VIII. CONCLUSION

The general trend of the Japanese labour market is the growing importance of non-regular workers both in terms of their number and their prevalence throughout the labour market. In terms of the number of dispatched workers used in the year 2000, the five most significant tasks were: (1) the operation of office equipment; (2) financial office-work; (3) mechanical design; (4) software development; and (5) filing (Ministry of Health, Employment and Welfare, *Rohdohsha Haken Ziggyoh* (Worker-Dispatching Business) 2002, p. 14). The concentration of worker-dispatching in data management-related jobs signifies the future role of temporary work in Japan. The government should take strong steps to promote the employment opportunities of dispatched workers, partly by following up the gradual abolition of regulations in this area with further deregulation, but also by providing appropriate education and training for dispatched workers. Both public and private vocational training is currently becoming out-of-date and inadequate as a result of rapid technological progress.

4. http://www.mhlw.go.jp/houdou/o9109/h0903-1.html

Table III. Monthly average wages for different types of employment

Type	*Thousand Yen*
Regular workers	312.5
Non-regular workers	140.8
Contract workers	237.9
Temporary workers	109.8
Short-term part-time	89.7
Other part-time	152.8
Dispatched workers	209.3
Registered dispatched workers	199.4
Regular-employment dispatched workers	230.7

Source: Health, Employment and Welfare Ministry, *Syuugyoh Keitai Tayohka ni Kansru Sohgoh Chohsa* (General Survey on Diversification of Employment Patterns), 1999.

Of similar significance is the gap in working conditions of regular and non-regular workers in spite of the growing importance of the latter. The wage gap is the most conspicuous and indicative of the general discrepancy (*see* Table III).

Promoting the interests of non-regular workers has been one of the most important governmental policies and will remain so in the future. The trade unions have been incapable of assisting non-regular workers because of the way they are organized. It is likely that a governmental initiative to stimulate the organization of non-regular workers will be needed.

10. Spain

Miguel C. Rodríguez-Piñero Royo

GENERAL INTRODUCTION: GENESIS AND EVOLUTION

Spain has a particular relationship with temporary work. On the one hand, it has traditionally resisted this form of employment, to the point where Spanish law has been among the last in Europe to recognize it as fully legal. On the other hand, once accepted by Spanish labour law, it has experienced an enormous growth in a relatively short span of time, so fast as to make temporary work in Spain one of the fastest growing markets of its kind in Europe. Unions and public opinion are still rather critical of this form of employment, whereas enterprises make extensive use of it, now that it is accepted as a useful means of HR management (Table 1).

The ambivalence towards temporary work has to do with the peculiar way in which temporary work agencies (TWAs) entered on the Spanish labour market. TWAs appeared at a time when labour law prohibited any leasing of employees, which was legally termed 'provision of workers' (*Cesión de trabajadores*). Provision of workers was deemed illegal in all circumstances, and was subject to an important number of civil, administrative and even criminal sanctions. This type of general prohibition, expressed in Article 43 of the Workers' Statute, applied without doubt to TWAs, and therefore the illegality of temporary work in Spain seemed at that time beyond discussion (Valdes Dal-Re, p. 7).

Nonetheless, over the years the prohibition was not strictly enforced by Spanish labour courts. A restrictive interpretation of Article 43 was adopted, in which some room for legitimate uses of employee leasing was left. Under this interpretation, application of Article 43 required some additional elements, without which a given managerial practice was not to be considered a prohibited form of employee leasing. Thus, while Article 43 defined 'management' in objective terms, labour courts demanded additional elements, such as fraudulent intent of the operation, the use of a non-existent company name or infringement of the rights of the workers. This way, not every form of employee leasing was deemed illegal in itself, and on the contrary some were tolerated. It was under this climate of tolerance that TWAs began operating in Spain, mostly under the guise of general services or subcontracting firms, and without regulation (Rodriguez Sañudo, p. 235). By the late 1980s, there was a significant number of TWAs operating in Spain, and multinationals in the sector began establishing themselves in the country; levels of activity were surprisingly higher than those of countries in which temporary work was legal.

The development of temporary agency work in Spain is not that different from parallel processes in the rest of Europe; even the case-law distinction between legal and illegal forms of '*marchandage*' was not exclusively Spanish. Peculiar to Spain was the fact that while the regulation of TWAs began in much of Europe in the 1960s,

R. Blanpain & R. Graham (eds.), Temporary Agency Work and the Information Society, 171–190

Table 1. Number of contracts provided by TWA

Year	*Number of contracts*	*1995: 100*
1995	378,739	100
1996	809,139	213
1997	1,309,021	345
1998	1,803,547	476
1999	1,993,221	525
2000	2,005,132	529
2001	1,901,352	502

Source: Anuario de Estadísticas Laborales.

and generally continued to develop in the following two decades, in Spain that process did not take place until the very beginning of the 1990s. Indeed, the 1980 Workers' Statute maintained a radical and indiscriminate prohibition on employee leasing, closing the door to temporary work agencies in Spain at a time when they were already well-established in almost all Europe. Together with Sweden, Greece and Italy, Spain strangely resisted TWAs, and these were the last countries to accept and to integrate them into their own labour markets. The reluctance to integrate TWAs was a distinctive feature of Spanish labour law regarding this kind of employment (Rodriguez-Piñero Royo, 2000, p. 180). Due to the time it took to admit TWAs, a wide debate on the subject took place in the country; by the time they were formally admitted to the labour market, TWAs were already well-known by all the actors within the industrial relations system, including labour authorities and social partners. Needless to say, not all were in favour of TWAs, and the unions particularly showed fierce resistance to their introduction into the labour market (Durán López & Martínez López, 1999).

The formal admission of temporary work did not take place until as late as 1993, when Royal-Decree 18/1993 amended Article 43 of the Workers' Statute to read that 'the hiring of a worker in order to provide him to another firm can be done only by temporary work agencies which are established legally'. The new text of the Workers' Statute set the basis for developing the legal framework for temporary work in the following years. In June 1994, Act No. 14/1994 on temporary work agencies was enacted, this being the basic and comprehensive legal text governing the sector. The act was complemented by a series of administrative regulations: Royal Decree 4/1995, on administrative aspects of TWAs; and Royal Decree 216/1999, on health and safety measures for workers employed by TWAs, the latter implementing EU directive 91/383.

A distinctive feature of Act No. 14/1994 is that it assumed a particular regulatory technique. Instead of creating a full code regulating temporary work, and covering all its aspects extensively, it dealt with some specific points, the rest being subject to customary labour and commercial law. This peculiar approach to temporary work has been called a 'minimalistic regulatory technique'; Act No. 14/1994 was a surprisingly short piece of legislation- far too concise to deal with all aspects of the trilateral contract of employment underlying temporary work. In applying the act over the past decade, this approach has proved to be completely inadequate, because traditional labour law, being based on strictly bilateral contracts of employment, gave no answer to many specific problems in temporary work. There is a widely held opinion that a more extensive legal treatment of temporary work was needed. Collective bargaining and case law have therefore played a very important role in trying to make up for the legislative shortcomings.

Table 2. Number of employment contracts registered by TWAs

Year	*Number of contracts*
1998	1,707,842
1999	1,892,284
2000	1,762,780
2001	1,639,764

Source: Anuario de Estadísticas Laborales.

The most significant characteristic of temporary work in Spain is its relatively fast growth. Spanish employers began making extensive use of TWAs, producing good profit-making opportunities, which attracted enterprises from all over the world; all large temporary work multinationals had soon entered the Spanish labour market, competing with national firms in a booming sector. The number of employment contracts registered by TWAs also increased substantially over the years (Table 2).

The basic legislation on temporary work underwent a number of small reforms through the 1990s until in 1999 major reform took place. Act No. 29/1999, of 16 July, was the result of opposition to the management of TWAs from their employees who objected to unfair treatment arising out of the model of temporary work which was designated by legislation (EIRR, 1999). Temporary workers had very short contracts, concentrated in low-skilled work, and with wages substantially lower than those of ordinary workers (Calvo Gallego *et al.*, 2000). Most contracts lasted under five days, and even though workers usually had several in one year, they had no stability or assured work. Many worked part-time. TWAs primarily provided workers for low-skilled jobs, mostly in the service sector; workers who found employment through a TWA consisted mainly of young, unskilled workers, who were most severely affected by unemployment. Finally, because of a practice of company-level bargaining, TWAs paid their employees rather low wages, creating unequal treatment with user firm workers. This contrasted with what the Government had in mind when introducing TWAs in Spain in 1993. Instead of increasing flexibility, and being a useful instrument for management of the workforce, temporary work had become a way of reducing labour costs in low-skilled jobs.

This situation gave rise to a widespread movement to reform Act No. 14/1994, in order to improve the working conditions of temporary workers. After much lobbying – including a proposal drafted by popular initiative – Act No. 29/1999 was passed, affecting the entire framework for temporary work; many of the reforms were also about to be introduced by a series of agreements signed over the previous decade (Rodriguez-Piñero Royo, 2000).

Later, other legislation with a general scope also dealt with TWAs, such as Act No. 45/1999, implementing Directive 96/71 on posted workers; and Royal Decree-Law No. 2/2000, on public contracts. The former, by regulating trans-border operations of TWAs, added a new chapter to Act No. 14/1994; the latter defined the cases in which TWAs can be used by public administrations (Calvo Gallego *et al.*, 2000), in such restrictive terms as to amount to a ban on their use.

The above regulations have been enacted by the State legislature, since labour legislation is a field in which it holds exclusive regulatory power; no regional legislation in this field exists. On the other hand, regional authorities exercise most administrative powers related to the implementation of national legislation on temporary work.

In addition to this legislation, collective bargaining has played a very important role in the development of temporary work in Spain. When TWAs were initially legalized, collective bargaining took place mainly at enterprise level. But by 1995 a state-wide, industry level bargaining unit was already established, and from that time on a single agreement has applied to the whole sector. There is a specific agreement for the region of Catalonia, and a handful of company agreements still in force. But the situation is now highly centralized, which has allowed social partners to introduce measures to govern the temporary work market through collective bargaining, and to advance many legal changes.

In 1999 Spain adhered to ILO Convention No. 181 of 1998. Previously, Convention No. 96, which justified the general prohibition of temporary work under Spanish law, had been applied.

I. TEMPORARY WORK

§1. Notion of Temporary Work

Temporary work is defined by Spanish law in Article 1 of Act No. 14/1994 as the putting of workers at the temporary disposal of a user firm. Putting workers at the disposal of a user is still prohibited on a general basis. Allowing temporary work is a unique exception to the general rule. According to Article 43 of the Workers' Statute, 'the hiring of a worker in order to put him at the disposal of another firm can be done only by legally established temporary work agencies'.

Temporary work is distinguished form other forms of employee leasing by a formal element, namely the fact that the hiring agency is 'legally established', which in practical terms means it has been granted authorization to operate as a TWA. All others forms of employee leasing are prohibited, and are subject to severe legal consequences under Article 43. First, both the hiring-out enterprise and the user enterprise will be held jointly liable for all economic consequences of the employment relationship. Secondly, the leased worker has the right to choose to become a fixed-term employee of either firm. Finally, administrative and penal sanctions are laid down in Article 43 to ensure enforcement of this prohibition.

Although this scheme of rules and exemptions seems to be clear enough, in practice there are still many problems regarding trilateral employment relations. Most importantly, besides temporary work there are still other forms of employee leasing, particularly between groups of enterprises and under service contracts between firms, which are admitted, despite lacking authorization. In addition, the distinction between contracting out and employee leasing, which is critical since the former is legal but the latter is not, has grown even more problematic. The distinction, based traditionally on ownership of the machinery and equipment used, is no longer helpful in the information society, where knowledge is the main economic asset (Cruz Villalon, 2000, p. 10).

§2. Cases in which Temporary Work is Allowed

As in most European countries, temporary agency workers cannot be used for any reason, and Article 6.2 of Act No. 14/1994 defines situations in which a user firm can legally hire their services. That is, in the same situations, and under the same conditions and requirements, as those provided by the Workers' Statute for fixed-term contracts of employment. Consequently, in any situation, all temporary contracts of employment, whether made directly with an ordinary firm or indirectly with a TWA, are permitted giving the user enterprise a choice between two alternatives.

More specifically, Article 15 of the Workers' Statute permits the use of temporary workers in the following situations: for a specific project or to perform a specific service, to adjust to temporary market needs and to substitute temporarily employees on leave of absence. There is a fourth case, introduced into Article 15 by an amendment made in 2001, which is to integrate certain groups of persons at risk of exclusion. This option was designed for use by public entities. It may apply to the use of temporary workers other than those provided by a TWA.

The use of temporary workers is further limited by certain prohibitions. Thus, Article 8 expressly prohibits the use of temporary workers in the following cases:

a) to replace employees on strike at the user firm;
b) to carry on activities considered particularly dangerous, according to a Royal Decree in force since 1999;
c) to provide workers to user firms that in the preceding twelve months have dismissed workers for economic reasons, with some exemptions – such as *force majeure* – or to provide workers to cover positions in the user firm which, in the last eighteen months, were held by temporary workers for over three months;
d) to provide workers to another TWA.

In addition to these express prohibitions, Article 12.3 states that it is impossible to use a temporary worker to fill a position in the user firm which has not had the appropriate risks-at-work evaluation. This proviso was set in order to make user firms fulfil their obligations in the field of health and safety.

II. THE LEGAL STATUS OF THE TEMPORARY WORKER

As a consequence of both the protective character of Spanish labour law and the way in which temporary workers appeared in the country, legal regulation of this type of work was particularly concerned with the legal status of the hired workers. In fact, most Spanish labour regulation can be interpreted from the perspective of the need to protect temporary workers, including those rules which do not directly concern their rights. For instance, the need for an administrative authorization for employment benefit temporary workers by excluding from the market those firms unable to grant its employees a minimum of economic security. The same can be said for limiting the use of temporary workers. By not presenting temporary work as a service to be used in any circumstance, the law protects the workers' right to be hired for an indefinite term, which is a general principle of Spanish labour law.

§1. Legal Qualification of the Relationship between the Temporary Worker and the Temporary Work Agency

Act No.14/1994 differentiates two kinds of workers employed by a TWA: those hired to work at the premises of the TWA which collective agreements call corporate staff (*Trabajadores de estructura*), and those hired to be put at the disposition of user firms (*Trabajadores en mission*), to whom I will refer as 'temporary workers'.

The act devotes a chapter to 'labour relations at the temporary work agency', and another to the 'relationship between the temporary worker and the user firm'; both apply only to temporary workers, corporate staff being subject to the general rules of the Workers' Statute.

Although no explicit declaration is made regarding this matter, it is clear from the regulation on temporary work that only one contract of employment exists, namely the one between the TWA and the temporary worker. That contract, which is not considered to have a special nature, does not qualify as an individually regulated 'special labour relation', and so is regulated by general employment legislation, as stipulated by Act No. 14/1994. This regulatory approach has been generally criticized, as the particularities of the trilateral employment relationship are not adequately dealt with by the Workers' Statute; many practical problems have arisen as a consequence of the absence of an adapted legal framework.

The temporary worker can be hired either under a fixed-term or an indefinite contract. A fixed term must coincide with the duration of the contract for services agreed by the TWA and the user, although after the 1999 reform Article 10.3 has permitted a single fixed-term contract for a number of assignments. For such a purpose, all the assignments must be clearly stated in the contract of employment, and must require the use of temporary work to adjust to market circumstances, based on Article 15.1.b of the Workers' Statute. For such workers a single contract of employment is signed with the TWA, and the contract will cover the series of assignments for each, though, a single document will be issued, the so-called '*orden de servicio*'.

In the case of indefinite-term contracts, the worker may be sent to successive user firms, maintaining a single employment contract with the TWA. For every assignment the worker will be issued with an '*orden de servicio*', specifying where the tasks are to be performed. Very few indefinite-term contracts are concluded, though, as Act. No. 14/1994 mostly provides for fixed-term employment. In fact, TWAs are the only employers allowed to hire on a temporary basis.

Part-time work is regulated by ordinary employment conditions, and is not mentioned in temporary work regulations. In practice, TWAs are among the major employers of part-time workers in a country with the lowest part-time employment in Europe.

The contract between the temporary worker and the TWA is regulated as follows. First of all, according to Article 10.2 TWAs are not allowed to hire temporary workers under special training fixed-term contracts (*Contratos para la formación*). Secondly, they may not obtain temporary workers from another TWA. Thirdly, Act 14/1994 imposes on TWAs an obligation to employ a given percentage of its workforce on a fixed-term basis. This obligation applies only to corporate staff, and it means that each TWA must employ a minimum of twelve workers on a fixed-term basis for each 1,000 contracts of temporary employment concluded in the previous year. The corporate staff can be hired under either full-time or part-time contracts. Only if the obligation is fulfilled can a TWA be granted the administrative authorization it needs to operate. It is justified as a means of providing that the TWA has 'an organizational structure that allows it to face the obligations that it assumes as employer in relation to its role as temporary work provider'. As an innovation of the 1999 reform, the obligation to use some fixed-term contracts addresses one of the main concerns about temporary work in Spain: the low quality of contracts of employment. It is a first attempt to control and reduce the high levels of instability though still rather modest in its objectives. The idea of imposing the obligation was originally conceived and applied by collective bargaining.

Temporary workers' contracts, regardless of their kind, must be in writing, following a model contained in Royal-Decree 4/1995. This is coherent with the general approach in Spanish legislation, which imposes a high level of formality in all temporary work operations, including written contracts, and duties to inform the labour authorities or the workers' representative bodies on the part of hiring-out and user enterprises.

No provision is made in Act No. 14/1994 regarding trial periods, therefore Article 14 of the Workers' Statute, which permits such periods under certain conditions, applies. This means that a trial period is permitted only if agreed between both parties to the contract at the moment of its conclusion and in writing, and is not permitted if the worker has already worked for the same employer. The trail period's duration is limited, depending on the work to be done. Collective agreements regulate the duration.

Act No. 14/1994 does not deal substantially with the content of the contract of employment, so the Workers' Statute and collective agreements regulate this agreement. Both Act No.14/1994 and collective agreements pay special attention to training temporary workers, especially with regard to safety measures. In fact TWAs are obliged to spend an annual sum on training which must be at least 1 per cent of the total amount spent on wages during the period. Collective bargaining has raised this proportion to 1.5 per cent.

§2. Remuneration

A crucial aspect of the regulation of temporary work is the remuneration of the workers. According to the original text of Act No. 14/1994, equal treatment of temporary workers in relation to the user firm's own employees was not required. By applying the TWAs' own collective agreement, a considerable gap opened up between their wages and those being paid at the user firm. This was interpreted as exploitation of temporary workers, brought about by the TWAs keeping their wage. Not surprisingly the remuneration of temporary work came under attack from many sectors, in large part causing the 1999 reform. Today Article 11 of Act No. 14/1994 states that workers on assignment in user firms are entitled to a remuneration that cannot be less than the overall pay to which the user's own employees are entitled under the applicable collective agreement.

Article 11 establishes a method of calculating this amount, which imposes on the hiring-out and user firms a duty to collaborate, in order to exchange the necessary information. It does not impose on the agency a duty to apply the user firm's collective agreement to its workers, nor even the given wage tables, as many demanded. It merely establishes a system to evaluate the adequacy of the temporary worker's overall pay which cannot be inferior to what he would have received had he been employed directly by the user firm. Overall pay should include, to that effect, compensation for weekly rest, extraordinary payments for holidays, and annual holiday payments.

This system, although not guaranteeing in all cases absolute equality of remuneration, is nevertheless effective in getting close to the principle of equal treatment that public opinion demanded. It is undoubtedly more effective than the system pursued by collective bargaining before 1999. In fact, the second national collective agreement for TWAs, signed in 1997, initiated a convergence process (*Proceso de convergencia*) aimed at narrowing the difference in wage for temporary and ordinary workers, using a comparison mechanism that would progress towards full equality in some three years. This mechanism did not account for all elements of the salary; took into consideration only industry-wide agreements applied to user firms; and operated in stages, reaching 70 per cent equality in the first year, 80 per cent in the second, until finally full equality was attained. Besides, since it was established by a collective agreement, it lacked the permanence the current Article 11 enjoys, as it depended on the agreement being in force. The legislative provision is more effective than the convergence rules. But it is clear that Act No. 14/1994 copied the mechanism first designed under the collective agreement, showing once again the strong connection between collective bargaining and statutory law in the temporary work sector, and the continuous exchange of ideas and problem-solving techniques.

§3. Social Advantages

As just noted, temporary workers are granted no equal treatment when working at the user firm's premises. Nonetheless they are granted by law equal access to most facilities and services at the user firm: according to Article 17.2 of Act No. 14/1994, they have the right to use transportation and other communal services during the assignment.

§4. Health and Safety

Spanish labour regulation shows a strong commitment to health and safety measures. This is a consequence of EU Directive 91/383, which develops the framework Directive 89/391 for this particular form of employment. But it must be emphasized that there is a particular concern about the level of risk at work in all forms of temporary work, whether fixed-term contracts or TWA assignments, because a strong correlation is found between short-term employment and the rise of work-related accidents and illness. This would explain why so much attention has been paid to this matter, both in specific legislation on TWAs and in legislation on general health and safety. For example, Article 28 of the 1995 '*Ley de Prevención de Riesgos Laborales*' – 'Act on the Prevention of Risk at work', which is the principal act on occupational health and safety – is devoted to the situation of temporary workers. It declares that they are entitled to the same level of protection from risk as any other worker. In order to enforce this principle, it makes the user firm responsible for ensuring that working conditions do not endanger the health and safety of temporary workers, and also establishes a number of duties to provide information concerning health and safety issues (EIRR, 1999). Articles 12.3 and 16 of Act No. 14/1994 also deal with these matters.

But the bulk of the regulation on risk at work is contained in Royal Decree 216/1999, which deals exclusively with these matters. This regulation was presented as implementing, with some delay, Directive 91/383 on the health and safety of temporary workers. The regulation is rather precise, and adequately implements the 1991 directive. A number of information and training obligations are imposed on both hiring-out and user firms, such as the duty to continuously exchange information on risk at work relating to future assignments, the profile of the hired worker, the training required to perform the job, amongst others.

Finally, there are specific tasks whose performance by a temporary worker is prohibited on health and safety grounds. This prohibition, required by Directive 91/383, was included in Act No. 14/1994 in its original version. But it could not be enforced, as Article 8 of the Act made only a general reference to the prohibition, referring identification of the prohibited activities to a subsidiary regulation which was not enacted until 1999. Without the list of excluded activities the prohibition was inoperative, and in practice TWA workers were used for all kinds of tasks, including those with high levels of occupational risk, which was a major concern for unions during this period. Royal Decree 216/1999 finally clarified this situation, by identifying the circumstances in which temporary work could not be used on health and safety grounds. First of all, positions in the user firm that had not undergone the appropriate risks-at-work evaluation were excluded, under Article 12.3 of Act No. 14/1994, as amended in 1999. Secondly, the use of TWA was forbidden for activities included in a list given in Article 8 of Royal Decree 216/1999, among which are mining activities, construction, jobs which require the use of explosives, etc. The list is not long, and scarcely concerns the work of TWAs, except for construction, regarding which the prohibition has provoked strong criticism from temporary work providers.

§5. Termination of the Contract

General rules on termination of employment apply to workers employed by a TWA, as full regulation of this matter is not covered by Act No. 14/1994. As indicated below, temporary workers can be hired either under a fixed-term or an indefinite contract. Under a fixed-term contract, once the contract for services agreed by both firms has come to an end the worker's contract of employment is also terminated, unless the worker continues performing tasks for the user firm. In this case, Article 7.2 of Act No. 14/1994 establishes a presumption that the worker has become employed by the user.

The only special provision established in Act No. 14/1994 regarding termination of contract is that the worker is entitled to a lump-sum payment equal to the wages of twelve days for each month of work performed. This indemnity – imported from French labour law – has been extended to most fixed-term contracts by an amendment to the Workers' Statute in 2001. Due to the extremely short length of most employment contracts between TWA and temporary workers, this indemnity has a very small practical relevance, and is largely symbolic.

§6. Freedom of the Temporary Worker to Conclude a Contract with the User

Act No. 14 tries to give the user firm an incentive to employ the temporary worker at the end of the assignment making temporary work a means of access to regular employment. In order to achieve this overall objective it sets out some rules regarding continued employment. First of all, Article 7.3 rules that any clause forbidding the worker to become an employee of the user firm at the end of the assignment will be considered illegal. Further, Article 7.2 rules that if at termination of the fixed-term contract the worker keeps on providing his services to the user firm, he will be deemed permanently employed. Finally, Article 12.4 considers null and void any clause of the employment contract of the temporary worker which may impose upon him the obligation to pay the TWA any amount of money on grounds of selection, training or hiring-out expenses.

The number of temporary workers subsequently employed by user firms cannot be known for sure, as there is no legal obligation to give information in this regard, and labour statistics give no indication. According to TWAs, the figure lies between 20 per cent and 40 per cent of all hired-out workers. Associations in the sector generally complain that many user firms hire temporary workers as a means of recruiting permanent workers.

III. THE LEGAL STATUS OF THE TEMPORARY WORK AGENCY

§1. Official Recognition

As explained at the beginning of this study, under Spanish labour law the distinction between legal and illegal employee leasing, between temporary work and provision of workers, is made by formal criteria, namely authorization of the TWA. Once the TWA is legally recognized, the activity of putting workers at the disposal of a user firm is classified as temporary work, and therefore legal. Act No. 14/1994 and Royal Decree 4/1995 devote much attention to the regulatory procedure and requirements needed to obtain recognition.

In order to be granted an authorization a TWA must meet a number of requirements. Most importantly it must have:

a) an organizational structure which allows it to fulfil the obligations that it assumes as employer in connection with its activity of temporary work provider;
b) temporary work as the only activity;
c) no pending obligation with Social Security or the Revenue Service;
d) the ability to guarantee, in a specified manner, payment of salaries and Social Security contributions;
e) no previous sanctions resulting in suspension of its activity on two or more occasions;
f) inclusion in their commercial name of the terms '*empresa de trabajo temporal*'.

Of all these perhaps the most relevant element is the requirement of having an organizational structure adequate for the firm's activity. This requirement was already imposed on TWAs in the original version of Act No. 14/1994; the 1999 reform developed it further, forcing the agency to hire a minimum number of employees for an indefinite period. This requirement relates to the corporate staff i.e. those hired directly by the TWA to work on its premises, and the minimum number required will depend on the size of operation, currently twelve for every thousand workers hired out.

One of the legal requirements of which TWAs are more critical is that of having temporary work as their exclusive activity. This obligation is by no means something initiated by the European legislation on temporary work, since it was traditionally imposed on firms operating in this sector as a way of guaranteeing their professional reliability. In the 1990s it has been considered too rigid a requirement, as a consequence of profound changes occurring in the Spanish labour market over the last decade.

It is true that this market has experienced two fundamental changes over these years. On the one hand, the traditional approach towards labour regulation has changed substantially, from complete state control to a system designed by a number of different actors, including private non-profit employment agencies.

On the other hand, business activities on the labour market have diversified, in response to new employer demands into for example outplacement, interim management and staff leasing. TWAs, as firms specialized in labour, are demanding the right to pursue such activities, being currently bound by the requirement to have temporary work as their exclusive activity. Most affected firms have navigated that requirement by establishing labour supply agencies of different kinds specialized in each activity. In practice each one of the large TWAs operates within a group of enterprises, among which are firms providing human resources consulting, outsourcing, outplacement and related services.

A final requirement for authorization as a TWA is the payment of a financial guarantee imposed by Act No.14/1994. This guarantee has a double purpose, as a means of financial protection for temporary workers and as a way of controlling access to the temporary work market. Such guarantees are common in Europe, and have been introduced to ensure that TWAs' obligations are fulfilled, regarding payment of wages and social security contributions (Blanpain, p. 13). In the Spanish case, this guarantee may take different forms, either as a deposit in cash or in public securities, a joint guarantee, or a bond posted by a bank or an insurance company. The required amount of the guarantee is based on the volume of activity in the TWA in the previous year, and should be ten per cent of its total payroll; the amount must be updated every year. Only in the first year of operation is this amount calculated on a different basis, as a fixed amount equal to twenty five times the annual minimum wage.

§2. The Agency as Employer

For all purposes the TWA is considered the sole employer, and even Article 1.2 of the Workers' Statute, which contains the legal definition of employer, was modified in 1994 in order to reflect this aspect of temporary work. Subsequently, Article 1.2 provided that an employer may also employ workers for hiring-out to a user firm.

Employer status has the following effects on a TWA. First of all, the TWA is directly responsible for legal duties imposed by both general and specific labour legislation. The liability of the user firm arises only where the law explicitly states. Secondly, all powers deriving from the employment contract remain at its disposal. Article 15 of Act No. 14/1994 allows the user firm to exercise directive powers for the period during which the temporary worker is assigned to it; this is a temporary and incomplete transfer of these powers, since the TWA retains the power to change the worker's assignment, amongst other things. Most interestingly, Article 15.2 does not transfer disciplinary powers to the user firms. In the event the user firm finds a temporary worker has breached his contractual duties, it may inform the TWA, which may exclusively apply disciplinary measures. These measures are carefully set out in the collective agreements signed for the temporary work sector.

IV. THE LEGAL STATUS OF THE USER

§1. The Relationship between User and Temporary Work Agency

The third element of the temporary work relationship, the user firm, is also the object of a number of rules under Act No. 14/1994, which devotes a whole chapter to this subject. Article 6 does not define a user firm, but instead defines the specific contract for services between the TWA and the user firm. The contract is subject to a specific regulation which requires it to be put in writing, and notified to workers' representative bodies at the user firm.

Spanish law defines the circumstances in which temporary work is allowed by enumerating the legal grounds for agreement of a contract between user and TWA. As indicated above, these circumstances are the same as the circumstances permissible for agreement of fixed-term contracts, specified in Article 15 of the Workers' Statute.

Both Act No. 14/1994 and the regulation derived from it provide for a mutual exchange of information between both firms, in a number of matters. Through this exchange they may co-operate in order to find a suitable worker for the job, to ensure that he has the qualifications needed, to guarantee that he receives the proper training, to supervise his performance at the user firm, amongst other things.

§2. The Relationship between User and Temporary Worker

Although Act No. 14/1994 devotes a whole chapter to the 'relationship between the temporary worker and the user firm', it is not legally defined. Implicitly a contract of employment must be excluded, to fit with the definition of the TWA as the sole employer. Although certain elements of the relationship between the user and temporary worker are regulated, the relationship falls short of a common private employment relationship.

During the temporary worker's assignment to the user firm, the firm will hold almost all prerogatives of management, particularly those of directing and controlling his activity. Disciplinary powers, on the contrary, remain in the hands of the TWA, as stated above. A number of duties are imposed on the user firms regarding hired workers. For instance, before actual work begins, the user firm must inform the temporary worker of the risks related to the activity he is going to perform, as well as of the protective and preventive measures in place (Article 16.1).

Spanish labour law extensively imposes liability in order to guarantee the worker protection in outsourcing, hiring between groups of enterprises and employee leasing. It was not strange, then, that the same approach was applied to temporary work as a new form of multilateral employment relation once it was admitted to the Spanish labour market. What was strange was the form of liability imposed. In fact, Article 16.3 of Act No. 14/1994 imposes on the user firm a subsidiary liability including payment of the temporary worker's wages; joint liability arises only in the case of irregular use of the TWA's services, outwith the legally permitted situations. For other multilateral employment relationships, joint liability is imposed. Although joint liability is ordinarily exceptional under Spanish private law, it is so extensively imposed in labour law that labour courts have concluded that it is the rule in all situations in which more than one employer is involved. In the case of TWA this rule, however, has not been followed, which has been criticized as proof of the favourable treatment of user firms. The explanation for the difference is explained by the existence of a financial guarantee provided by the TWA, to underwrite payment of its employees. According to Royal Decree 4/1995, in the case of delay in the payment of wages, workers are allowed to claim compensation from this guarantee failing which the user becomes liable.

In the case of health and safety measures, on the contrary, direct liability is the rule (Article 16.2) since in many cases it is derived from infringement of safety duties legally imposed on the user firm. This is more coherent with the general rules of Spanish labour law, which, in the field of health and safety, tends to concentrate duties and liabilities on persons who retain control of the working environment, regardless of the question of who is the employer.

V. COLLECTIVE LABOUR RELATIONS ASPECTS

In collective rights the legal status of the temporary worker is less clearly defined. Act No. 14/1994 does not offer a complete and coherent regulation of the matter, so that the general regulation of collective labour relations applies. This has had its limitations, and it is in collective relations that the most significant problems for the sector have arisen. It is not surprising, then, that all amendments of Act No. 14/1994 during the 1990s have dealt with aspects of collective labour relations.

§1. Representation of Temporary Workers

Act No. 14/1994 makes clear that the TWA is the sole employer in temporary work operations. The main consequence for collective labour relations is that all representative functions will take place at the TWA itself. All workers employed by a TWA, both corporate staff and temporary workers, are considered to be part of the same workforce for representation purposes, regardless of the fact that most of them will perform their tasks at user firms. It is within the TWA that representative bodies, required by the Workers' Statute, are to be established, and all their tasks will be performed with regard to the TWA. Another consequence of the TWA's continuous employer status is that temporary workers cannot be represented by the representative bodies at the user firm. Equally, they cannot participate in the election of these bodies.

This approach to temporary worker representation has serious limitations. From the TWA's pespective, the physical dispersal of workers and their continuous rotation make it very difficult to organize a valid election, and an operative representation. Regarding the situation at the user firm, the exclusion of temporary workers from its representative bodies denies them representation at the firm in which most work-related problems arise.

In the light of these problems, Act No. 14/1994 allowed temporary workers to make complaints through the representative bodies at the user firm. This rule was amended in 1997, following a national agreement on the promotion of employment stability. According to the terms of the new Article 17, temporary workers can be represented at the user firm by its workers' representative bodies. Workers on temporary assignment to user firms may use their representative bodies, in order to make complaints; but they will not be taken into account when calculating the number of represented workers at the user firm, which is based on the workforce size. This is coherent with the fact that they are generally ignored in the calculation of the number of employees in the user firm for all purposes.

As indicated above, information rights have been extensively provided throughout Act No. 14/1994. Article 9, amended in 1999, obliges the user company to supply its workers' representative bodies with complete information on all the contracts concluded with TWAs, including their justification, within ten days of their agreement. A basic copy of the contract of employment of a temporary worker must also be given, within ten days. For that reason, the TWA is obliged to provide the user firm with the contract. This right to be informed is similar, in its content, to the right granted by the Workers' Statute to any workers' representative bodies regarding workers employed by the firm in which they operate. From this point of view it is a clear exception to the general principle that temporary workers are to be represented exclusively at the TWA.

§2. Collective Bargaining

With regard to collective bargaining, Act No. 14/1994 follows its own guiding principles on temporary work. As a TWA is the only employer of temporary workers, their employment is regulated by the collective agreements applicable to such firms, and consequently is not regulated by those applicable to user firms. Collective bargaining which affects temporary workers must take place between their representatives and the TWA. However, Article 13 of Act No. 14/1994 states that in the absence of representatives of their own, most representative unions are authorized to bargain collectively on behalf of TWA employees. This special rule, which differs from the general rules on collective bargaining stated in the Workers' Statute, has been crucial in order to make industry-wide agreements possible. And this pattern of collective bargaining has also been absolutely essential for the re-structuring of the TWA sector in the second half of the 1990s.

This general entitlement allowing most unions to act as bargaining agents for temporary workers was reasonable, in that under Spanish collective labour law these workers were most likely to face serious difficulties in organizing representation of their own. The first mistake made by Spanish law-making bodies was to establish this rule on a subsidiary basis, so that it operated only in bargaining units in which no temporary workers' representative bodies had been established. A second mistake made in Act No. 14/1994, was that temporary workers were to be paid according to the collective agreement of the user firm only in cases in which the TWA was governed by no collective agreement of its own. This rule acted as a strong incentive for TWAs to have agreements of their own, in order to avoid equal treatment on wages. Equal pay was probably one of the objectives of Act No. 14/1994, assuming that collective agreements applying to user firms would be bargained for by the most representative unions and that their quality would be guaranteed. But the TWAs managed to avoid wage regulation by a users' collective agreement by promoting the creation of workers' representative bodies of their own, sometimes directly controlled by management, or staffed by high-level managers themselves.

The development of collective bargaining in the TWA sector was impressive. In a few months most TWAs had signed company-level agreements, which naturally favoured their interest. Wages were set extremely low, and working conditions at a low standard. The agreements were of great use to the TWAs, which thanks to the low wage scales could operate at reduced labour costs, and thus offer their services at very competitive prices. For some years it was cheaper for a firm to cover a position with a temporary worker hired through a TWA than to hire directly a worker with a fixed-term contract. This fact explains, of course, the enormous growth of temporary work in the Spanish labour market in the years following 1994.

The practice of company-level bargaining had rather negative effects both on temporary workers – whose wages and working conditions were of a poor standard, and on the market as a whole, as temporary workers became a means of reducing labour costs, instead of an instrument for flexibility in HR management. Both unions and the major firms in the sector became aware of these effects, and they looked for an alternative to company-level collective bargaining in the sector. By 1995 they managed to start a process of industry-wide bargaining, that has produced three National Collective Agreements for Temporary Work Agencies, the last of which came into force on 1 January 2001.

The importance of national collective bargaining must be underlined for a number of reasons. Firstly it stopped the deterioration of conditions of temporary work which was being produced by company-level bargaining. Secondly it improved consistently pay and other conditions of workers employed by TWAs. Thirdly it substantially altered the model of temporary work in Spain: as this form of work became more expensive, it began to be used more carefully and more strategically by user firms, rather than to reduce labour costs. Finally, and most interestingly, the national agreements introduced some measures that preceded the 1999 reform of temporary work legislation, in particular the principle of equal treatment in pay for temporary workers, which was progressively put into practice by the second national agreement in 1997. This and other measures produced by the collective bargaining process are now present in the text of Act No. 14/1994.

Another noteworthy aspect of collective bargaining in temporary work is its treatment in the collective agreements applicable to the user firms. In the mid-1990s the nature of temporary work at the time encouraged its regulation under the collective agreement applicable to the user firm. As low-paying employers setting low-standard working conditions, a great resistance towards TWAs grew among the unions, who aimed to discourage the use of temporary workers as much as possible, or at least to force TWAs to improve the standard of their employment practices. Therefore industry-wide agreements began including clauses on the use of temporary work, permitting it where the hiring-out firm was subject to a national agreement for TWAs, or obliging TWAs to pay temporary workers the same wages received by the user firm's workers.

In all cases some kind of 'hot-cargo clause' was used. The use of these clauses, along with their impact on the ability of TWAs to supply their services to key sectors of the Spanish economy, produced an important debate on their legality. TWAs claimed they could not be enforceable on a number of grounds. Firstly, these clauses were a breach of the right to free enterprise, granted by the Spanish Constitution; secondly, they harmed third parties' rights, which is unlawful under Spanish law on collective bargaining; thirdly, they breached competition law, by granting in some cases more favourable treatment to TWAs subject to national collective agreements. The conclusion of the third National Agreement and the 1999 reforms deprived this strategy of most of its purpose, and these clauses are no longer so relevant. Though still present in a number of industry-wide agreements, they have little practical effect.

§3. Role of Codes of Conduct

Despite the widespread importance of Codes of Conduct in contemporary labour relations, in Spain they are almost non-existent. The few in operation have mostly been introduced due to European initiatives, such as the 1990 code of conduct to prevent sexual harassment in the workplace. Spanish labour law is strange to such 'soft law', generally speaking.

Unions prefer collective agreements as a regulatory technique in this area, and in temporary work they are particularly suitable since collective agreements in Spain are vested with an *erga omnes* effect. The existence of a national bargaining unit further enhances the regulatory effectiveness of collective agreements. The existing codes of conduct in temporary work apply unilaterally to all TWAs and associations of TWAs.

The only exemption to the general lack of collectively agreed codes of conduct is in Catalonia, where under the promotion of the Regional Labour Office a code was agreed upon in 2002. This code, drafted on the basis of almost a decade of experience in temporary work, is focused on the resolution of the main problems identified.

VI. ROLE OF THE GOVERNMENT

As in every other European country, the role of the State in the development of temporary work has been central, both in controlling the activity of the TWA and as a protector of temporary workers' rights. In the Spanish case this role has been particularly important, given the resistance to this form of employment. Weakness of unions and the absence of workers' representative bodies in the TWAs also explain the high degree of administrative control. Finally, administrative intervention in the labour market is widespread.

§1. Recognition of Temporary Work Agencies

As outlined above, a firm planning to operate as a TWA must obtain an administrative authorization, which is the basic instrument by which the State exercises control of the temporary work market. The authorization is the sole means of distinguishing lawful temporary work from prohibited forms of employee leasing, which is clearly only a formal distinction. In Spanish labour law there is currently no substantial difference between legal and illegal trilateral employment relationships. Labour authorities are therefore not required to supervise the actual operation of all firms leasing workers.

Inherently, the authorization performs a number of other functions related to the supervision of the TWA. First of all, it controls access to the temporary work market, which the State considers should be restricted by its authorization. Secondly, through the application process labour authorities can check the fulfilment of all requirements imposed on TWAs. Thirdly, authorization gives the TWA a registration number, which permits its entry in a specialized register (the registration number acts must be used by the agency in all its operations, and included in all its publicity). Fourthly, the State uses authorization status as a punitive instrument: under Act 14/1994 its withdrawal by the labour authority is the most severe sanction against the TWA in cases of serious breach of legal and contractual obligations.

It is no surprise, then, that authorization is commonly used as a permanent control of labour market activities (Blanpain, p. 12). In Spain it is also used to control employment agencies, which need a specific administrative authorization prior to starting business. In temporary work, it is relevant that all European legislation on temporary work requires obtaining and maintaining authorization. The EU proposals on harmonization of national legislation on temporary work in the 1980s and the 1990s, and the recent proposal foresee a similar system of administrative authorization.

Furthermore, international labour legislation uses authorization as a central element of regulating temporary work: ILO Convention No. 181, which deals in a single text with both TWAs and private employment agencies, demonstrates the point. According to Article 3.1, 'a member shall determine the conditions governing the operation of private employment agencies in accordance with a system of licensing or certification, except where they are otherwise regulated or determined by appropriate national law and practice'.

The conditions required by Act No. 14/1994 to have an administrative authorization were set out above. Which authority has power to grant it depends on the territorial scope of the TWA: if local, the provincial labour delegate has power of authorization; if regional, the regional ministry of labour exercises the power. In both cases it falls within the competence of the regional governments (*Comunidad Autónoma*). Only for TWAs planning to operate throughout Spain will the central government labour department intervene.

Administrative authorization has a territorial scope, which has produced problems for TWAs providing services outside the territory in which they are authorized. Labour courts were not unanimous in the resolution of these cases, but most tended to consider such hiring-out as a form of illegal employee leasing, as it was not covered by any authorization. Act No. 29/1999 introduced a new proviso according to which a TWA will be allowed to hire out with the territorial scope of its authorization, subject to a legal duty to inform the labour authorities of the territory where these particular services will be performed.

The authorization also has a peculiar temporal scope. When granted, it lasts for one year, and must be renewed on a yearly basis. After the second renewal it becomes permanent, although, as explained below, it can be withdrawn on justified grounds. During the first three years a number of controls are used, in order to verify whether the TWA has fulfilled all its legal obligations. This acts as a sort of trial period, in which the TWA must earn the trust of the labour authorities (Durán López & Martínez Rodríguez, 1999).

With hindsight, the authorization has fallen short in regulating access to the market of temporary work, and monitoring TWAs. Almost ten years after Act No. 14/1994 was brought into force, its inadequacy in these respects is clear. Many of the TWAs which have been authorized are small, which in many cases has disadvantaged the treatment of their workers. The 1999 reform aimed to avoid this effect by demanding that TWAs have an 'adequate structure'. This requirement, together with the impact on wages of applying the equal treatment principle, has had the effect of reducing the number of TWAs operating in the Spanish labour market. (*See* Table 3.)

As well as administrative authorization, Act No. 14/1994 provides for another instrument for the control of temporary workers: TWAs must enter themselves in a special register at the labour authority which granted the authorization. The registration entry must give certain data, sufficient to identify the TWA. Each TWA is given a registration number upon fulfilment of this obligation, and this number operates as a means of identification for a number of purposes.

§2. Follow-up, Supervision and Sanctions

A number of measures are contained in Act No. 14/1994 to allow supervision of the operation of TWAs. To begin with, Article 5, as amended in 1999, obliges the TWA

Table 3. Number of TWAs (according to the scope of their operations)

Year	*Total*	*Nation-wide*	*Region-wide*	*Province-wide*
1994	86	18	46	22
1995	316	66	119	131
1996	399	92	158	149
1997	428	109	158	161
1998	435	112	158	165
1999	411	112	148	151
2000	364	108	136	120
2001	346	109	124	113

Source: Anuario de Estadísticas Laborales.

to inform the labour authorities of all its contracts, including their starting and ending dates. Further, temporary workers may attract the attention of the labour authorities by using the different channels provided by Spanish labour law, particularly the Labour Inspectorate. And, of course, the provisions concerning the use by temporary workers of the representative channels at user firms may result in them presenting grievances to the labour authorities. Finally, the Labour Inspectors themselves have the right to inspect at any moment the situation of temporary workers both at the user firm and at the TWA, and special surveillance campaigns are organized periodically, in the target sector.

In order to enforce these supervision techniques, and to guarantee at the same time that all legislation on temporary work is respected, Act No. 14/1994 contains a special chapter on infringements of its regulations, and their sanctions. In doing so, it followed a long tradition of administrative sanctions in labour law, which empower the labour authorities with means to guarantee the effectiveness of regulations on the use of work. This chapter was later on removed from Act No. 14/1994, to be included in a general act on labour infringements and sanctions (Royal Legislative-Decree 5/2000 of 4 August 2002). Subsequently, all these issues were to be dealt with in a special and comprehensive act on infringements and sanctions, rather than in each specific labour act.

Sanctions are divided into three categories, minor, serious and very serious, according to the importance of the duty breached. Sanctions take the form of fines, calculated on the basis of rules given in the general act of 2000. Broadly speaking infringements of rules on temporary work do not receive a harsher sanction than those of any other area of work.

A specific sanction is still separately provided by Act No. 14/1994, although it is of a completely different nature and scope: the suspension of activities of the TWA. Suspension is imposed in the case of repeated breach of duties classified as very serious, and is currently regulated by Article 41.3 of Royal Legislative-Decree 5/2000. Article 2.1 of Act No. 14/1994, in its current form, includes among the conditions required for authorization as a TWA 'not to have been sanctioned with suspension of its activity on two or more occasions'. Consequently suspension of activity, which is normally a sanction of a temporary nature, becomes permanent in the case of a repeated breach. A third suspension is definitive, and authorization is withdrawn.

Article 2.5 of Act No. 14/1994 provides that the administrative authorization will be withdrawn by the labour authority in the event that the TWA does not maintain an 'organizational structure that allows it to fulfil its obligations as employer in connection with providing temporary work'. Although the regulation of withdrawal in these circumstances is not clear, it seems it can be partial or total, depending on the extent of infringement and on the territorial scope of activity of the TWA. This is a special rule which only relates to the organizational and structural requirements of a TWA, and was introduced at the same time as these requirements were defined in detail in Act No. 29/1999.

CONCLUSIONS

Temporary work has undergone a number of changes in the Spanish labour market in a very short time. It has been able to reach a remarkable level of activity in just a decade in the country, since Spain permitted it as a lawful form of employment. It has evolved considerably through this period, in which two models of temporary work have been in practice. At the outset, temporary work was primarily a means of reducing labour costs for low-skilled and low-paid jobs. The operative model of employment was based on short contracts, without prospect of permanent employment. Generally speaking, temporary workers were at a disadvantage under this model, and they used TWAs in order to search for better employment. Resistance to the activities of TWAs grew fast, and a number of legal reforms were made to dismantle this model by changing its legal basis, affecting principally the regulation of temporary workers' wages. These reforms were to some extent successful, and subsequent to their implementation one can find signs that a new model of temporary work was put into practice, in which TWAs are no longer a means of reducing labour costs, but an instrument for flexible management of the workforce. The principle of equal treatment in wages increased costs for TWAs, which together with the introduction of stricter organizational and financial requirements, reduced the number of TWAs. Now hiring temporary work is a considerable expense for Spanish firms, and requires good reasons. The use of temporary work is now a general element in HR policy in user firms, which in many cases design their policy in collaboration with the temporary work providers they use.

Probably the most interesting feature of the Spanish experience with temporary work is the regulation of this market through a centralized collective bargaining practice which has contributed substantially to the change in the model operating in the sector. In fact, many elements of the currently operative model of temporary work were designed and implemented by the social partners, in some cases preceding legislative incorporation. The role of centralized collective bargaining has been one of major importance. In the successive national agreements a number of core topics have been dealt with, which have introduced some aspects into Spanish industrial relations for the first time. Those agreements regulated matters related to the temporary work market and to the operation of TWAs producing a negotiated model of temporary work. The understanding between State unions and major TWAs was essential in this process. Some of the most important reforms of temporary work were produced by employment firms and unions working together. Large TWAs came to realize that low-skilled and inexpensive hiring-out had no long-term future, and that public acceptance was required to guarantee their future. Consequently they supported some reforms, such as increased wages and a reduction in their overall volume of activity.

The State, on the contrary, has not been particularly diligent in regulating temporary work, and is responsible for creating many of the problems arising in its development. To begin with, failure to implement the prohibition on temporary work before 1993 determined the way TWAs operated, namely without regulation and tolerated by the authorities. When regulation was introduced, it was difficult to remove unregulated practices. Secondly, Act No. 14/1994 was defective in its general design – the so-called 'minimalistic approach' – and in different aspects of its regulatory scheme. Many of the most significant problems in temporary work were not anticipated, allowing unacceptable practices in some TWAs. Successive reforms, effective as they were in solving some of the most important problems, were not able to give an overall solution to regulation of the sector. The consequence of this legislative deficiency is that some matters relating to the regulation of TWAs and their operations remain unsolved, transferring their resolution to the labour courts. The regulation of temporary work still requires much work before it is complete.

BIBLIOGRAPHY

Calvo Gallego, J.; González Rendón, M., & Rodríguez-Piñero Royo, M., *El impacto de las empresas de trabajo temporal en España: de la legalización a la reforma*, Colección Andaluza de Relaciones Laborales, Madrid, 2000.

Cruz Villalón, J., 'El marco jurídico de las empresas de trabajo temporal', in Alarcón Caracuel, M.R. (ed.), *La reforma laboral de 1994*, Marcial Pons, Madrid, 1994.

Cruz Villalón, J. (ed.), 'Número monográfico sobre relaciones triangulares de trabajo', in *Temas Laborales*, No. 57, 2000.

Durán López, F., & Martínez Rodríguez, F., 'Spain', in Blanpain, R. (ed.), *Private Emplyment Agencies*, Bulletin of Comparaive labour Relations, No. 36, 1999, p. 313.

Escudero Rodríguez, R. (ed.), *Las empresas de trabajo temporal. Crónica de un debate*, Consejo Económico y Social de Madrid, Madrid, 2001.

García Murcia, J., 'Una primera aproximación a la Ley 10/1994 y normas concordantes: las nuevas normas sobre colocación y cesión de trabajadores', in *Temas Laborales*, No. 31, 1994.

Galán García, A. (ed.), *Inserción Laboral*, Servicio de Publicaciones de la Universidad de Huelva, Huelva, 1999.

Rodríguez Sañudo, F., 'Temporary work in Spain, in Blanpain, R. (ed.), *Temporary work and labour law*, Kluwer, Deventer, 1993.

Rodríguez-Piñero Royo, M., *Cesión de trabajadores y empresas de trabajo temporal*, Ministerio de Trabajo y Asuntos Sociales, Madrid, 1992.

Rodríguez-Piñero Royo, M.; *Público y privado en el mercado de trabajo de los noventa*, Servicio de Publicaciones de la Universidad de Huelva, Huelva, 1992.

Rodríguez-Piñero Royo, M., 'La legalización de las empresas de trabajo temporal en España: crónica de un fracaso legislativo', in *Temas Laborales*, No. 57, p. 177, 2000.

Rodríguez-Piñero Royo, M., 'Temporary work and employment agencies in Spain', in *Comparative Labor Law and Labor Policy Journal*, forthcoming.

Valdés Dal-Ré, F., 'Las empresas de trabajo temporal: notas de un debate no tan ajeno para un próximo debate propio', in *Relaciones Laborales*, No. 7, 1993.

Valdés de la Vega, B., *Las empresas de trabajo temporal*, Editorial Comares, Granada, 2001.

11. Sweden

Birgitta Nyström

1. APPROACHES TOWARDS TEMPORARY WORK

1.1 Introduction

The Swedish labour market – as in other industrialized countries – has undergone considerable change in the last decades. Industry's share of employment is diminishing, and previous growth in the public sector has become stagnant. The private service sector has, on the other hand, increased rapidly since the 1980s as has the demand for flexible labour and specialized employees.

All this influences the organization of work. One tendency is that the 'typical employment relationship', defined as a full-time employee hired for an indefinite period and performing work at the employer's workplace, is increasingly replaced by other forms of work. Only a core of employees is employed on a full-time basis and with a permanent employment contract. Various forms of so-called 'atypical work' have contributed to greater flexibility in Swedish working life, with *part-time* and *fixed-term employment* as well as *temporary work* becoming more and more common. Almost a fourth of the Swedish workforce consists of part-timers, of which most are women. In 1996, fixed-term employees comprised more than 10 per cent of the Swedish workforce and in 1999 the figure had risen to 14 per cent.[1] It appeared to have remained at this level. Many of these employees nevertheless have strong ties to the workplace and stay there for considerable periods.

Economic crisis and changes in production methods, such as moves to order-related production, have contributed to a new style of business organization using a minimum of permanent staff. Swedish employers also maintain that labour law obstructs greater employment. Business organization is so streamlined today that in case of illness, maternity leave or peak business periods it is not possible to find the labour required simply by transfers among ordinary employees. In response, the use of temporary workers is one tactic. Employers also occasionally seem to use temporary employees as a means of recruitment. Temporary work is a way of trying out the employee without dealing with the limitations in the Employment Protection Act (*see, infra,* Section 1.3.1). Statistics indicate that the majority of temporary employees seem to get permanent employment at the user after some time.

Public employment services enjoyed a monopoly in Sweden between 1935 and 1993. Temporary work[2] was in principle prohibited in the years 1942–1991.

1. The Social Situation in the European Union 2001, eurostat.
2. The concept of '*temporary work*' is not used in Sweden. This expression can be confused with short-term/fixed duration/fixed-term employment, temporary and casual employment which all are opposites of more permanent engagements. The Swedish expression is '*hiring-out of labour*' or '*hiring-out of employees*'.

R. Blanpain & R. Graham (eds.), Temporary Agency Work and the Information Society, 191–224

In recent years employment exchange and temporary work legislation have changed entirely. Deregulation was completed in 1993.

Private employment agencies and temporary work are addressed in the same Swedish Act and it is sometimes difficult to draw a distinction between them. The emphasis in this report is on temporary work, but in places it is necessary also to discuss other activities of private employment agencies for a full understanding. The relevant legislation is applicable to all types of employees, blue-collar and white-collar, private and public, and as a general rule both to Swedish and foreign employees.[3]

Since the deregulation process started at the beginning of the 1990s, the sector has expanded very quickly. Private employment agencies are still not common in the Swedish labour market and temporary work employs only a small number of employees. The European Foundation for the Improvement of Living and Working Conditions established in 2001 that within the European Union, the Nordic and the southern European countries had the lowest levels of temporary workers, but the countries where this form of employment was currently increasing most rapidly were Italy and Sweden.

Temporary work has always been and remains most common in office and financial work, but features in other trades, e.g. technical and computer services, stock-room work, nursing, education, transport, retail, construction and manufacturing. It is common in expert knowledge-based businesses. There are no official statistical data relating specifically to temporary work. It is difficult to say how many temporary employees there are in the Swedish labour market today, but it is less than 1 per cent of the workforce. In December 2001, the sectoral organization SPUR estimated that 38,000 employees, or 0.87 per cent of the workforce were temporary employees[4] (more figures are given below in Sections 3 and 5).

This report indicates that there are difficulties in aligning temporary work to general Swedish labour legislation. It also demonstrates that the different players in the labour market have – after an initially rather negative reaction from the trade union-side – integrated temporary work into the ordinary 'Swedish model' for labour market relations by means of collective agreements. Consequently, there are variations in working conditions between different categories of temporary employees owing to the applicable collective agreement (concerning collective agreements in the temporary work sector, *see further, infra,* Section 6.3)[5].

1.2 Developments in the Regulation of Temporary Work

Private employment agencies have existed for a long time in the Swedish labour market. The agencies were often fee-charging and profit-oriented. Job seekers were frequently given unsatisfactory conditions, charged high fees and sometimes were assigned jobs that did not exist. Over a century ago, the Swedish government tried to gain some control of employment services by a system of recognition. At the beginning of the twentieth century, municipal public employment agencies were set

3. Non-EEA citizens need a labour permit, though.
4. Others have estimated these figures to be a bit lower.
5. Parts of this report are under publication in the International Labor Law and Policy Journal (Nyström, B. 'The Legal Regulation of Employment Agencies and Employment-Leasing Companies in Sweden').

up, which eventually became state public employment services. In 1935, a statute on employment agencies was enacted to comply with the 1933 ILO Convention No. 34 concerning Fee-Charging Employment Agencies. The 1935 Act outlawed profit-oriented employment exchange. The private employment agencies, which were generally very small and concentrated on the labour market for women, were gradually wound up.[6]

In 1942, the 1935 Act was amended so that temporary employment under certain circumstances was regarded as employment exchange undertaken as a profit-making occupation, which was prohibited. At this time, even under circumstances in which temporary work was allowed it was looked upon with disapproval, and almost not tolerated. The legislation was also adjusted to conform with the 1949 ILO Convention No. 96 concerning Fee-Charging Employment Agencies.

In 1976, the 1935 Act was further amended and profit-oriented international exchange of musicians and stage artists was allowed under certain conditions. The arts sector was considered to be very particular and it has continually been debated in what way employment exchange should best be organized in the sector.

By permission of the *Labour Market Board*, which is a government agency responsible for implementation of the government's employment policy, non profit-oriented fee-charging employment exchange was allowed under certain conditions under the 1935 Act. In practice, few organizations of employers or of employees or of both were granted the permission. Non-profit oriented employment agencies charging no fee had to notify the Labour Market Board of their activities.

Profit-oriented employment exchange was considered a crime under the 1935 Act as was the use of employees assigned by a profit-oriented employment agency.

In spite of the restrictions in the 1935 Act, temporary work firms had to some extent long been in operation in Sweden. That was especially the case in the typewriting business, the so-called 'flying' typewriting firms, but also in areas like transportation, printing and the arts. Their legality was questionable, and sometimes they were found to be in contravention of the ban on temporary work, but the line between legal and illegal was difficult to ascertain. Applying the prohibition caused much confusion. In court, the 1942 amendment was applied to typewriting agencies that had sent their employees to user undertakings to perform work. If the employment contract remained with the typewriting firm but it was the user who directed and allocated the work, and the employee was integrated into the user organization, the prohibition applied. Developments in the labour market gradually led to a situation where the notion of employment exchange was difficult to determine. Many small companies offering different kinds of services emerged, for instance in the cleaning, accounting and computer businesses. Regarding many of these firms' activities, it was uncertain if they were carried out as contract work or temporary work. Temporary work agencies in the office staff sector were therefore common and could operate quite openly. Users of temporary work agencies could be found even in the public sector, some even concluding collective agreements with trade unions already in the 1980s, which was confirmation of their maturity.

The amount of litigation on temporary work was very small. This is partly explained by the prevalence of the notion that some temporary work firms (principally the flying typewriting firms) were in fact accepted, perhaps desirable, although

6. For historical developments, *see also* e.g. Fahlbeck (1995:1), pp. 593–597, and Nyström (1999), pp. 338–340.

illegal. All the same, public opinion and the trade unions were rather concerned about sanctioning such firms, and the Labour Market Board did not accept the state of affairs. The legality of temporary work agencies was debated for many years and has been thoroughly discussed in Swedish legal thought and by state committees.[7]

In the 1980s, discussions aimed at a more favourable attitude towards temporary work began. There were several proposals on amending the 1935 Act. The debate was more or less concentrated on temporary office work, and the existence of and need for the flying typewriting firms. Office work underwent radical changes during the 1970s and 1980s, and there was an enormous growth in the number of flying typewriting firms during the 1980s.

In 1991, the Job Placement and Hiring-Out of Labour Act was passed, with an entirely new approach to temporary work.[8] Temporary work was in principle legalized. It was distinguished from, and no longer to be considered as a form of employment exchange. The close connection between temporary work and employment exchange is nevertheless clear from the fact that they are regulated by the same statute. Still, private profit-oriented employment exchange was considered criminal. An additional exception, besides the one for profit-oriented international exchange of musicians and stage artists, was added in the 1991 Act: head-hunting. For a long time there had been businesses operating to recruit highly qualified employees, mainly business executives. The agencies argued that their activities did not constitute employment exchange since all they were simply proposing the best candidates to a future employer, and so their activity was formally legalized. The Labour Market Board could give licences for headhunting agencies as well as musicians and stage artists agencies lasting for a year. Non-profit oriented fee-charging agencies also had to hold licences granted by the Labour Market Board.

Fairly strict limitations on temporary work remained. *Inter alia*, the user had to show that there was a temporary need for extra manpower, and the possibilities for temporary work firms to use employees under fixed-term employment contracts were limited compared to the generally applicable rules under the 1982 Employment Protection Act. It was not possible to post a temporary employee at a user for longer than four months. But temporary work was not dependent on any form of permission from public authorities.

The 1991 Act was introduced by a social democratic government. In 1993, an entirely new Act introduced by a non-socialist government did away with the rest of the restrictions.[9] The explicit aim was to improve the operation of the labour market. The public monopoly on employment exchange was abolished.

The 1993 Private Job Placement and Hiring-Out of Labour Act[10] legalized profit-oriented private employment services as well as temporary work firms and treated them as any other business. The only remaining restriction is that private employment services and temporary work firms are prohibited from charging job seekers and employees any kind of fee. It is still a criminal offence to do so. The recognition and surveillance system undertaken by the Labour Market Board was abolished by the 1993 Act, as were rules allowing temporary work only in specific circumstances of need, prescribed time-limits and restrictions on use of fixed-term

7. For earlier discussions, *see* e.g. Sigeman, *Contract Labour in Sweden*, 1970; Adlercreutz, *Temporary Employment*, 1970.
8. *See also* Fahlbeck (1995:1) pp. 597–599.
9. *See also* Fahlbeck (1995:1) p. 599.
10. *Lag (1993:440) om privat arbetsförmedling och uthyrning av arbetskraft.*

contracts. The Employment Protection Act nowadays applies to temporary workers in the same way as to other employees.[11]

The prohibition of profit-oriented private employment agencies and temporary work firms was founded on ILO Convention No. 96 of 1949 concerning Fee-Charging Employment Agencies. Sweden had to denounce from that ILO Convention in order to enact the 1993 Act. It ceased to be bound by the Convention in June 1993, and the new Act came into force in July of the same year. Like many other countries, Sweden found that ILO Convention No. 96 no longer corresponded to the realities of the modern labour market. But as Sweden has traditionally been at the forefront of the work of the ILO, the move was highly disputed. The contribution of *bona fide* private employment agencies to a well-functioning labour market was, however, widely recognized. The intention behind the 1930s legislation – preventing exploitation of job seekers and employees – was still valid, but had to be viewed in the light of well-functioning public employment agencies, strong trade unions and extensive protective legislation in the social policy field.

After the 1993 Act, Sweden was amongst the countries with the least legislation on temporary work. It was decided that the effects of the new regulation (or rather deregulation) should be evaluated after three years. Especially important was the assessment of the effects of deregulation on temporary work. The State Committee for Evaluation of the Deregulation of the Monopoly on Employment Exchange was set up in 1996 with a single investigator,[12] who reported to the committee in March 1997.[13] The Committee found that temporary work was an efficient way of organizing different forms of work for a limited duration and stated that there was no reason to believe that temporary work agreements led to a diminishing amount of permanent employment contracts. The Committee was nevertheless not satisfied with the situation concerning private stage artists' agencies, where several agencies were found to be charging the job seekers fees. The Committee proposed that, contrary to the prevailing state of affairs, employment exchange and other services should be strictly separated.

The nature of temporary workers' employment was, however, in some ways considered a problem by the 1996 Committee. Some temporary employment agencies engaged employees only assignment-by-assignment.[14] The economic situation for hired-out employees was insecure according to the Committee when only certain temporary work agencies used permanent employment contracts and guaranteed wages. The Committee proposed the appointment of a Public Board consisting of representatives from the business sector, labour market representatives and independent lawyers. Temporary employment agencies with staff would have to be registered with the Board and certain financial and labour law standards had to

---

11. Representatives in the temporary work labour market have to some extent taken the opportunities available to deviate from the Employment Protection Act by collective agreements, *see further, infra,* Section 6.3.
12. The investigator Mr. Björn Rosengren was the former president of the Central Organization of Salaried Employees (TCO) and has later been cabinet minister in a social democratic government.
13. SOU 1997:58 *Personaluthyrning. Slutbetänkande av Utredningen för utvärdering av avregleringen av arbetsförmedlingsmonopolet* (Temporary Work. Report from the State Committee Evaluating the Deregulation of the Monopoly of Employment Exchange).
14. An employment contract for an indefinite period not only gives job security; it is also important for instance when the employee wants to borrow money from a bank, obtain a credit card or rent a flat.

be fulfilled for registration. The Board should survey the activities of the registered firms and have the opportunity to withdraw recognition. The Committee also proposed that it should be clear from the wording of the act that assignment-by-assignment employment was in principle prohibited and that the employment contract with the temporary employment agency was, as a rule, for an indefinite period.

The Committees' report did not lead to any legislation. The government explained its lack of response by referring to emerging voluntary sectoral registration (*see further*, *infra*, Section 6.2), and the growth of collective agreements in the area (*see further*, *infra*, Section 6.3). The government stated though that it intended to follow developments closely, and if needed would suggest new legislation. In 2002, a government working group was appointed comprised of representatives from the government and labour market representatives to follow developments in the area (*see*, *infra*, Section 1.4).

1.3 Other Relevant Legislation

1.3.1 Security of employment

The 1991 Job Placement and Hiring-Out of Labour Act limited the possibilities of using temporary employees under fixed-term contracts compared to the generally applicable rules in the Employment Protection Act. In the 1993 Act there are no special rules regarding fixed-term contracts and the Employment Protection Act is today fully applicable to temporary employees.

Fixed-term employment is regulated in detail by collective agreements and by the 1982 Employment Protection Act. A Swedish employer with a temporary shortage of labour can hire an employee for a fixed term of employment in specific situations described in the Act. In 1974, the first Employment Protection Act introduced into Swedish labour law the principle that an employment contract as a rule lasts for an unspecified period (permanent employment). The employer must show just cause for ending the employment relationship and the employee is entitled to one to six months' notice (often more under collective agreements). Hiring agreements of a limited duration can only be concluded in certain particular cases, i.e. when the employment contract was concluded for a season, for a specific task and if required by the special nature of the job, for replacement work, or for practical work experience.

The 1974 Act was replaced by the new Employment Protection Act in 1982. The main reason for passing the new Employment Protection Act in 1982 was to extend the right to use fixed-term contracts. The 1982 Act permits probationary employment agreements not exceeding six months and contracts referring to a certain period of time (not exceeding six months in a two year contract) due to a temporary build-up of work. In amendments of the Act in 1996, a new form of fixed-term employment, other than those already mentioned, was introduced. For no special purpose a fixed-term employment contract may be agreed for a total of twelve months (in certain cases eighteen months). An employer is only permitted to have at the most five persons employed under this form of employment to encourage small undertakings to employ new personnel. The regulations governing fixed-term employment in the Employment Protection Act may be replaced by collective agreements. Players in the labour market have made considerable use of this option. Certain collective agreements are more generous than the Act in these respects, though others are more restrictive. (Concerning fixed-term employment and collective agreements regarding temporary work, *see further*, Section 6.3.)

The option of hiring employees for limited periods has been one of the most frequently discussed issues between employers and trade unions since the legislation on security of employment was enacted at the beginning of the 1970s. Developments during the 1990s in the face of high unemployment rates and calls for flexibility in production have drawn further attention to the issue. The government has variously tried to encourage the labour market representatives to formulate a solution themselves. But for the employers' organizations, flexibility has been the answer to most problems, and on the trade union side every suggestion of change has been considered a serious attack on employees and their job security.

In 2000, a state research institute was given the task of reviewing central aspects of Swedish labour law, including fixed-term employment. The institute had an expert panel with labour market representatives at their disposal. The review was finished at the end of 2002.[15] The report underlines that employment contracts as a general rule are for an unlimited period and suggests the abolition of the different types of fixed-term work set out in the Employment Protection Act. Instead, it should be possible to conclude fixed-term contracts for up to eighteen months for whatever reason[16] within a reference period of five years. If a fixed-term contract lasts longer, the employer will, according to the proposal, not be liable to pay damages, which is the general penalty for violation of labour law; instead the employer shall pay special compensation amounting to one third of the employee's monthly salary for every month the employment relationship endures, or at least three months' pay. There does not seem to be much enthusiasm for this proposal, and it is not a very daring speculation to presume that it not will lead to new legislation.

1.3.2 The trade union veto

It has always been permissible to use contract work and subcontracting in Sweden. Before the de-regulation of temporary work, therefore, the demarcation between contract work and temporary work was critical. With the enactment of the Co-determination Act in 1976,[17] a right of veto was introduced for national trade unions for use under certain conditions when an employer intends to give a job to someone not employed by him. The intention was to counteract the evasion of employer obligations that could arise in such situations. In some trades, e.g. the construction business, a complex system of contractors and sub-contractors is not unusual. This creates opportunities for employers for the evasion of tax and social security contributions. In temporary work, the employer also sometimes intends to circumvent legislative provisions and collective agreements.

---

15. Ds 2002:56 *Hållfast arbetsrätt – för ett föränderligt arbetsliv* (Stable labour legislation – for a flexible working life).
16. With the exception of probationary employment agreements, where no changes are proposed, i.e. such agreements are permitted if the probation period does not exceed six months. For replacement 18 + 18 months should be possible.
17. Also known as the Act on Joint Regulation in Working Life, or the 1976 Act on Employment Consultation and Participation in Working Life.

If an employer intends to use a contractor for the performance of a certain task or otherwise to allow non-employed persons to perform work, the employer is, according to the Co-determination Act, obliged to initiate negotiations in advance with the trade union to which he/she is bound by the collective agreement covering the work in question. The employer must give all information that the trade union might need and must postpone the decision on the use of the contractor until the negotiations have been concluded. If the decision which the employer intends to take can be presumed to involve the setting-aside of law or of a collective agreement for the work, or of what is otherwise generally approved within the industry concerned, the union has the right to block the proposed decision. This is very rarely the case. Nevertheless, the employers' duty to initiate negotiations informs the trade union of the situation and allows it to influence the employers' decision. The right of veto is not to be used to protect the jobs of union members, and does not authorize the union to veto contract work or temporary work situations as such. It merely confers upon unions the authority to veto illegal practices.

The employer is not obliged to initiate negotiations if the planned arrangement essentially corresponds to what was earlier approved by the trade union. Still, in this situation it is possible for the trade union to request negotiations with the employer. Another general exemption from the employers' duty to enter into negotiations regarding occasional and short-term work, or work which requires special expert knowledge, is not applicable to temporary work. It is possible for the labour market representatives to conclude collective agreements and deviate from the veto rules. For instance, under certain agreements the employer is exempted from the duty to negotiate when engaging certain specified contractors.

The employer may in certain cases (for urgent reasons) be exempted from the duty to postpone the decision until the negotiations are concluded. The employer may also disregard the veto if the union lacks good reason for it. If the employer sets aside the duty to negotiate or overrules the veto he/she may be liable in damages to the union concerned.

Criticism has sometimes been voiced against the right of veto and its controversial rules were revoked in 1991 by a non-socialist government, but were reintroduced with some amendments in 1994 when a new social democratic government came into power. In the case of purchase in accordance with the 1992 Public Procurement Act, which is based on EC law, a union veto may be imposed only if it is based on certain circumstances enumerated in the Act, e.g. that the supplier has been declared bankrupt. In legal discourse it has been questioned if the right of veto is in accordance with EC law regarding discrimination. But a discriminatory veto is probably illegal according to the Co-determination Act. The veto rules have also been questioned because there is no possibility for a contractor who does not receive the assignment due to a veto to appeal to any kind of authority or to litigate.

From the foregoing, it is clear that as a general rule it is not possible to use the right of veto in a situation where an employer uses temporary workers instead of hiring in new employees. In a case before the Swedish Labour Court in 1980, a similar situation was discussed.[18] The circumstances in the case were the following: an employer had dismissed employees because of redundancy. According to the Employment Protection Act, former employees dismissed for reasons of redundancy

18. AD 1980 No. 54.

enjoy a preference for being taken back into employment in the enterprise where previously employed within nine months from termination of the previous employment (preferential right of re-employment). In this case, the employer had loaned employees from another employer instead of taking back former employees. The Labour Court found that this was not a circumvention of the Employment Protection Act. One of the main reasons for that conclusion was that the loan of workers was for a limited period and not aimed to be permanent. The legal boundaries, however, are not entirely clear. A recent case, where the Swedish Metal Workers' Union sued an employer who engaged temporary workers instead of taking back former employees with preferential right to re-employment, has been followed with great interest in Sweden. The Labour Court's judgement was given on 15 January 2003.[19] The Labour Court found that in the circumstances no circumvention of the Employment Protection Act had occurred. The Court referred to the 1980 case, and considered that since 1992 temporary work had been permitted in Swedish law, so there was no reason for a more strict interpretation than that given in the 1980 case. In the 2003 case, there was nothing indicating that the employer used temporary employees for reasons other than difficulties in planning the work.

The cases indicate though that there might be situations where dismissals followed by the engagement of temporary workers, during the period in which the dismissed employees still have preferential right of re-employment, could be considered a circumvention of the Employment Protection Act.

1.4 EC Law

EC law has brought a number of changes to Swedish labour law, and has to some extent also influenced temporary work. Regarding working conditions, Directive 91/383/EEC aimed to improve health and safety for temporary employees[20] and has been implemented by the Swedish Work Environment Act (*see*, *infra*, Section 4.2). Directive 96/71/EC on posting of workers guarantees temporary workers hired out to a user in another Member State some of the important terms and conditions of employment in the Member State where the work is carried out.[21] Special Swedish legislation on posted workers has implemented this Directive.[22] However, cross-border temporary work is so far rare in Sweden.

In Sweden there are no statutory rules or formal procedures concerning the employment contract. Implementation of Council Directive 91/533/EC on the employer's obligation to inform employees of the conditions applicable to the employment contract[23] has not brought any changes in this respect. In 1993, a new rule was added to the Employment Protection Act which prescribes that employers generally have a duty to inform a new employee in writing of certain details

19. AD 2003 No. 4.
20. Council Directive 91/383/EEC of 25 June 1991 supplementing the measures to encourage improvements in the safety and health at work of workers with a fixed-duration employment relationship or a temporary employment relationship, OJ L 206, 29 July 1991, SS. 19–21.
21. Directive 96/71/EC of the European Parliament and of the Council of 16 December 1996 concerning the posting of workers in the framework of the provision of services, OJ L 18, 21 January 1997, S. 1.
22. *Lag 1999:678 om utstationering av arbetstagare* (Law about posted workers).
23. OJ L 288, 18 October 1991, S. 32.

concerning the employment agreement. A similar rule in the 1993 Act on Private Job Placement and Hiring-Out of Labour was then repealed.[24]

At the European level, the European federation for temporary work agencies (CIETT-Europe) and the trade union for agency workers (Uni-Europa) signed a joint position for a European directive on agency work in October 2001. The declaration was negotiated in the framework of the European social dialogue committee for hiring-out of labour. During the social dialogue UNICE, ETUC and CEEP had tried to negotiate a framework agreement but the negotiations broke down. The Commission proposed in March 2002 a Directive on working conditions for temporary workers.[25] The proposed Directive is based on the principle of non-discrimination and that a temporary worker should not be treated less favourably than comparable workers in the user company, unless different treatment is justified for objective reasons.

If the proposed Directive is accepted, Swedish labour legislation will have to be supplemented with the principle of non-discrimination as elaborated in the Directive (Articles 5 and 3 of the proposal). According to Article 6 of the proposed Directive, the user will have some duties, and Swedish implementation of the proposed Directive will need new legislation about information on vacancies in the undertaking (Article 6.1 of the proposed Directive). Regarding the proposed Article 6.4 (access to the social services of the user undertaking), it is difficult to ascertain what is meant by social services here: social insurance, health care or childcare facilities, free coffee? Swedish temporary workers – as other workers – benefit from the state social insurance system, and sometimes some complementary social insurance or social benefits from their employer, the temporary work agency, such as company medical service (*see further*, *infra*, Section 5.3). The proposed Article 7 (representation of temporary workers), and Article 8 (informing workers' representatives) will not require new Swedish legislation.

In Sweden there is an ongoing discussion regarding the possibility of regulating wages in an EC Directive. The non-discrimination principle in Article 5 of the proposed Directive includes wages. It is argued, largely by Swedish employers, that wages explicitly fall outside the Treaty. The proposed Directive is based on Article 137(2), and it is clear from Article 137(6) that Article 137 is not applicable to wages. EC law, on the other hand, already has several regulations regarding wages: the Directive on Equal Pay, the Directive on Posting of Workers, the Directive on Transfer of Undertakings, the Directive Establishing a General Framework for Equal Treatment in Employment and Occupation etc. The proposed Directive on Temporary Work seems to have a similar aim to these regulations; to protect an employee against discrimination or to protect his/her wages from deteriorating. This supports those (mainly on the trade union side) who argue that the Directive is within the competences of the EC.

There is a consensus in Sweden that wages are a subject for the national social partners and collective agreements and/or individual employment contracts only. There is no tradition of wage-legislation or state wage-policy.

Swedish employers are rather resistant to the proposed Directive, and doubt that temporary work is a subject well-suited for EC regulation. On the employee side, the Swedish trade unions are cautiously positive; they want an EC directive with minimum

24. The abolished rule in the 1993 Act prescribed a written contract regulating the type of employment, salary and other general conditions of employment. The new rule in the Employment Protection Act requires more specific particulars. However, in reality it seems to have less strict conditions, because it only requires written information and not a written contract.
25. COM (2002) 149 final, 20 March 2002.

standards and a principle of non-discrimination in order to prevent social dumping. They underline it is important that implementation of and derogation from the directive should be by collective agreement, in accordance with established Swedish traditions. The proposed Article 5(1) therefore is important. The Swedish Federation of Trade Unions (LO) and the Federation of White-Collar Workers (TCO)[26] are also critical of the proposal in parts. They do not approve of the proposed option of deviating from the Directive with regard to employees with an indefinite employment contract and to postings shorter than six weeks, because this in their opinion will only lead to circumvention of the Directive. They want a new rule about prevention of abuse of temporary employment, *inter alia* that it should be illegal for an employer to dismiss his/her own employees and replace them with temporary workers. (*See also* the referred case from the Swedish Labour Court, above Section 1.3.2.) They also demand a provision prescribing permanent employment contracts as a general rule and that the employer should be obliged to negotiate with, or at least to consult, the trade union at the workplace before he/she decides to use temporary workers. (Concerning the SPUR trade association, and its views on the Directive, *see*, *infra*, Section 6.2.)

The previously mentioned government working group for temporary work was supposed to have completed its work in November 2002 with a report to the government. In fact, the working group awaits new instructions from the government to follow the implementation of Directive 2000/78/EC, Directive 2000/43/EC[27] and the expected Directive on temporary work, which are of course of fundamental importance for the working group's report and its proposals.

2. DEFINITIONS AND POSSIBLE CHANNELS

2.1 Legal Definition of Temporary Work

Temporary employment (or, as it is called in Sweden, hiring-out of employees) was introduced as a legal concept in 1991, and is defined as a legal relationship between a client and a temporary employment agency whereby the agency, in return for a fee, places its own employees at the disposal of the client (the user) to perform work in the latter's business. In other words, two conditions must be met: that it is a remunerative relationship, and that the third party (the user) has a business where the employee shall perform work.

If the temporary work agency does not charge the user a fee, the agreement seems to be a loan of workers rather than hiring-out of labour. Temporary work should also be distinguished from employment exchange, which is found for instance where the employment relationship between the worker and the temporary work agency seems fictitious (*see further infra*).

2.2 Some Definitions and Demarcations

One means of obtaining competent extra manpower at short notice, especially for large companies and large employers in the public sector, is through a *personnel pool*

26. About LO and TCO, *see*, *infra*, Section 6.1.
27. The Directive 2000/78/EC shall be implemented by 2 December 2003 at the latest, and Directive 2000/43/EC on 19 July 2003 at the latest. Swedish legislation is under preparation. SOU 2002:43 *Ett utvidgat skydd mot diskriminering* (A Wider Scope for Protection Against Discrimination).

or a *manpower pool*. Employees (initially often a surplus of manpower resulting from organizational changes) are placed in a pool, and are called to perform work in different parts of the organization. This differs from employment exchange and temporary work in that all tasks are performed for the employer himself.

Another kind of manpower pool, in which several employers share, is more closely adapted to small undertakings and has become increasingly common. Due to a decrease in labour needs, several employers put their redundant employees in the same pool to be hired when needed, as temporary workers. Instances of special agreements on lending or hiring in or out manpower between different employers are to be found in the construction business and in the hiring of pilots. These arrangements are often short-term and aimed at avoiding a situation where one employer is temporarily short of manpower while another is above strength. Lately, use of such arrangements has been growing. For employers, this system is cheaper than using the services of a temporary work agency. For the employee, his/her employment contract remains with the old employer and it is therefore considered to give greater security.

The difference between temporary work and *lending of manpower* is unclear. Frequently, an employer temporarily requires manpower from another enterprise, for instance for the performance of a task demanding particularly skilled labour, or to meet a temporary increase in work. There are also examples of employers lending or hiring out their employees on a more permanent basis, for instance within groups of companies where the employees are employed by the parent company but perform work permanently for a subsidiary. Rights and obligations between the three participants and the legal status of their relationship can be somewhat unclear.

Contract work, subcontracting, franchise, consultancy and freelance work are examples in which the person who has undertaken the work is an independent contractor, and where no employment relationship exists. The boundaries are, however, difficult to establish, as with the difference between a temporary work arrangement that lasts for a long time and a contract work situation. The former is a contract for supplying labour (manpower) and the latter a contract for completing particular work. In practice the dividing line may be blurred. *Contract work* is common in Sweden.

A new phenomenon, *outsourcing*, in which temporary workers or contractors perform work instead of the user's employees, has become widespread. A common application is to reduce the number of divisions so that only the essence of the business' activities remain, cutting out, for instance, service-, repair- and training divisions. Employees who used to work in those divisions often continue to perform the same work but now as independent contractors or subcontractors receiving most of their commissions from the former employer. To take another example, business A closes down its telephone exchange, staff restaurant and porter's office, contracting out those functions to contractor B. The former employees in A's business continue to perform their usual work in the same workplace but are now employed by contractor B.

Call-centres have grown in popularity in recent years. Employers contract out their telephone operating and booking services to a call-centre, which is often situated in a geographical region where unemployment is high. Communication is by telephone, data-operating or the like, so that geographical distance is immaterial. Call-centres can serve firms and customers all over the country.

The above-mentioned examples of new and flexible forms of working often create difficulties in establishing what kind of contract has been made. To summarize, agreements to perform work fall on the whole into two main categories: *employment agreements* and *independent contract work agreements*. The distinction between them is critical. Only the employment relationship is covered by labour law, which on the whole aims at protecting the weaker party, i.e. the employee. There is no legal definition of an *employee*. The Swedish definition of employee has arisen from the application of several different statutes, and legal interpretation has given it a wide scope. In most cases there is no difficulty in deciding whether an employment relationship exists or not. Employees are dependent on the other contracting party, whereas *contract workers* are more independent. In difficult situations, a thorough investigation is carried out of several circumstances established in the employment contract and the factual circumstances in which the work is performed. The rules on determining employee status are mandatory in order to protect the individual who performs work.

The increase in atypical work arrangements is often seen as problematic by the trade unions and also to some extent by the legislator. Atypical work agreements can undermine the employees' position, protection achieved through labour legislation and collective agreements. Labour and social laws are to a considerable extent modelled on the 'typical employment relationship' and are more or less applicable to 'atypical work'. To give some examples with reference to the above-mentioned situations: employees who after outsourcing become independent contractors are not covered by labour law, and social security rules apply to them in a different way.[28] Temporary workers are employees and covered by labour law. But most of the rights they are entitled to under labour legislation, e.g. co-determination and security of employment, can only be enforced against the temporary work agency and not against the user firm where they work. It may be that, in the same workplace, there are workers with a permanent employment contract, employees with fixed-term contracts, temporary workers, workers loaned from a subsidiary, contractors with their own employees, consultants and free-lancers. All these persons may perform practically the same job, but different rules apply and conditions may differ considerably.

3. TEMPORARY WORK ORGANIZATIONS

3.1 Some Definitions and Demarcations

Before the 1991 Act, temporary work agencies were in principle prohibited. They were legalized under that Act and have since worked under the same regulation as other organizations. Since the 1993 Act there has been no system of licensing. The temporary employment agency holds all employers' rights and responsibilities towards the temporary employee, except regarding working conditions at a user company, where the user has the authority (*see further*, *infra*, Section 4.2). Labour and social security legislation is generally applicable to the employment contract; i.e. to the temporary employment agency and not to the user. It is the temporary employment agency which pays the wages and taxes of the temporary employee.

As indicated above, *labour exchange* is defined in the 1993 Act as an activity aimed at procuring work for applicants or manpower for employers, which is not *temporary work (hiring-out of labour)*. It is, however, as mentioned previously, not always possible to distinguish between different types of business here. In principle,

28. There are only estimated figures, but in 1999, over 10 per cent of the working population in Sweden were self-employed, The Social Situation in the European Union 2001, Eurostat. The self-employed are covered by some protective legislation.

the market for private employment agencies could be divided into different categories, temporary work, recruitment and outsourcing (contract work).[29] Other categories are search (headhunting), selection and outplacement. Demarcations between different kinds of activities (temporary work, employment exchange, contract work etc.) are very difficult to ascertain and in Sweden most agencies are active in several areas.

Recruitment agencies handle employment exchange for different kinds of specialized and qualified staff. They work at the employer's request but interested applicants contact the employment agency themselves. The need for recruitment of specialized manpower was recognized many years before the new legislation and different types of private, 'middlemen' services emerged, although they bordered on the illegal. *Headhunting* was legalized by the 1991 Act. *Search* agencies carried out headhunting, searching for candidates with the profile described in an employer's request. *Executive-search* concerns executives and managing directors and is a small market. Most search agencies in the Swedish labour market are owned by foreign undertakings.

Selection agencies do not search for candidates. Their main task is to form an opinion of job candidates. They advertise for job applicants and then grade the interested applicants and advise the employer accordingly.

On commission from an employer, an *outplacement* agency tries to help redundant executives and other redundant employees to find new jobs or to develop a self-employed activity. Outplacement agencies work mostly using analyses and consultations. They carry out more of an advisory than a placement activity. Because of high unemployment (by Swedish standards) since the beginning of the 1990s, outplacement activities have also increased.

A few large companies dominate the *temporary work* sector in Sweden. However, many temporary employment agencies are small. Some of the largest firms operating in Sweden are foreign-owned and belong to a group of companies operating in several countries. They have expanded their activities in recent years, and are also carrying on contract work, recruitment and selection, as well as training of personnel.

The geographical region with most private employment exchange and temporary work agencies is the capital, Stockholm, with more than 50 per cent of the sector's activity. Four large firms employ about 90 per cent of the temporary employees in the region. The largest companies have about 10,000 employees or more, but in total there are no more than about 230 private employment agencies or temporary work firms with ten or more employees in Sweden.

Certain agency functions are also carried out by various councils set up by the labour market representatives in collective agreements to place employees in danger of becoming unemployed as a result of streamlining, cuts in operation costs and such like. These so-called redundancy programme agreements contain rules on help with training, outplacement, and financial support in redundancy situations. The councils work on behalf of both employer and employees. As early as the 1970s, a council established by the Swedish Employers' Federation (SAF) and the Private Sector White-Collar Workers' Cartel (PTK, a 'negotiation cartel' for trade unions in the private sector) offered outplacement assistance. About 30,000 private businesses are associated with the council, and at most (in 1993) almost 50,000 redundant white-collar employees were registered at the council. There is a similar council for state employees and discussions continue between the social partners about a similar body

29. For 2001, the figures were 86 per cent temporary work, 6 per cent recruitment and 8 per cent contract work.

for private sector blue-collar employees.[30] Some employers associated with one of the councils have also engaged a temporary work agency, to work with the council on the redundancy situation.[31]

3.2 Rules Governing Temporary Work Agencies

There is a prohibition in the 1993 Act on payment from job applicants or employees in exchange for offering or referring work to them. This includes all kinds of registration- and placement fees as well as compulsory services charged. It was considered important to explicitly mention this in the Act. The agencies must charge their customer to finance their business. They can charge any fees they choose, with one exception: fee-charging labour exchange for sea crew is prohibited.[32] There is no prohibition on using sea crew as temporary employees, though.

According to the State Committee for Evaluation of the 1993 Act, the temporary employment agencies charge for the costs of the employee (wages, taxes, social security fees etc.) plus 30–40 per cent of the administrative costs of providing the employee. The last figure seems to vary a lot, but it is a fact that due to these costs most commissions are of a relatively short duration: generally two to three weeks for secretaries and other relatively low-qualified personnel, and two to six months or more for high-level personnel, though the full range is from a couple of days up to a year. When a temporary employment agency undertakes contract work the employees can be hired out for years.

Temporary work agencies must not in any way prevent employees from accepting employment from a user for which the employee is or has been working. An employee who has terminated an employment relationship and then accepts a job with a temporary work agency must not be hired out to his/her previous employer earlier than six months after the employment relationship ended. An employer violating these rules could be fined. The first rule aims at protecting the employee from unwanted restrictions on working for any employer he wishes. A clause in a contract between the temporary work agency and the user where the user promises not to employ a temporary worker is not binding upon the employee.[33] The second prohibition aims at preventing circumvention of labour law and socially unwanted recruiting techniques by temporary employment agencies.[34] The motives for termination of the employment relationship are not relevant. The temporary employment agency may in both situations be liable to pay a fine. In this latter case, there is also a possibility that a court would find that there is no employment relationship between the agency and the worker. The employment relationship between them is fictitious and the worker legally considered an employee of the user.

It has already been mentioned that nowadays no prior permission is required to establish a temporary work agency. There is no obligation to notify the authorities about the type of business that will be conducted. Like all other businesses, these firms are of course subject to general obligations pursuant to the law of association.

---

30. The state is attempting to stimulate the development of voluntary agreements in this area to cover the whole labour market.
31. The employer engages the private employment agency. The council works on behalf of both parties.
32. This is in accordance with the 1920 ILO-Convention No. 9.
33. The user may be liable in damages under contract law towards the temporary work firm, though.
34. It has been argued that the second prohibition prevents job creation, and this rule may be abolished.

In the discussions leading up to the 1993 Act, some consideration was given to whether personal qualifications or personal suitability of the person(s) in charge of the exchange was required for registration. Both the LO and the TCO wanted registration, but this idea was rejected, *inter alia*, with reference to the voluntary sectoral organization (*see further*, *infra*, Section 6.2). The State Committee for Evaluation of the Deregulation of the Monopoly on Employment Exchange proposed in 1997 that registration of temporary employment agencies should be required. But this proposal has not yet led to any changes. The present government's Working Group for Temporary Work is, among other things, discussing possible licensing, which is a demand which has come from the trade union side.

Both the changing economic environment and an increasing demand for qualified and flexible workers in some parts of the labour market has led to a growth in private employment and temporary work agencies in the last few years. The State Committee for Evaluation of the Deregulation reported in 1997 that the temporary work sector had expanded quickly since the 1993 Act came into force, but on the whole still represented a very small part of the Swedish labour market. At the end of 1996 there were just over 9,400 persons (0.2 per cent of the workforce) working in temporary employment agencies. But this figure included about 2,100 one-man firms, namely self-employed persons who hire themselves out to perform office-work, bookkeeping and such like. Many of these one-man firms lasted only a short time and were not a full-time activity for the owner.

Temporary work figures are now rising quite fast. In December 1997, there were about 14,000 persons (0.33 per cent of the Swedish workforce), working in the temporary employment business according to SPUR, the sectoral organization for private employment and temporary work agencies,[35] whose members comprise about 85 per cent of the sector. (This figure included the self-employed.) 42,000 persons (0.96 per cent of the Swedish workforce) were employed by private employment agencies in 2000; 89 per cent of those worked in temporary work, 6 per cent in contract work and 5 per cent in recruitment.

In 2001, 38,000 persons (0.87 per cent of the Swedish workforce) were employed by private employment agencies according to SPUR's statistics. 86 per cent of those worked in temporary work, 8 per cent in contract work and 6 per cent in recruitment. The agencies that belong to SPUR estimated in 1997 their activities at 75 per cent office and financial work, 6–8 per cent stockroom work, 2 per cent retail trade and 1–2 per cent nursing.

In 1999, turnover in the employment services sector increased by 71 per cent. Eighty-eight per cent of the turnover came from hiring out labour. For the hiring-out firms, office work represented about 40 per cent and financial work 25 per cent of the turnover. The most significant growth areas during 1999, however, were stockroom work and industry, with an increase of 158 per cent, and nursing, with an increase of over 170 per cent. The sector has handled certain employees for the first time, such as lawyers. In 2000, turnover in the sector increased by 68 per cent. Around 5 per cent came from contract-work and recruitment. Almost 90 per cent came from temporary work. Recent figures seem to indicate that the rapid growth of temporary work has stopped, but this is probably due to the general economic recession in Swedish society currently. For 2002, turnover according to SPUR seems to have stayed at the same level as the previous year, except for nursing which continued to increase.

35. Concerning SPUR, *see further*, *infra*, Section 6.2.

4. THE USER OF TEMPORARY EMPLOYEES

4.1 The User and the Temporary Work Agency

The main reason for using temporary employees is for extra manpower in cases of sickness or temporary increases in work. There are also businesses that use temporary workers for work concentrated in a particular period of the year. A Swedish employer with a temporary shortage of labour has several possibilities: he often tries in the first instance to meet the temporary shortage by using overtime work from the ordinary work force. He can hire employees under fixed-term contracts under the conditions laid down in the Employment Protection Act. He can use contractors or sub-contractors. He can also hire in temporary workers. In that case, he enters into an agreement with a temporary employment agency. The relationship between the temporary employment agency and the user is a contract under standard contract and commercial law. The 1993 Act does not set any stipulations regarding this contract. There are no demands for a written contract or for any particulars.

Users of temporary employees carry out all kinds of business, are big and small companies, and are found in the private and public sectors, the service and the manufacturing sectors.[36] There are even examples of temporary workers performing tasks which required the exercise of public authority!

The 1993 Act contains no rules aimed at the regulation of the user companies. But before the 1991 Act,[37] the use of temporary employees was criminal. When temporary employment was legalized by the 1991 Act, there still remained a few restrictions on users. They had to have a temporary need for extra manpower, they were not allowed to use temporary employees for more than four months at a time, and the possibility of using fixed-term contracts was limited. A user was also prohibited from hiring in an employee who had had an employment contract with the user within six months of termination of the employment relationship. Further, the user was not allowed to aid the prevention of temporary employees accepting employment in his/her undertaking. The latter prohibition remains in place for the temporary work agency, but not for the user (*see* Section 3.2, *supra*). Some wanted to keep these restrictions, but they were considered ineffective and, according to the legislator, it was unlikely that hiring-in of the same person would go on for a very long time, because of the high costs involved.

4.2 The User and the Temporary Employee

There is no contractual relationship between the user and the temporary worker and the 1993 Act does not deal with this relationship at all. The temporary worker is part of the user's business organization during the posted period. It is the user who supplies the working material and a working environment. The worker is subject to the managerial authority of the user, as regards following orders and safety regulations, and the user has to follow good labour market practice regarding the treatment of temporary workers. The user's authority is however restricted according to the employee's professional qualifications, so that he cannot for instance order a person hired in to do secretarial work to work in the staff restaurant instead.

---

36. Even trade unions are customers of temporary employment agencies.
37. In the years between 1972 and 1992.

The special task the employee has to perform is designated by the employment relationship with the temporary employment agency and the contract between the temporary employment agency and the user.

The employment-leasing firm is always considered to be the employer, even when the employee is working at a user company. There is one aspect though where both the hiring-out firm and the user are jointly responsible as employers and that is regarding the working environment. The 1977 Work Environment Act was amended in 1994 to adapt to the new situation created by the legislation on hiring-out employees, and to transpose Directive 91/383/EEC[38] into Swedish law.

The temporary work agency, as employer, cannot easily influence or control the working conditions at the user firm. Therefore the user has a far-reaching obligation to provide safe working conditions for hired-in workers. That responsibility is, in principle, the same as for his/her own employees, obliging the user to take the same safety precaution for both sets of employees. The user's responsibility for temporary workers is limited to the specific work conducted on the premises and does not include long-term measures such as rehabilitation,[39] which is the sole responsibility of the temporary work agency. As a general rule, safety representatives for the employees must be appointed from among the personnel in a workplace where at least five employees work. The employee safety representative of the temporary employment agency is allowed to enter the user's premises if that is necessary in order to fulfil his/her duty. If the user tries to obstruct the safety representative from the temporary employment agency in any way he may be liable in damages. A study on work environments in the staffing industry from 2002 has shown that the activities of the safety representatives did not work well for hired-out employees.[40]

In autumn 2000, the Labour Inspectorates[41] conducted a survey of the 37 largest temporary work agencies – 193 work places in total. The results were predominantly positive, but criticism was raised about contact with the employer during hired-out periods and routines in managing work environments for hired-in personnel.

There is no legal prohibition on the user hiring out the employee to a sub-user. Neither is there a limit to the amount of subsequent hiring-out.

5. THE TEMPORARY WORKER

5.1 Legal Status of the Temporary Worker

The temporary worker is always considered to be an employee, holding an employment contract with the temporary work agency. As mentioned above, in Section 4.2, there is only one situation, concerning the work environment, when the temporary employee has rights according to labour legislation enforceable against the user undertaking.

38. *See*, *supra*, Section 1.4.
39. Rehabilitation is aimed at reintegrating an employee into working life, after a return to work after illness, which is an employer's responsibility under Swedish legislation.
40. *See*, *infra*, Section 5.1 on the situation in which a user refuses to hire in a special group of employees, e.g. women or handicapped.
41. Local authorities responsible for supervision of the work environment at individual places of work. In 2001 they amalgamated with the Board of Inspectorates to form the Work Environment Agency (*Arbetsmiljöverket*).

Swedish labour legislation applies to temporary employees in the same way as to other employees. Three parties are involved in a temporary work arrangement: the temporary work agency, the worker and the user. This makes it sometimes difficult in practice to apply ordinary labour legislation, which is aimed at regulating the relationship between an employer and an employee.

One example where problems can arise concerns employees' rights to business information and the possibility of influencing working conditions. The employers' obligations, according to the Co-determination Act, rest with the temporary employment agency. The employees in question and their trade unions have no opportunities to influence the user firms. Even if a temporary employee may sometimes refuse a specific assignment and thereby in a way influence his/her own working-conditions, it is in practice impossible to express an opinion on conditions in the user firm. It should be clear from Section 1.3.2, *infra*, that the 1976 Co-determination Act, however, gives trade unions in the users' firm special rights, concerning information and negotiations prior to the employer's decision on use of non-employed personnel and the right to block the employer's decision under certain circumstances.

It is also very difficult for employment service trade unions to work when their members are spread out in many different workplaces and far from their employer. The Union of Salaried Employees and the Swedish Service Employers' Association (*see*, *infra*, Section 6.3) have agreed that, due to the specific nature of their business, it is important to facilitate local trade union activity.

There have been discussions on potential discrimination and/or circumvention of employment security when a user refuses to hire a specific employee or category of employees, because he believes he cannot make good use of the employee or category of employees, potentially causing their dismissal by the temporary work agency. Here, the legal situation is unclear, and it is difficult to say when a situation like this constitutes a violation of the law. It is clear, however, that it is not acceptable for an employer to discriminate with reference to his clients' wishes.

5.2 Who is the Temporary Worker?

Less than 40,000 employees – though some have estimated less than 30,000 employees – are employed in temporary work in Sweden. That is less than 1 per cent of the workforce, which is less than average within the EU.

There are more immigrants employed by temporary work firms than in the Swedish labour market generally. Almost half of all agency workers have some kind of university education – which is more than the average on the labour market – and women dominate the group, representing about two thirds of temporary employees. It must, however, be noted that the trades and professions in question are typically 'women's jobs'. During the last years when stock-room work and industry have expanded, the male proportion of temporary employees has increased. The Swedish Equal Opportunities Ombudsman has recently intensified its supervision of the sector.

Those who start working as temporary employees more often arrive from other jobs, rather than from unemployment. Hired-out staff are on average of relatively low age, just below thirty years. Most of them stay in the sector for a short period. There are two main categories of hired-out employees, those staying for a very short period and those working in the business for many years because they like this form of work. Average length of employment in a temporary employment agency is just over a year, but about one fourth of employees stay for many years.

When a temporary worker leaves his/her job it is often to become employed by a user. From the point of view of temporary employment agencies, this is satisfying, but problematic. It shows that they have succeeded in recruiting and training competent employees. On the other hand, the temporary employment agencies always face problems in recruiting new employees.

5.3 Social Security, Unemployment Benefits

A temporary worker has the same right to social security as other employees. Sweden has a state social insurance system that guarantees sickness benefit, parental allowance, and a pension amongst other things. Employees engaged by employers under collective agreements are also entitled to supplementary pensions and further labour market insurance. Labour market insurance consists of collective insurance schemes, which supplement state social insurance and are based on collective agreements. Employers bound by such agreements are under an obligation to keep their employees insured. Social security and the insurance schemes are financed by employers' contributions, *inter alia*, from temporary work agencies.

The only benefit that has caused noticeable problems for temporary employees is unemployment benefit. Swedish unemployment insurance associations are closely linked to the union movement. The system is financed up to around 95 per cent by state sources, *inter alia*, from social security contributions which employers are required to pay in respect of their employees. There is a compulsory basic insurance and a voluntary loss-of-earnings insurance. The latter applies to those who have belonged to an unemployment insurance association for at least twelve months and have completed a qualifying period of employment.

As mentioned in Section 1.3.1, the Employment Protection Act is fully applicable to temporary work. It follows that the employment relationship is normally for an indefinite period. Here, it must be underlined that although a permanent employment relationship exists, the employer is not obliged to provide paid work all the time. In the larger temporary work agencies employment for an indefinite period is the rule, but here as well as in many small temporary work agencies employment assignment-by-assignment can be found. Both employers and trade unions estimate that about 80 per cent of temporary employees are hired for an indefinite period. The Swedish Labour Court has interpreted the Employment Protection Act very restrictively when it comes to repeated fixed-term employment. Yet, the legal situation is somewhat unclear, because a few collective agreements permit assignment-by-assignment employment. Other courts have, in the interpretation of rules regarding unem-ployment benefits and other social security benefits, stated that those regularly occupied by a temporary employment agency should be considered as employed for an indefinite period (irrespective of whether the employment contract says otherwise). On that interpretation, the temporary worker is considered to be at the disposition of the temporary work agency on an indefinite employment contract and not to be unemployed.

In 1996, the Labour Market Board noticed that different unemployment insurance associations interpreted the rules on part-time unemployment in various ways. The Board emphasized therefore that, according to well-established court practice, temporary employees did not have the right to unemployment benefits during periods when they were not posted at a user's firm. Social security was not supposed to subsidize the temporary agencies' staff expenses. In 2001, the Labour Market Board had to clarify this earlier statement to avoid coming into conflict with statutes regarding discrimination and competition. Its 1996 statement should only be applied to workers employed only to be hired out, *inter alia*, temporary workers. Other employees in private employment agencies, such as persons employed in order to do contract work, should not be affected.

The issue concerning unemployment benefits affects increasingly less employees, because a growing number are guaranteed full pay regardless of whether they are hired out or not (*see further*, *infra*, Section 6.3).

It is estimated that 90 per cent of employees currently working for temporary work agencies have some kind of wage guarantee. Employees without a wage guarantee are not only paid for time in which they are not hired out, but also not entitled to sickness benefits for an illness not occurring during hired-out time.

5.4 Strikes

There are no statutory rules in Sweden regarding temporary work and strikes. The government does not interfere in collective bargaining and disputes between the labour market representatives. In other words, the state is strictly impartial. This has always been an important principle in public employment exchange. The Public Employment Service is, in the interests of impartiality, to continue providing its services during a lawful labour dispute. Workers involved in a dispute retain their employment contracts and cannot be permanently replaced. According to well-established traditions in the Swedish labour market, it would be almost impossible for an employer to use temporary employees in case of a strike or a lockout in his/her enterprise. The issue is not regulated and no legal obstacle could be raised if an employer should decide to replace the striking workforce. The replacement employees would, however, be condemned by the trade unions. (SPUR's ethical rules deal with this issue; *see*, *infra*, Section 6.2; and the collective agreement for blue-collar temporary workers contains a rule on neutrality; *see* Section 6.3). There have been no instances of employers seeking to hire other available labour to do strikers' work over the past few decades in Sweden.

5.5 To Work as a Temporary Employee

Several surveys have been conducted regarding working conditions for temporary employees.[42] Other than scientific research, both the principal trade union in the hiring-out of labour business, the Union of Salaried Employees (HTF), and the business organization, SPUR, have sent out questionnaires to temporary workers asking them their opinions of their working conditions.[43] The different studies are not comparable, but they show a number of similar results: most hired out

42. Bellaagh/Isaksson, Uthyrd men fast anställd (*Employed as a 'temp'*), Arbete och Hälsa (1999:6); Isaksson/Bellaagh, Anställda i uthyrningsföretag – vilka trivs och vilka vill sluta? (*Employed by temporary work agencies – who gets on and who wants to quit?*), Arbete och Hälsa (1997:7); Wadensjö, Personaluthyrningsföretag – en bro till arbetsmarknaden? (*Temporary work – a Bridge to the Swedish Labour Market?*) Institutet för social forskning (SOFI), Stockholms universitet & Inregia AB, 2000. In 2002, the Swedish Environmental Research Institute Ltd. conducted a study on management of work environments in the staffing industry.
43. HTF in 1996, 1998 and 1999. SPUR in 1996, 1998, 2000 and 2002.

employees work for more than half the length of full-time hours, mostly at least 75 per cent of full-time hours, and the majority is satisfied with their working hours, although one third would prefer more. Those with shortest working hours would like more. Most employees are satisfied with their work, but many also say that they would take an offer of a permanent job. Most satisfied are nurses and teaching personnel.

Advantages of temporary work are, according to the employees, the variety and the chance to improve skills, flexibility with regard to working hours and workload which allows reconciliation of work and family life. The greatest disadvantage is the economic insecurity, but lack of responsibility and discontinuity of social relations at the workplace are also negative aspects. Collective agreements have lately tried to give temporary workers financial security and employment security on a level with other employees, *see further*, *infra*, Section 6.3. According to trade unions and SPUR, about 80 per cent of temporary workers were permanently employed and 90 per cent enjoyed some kind of guaranteed wages when not hired out. This seems to be reflected in the latest questionnaire, in which a smaller group of temporary employees say that one of the disadvantages with the work is financial security.

Studies indicate that the average pay for temporary employees is comparatively low, but some categories of employees, especially in the public sector, such as physicians, nurses, dentists and teachers, often can increase their salaries if they quit public employment and start work as temporary employees. In nursing, salaries can increase almost 30 per cent for an employee who quits public employment to be a temporary employee. It has been debated whether this could be a means of raising wages in low-paid women's jobs by creating competition between employers. But many public employers have decided not to use temporary workers because of the high costs. In spite of this, the number of temporary workers in nursing and education is increasing.

A survey on nurses leaving public employment for temporary work agencies has shown that the nurses are very unsatisfied with public employment and find it easier to limit their engagement in difficult working situations if they are hired out to different employers. Satisfaction with working as a temporary employee was mainly due to the fact that the nurses considered they could concentrate on the patients. It was considered an advantage not to be involved in administration in the workplace. On the other hand nurses find it easier to develop their skills when in public employment.[44]

The right to a trial work period at the user firm can be established in the contract between the temporary employment agency and the user. The larger firms particularly are interested in developing competence among their employees to forestall the need for trial periods. Consequently, a second temporary worker is assigned to the user firm, at the temporary employment agency's expense, only to 'understudy' the work there. So-called 'back-up agreements' mean that the temporary employment agency and user agree an obligation on the hiring-out firm to supply the user with temporary employees who are acquainted with the user's firm. In many situations the user expects no trial period for a temporary worker.

Training arranged by the employer to develop the skills of employees has become important for all kinds of employees. There is no legislation on the matter in Sweden, although it has been discussed. There are collective agreements including schemes for skills development in some areas of the labour market, but these are not common.[45] The employer can of course voluntarily train his/her employees.

44. Michael Allvin and others, National Centre for Work Life Research, 2003.

45. The main agreements concerning hiring out of blue-collar and white-collar employees have special rules on training, *see*, *infra*, Section 6.3.

The largest temporary work firms have quite extensive training opportunities for their employees. The training takes place mostly outside working hours, and is therefore unpaid.

6. THE ROLE OF THE SOCIAL PARTNERS

6.1 Trade Unions and Employers' Organizations

One reason for the smooth deregulation of private employment services and temporary work in Sweden is the role of strong labour unions covering virtually the whole labour market. The Swedish labour market is highly organized. The overall rate of unionization is above 80 per cent of the working population. Although figures from most recent years seem to indicate that a decreasing number of employees join trade unions. Unionism is evenly distributed among the three main parts of the labour market: private, local government and state (central government). It is divided into three main federations; one for blue-collar employees, one for white-collar employees and one for professionals. The Swedish Federation of Trade Unions (LO) is a confederation of national trade unions in the blue-collar sector. White-collar employees are unionized in national trade unions belonging to the Federation of White-Collar Workers (TCO). Professionals belong to national unions amalgamated into the Swedish Federation of Professional Associations (SACO).

The trade unions try to organize temporary and other atypical employees as well as typical workers. One of the largest unions within the TCO, the Swedish Union of Salaried Employees (HTF), organizes the majority of the temporary workers.

It has sometimes been estimated that less than 40 per cent of temporary employees are unionized. This has increased during the last years when hiring-out of labour has expanded to take in more groups of employees. The Swedish Union of Salaried Employees estimates that, in their area, they organize over 70 per cent of temporary employees. Many work as temporary employees only for a short period of their working life, and if they have already joined a trade union and are established in the labour market before they start to work as temporary employees, they remain union members. Still, it is difficult for the trade unions to attract young people who enter the labour market as temporary employees.

To a large extent it is the trade unions which are responsible, on behalf of their members, for supervising the application of both collective agreements and labour legislation in Sweden. Some of the rights given to employees are to be exercised through the unions and are only given to trade unions governed by a collective agreement. One could say that these are the 'established trade unions'. For instance most of the rules in the Co-determination Act aimed at industrial democracy require a collective agreement, as do rights to representation by trade unions pursuant to the 1974 Workplace Union Representatives Act, *inter alia*, conducting trade union activities during paid working time.

Employers trade organizations in the private sector have, since 1902, been associated as the Swedish Employers' Confederation (SAF). SAF amalgamated in 2001 with the leading trade organization, The Federation of Swedish Industries, forming the Confederation of Swedish Enterprise (SN). In the public sector there is one agency representing the state as employer and one central agency for local government of which the local municipalities are members. One of the largest trade associations within SN is the Swedish Federation of Trades and Services. One of its member organizations is the Swedish Service Employers' Association, which has concluded collective agreements with the Swedish Union of Salaried Employees for hired-out employees since the 1980s. Most of the larger temporary employment agencies are members of the Swedish Service Employers' Association.

The labour market parties play an important role in rule-making in the Swedish labour market. Terms and conditions of employment are usually set by standards laid down in collective agreements. Collective bargaining in Sweden is highly centralized, although a process of decentralization began in the 1980s and still continues. Collective bargaining can take place at several levels, but today the focus of bargaining is at the industry-wide level. Industry-wide collective agreements cover every sector of the Swedish labour market. Legally binding agreements can be concluded at all levels of bargaining. Most workplaces, with the exception of very small ones, are covered by collective agreements and an overwhelming majority of Swedish employees is covered by collective agreements. These figures are lower in the temporary work sector.

Regulation in collective agreements covers most areas of the individual employment relationship, although labour legislation has been extensive since the 1970s. Most labour legislation is constructed so that it is possible to agree upon further terms in a collective (but not individual) agreement. There is no legislation regarding pay in Sweden, not even a minimum wage. Here, collective agreement regulation is more or less exclusive – to some extent supplemented by individual agreements between employer and employee in recent years.

Collective agreements also have an impact on the working conditions of non-unionized employees, according to labour market practice and case law. Although they are not directly covered by the agreement, it is a general principle that the employer is considered to be obliged to apply collective agreement provisions also to non-unionized employees and employees belonging to a different union from the signatory union to the agreement, unless anything to the contrary has been agreed with the signatory union. But it is not possible under Swedish law to give collective agreements an *erga omnes* effect.[46] The working conditions for employees who work for employers not bound by any collective agreement are regulated by labour legislation and individual employment contracts.

LO and TCO have traditionally opposed temporary work as well as private employment exchange. Employers in SAF, which for a long time supported the ban on profit-making employment agencies, were in favour of less strict limits on private employment exchange in general and of legal authorization of the typewriting firm activities. The 1980s saw changes in position. SAF supported deregulation as did SACO. LO and TCO had apprehensions that deregulation would lead to a segregated market. They both opposed the changes in the 1993 Act and wanted to keep the system of authorization of temporary employment agencies from the 1991 Act. The veto rules in the Co-determination Act were not considered sufficient; state control was in their opinion also needed. The trade unions have nevertheless gradually accepted private employment agencies and their different activities. Today trade unions generally recognize that there is a need for temporary employees and have directed their work to secure working conditions at the same level as 'typical' employees. A result of the 'Swedish model' is that rather than being resisted, the employment agencies

46. In many countries, e.g. the majority of the European Union Member States, there is a mechanism for the extension of collective agreements whereby they are automatically rendered applicable to all employers and employees falling within their ambit, an *erga omnes* effect.

and employment leasing companies have been increasingly integrated into the normal system of labour relations and collective agreements. It started with an appendix, regulating some aspects of the working conditions for temporary employees, to the regular collective agreement for white-collar workers in the services sector. Today there are special industry-wide collective agreements for both white-collar and blue-collar temporary employees. Concerning collective agreements, *see further* Section 6.3, *infra*.

6.2 Trade Association, Ethical Rules

There is an important trade institution working to support good business practice in temporary workers, which has been mentioned above. The Swedish Association of Temporary Employment Business and Staffing Service (SPUR)[47] organizes employment exchange and temporary employment agencies, and covers about 85 per cent of the sector. SPUR is entirely a trade (and not an employers') organization, and does not for instance conclude collective agreements. Its main aim is to work for high quality, ethics and sound personnel policy in the business. Its members include businesses operating in temporary work, employment exchange, recruitment, headhunting, selection, contract work, and education.

An agency must fulfil certain conditions to become a member of SPUR, regarding its activity, turnover, insurance and qualifications.

SPUR has worked intensively to build up a self-regulating system in the business and has adopted a number of ethical rules in order to combat employers' malpractice in this quickly expanding sector. The ethical rules should be guiding principles, implying in short: when a member employs someone, a written employment contract is necessary, and terms and conditions consistent with collective agreements should be followed. A member is obliged to see that his administrative staff have relevant knowledge of labour law and collective agreements, and that bookkeeping and accounting follows law and good practice. In relation to other businesses, a member should follow business ethics, and when an industrial dispute occurs should be considerate to both parties. In relation to customers, a member should be discreet and must inform employees of the need for secrecy, asking them to sign a secrecy clause.

SPUR has appointed a council of ethics, consisting of three persons without connections with temporary work or employment exchange businesses, for supervising members' observance of the ethical rules. If SPUR is notified that a member or a non-member has failed to comply with the rules they will conduct an investigation. A member could be cautioned and in grave cases expelled from the membership. Hitherto about ten matters have been dealt with, but no member has been expelled. A non-member is affected by a statement from SPUR in that the decision is published and the firm may be denied membership.

Law-abiding employers in the sector are troubled by the fact that other employers sometimes emerge who evade payment of taxes or social security contributions, or who hire out employees that officially are unemployed or sick and therefore enjoy sickness-pay or unemployment benefits. These illegally operating employers lower costs and this constitutes unfair competition in relation to law-abiding employers. Trade unions and the authorities of course also follow such malpractice (*see also*, *infra*, Section 6.3).

47. The predecessor to SPUR was organized in 1967.

Another important role for SPUR is raising awareness about the sector and its importance on the labour market. SPUR also gives qualified services to its members, formulates standard-contracts to be used in relation to the user firms, formulates quality rules for different kinds of work, such as a policy on quality-control of users and how to direct them for SPUR's members who hire out employees to schools. It also acts as a policy-maker. On policy, SPUR often co-operates with SN and in international matters with CIETT (*Confédération International des Entreprises de Travail Temporaire*). Sometimes SPUR also collaborates with the Labour Market Board and other public authorities in the labour market, in order to find new ways to help workers who due to unemployment or sickness have been out of the labour market for a long time.

According to SPUR, the proposed EC Directive on temporary work is not necessary, and from a Swedish perspective could be counterproductive, impeding further developments in collective agreements and other means of improving standards for both employees and users. SPUR also considers that the proposed Directive discriminates against temporary work agencies, because it will be the only sector on the labour market where employers will not be able to decide working conditions for their employees, not even by collective bargaining with trade unions.

6.3 Developments in Collective Agreements

Collective agreements on temporary work, which regulated temporary work agencies, emerged before the beginning of the deregulation process. The Union of Salaried Employees (HTF)[48] concluded a collective agreement with the Swedish Service Employers' Association[49] in the mid-1980s. This agreement on hiring-out of labour was for a long time the model agreement in the temporary work business and was most frequently used. The general collective agreement for white-collar employees in the trade and services sector, with general rules on hiring arrangements, remuneration, holidays, other forms of time-off and leave of absence, sick-pay, termination of the employment relationship, and occupational social security, was applied as widely as possible. But the special supplementary collective agreement on hiring-out of labour applied to matters to which the general agreement was not applicable.

On the strength of earlier agreements, workers were guaranteed an average twenty working hours weekly over a period of one month. It was, however, possible to deviate from this provision. In 1998, a new agreement entered into force with an important innovation: temporary workers were guaranteed hours equal to 75 per cent of ordinary full-time work (normally translating as thirty hours' guaranteed pay) a week. It was possible to deviate from this new provision, but only at the employee's request and the local trade union could demand to be informed.

Recently, temporary work has been used in increasingly more trades. As a result, other trade unions started to conclude collective agreements at national level. In May 1997, a collective agreement with the Transport Workers' Union (associated with the LO) covering the whole country was concluded. This was the first nationwide agreement outside the area of office work. Agreements also emerged in the metal industry, nursing, the hotel and restaurant sector, and transport.

---

48. *Tjänstemannaförbundet HTF* (sometimes translated: The Swedish Union for Commercial Employees).
49. *Tjänsteföretagens arbetsgivarförbund* (a part of the Swedish Federation of Trade and Services, associated with SN).

In 2000, the first collective agreement dealing solely with hiring-out of labour was negotiated between LO and the Swedish Service Employers' Association. It regulates the working conditions for all temporary employees belonging to a trade union associated with LO. It was signed by all nation-wide blue-collar federations associated with LO.[50] The agreement is only applicable to temporary work, and not to outsourcing (contract work). The agreement stipulates a wage guarantee of 85 per cent, rising to 90 per cent from October 2002 for employees with at least six months' employment. When hired out, the working conditions that are applicable to comparable employees in the user firm should apply to the hired-in employee. This means that, for example, wages should be the same as for comparable employees at the user firm. The employee has a right to refuse a particular assignment without reduction in pay for compelling reasons, such as extreme length of commuting distance or harassment at the user firm.

Under the agreement, permanent employment is the general rule, but there are certain provisions for employment for a limited period. A limited employment contract should only last for six months, but – if the local trade union agrees – it is possible to conclude a fixed-term contract for twelve months. Fixed-term contracts are furthermore allowed for replacement and for practical work experience, but the possibilities to conclude fixed-term employment contracts under the agreement are on the whole more limited than under the Employment Protection Act. The agreement also contains a provision on neutrality regarding work provided to a user undergoing a labour dispute. The hired-out employee is explicitly not prevented from taking a job at the user firm after termination of the employment contract and the applicable notice period.

A new agreement between LO and the Swedish Service Employers' Association was concluded in December 2002. It brings a few changes to the earlier agreement, most of which attempt to clarify previous provisions. From January 2004, the wage guarantee is to be increased after three months' uninterrupted employment. Between January and April 2004, the wage guarantee remains 85 per cent, and in May 2004 it rises to 90 per cent from the first day of employment. The method for calculating wages when hired out has caused problems, so the new agreement tries to identify the relevant reference group at the user firm. The provision regarding the geographical area within which a temporary worker may be sent has also caused problems. In the new agreement, it is stipulated that a reasonable travelling distance should be agreed when the temporary worker is hired by the temporary work agency. The trade union may participate in that negotiation process, and if the parties cannot reach a conclusion, the local municipality is normally determined to be the geographical area in which the employee is obliged to work for different users.

The parties to the LO-agreement have set up a joint working group through which they will follow the application of the agreement, try to simplify it and work for fair competition because they have noticed employers' malpractice in the sector. It is also noted that the LO has begun to consider introducing licences for temporary work agencies which are granted by the social partners.

In autumn 2001, the Swedish Union of Salaried Employees, eight unions belonging to SACO and the Swedish Service Employers' Association concluded a new agreement with the assistance of a conciliation board, which is applicable from April 2002. This agreement is – like the LO agreement – comprehensive in that it

---

50. The LO has negotiated, but has no competence to conclude a collective agreement on behalf of its member unions. It is the nation-wide blue-collar federations associated with the LO that have to sign the agreement before it enters into force.

regulates all aspects of hiring-out of labour and does not rely on any other agreement. In other words, it is no longer a supplement to the general agreement. As a general rule, the employment relationship is permanent, but the agreement allows a fixed-term agreement in several situations. According to the new agreement, all temporary employees with more than eighteen months of employment receive 100 per cent of full-time remuneration irrespective of whether they are hired out or not. Those who have been employed less than eighteen months receive first 75 per cent of full-time wages guaranteed followed by an 85 per cent guarantee. The agreement also contains rules on confidentiality regarding the affairs of employers and users, on the notice period in case of termination of the employment agreement, overtime pay, holiday pay, sickness pay, parental leave pay, amongst other things. A special working-time agreement and an agreement on training employees are supplemented.

The above-mentioned agreements, firstly that between the Swedish Service Employers' Association and the Union of Salaried Employees and secondly that between the eight SACO-federations and the LO-federations, are the most commonly applicable. It is noteworthy that these two leading agreements have an entirely different approach to wages. According to the LO-agreement, wages for temporary workers should be the same as for comparable workers at the user firm. (This is the same principle used in the proposed EC Directive.) The HTF-agreement gives the temporary worker a monthly salary which is the same irrespective of the user firm.

There is also an important collective agreement for temporary work on health care concluded in 1999. It is constructed as a special agreement to supplement the main collective agreement in the private health care sector covering all employees except doctors and dentists. Guaranteed wages are 75 per cent of full-time pay. The temporary employee can refuse to be sent to a user under particular circumstances, such as where he/she has previously been harassed at the user firm, without reduction in pay. The temporary employee has a right to a trial period with the user. Fixed-term contracts are allowed in situations where there is a need for extra employees for a short period or where there is need for special competence, but not where there is a permanent need for extra labour. It is emphasized that skills development is a common responsibility for the temporary work agency and the temporary worker. The agreement also contains rules on pay, working time, and insurance.

In 2001, for the first time, a collective agreement for the call-services sector was concluded between the Union of Salaried Employees and the Swedish Service Employers' Association. This is only a supplementary agreement to the general collective agreement for the white-collar services sector. A new supplementary collective agreement, which is applicable from April 2003, has recently been signed. As a general rule, the employment relationship in this sector should be permanent. But other than the possible fixed-term agreement situations specified in the Employment Security Act and the general collective agreement for the white-collar services sector, work for a fixed-term period is possible in situations where there is a need for extra employees for a short period or where there is a need for special competence or the employee asks for a fixed-term contract, but not when the need for extra labour is permanent. If under such fixed-term agreements working hours exceed 832 hours during a twelve-month period, the employee must be offered a permanent contract. The agreement also contains rules on working time, holiday pay and wages.

The formula used in several collective agreements that temporary employees are employed for an indefinite period and have 100 per cent guaranteed pay, irrespectively of whether they are hired out or not, has caused debate. It is alleged that it encourages the temporary work agency to hire out its employees for any job, regardless of their qualifications, or to use them in a position for which they are not qualified at the hiring-out agency.

7. THE ROLE OF GOVERNMENT

As previously explained, Sweden denounced from ILO Convention No. 96 of 1949 in order to enact the 1993 Act. There was a general feeling that Convention No. 96 was outdated and failed to recognize the increasing role of new types of private employment agencies in the labour market, and in 1997 Convention No. 96 was replaced by ILO Convention No. 181 on Private Employment Agencies, and by Recommendation No. 188. in 2001, Sweden decided not to ratify ILO Convention No. 181 for the time being.[51] Principal reasons for this decision were the establishment of the above-mentioned government working group (Section 1.2) and the ongoing discussion on EC regulation. There do not seem not to have been particular legal obstacles to ratifying Convention No. 181. Still, some minor questions could be discussed.[52]

Although Sweden has been a member of the European Union only since 1995, the judgement of the European Court of Justice in 1991 in *Höfner and Elser* v. *Macrotron GmbH*,[53] concerning the monopoly of public employment agencies, was one of the motivations for Sweden's abolition of the public monopoly. The case *Job Centre coop. Arl* followed in 1997.[54] In both cases, the Court held that a public placement office could be classed as an undertaking for the purpose of Community competition rules. An undertaking vested with a legal monopoly might be regarded as occupying a dominant position within the meaning of Article 86 in the EC Treaty.[55]

Supplying labour and arranging employment is traditionally regarded in Sweden as a job best undertaken by the public authorities, and when the 1993 Act was passed it was not expected that private employment exchange would be very extensive. Private job placement was supposed to complement the public employment service in certain parts of the labour market especially regarding headhunting for executives, but also for specialists and certain professions and trades. Public job placement was introduced in Sweden in the early 1900s. There are local Public Employment Service Agencies throughout the country. The labour market representatives sit on the Board of the Employment Service. Public job placement is non-fee-charging. It is supposed to counteract segregation in the labour market and is also an important instrument of labour market policy. Employers are under an obligation to report vacancies to the Employment Service, though an employer looking for labour is not required to appoint a person suggested by the Employment Service. However, most employment arrangements are concluded without the help from the Employment Service, presumably as a result of personal contacts.

It is clear that private employment exchange is relatively insignificant, but it has nevertheless influenced public employment exchange. Quite a few public employment agencies have now arranged special exchange services for fixed-term and casual work and there are examples of special services for certain groups of employees. There are also examples of employment policy programmes in which the

51. Government Bill 2000/01:93.
52. *See* Nyström (1999) s. 356.
53. Case C-41/90 [1991] ECR I-1979.
54. Case C-55/96 [1997] ECR I-7119.
55. *See also* case C-163/96 *Silvano Raso and others* [1998] ECR I-533 (dock work monopoly).

long-term are trained and employed by an organization, and in which the public employment agency, trade unions, adult educational associations, municipalities, and local enterprises are involved. The organization hires out the employees with the aim that they will subsequently receive indefinite employment contracts. Together with the local municipalities, public employment agencies have started so-called job centres. In a job centre, unemployed people can choose a combination of education and temporary work. In terms of social security, they receive unemployment benefits or other public benefits when they are not hired out. Different kinds of state subsidiaries are also involved with some call-centres, which can be placed in geographical areas with high unemployment.

These public authority activities have drawn the attention of competition watchdogs. Assistance given by state subsidiaries to groups with difficulties in accessing the labour market could be seen as distorting competition. Between 2000–2001, the Parliamentary Auditors[56] conducted studies concerning temporary work and labour market policy from a competition perspective. The Auditors have established that there have been forms of labour market policy, especially the introduction of so-called job centres, which have distorted competition. Owing to current labour market policy and a new policy from the Labour Market Board, this decision has not yet been followed up by the Auditors. The authorities working in this area have instead been urged to co-operate with private employment exchange firms. The Labour Market Board has for example initiated co-operation activities involving immigrants and the elderly. In 2000, the Labour Market Board was commissioned by the government to initiate a project in which private employ ment agencies are supposed to be a complement to public employment agencies. A report from the Department of Industry indicates that it is easier for immig rants to find employment with temporary work firms than to obtain other forms of employment.

8. CONCLUSIONS

The proposal from the State Committee for Evaluation of the Deregulation of the Monopoly on Employment Exchange in 1997 (*see* above Section 1.2) has not led to legislation. There are several reasons for this: negotiations and collective agreements in the area are flourishing. A government working group was established in 2002, which together with labour market representatives shall survey working terms and conditions for hired-out employees and make an inventory of problems in the sector. There are also developments in the area at European Community level. The growth of a self-regulating system from the work of the business organization, SPUR, also explains why further legislation was not required. There is no tradition in Swedish labour law to legislate where the labour market representatives can provide a solution.[57] From the trade union's point of view, it is nevertheless unsatisfactory to have a self-regulating system which is not readily accessible to employees. Therefore some continue campaigning for a public authorization system.

56. The Parliamentary Auditors investigate and examine all kinds of state activities, mainly by performance-auditing, and endeavour to promote sound management of state funds and rational use of state assets.

57. In fact, in the middle of April 1998 the Swedish government stated that – due to self-regulation and the extended use of collective agreements – it did not intend to legislate in this area.

A change in attitude towards temporary work has emerged in recent years; using temporary employees is more seriously considered. Good private and public employers use temporary workers without much hesitation. However, some public employers, such as hospitals, have a policy not to hire in labour, because they regard it as too expensive and are afraid that their own employees will be tempted to start work with a hiring-out firm because they would be better paid. A non-socialist government introduced the 1993 legislation, but the social democrats made no changes to it when they returned to power. Instead, they have acceded to the trade unions' demands by appointing the government working group. By and large, the trade unions are opposed to temporary work, but they seem to be adapting to its existence and try to exert some influence on the sector by concluding collective agreements. As a form of work, it seems to be gradually more accepted and at the same time better integrated into the traditional Swedish model of labour relations. The trade unions indicate that they have accepted temporary work, and are now determined to obtain as good working conditions as possible for the employees. The growth of collective agreements clearly shows the line taken by the Swedish trade unions: if you cannot beat them, join them. The Swedish labour market and labour law have to adapt to current changes, and they have successfully managed to do this in a traditional way: by securing labour standards for 'atypical employees' at the same level as for 'typical employees'.

This quickly expanding area of Swedish working life has recently attracted interest from social science research. Several research projects have examined private employment agencies and temporary work from different perspectives. Research results give a somewhat contradictory picture. Most temporary employees say that they like their job, yet the average time of employment with an employment leasing company is only a year. One of the reasons for this extreme mobility is economic insecurity. Wage security has advanced considerably in the last years. Initially, there was no wage guarantee for a temporary employee who was not hired out. In 1996, about 35 per cent of temporary employees had some kind of wage guarantee, which was often 50 per cent of normal pay. In 1998, the majority received 75 per cent of normal pay when not hired out, and today the majority have full or almost full pay regardless of whether they are hired out or not. There are also groups of temporary employees who are much better paid in working as temporary employees than in ordinary employment performing the same job.

Conclusions drawn from surveys about temporary work have recently also inspired discussions regarding stress and over-demanding working conditions in the Swedish labour market, which seem to be one of the reasons for extremely high absence from work due to illness. Streamlining of operations in the last decade, especially in the public sector, has led to a situation where many (mostly rather low qualified) service- and other supporting jobs have been outsourced. The remaining employees are supposed to perform administrative and service tasks alongside their ordinary assignments. By comparison, temporary employees have the advantage of performing the tasks for which they have been trained and restricting the extent of their engagement in the workplace.

In summary, temporary work plays a minor role in the Swedish labour market. Despite a considerable rise in the number of temporary workers in the last years, temporary work affects an insignificant part of the labour market. So far there has not been extensive use of temporary workers. Its advantages and disadvantages are still under discussion. A prevalent view is that temporary work is needed along with other forms of more flexible working; but that it may give rise to a dualistic labour market, with a core of employees that enjoy security of employment and other benefits by virtue of labour and social security legislation as well as collective agreements, and groups on the margin with greater employment insecurity and less social security. It is nevertheless likely that the temporary work sector will continue to grow in Sweden. There is still demand from user companies, temporary work agencies are very competent in specific areas, and they can offer competence and specialized employees at short notice. On the whole, temporary workers are well protected by the legal framework, most of them working on open-ended contracts and being on average well-informed as to their rights. The 'typical employment relationship' continues to be the model on which Swedish labour legislation is shaped. This relationship is in practice increasingly replaced by other 'atypical' ways of performing work. In other words, the 'atypical' is on its way to become 'typical'. Labour and social security legislation should now be considered with this in mind.

BIBLIOGRAPHY

Adlercreutz, A., 'Sweden', in Blanpain, R. (ed.), *International Encyclopaedia of Labour Law and Industrial Relations*, Kluwer 1998.

Adlercreutz, A., *Temporary employment*, Acta Instituti Upsaliensis Iurisprudentiae Comparativae XII, 1970.

Eklund, R., 'A Look at Contract Labour in the Nordic Countries' in *Juridisk Tidskrift* 1995/96 No. 3, pp. 625–654.

Eklund, R., 'Public Employment Exchange and the Use of Temporary Employment Agencies in the Nordic Countries', in *Recht in Europa: Festschrift für Hilmar Fenge*, Verlag Dr. Kovac, 1996.

Eklund, R., 'Deregulation of Labour Law – the Swedish Case', in *Juridisk Tidskrift* 1998/99 No. 3, pp. 531–551.

Fahlbeck, R., 'Employment Exchange and Hiring Out of Manpower in Sweden: From Rigid State Planning to Freedom of The Market' in *Yearbook of Polish Labour Law and Social Policy* Vol. 7, 1995, pp. 247–267 (also contains an unofficial translation of the 1993 act).

Fahlbeck, R., 'Employment Exchange and Hiring Out of Employees in Sweden', in *Tidsskrift for Rettsvitenskap*, 4/95 pp. 589–622 (Quoted as Fahlbeck (1995:1)).

Fahlbeck, R., 'Past, Present and Future Role of the Employment Contract in Labour Relations in Sweden', in Betten, L. (ed.), *The Employment Contract in Transforming Labour Relations*, Kluwer 1995.

Fahlbeck, R., 'Labour and Employment Law in Sweden', in *Juristförlaget i Lund* 1997.

Fahlbeck, R., 'Nothing Succeeds Like Success. Trade Unionism in Sweden', in *Juristförlaget i Lund* 1999.

Fahlbeck, R., and Sigeman, T., *European Employment and Industrial Relations Glossary: Sweden*, European Foundation for the Improvement of Living and Working Conditions. Sweet and Maxwell, 2001.

Numhauser-Henning, A., 'Hiring procedures in Sweden', in *Juridiska Föreningen i Lund* 1986.

Numhauser-Henning, A., *Fixed-Term Contracts of Employment and Temporary Work in Sweden*. Report to ILO 1988 (unpublished).

Nyström, B., 'Sweden', in Blanpain, R. (ed.), *Private Employment Agencies*. Bulletin of Comparative Labour Relations 36, Kluwer 1999.

Nyström, B., 'The legal regulation of Employment Agencies and Employment-Leasing Companies in Sweden', in *International Labor Law and Policy Journal* (in publication).
Sigeman, T., *Contract Labour in Sweden*, Annales Academiae Regiae Scientiarum Upsaliensis, 14/1970.

12. The Netherlands

Dieuwke Visser, Willem Plessen and Antoine Jacobs

1. INTRODUCTION

Flexibility in employment is not just a 20th century phenomenon. It and temporary employment have always been needed since full-time, year-round employment has never been the only form of labour required. The Bible's book of Matthew (20: 1–16) recounts a story describing a form of flexible working where workers were employed by the hour or by the day to bring in the harvest. Closer to home, the Netherlands' Civil Code of 1811 contained two articles concerning the hiring and provision of services and the 1838 Civil Code contained an article on the hiring of domestic servants and working folk. The employment contract was added to the Civil Code in 1907 and the temporary employment contract was added to the Civil Code in 1999.

Private enterprises were established to service the labour market in the 19th century. Temporary work really became a profit-making business in the Netherlands in the second half of the 20th century, reaching a high-point in the 1990s. Under increasing competition, businesses have been forced to organize themselves in an increasingly flexible manner to respond to the changing external conditions. The need for flexibility and the way temporary work agencies offered their services made agency work ever more important in the Netherlands.

Some facts and figures

In the Netherlands in 2001, temporary work agencies employed about 725,000 temporary workers,[1] 245,000 of which found employment either with a user company or with another company. Of all temporary workers about 20 per cent belong to so-called target groups, such as the long-term unemployed or disabled, immigrants and people re-entering the labour market. About 50 per cent of temporary workers work full-time. The total number of hours worked by temporary workers in 2001 was 367.2 million (*cf.* 1996: 306.1; 1991: 195; 1986: 155.5 million). A good 3 per cent of the total working population in the Netherlands works for a temporary work agency.[2]

A body of laws and regulations apply to temporary workers and temporary work agencies. Some of these specifically provide for temporary work agencies and/or temporary workers, others are general laws that apply equally to employers and employees in general. This chapter begins with a short summary of the history of temporary employment in the Netherlands (Section 2). Section 3 describes the legal framework for temporary work agencies as given by the Act on Allocation of

1. 85 per cent in Phases 1 and 2, 15 per cent in Phases 3 or 4 or with a regular employment contract (*see* Section 5 for further explanation).
2. *Source*: Instroom uitzendkrachten 2001 Algemene Bond Uitzendondernemingen, and Central Bureau for Statistics.

R. Blanpain & R. Graham (eds.), Temporary Agency Work and the Information Society, 225–246

Employees by Intermediaries. The temporary employment contract as defined in the Civil Code as well as other relevant articles in the Civil Code on the employment contract are dealt with in Section 4. This is followed by Section 5 on the Collective Labour Agreement for Temporary Workers as concluded between the three major trade unions[3] and the major employers' federation for temporary work agencies, the *Algemene Bond Uitzendondernemingen* (ABU). This collective agreement will be referred to as the ABU CLA. Section 6 deals with some other relevant issues related to temporary agency work, such as a special procedure for dismissal and the EU directive on fixed-term contracts.

2. HISTORY (THE LEGAL SITUATION AND ITS CONTEXT – PAST AND PRESENT)

2.1 Past

Temporary work agencies existed before World War II, but their number was negligible. In 1930 a law was passed introducing a public employment service for each municipality (Job Placement Act, *Arbeidsbemiddelingswet* 1930). The public employment service became state-run in 1940, and was placed under the supervision of the Ministry of Social Affairs in 1954. The 1930 *Arbeidsbemiddelingswet* prohibited profit-making employment services. However, as there were many gaps in this act, commercial enterprises for temporary work, recruitment and outplacement offices and job hunters emerged all the same. In the 1950s the number of private temporary work agencies increased rapidly. Different sectors of industry in need of extra labour offered attractive possibilities for temporary workers. But also employees doing office work – such as shorthand typists – started to work by means of a temporary work agency. These were mainly women, often working part-time.

In 1958 the judgement of a magistrate in the Amsterdam Court stated that working through a temporary work agency was not a form of 'job placement' as prohibited by the *Arbeidsbemiddelingswet*. This judgement was confirmed by the Supreme Court in later rulings. The same issue produced considerable litigation because temporary employment was not only provided by agencies. There were also quite a number of outlawed activities in this field. In the shipbuilding and steel industries 'press-ganging', moonlighting, failure to pay taxes and social security contributions and non-observance of regulations on working time were common. Despite these malpractices, cases brought in order to prohibit private temporary work agencies were not successful.

In 1962, to prevent the activities of fraudulent contractors paying higher wages and to prevent abuses in the shipping industry a governmental wage control measure was issued. Employees hired out to user companies were to be paid at the level of wages paid to the employees of the user enterprise. This wage control measure was not successful. Other regulations to protect labour relations followed. In 1965 the Temporary Agency Work Act (*Wet op het ter beschikking stellen van arbeidskrachten, Wet TBA*)[4] was introduced. Temporary employees working for temporary work agencies were regarded equal to 'normal' employees under the social security and tax laws. Furthermore this act gave the possibility to create a licence

3. These trade unions are: *FNV Bondgenoten, Dienstenbond CNV* and *De Unie*.
4. Wet op het ter beschikkingstellen van arbeidskrachten, *Staatsblad* 1965, 379.

system for temporary work agencies. It was not until 1970 that the licence system[5] for temporary work agencies became obligatory. The licence contained a number of conditions to be fulfilled by agencies, such as: temporary work was only allowed for temporary assignments, the duration of assignments was limited by a maximum period (over the years this has varied from 3 to 6 months or 1,000 hours), temporary agency work was forbidden in the construction and road haulage industries. Temporary workers' wages had to be equal to the wages of employees in the same or similar jobs in the user enterprise.

The reason for introducing the licence system was the occurrence of riots in the steel industry and wage differences between steel industry employees and the temporary workers provided by agencies, with temporary workers often earning considerably more. Of the 1,500 licenses requested, only 400 were awarded to temporary work agencies. Initially, a new licence was required each year, but as of 1985 renewal was required every four years.

On 1 January 1991, the Employee Placement Act (*Arbeidsvoorzieningswet*)[6] came into force, providing the legal framework for temporary employment and replacing both the 1930 Job Placement Act and the 1965 Temporary Agency Work Act. The licensing system was continued, but licences were no longer limited in duration. Conditions attached to the licence were given in the Regulation for the Allocation of Workers (*Regeling voor het ter beschikking stellen van arbeidskrachten*).[7] These included conditions on the maximum duration of an assignment, the prohibition on preventing a temporary worker from entering employment with another company, the prohibition on using temporary workers in the construction industry, and the wage ratio rule (*see* Section 3).

2.2 Present: Flexibility and Security

In the 1990s social-cultural changes in employment as well as the economic situation (and the rise of information technology), made clear that changes in labour law were required. There was a clear need for greater flexibility in labour relations, and this was increasingly demanded by employers. Furthermore it had become clear that the allocation function of temporary work agencies could no longer be ignored. Trade Unions reluctantly accepted this demand for flexibility and in return demanded a substantial improvement in the rights of (temporary) workers. In 1996, employers' organizations, unions and government – united in the Labour Foundation StAR (*Stichting van de Arbeid*) – gave a unanimous recommendation to the Minister of Social Affairs and Employment on modernizing labour law, entitled: Flexibility and Security.[8] Employers were to be awarded greater flexibility in their relationship with their employees, and on the other hand more security was to be granted to employees. It aimed at a well-balanced system taking into account the interests of all parties involved, based on the so-called Dutch Polder model.

The recommendation had far reaching consequences for private agencies, both in the rules and regulations comprising the framework on temporary employment (formerly consisting of the licensing system, the Regulation for the Allocation of Workers

5. Decree of 10 September 1970, *Staatsblad* 410.
6. Arbeidsvoorzieningswet, *Staatsblad* 1990, 402.
7. Decree of 17 December 1990 by the Minister of Social Affairs and Employment, Regeling voor het ter beschikking stellen van arbeidskrachten, *Staatscourant* 245.
8. Stichting van de Arbeid, Nota '*Flexibiliteit en Zekerheid*', 3 April 1996 (publication number 2/96).

and the 1991 Employment Services Act) as well as in their relationship with temporary workers. Included in the Flexibility and Security recommendation was a proposal, resulting from an agreement between two federations of temporary work agencies and the three major trade unions, for a new system for hiring out temporary workers by private temporary work agencies. This proposal formed the basis for the collective agreement for temporary workers 1999–2003 (*see* Section 5). It insinuated that the longer the relationship between agency and temporary worker was continued, the more secure the labour contract: from a hire and fire system in the first year, to fixed-term contracts in the second and third year and an indefinite employment contract after three years. The Minister of Social Affairs and Employment embraced the recommendation and proposals for new legislation followed. The Act on Allocation of Employees by Intermediaries[9] (Section 3) came into force on 1 July 1998, and the Flexibility and Security Act[10] was integrated into the Civil Code as of 1 January 1999 (Section 4).

3. ACT ON ALLOCATION OF EMPLOYEES BY INTERMEDIAIRIES

As of 1 July 1998 the framework in public law for temporary work agencies is given in the Act on Allocation of Employees by Intermediaries, the 'Waadi'. This act sees to the regulation of the activities of both temporary work agencies and recruitment agencies.

3.1 Introduction

The Flexibility and Security discussion showed that regulations regarding employment in many cases imposed limitations on the ability of temporary work agencies to carry out their business effectively. According to the StAR and the government, the need for state intervention in the Dutch labour market was no longer required to the same extent. This resulted in the abolition of the licensing system, and most of the conditions that were linked to it. The ban on temporary workers in construction and road haulage was permanently lifted. Furthermore the maximum duration for an assignment was abolished; the Waadi does not limit the duration of an assignment with the user enterprise in any way. As the position of the temporary employee in relation to the temporary work agency improved because of the changes that Flexibility and Security brought to the employment contract, there were no serious objections to long-term assignments.

Despite deregulation, not all obligations and prohibitions continued in the former Employment Services Act and Regulation for the Allocation of Workers were abolished. The Waadi contains four regulations governing temporary work agencies. The most important of these concerns wage-levels for temporary workers (Article 8 Waadi, *see* Section 3.2), the 'wage ratio rule'. Other regulations (*see* Section 3.3) concern:

- no fee-charging of any kind to temporary workers (Article 9 Waadi);
- no additional temporary workers for companies experiencing a strike (Article 10 Waadi);
- providing temporary workers with information on occupational qualifications and safety rules (Article 11 Waadi).

9. Wet allocatie arbeidskrachten door intermediairs (Waadi), Act of 14 May 1998, *Staatsblad* 306 (latest amendment by Act of 29 November 2001, *Staatsblad* 625).
10. Flexibliteit en Zekerheid, Act of 24 December 1998, *Staatsblad* 741.

3.2 The Wage Ratio Rule

Article 8.1 Waadi states that the temporary work agency has to pay the temporary worker wages and other expenses equal to those paid to employees working in the same or similar jobs/positions with the user enterprise itself. There are two exceptions to this rule. If there is a collective agreement applicable to the temporary work agency that determines wages and additional expenses (such as overtime, shifts, costs) for temporary workers, that level of remuneration has to be paid to the temporary worker (Article 8.2). If there is a collective agreement applicable to the user enterprise containing a provision on the remuneration of temporary workers, the user enterprise has to make certain that remuneration paid to temporary workers is in conformity with this provision (Article 8.3). Neither of Articles 8.2 and 8.3 takes precedence over one another. Their relationship is to be negotiated by social partners in collective agreements. Evidently, a good deal of self-regulation is expected of social partners. Articles 8.2 and 8.3 may then cause problems where both collective labour agreements for the temporary work agency and for the user enterprise contain a provision on the wages to be paid to the temporary workers (*see also* Section 3.4).

For that matter, the ABU CLA itself provides a solution for user enterprises wishing that their collective agreement remuneration provision applies to temporary workers: the wage provision should be notified to the Foundation Notification Office for the Temporary Agency Sector (*Stichting Meldingsbureau Uitzendbranche*, SMU). This arrangement was set up by the employers' federation and trade unions for the temporary agency sector, and incorporated in the collective agreement for temporary workers. It gives priority to wage provisions for temporary workers in other collective agreements over the wage provisions in the collective agreement for temporary workers, provided the 'other' wage provision has been notified to the SMU.

Recently the ABU fundamentally criticized Article 8 of the Waadi. In its opinion Article 8 must lapse: only the employers of the temporary workers, that is the temporary employment agencies (*see* Section 4), should have competence to negotiate their employment conditions. The ABU considers that Article 8, by giving to other employers and trade unions the competence to negotiate employment conditions of their workers to other employers and trade unions, infringes upon the right of the ABU to bargain collectively – as established in ILO Conventions 87 and 96 and in Article 6 European Social Charter. Furthermore because of this provision temporary employment agencies might be forced to pay temporary workers performing the same work for different user enterprises unequally, thus violating the principle of equal treatment. This opinion is now under discussion in the StAR.

3.3 Conflict of Scope

An additional problem is that some collective agreements, under provisions on their scope, regard regulation of temporary workers, and sometimes temporary work agencies in their sector, as within their remit. Consequently, not only wages and other expenses would have to be paid to temporary workers, but all other employment conditions (permitted types of employment contract, pension scheme, training funds, additional insurance et cetera) would equally apply. Such a provision in another sector's collective agreement results in a conflict of scope. In that instance, one and the same temporary worker and temporary work agency are covered by two different collective agreements. Solutions to specific conflicts were provided by sectoral employers' federations and unions, but this problem required a more comprehensive solution. In October 2001, the StAR sent a recommendation on the demarcation of employment conditions for temporary workers in the collective agreement for temporary workers and in other collective agreements.

The essence of the recommendation is the 'majority criterion': in general the collective agreement of the temporary work agency sector applies to temporary workers, unless the temporary work agency mainly (i.e. more than 70 per cent of cases) hires out temporary workers in one and the same sector. In that case it is the collective agreement of the particular sector which applies.

3.4 Other Regulations of the Waadi

The temporary work agency will charge a fee to the user enterprise based on wages, taxes, social security contributions, holiday pay etc., and of the expenses for the services rendered by the agency. However, as Article 9 of the Waadi states, under no circumstances can any kind of fee be charged to the temporary worker for being given an assignment through a temporary work agency.

Article 10 of the Waadi prohibits temporary work agencies from providing services to companies experiencing a labour conflict, whether it is a strike, a lock-out or occupation by the user enterprise personnel. The prevailing view on this is that the ban only concerns providing extra personnel so as to prevent the use of temporary workers to break a strike or other labour conflict.[11]

According to Article 11 of the Waadi, the temporary work agency has to obtain from the user enterprise all relevant information on occupational qualifications as well as information on the health and safety rules for the job concerned, before sending a temporary worker on an assignment with the user enterprise. This information has to be passed in writing to the temporary worker before the start of the assignment.

4. THE DUTCH CIVIL CODE AND THE TEMPORARY EMPLOYMENT CONTRACT

In addition to the Waadi, there are many other rules and regulations of both private and public law concerning temporary workers. The main private law rules are given in the Civil Code, Book 7, in the chapter on employment contracts. This section deals with the temporary employment contract and the Civil Code in general (Section 4.1), and with the three most relevant articles regarding the temporary employment contract (Sections 4.2–4.4). Other rules and regulations can be found in the Act on Occupational Health and Safety, the Working Hours Act, the Works Council Act, non-discrimination acts etc. Some of these will be discussed in Section 4.2 as well.

4.1 The Civil Code and the Temporary Employment Contract

Before 1 January 1999 there was little certainty on the status of the temporary employment contract. It was regarded as a regular employment contract by some.[12] Others argued it was not a regular labour contract because not all requirements for

11. President Rechtbank (Tribunal) Roermond, 2 July 1996, KG 1996, 257.
12. Hoge Raad (Supreme Court) 23 May 1988, NJ 1980, 633.

such a contract (as stated in the Civil Code, chapter on labour contracts)[13] were fulfilled. Generally it was accepted that a contract existed for the duration of an assignment, which terminated at the end of the assignment. This was to be agreed upon by the user enterprise, taking into account the regulation on the maximum duration of an assignment. Under tax law and social security law the temporary workers were regarded as employees of the work agency (with regard to liability for income tax and social security contributions; *see also* Section 6.3). Many other issues were taken care of in the Collective Labour Agreement for Temporary Workers (*cf.* Section 5). The temporary employee was only paid for the hours worked, and was entitled to holiday pay and a number of paid holidays. When sick, the assignment ended and generally the (former) temporary employee was then entitled to social security sickness benefit. Where there was no new assignment at the end of an assignment, the temporary employee became unemployed and could be entitled to unemployment benefit.

As mentioned in Section 2 above, the Flexibility and Security Act that came into force on 1 January 1999, created several changes in the chapter on employment contracts in the Civil Code (Book 7, Chapter 10). An important change for the temporary work agencies was a new Section on 'special provisions regarding the temporary employment contract', containing two Articles (7:690 and 7:691 CC) in the CC chapter on employment contracts. No more discussions as to the legal status of the temporary employment contract or the temporary worker: the temporary worker is an employee of the temporary work agency. Another important new article was the article on fixed-term contracts (Article 7:668a CC allowing three fixed-term employment contracts over a period of three years).

The chapter on employment contracts in the Civil Code (Book 7) contains the general provisions that apply to the employer and employee relationship. Some of these provisions are mandatory. Many, however, are not mandatory, allowing deviation by means of individual employment contract or by collective agreement. Provisions that allow express deviation by individual contract are termed 'semi-mandatory'; provisions that allow deviation by collective agreement are called 'three-quarters mandatory'. The Collective Labour Agreement for Temporary Workers contains many articles that deviate from the Civil Code provisions, thereby creating an even more flexible system of temporary employment contracts than would otherwise be allowed under the Civil Code (*see* Section 5).

4.2 The Temporary Employment Contract, Article 7:690 CC

> 'The temporary employment contract is an employment contract whereby one party, the employee, is hired out by another party, the employer, in furtherance of the employer carrying on its profession or trade, to a third party in order to perform work under the supervision and direction of that third party pursuant to an order placed by the latter with the employer.'

This definition contains six main elements:
(1) the employee (the temporary worker);
(2) the employer, carrying on its profession or trade (the temporary work agency);

13. The three requirements given by Article 7:610 CC, carrying out work, remuneration and, in particular, a relationship of authority were not always fulfilled in the relationship between temporary worker and temporary work agency.

(3) hiring out to perform work;
(4) under the supervision and direction of a third party;
(5) the third party (the user enterprise);
(6) pursuant to an order placed by the third party with the employer.

The temporary worker thus is a 'normal' employee within the meaning given in the Civil Code, with all due rights and obligations of employees. Such rights include for instance (minimum) wages, paid holidays and holiday allowance, payment of salary during sickness, parental leave, adjustment of working hours et cetera.

The employer is a temporary work agency carrying on its profession or trade. A definition of this notion is given in the Collective Agreement for Temporary Work in the article on the scope of the agreement: of the annual wages paid by the agency, which are assessable under the national insurance scheme, at least 50 per cent must be paid under temporary employment contracts. So the special provisions for temporary employment contracts only apply to employers actually performing the allocation function.

The temporary worker is hired out by the temporary work agency to perform work within a user enterprise. The work is performed under the supervision and direction of the user enterprise, the third party. This means that the user enterprise has the authority to give instructions to the temporary worker regarding the work to be performed. Authority to give instructions on other issues related to the employment contract remains with the employer, the temporary work agency. The temporary worker has to follow the instructions given by the user enterprise and has to comply with all rules that apply within the user enterprise, for instance on health and safety rules.

The definition of the temporary employment contract makes clear the triangular relationship between the three parties involved. But, however, much authority the user enterprise holds, there is no contractual relationship between it and the temporary worker. Rather, it has a contractual relationship with the temporary work agency, as the user enterprise places an order with the temporary work agency, to which the agency then responds by providing the temporary worker.

However, regardless of the fact that there is no contractual relationship between temporary worker and user enterprise, the user enterprise is assigned by law certain tasks and responsibilities of an employer.

Both the Act on Occupational Health and Safety (*Arbeidsomstandighedenwet*)[14] and the Working Hours Act (*Arbeidstijdenwet*)[15] regard the user enterprise as responsible for fulfilling their requirements in relation to temporary staff working under the user's supervision and direction. Health and safety rules, working conditions, working hours, days and shifts for both user enterprise staff and hired temporary workers must comply with labour regulations. These responsibilities cannot be taken on by the temporary work agency as they are beyond its control. As an employer, the temporary work agency does have its own responsibilities under the Act on Occupational Health and Safety and Working Hours Act, such as on absenteeism policy. Under Article 7:658 CC, the employer (agency as well as user enterprise) is obliged to ensure safety in the workplace for his own employees and temporary workers. The employer (agency and user enterprise) is liable for any injury the

14. Arbeidsomstandighedenwet 1998, Act of 18 March 1999, *Staatsblad* 184 (latest amendment by Act of 6 December 2001, *Staatsblad* 584).
15. Arbeidstijdenwet 1995, Act of 23 November 1995, *Staatsblad* 598 (latest amendment by Act of 18 March 1998, *Staatsblad* 184).

employee suffers in performing his work, unless the employer can prove that he had fulfilled all safety obligations, or that an accident at work was caused by the deliberate recklessness of the employee.

Another act that treats the user enterprise as the temporary worker's employer is the Works Councils Act.[16] Temporary workers have employee participation rights, as deprived by the act, in the temporary work agency from the first day of employment. In this they are equal to temporary work agency corporate staff. Temporary workers who have performed work in the user enterprise for a period of at least 24 months are to be regarded as employees of the user enterprise under all provisions in the Works Councils Act as well. They have to be informed in the same way as user enterprise staff. They are entitled to vote after having worked in the user enterprise for 30 months, and are eligible as members of the user Works Council after working in the user enterprise for 36 months, which is, in practice, an infrequent occurrence.

4.3 Some Special Provisions, Article 7:691 CC

1. Article 7:668a CC shall not apply to the temporary employment contract until temporary work has been performed for more than 26 weeks.
2. The temporary employment contract may contain a written clause stipulating that the contract will terminate if the assignment for which the temporary worker is hired out by the temporary work agency to the third party as described in Article 690 is ended on the request of the third party. If the temporary employment contract contains such a clause, the employee can immediately terminate the temporary employment contract.
3. A clause of the type described in paragraph 2 is no longer effective if the employee has been working for more than 26 weeks for the employer. After the expiry of this period the employee may no longer terminate the contract as described in paragraph 2.
4. For the calculation of the periods, referred to in paragraphs 1 and 3, periods in which work is performed with intervals of less than one year are taken into account.
5. For the calculation of the periods, referred to in paragraphs 1 and 3, periods in which work is performed for different employers where, with respect to the work performed, a later employer must reasonably be considered to be the successor of an earlier employer, have to be taken into account.
6. This article does not apply to a temporary employment contract whereby the employer and the third party belong to the same group of companies as described in Article 2:24b CC or for which one company is a daughter company of the other company as described in Article 2:24a CC.
7. Deviation to the detriment of the employee from the terms referred to in paragraphs 1, 3, 4 and 5 is only possible by collective labour agreement or by a regulation by or on behalf of an authorized government/administrative body.

Article 7:691 CC gives the extra flexibility that was common practice in temporary employment contracts in the past (with a restriction on the duration of an

16. Wet op de Ondernemingsraden, Act of 28 January 1971, *Staatsblad* 54 (amendments in 2000 and 2001, latest amendment by Act of 20 December 2001, *Staatsblad* 692).

assignment). However, now this highly flexible system limits the length of an assignment to 26 'worked' weeks – meaning only the weeks in which the temporary worker actually works are counted. After 26 worked weeks the regular labour law contract as defined in Article 7:668a CC applies (*see* Section 4.4).

Article 7:691.2 CC gives a description of the so-called temporary stipulation: the contract ends the moment the assignment at the user enterprise ends, which is to be decided by the user enterprise. This is a unique way of ending an employment contract in the Netherlands in that termination is not determined by objective conditions.[17] It is this temporary stipulation that makes this a highly flexible 'hire-and-fire' system. The assignment begins the moment the temporary worker starts working at the user enterprise and ends either the moment the user enterprise decides it should, or the moment the temporary worker decides that he/she no longer wishes to work at the user enterprise. So there is extreme flexibility, for both user enterprise and for temporary worker. On the other hand, flexibility creates a great deal of uncertainty for both parties as little contractual obligations exist between the employer and the employee. It is remarkable is that the employer – the temporary work agency – has no say in the termination of the temporary employment contract during this first period of 26 worked weeks. After the period of 26 worked weeks has expired, the temporary stipulation can no longer be used in the contract. As of that moment, the employer has to conclude a fixed-term contract with the temporary worker. 'Normal' CC-rules and such like apply to both the agency and the temporary worker.

As already mentioned, during this period of 26 weeks, only weeks in which the temporary worker has worked are taken into account. Weeks not worked – due to lack of assignments, or because the temporary worker is sick or on holiday, or for any other reason – are not counted. Unless there is a break of one year or more between two worked weeks, the counting of weeks is not interrupted (Article 7:691.4 CC). In theory, this period could last as much as 26 years.

In Article 7:691.5 CC, the obligation to take into account work performed for successive employers is provided. This situation arises where a temporary worker continues to perform the same work either at the same user enterprise for different employers, or with the same employer for different user companies. The resulting obligation is the outcome of case law addressing abuse of the method of calculating the 26 worked weeks.[18] For example, an agency may first provide a temporary worker to a user enterprise, a fixed-term contract may subsequently be agreed with the user enterprise, followed by the same worker being provided by the temporary work agency at the same user enterprise and so on, in an effort to avoid permanent employment with the user enterprise. This was called the 'revolving door construction'. The notion of successive employers applies to various situations: the employers may be two different temporary work agencies or a temporary work agency and the same user enterprise.[19]

---

17. Normally fixed-term contracts terminate automatically by law on expiry of the agreed term (or for another objective reason such as completion of a specific task or the occurrence of a specific event), and permanent contracts end by taking into account a period of notice (for which the employer requires a dismissal permit from the Legal Officer of the Centre of Work and Income).
18. Two examples: Rechtbank (Tribunal) Amsterdam 20 May 1969, Prg. 1970, 694, and Hoge Raad (Supreme Court) 22 November 1991, NJ 1992, 707.
19. For example, the temporary worker may be working for one temporary work agency at user enterprise X. When X decides do business with another agency, the same temporary worker could continue the assignment by working as a temporary worker for the other agency. Only those weeks worked on the assignment for user enterprise X have to be taken into account by the

The provisions of this article do not apply to hiring out temporary workers within the same group of companies or in case of a mother-daughter company structure (dealt with in Article 7:691.6 CC). The prohibition on such hiring-out is to prevent any company using the flexibility created by this article in order to organize its own flexible working system within the company. The provisions of Article 7:691 CC were explicitly created for companies that are regarded as having an allocation function in the labour market, namely the temporary work agencies.

Paragraph 7 of Article 7:691 CC allows deviation by collective agreement from the terms given in paragraphs 1, 3, 4 and 5. This allows extension of the term in which the temporary employment contract may contain the temporary stipulation, and accordingly in which the temporary worker can immediately terminate the contract. This option is exercised in the ABU CLA (*see* Section 5.2). After this term has expired, the regular (fixed-term) employment contract rules as given in Article 7:668a CC, apply.

4.4 A Series of Fixed-Term Employment Contracts, Article 7:668a CC

1. From the day on which between the same contracting parties
   a. fixed-term employment contracts have succeeded one another over a period of 36 months or more at intervals of no longer than three months, accounting also for those intervals, as of that day the last employment contract shall be deemed to have been concluded for an indefinite term;
   b. more than three fixed-term employment contracts have succeeded one another at intervals of no longer than three months, the last employment contract shall be deemed to have been concluded for an indefinite term as of that day.
2. Paragraph 1 accordingly applies to consecutive employment contracts between an employee and different employers, where a later employer must reasonably be considered to be the successor of an earlier employer with respect to the work performed.
3. (...)
4. (...)[20]
5. Deviation to the detriment of the employee under paragraphs 1 to 4 is only possible by collective labour agreement or by regulation of or on behalf of an authorized government body.

Article 7:668a CC sets out the regular system for fixed-term employment contracts as it was introduced by implementation of Flexibility and Security: namely a maximum of a 'chain' of three fixed-term contracts over a period of three years.

other agency. Weeks worked on earlier assignments are not included. In another example, an employee works on a short fixed-term contract for company X. For some reason the contract is not renewed, but the same worker can continue performing the same work for (user) company X on an assignment by a temporary work agency. A final possibility is the situation in which user enterprise X is taken over by or merges with another company and the temporary worker continues to perform the same work for the 'new' company. Again, only weeks worked on the same assignment or job are taken into account for the counting of 26 worked weeks.

20. Article 668a CC, paragraphs 3 and 4:

'3. Paragraph 1, division (a) and the final clause do not apply to an employment contract concluded for a period of no longer than three months which immediately succeeds an employment contract concluded between the same parties for 36 months or longer.
4. The term of notice is calculated as of the first day of the first employment contract as meant in (a) or (b) of paragraph 1.'

Contracts can succeed immediately or at intervals of no longer than three months, intervals inclusive. Once an interval is longer than three months[21] the chain is broken and a new series of contracts may begin. Apart from the maximum term of three years (intervals inclusive) and the maximum number of three contracts, there is no restriction as to the duration of a contract, nor as to its reason.

Each of the contracts ends on its last day. Neither employer nor employee can prematurely terminate a fixed-term contract (unless this is specifically agreed in either the individual employment contract or the collective agreement). Once the term of three years or the number of three contracts is exceeded, the contract last concluded is converted to a contract for an indefinite period.

The notion of successive employers with respect to the work performed equally applies to regular employment contracts as to temporary employment contracts (*see, supra,* Article 7:691.5 CC). Again, Article 7:668a CC allows the deviation to the detriment of the employee by collective agreement. This option is also exercised in the ABU CLA.

5. COLLECTIVE LABOUR AGREEMENT FOR TEMPORARY WORKERS

5.1 Outline

The Collective Agreement for Temporary Workers dealt with in this paragraph was concluded between the three major trade unions[22] on the one side and the employers' federation for temporary work agencies, the ABU (*Algemene Bond Uitzendondernemingen*) on the other side. It is referred to here as the ABU CLA.

In 1972, the first collective agreement for temporary workers in the office and administrative sector was signed between three unions for office staff on the one hand, and the ABU on the other hand. In 1973, this first ABU CLA was declared 'generally binding' by the Ministry of Social Affairs, so that it applied to all temporary work agencies and all 'office/administrative' temporary workers working for them. It was not until 1987 that the ABU CLA for *all* temporary workers was concluded (covering office, administrative, industrial, skilled and unskilled workers). It was declared generally binding that same year. Since 1990, the collective agreement for temporary workers contains its own remuneration system, the lowest pay level being the statutory minimum wage. The early collective agreements were elementary in that the temporary employment contract had no real legal status and provided for a simple hire-and-fire system with few obligations between temporary worker and temporary work agency.

However, with the introduction of the Flexibility and Security Act, a new collective agreement for temporary workers was introduced, the ABU Collective Agreement for Temporary Workers 1999–2003.[23] Most of its provisions were concluded for a five-year period, particularly those on the legal position of temporary

21. Before Flexibility and Security the interval was 32 days.
22. These trade unions are: *FNV Bondgenoten, Dienstenbond CNV, De Unie.*
23. The ABU CLA covers over 80 per cent of the temporary employment market. All big and most middle-sized temporary work agencies are members of the ABU, as are quite a number of small agencies. Apart from the ABU Collective Labour Agreement, there is also the NBBU Collective Labour Agreement (*Nederlandse Bond voor Bemiddelings- en Uitzendondernemingen*, Dutch Organization for Placement and Temporary Work Agencies), which was concluded with a (very) small trade union, the LBV (*Landelijke Belangen Vereniging*, Nation Association for Workers Interests). The NBBU CLA covers about 5 per cent of the temporary employment market. NBBU members are small and medium-sized temporary work agencies. The NBBU will not be dealt with in this chapter.

workers. Some provisions have a one-year validity and can be renewed or renegotiated on a yearly basis.

This new ABU CLA is more substantial than previous ones. It contains a number of articles on the temporary employment contract, but also articles on remuneration, working time, days of holidays, holiday allowance, special leave, rules that apply during sickness, pensions and training, amongst other things. It envisages the employment contract in a number of varieties, according to two different systems of contracts: the phases system (Section 5.2) and the chain system (Section 5.3). Both systems start with the flexibility of Article 7:691 CC, and end in a permanent employment contract. The chain system closely follows the systems set out in Articles 7:691 CC and 7:668a CC; the phases system makes ample use of the option of deviating from these articles by collective labour agreement. The termination of a temporary employment contract varies with the type of contract concluded (Section 5.4) as does the remuneration (Section 5.5). To conclude this section on the ABU CLA, some other relevant provisions will be briefly discussed (Section 5.6).

5.2 The Phases System

The phases system consists of four consecutive phases, progressing from extreme flexibility with little security for the employee to security for the employee with little flexibility over a period of three years.

Phase 1 is the period of 26 worked weeks as defined in Article 7:691 CC. Only weeks in which the temporary worker actually works are counted to make up this period, regardless of the number of days or hours worked during a week. Weeks of holidays or sickness do not count. Only in the case of an interruption of more than 52 weeks in which the temporary worker has not worked for the temporary work agency, does the phase recommence. During Phase 1 it can be stipulated in writing that the temporary employment contract will terminate if the assignment for which the temporary worker is hired out by the temporary work agency to the user enterprise is terminated at the request of the user. This is a temporary employment contract with a temporary stipulation.

Phase 2 is a period of six months, commencing on continuation of temporary work within a year after Phase 1 has ended. Again, in Phase 2 the employment contract may contain the temporary stipulation, deviating from Article 7:691 CC by collective agreement. To calculate the period of six months, comprising Phase 2, breaks of no longer than three months between two temporary employment contracts will be counted. The counting of Phase 2 recommences after a break between two contracts lasting more than three months, but less than one year. After a break of one year or more, Phase 1 recommences. Any temporary work contract in Phase 2 ends at completion of the six-month period.

Phase 3 comprises a period of 24 months. From the start of Phase 3, the temporary stipulation can no longer be used in the employment contract. On continuation of temporary work immediately following or not more than three months after Phase 2 has ended, the temporary worker is working on a 'regular' fixed-term employment contract as referred to in Article 7:668a CC.

Again the option of deviation by collective labour agreement is used. The period of 36 months has been reduced to 24 months, but the restriction of a maximum of three fixed-term contracts is increased to a maximum of eight fixed-term contracts – with a minimum duration of three months each. In Phase 3, the same interruption rule applies as in Phase 2. In computing 24 months, breaks of no longer than three months are included. After a break between two contracts lasting more than three months, but less than one year, the counting of Phase 3 recommences. After a break of one year or more, Phase 1 recommences.

Once the temporary worker continues working for the temporary work agency after completing Phase 3, immediately or within a period of no longer than three months, the temporary worker is employed under Phase 4. However, there is another means of arriving at Phase 4 – even before finishing the period of 24 months in Phase 3 – which is by working for the same user enterprise for a period of 18 months. Weeks worked in Phase 1 are converted into months and intervals of no longer than three months in Phases 2 and 3 are included in computing these 18 months.

In Phase 4 the temporary worker and the temporary work agency conclude a permanent employment contract. This is more or less the end of flexibility. Both in Phases 3 and 4, all contracted hours have to be paid to the temporary worker for the duration of the employment contract, including during illness and idle time (*see also* Section 5.5).

5.3 The Chain System

The chain system follows the system as given by Articles 7:691 and 668a CC, not allowing any deviations to the detriment of the temporary worker. Just like the phases system, it starts with a period of 26 worked weeks, Phase 1. Either during these 26 worked weeks or ultimately on continuation within a year after finishing the period of 26 worked weeks, the parties to the temporary employment contract may decide to continue according to the 'regular' law governing employment contracts. This is known as the chain system of three fixed-term contracts within a period of three years, governed by Article 7:668a CC. Once this system has been chosen, it is no longer possible to opt for the application of the phases system (unless of course there is an interruption of a year or longer).

As the chain system only offers the possibility of three fixed-term contracts for a period of maximum three years it is significantly less flexible. So why make use of the chain system? The chain system is often used when it is clear in advance that an assignment with the same user enterprise may last longer than 18 months. In this way, the significance of the 18 months under the phases system (resulting in a permanent employment contract) is avoided and the obligation of a permanent employment contract is postponed till after 26 worked weeks and an additional three years (maximum). Another reason for using the chain system – especially in times of scarcity of temporary workers, as in 1999 and 2000 – is to offer more security to a temporary worker, in order to retain the worker for a longer period. Just like the phases system, the chain system eventually ends in a permanent employment contract (after maximum 26 worked weeks and a further three years).

5.4 Possibilities for Termination

As stipulated in Article 7:691 CC, the temporary worker may at any time terminate a temporary employment contract containing the temporary stipulation with immediate effect (during Phases 1 and 2). According to the ABU CLA, the temporary worker must notify the temporary work agency of the intention to terminate the contract prematurely no later than one working day prior to termination. This gives the agency some time to seek a substitute for the user enterprise. The temporary work agency will notify the temporary worker of the imminent termination of the assignment and temporary employment contract accordingly, unless the contract has lasted for two months or more. In that case the temporary worker has to be notified seven calendar days prior to the end of the assignment.

Fixed-term temporary employment contracts terminate by law – without any notice being required – by expiry of the term. A temporary worker may prematurely terminate a fixed-term contract, so long as the applicable term of notice is observed. This term of notice is one week for contracts lasting three months or less, of two weeks for contracts lasting more than three months but less than six months, and of one month for contracts lasting more than six months and permanent contracts. In all cases the period of notice that should be given by the temporary work agency is the statutory period of one month (also requiring a dismissal permit of the Legal Officer of the national Centre for Work and Income, CWI[24]).

5.5 Obligations in Case of Loss of Temporary Work ('Idle Time')

There is ageneral provision in the Civil Code stipulating that the employer has to pay wages for all contracted hours for the duration of the employment contract (Article 7:628 CC). However, this provision is semi-mandatory during the first six months of an employment contract and three-quarter-mandatory after six months. The ABU CLA exercises the option of deviating from this statutory obligation to pay wages for all contracted hours. During Phases 1 and 2 in contracts containing the temporary stipulation, the temporary work agency is only under an obligation to pay a temporary worker for the period(s) in which the temporary worker actually performed work.

In case of a regular fixed-term contract (under the chains system), it is only possible to make use of the provision precluding the obligation to continue to pay wages for a period of six months, following the first 26 worked weeks. This provision will not apply under a fixed-term contract in the event that the temporary worker is sick, if the contract is at that time still in force.

For Phases 1 and 2, the situation is quite straightforward: hours worked are paid and the moment the assignment ends, the obligations between temporary work agency and temporary worker also end. If fulfilling the requirements for unemployment or sickness benefit, the temporary worker will be entitled to such a benefit once the assignment has ended.

For fixed-term and permanent employment contracts, however, the situation is more complicated. The general rule that wages have to paid for all hours worked (Article 7:628 CC) does apply to all fixed-term employment contracts under Phase 3, which do not contain a provision precluding the obligation to continue paying wages, and to permanent employment contracts. Therefore, where under such a contract, the assignment ends before the contract ends, the temporary work agency is obliged to continue paying in full the agreed wage during this 'idle time' for the duration of the temporary employment contract. Yet, the collective agreement also obliges both the

24. The CWI is a public institution with representatives from employers' and employees' federations and municipal authorities, responsible for, amongst other things, unemployment benefits, work permits and dismissal permits. *See also* www.cwinet.nl

temporary work agency to look for suitable substitute temporary work to offer to the temporary worker and the temporary worker to accept suitable work. Suitable work according to the ABU CLA is work of the same level or not more than two levels lower than the last job performed, involving average hours of work per week/period/month equal to the hours of work agreed in the temporary employment contract. Until suitable substitute work has been offered and accepted or refused, the wages for the previous assignment have to be paid. If work is offered and accepted for fewer hours than the hours agreed in the previous assignment, the agency is obliged to top up the temporary worker's wages to the previously agreed wages. If the temporary worker has refused a reasonable offer for suitable substitute work, the temporary work agency is no longer under the obligation to pay wages to the temporary worker.

As long as no suitable substitute work is found for the temporary worker, the temporary work agency will use its best efforts to find and offer the temporary worker concerned suitable work. In order to achieve re-employment during the period of idle time, the agency and the temporary worker discuss opportunities, wishes and possibilities as well as the possibility of additional training. The obligation to search for suitable substitute work of course ends when a fixed-term employment contract terminates. However, after sufficient re-employment efforts, it may become clear that there is no suitable employment available for the temporary worker and re-employment for the remaining period of the employment contract has proved impossible. Thus the temporary work agency may establish that, for reasons of business economy, the job of the temporary worker concerned has to be terminated. The agency may apply to the Centre of Work and Income, legal department, for a permit to dismiss the temporary worker. The request for a permit to dismiss the temporary worker who has worked less than five years for the agency may not be made earlier than one month after the last assignment has terminated (five to ten years: three months; ten years or more: four months).[25] This point is further discussed in Section 6.1 on the directive on dismissal of temporary workers.

5.6 Other Provisions

Before concluding this section on the ABU CLA, some other provisions of the collective agreement should be dealt with, namely those dealing with holidays, pension scheme, training and remuneration.

As mentioned before a temporary worker is entitled to paid holidays. A temporary worker acquires the right to sixteen hours of holiday for each working month fully worked, or a proportionate part thereof if a working month has not been worked in full, amounting to 24 days per year fully worked. This is four days more than the statutory minimum of 20 days (Article 7:634 CC). Furthermore the temporary worker is entitled to a holiday allowance of 8 per cent of the basic hourly wage earned monthly for normal hours worked. The holiday allowance is paid out once a year in June, or, where a temporary employment contract ends and is not renewed, ultimately six weeks after termination of the contract.

The 1999–2003 ABU CLA for the first time includes a provision on a pension scheme for temporary workers. All temporary workers that have been employed for at least 26 weeks by one temporary work agency and who are aged 21 years or older

25. For calculating these periods, all phases and chains are included, Phases 1 and 2 together counting as one year worked, intervals of less than three months between fixed-term contracts inclusive.

are covered by this pension scheme for temporary workers. It takes the form of a pension scheme based on a defined contribution, with the premium being 3.5 per cent of gross wages. A temporary work agency may charge a maximum of a third of the pension premium to the temporary workers, deducting this from the remuneration to be paid to the temporary worker.

Another new element in this collective agreement is training, defined as any form of structured activity aimed at the temporary worker acquiring, keeping up, expanding or gaining more in-depth knowledge and/or skills. As soon as a temporary worker has performed work for at least 26 weeks for one agency, the agency must discuss with the temporary worker his/her training needs. The temporary work agency is by collective agreement required to spend a certain percentage of the aggregate of the annual wages payable to temporary workers on training (2001: 0.82 per cent; 2002: 0.92 per cent).

The wage ratio rule was already described in Section 3. In practice, wages should be paid to temporary workers either according to the remuneration system of the user enterprise (in case of notification of the user's remuneration provision to the SMU) or according to the pay scheme for temporary workers. The pay scheme for temporary workers includes a table to determine the basic hourly wages according to the categorization, by function group, of the work performed and an increment based on number of weeks worked for the temporary work agency. The function group (1–9) is determined by taking into account the nature of the work, the required knowledge, skills and experience and the required degree of independence.

Function group 1, increment 1 starts with an hourly wage that is little more than the statutory minimum wage. For so-called target groups the pay scheme also contains a special 'starters-table' for function groups 1–3, all beginning with an hourly wage at the statutory minimum. The starters-table applies for a maximum period of one year (26 worked weeks plus six months). Temporary workers belonging to the target groups are: temporary workers with no prior working experience, formerly (long-term) unemployed and incapacitated/disabled workers, people re-entering the labour market, school-leavers and holiday workers. After one year they enter the regular table. The pay scheme also includes compensation for working overtime and irregular hours.

6. SOME OTHER ISSUES RELATED TO TEMPORARY AGENCY WORK

In this section, three additional issues that are relevant to temporary agency work will be briefly discussed: the Decree on dismissals and Appendix B relating to dismissals of temporary workers (Section 6.1), new legislation as a result of the EU Directive on fixed-term work (Section 6.2) and (liability for) payment of social security contributions and taxes for temporary workers (Section 6.3).

6.1 Decree on Dismissals, Appendix B

Before the introduction of the article on the temporary employment contract in the Civil Code, termination of a temporary employment contract was simple. Each contract ended at the end of the assignment, and in any case at the end of the maximum term of assignment. Notice by the employer of termination of a permanent employment contract[26] requires a permit from the Legal Officer of the Centre for Work and

26. Also for the premature termination of a fixed-term employment contract containing a term of notice.

Income (regulated in the Extraordinary Labour Relations Decree 1945 and the Decree on Dismissals).[27] Until such a permit is obtained, any notice given by the employer is null and void, and does not terminate the employment contract. One of the grounds for dismissal – which must be given and substantiated when applying for a permit – is business economy.

With the introduction of Flexibility and Security, flexibility in temporary employment contracts has become limited in time. As the relationship between temporary worker and temporary work agency proceeds, at some point a long-lasting fixed-term or permanent employment contract may follow. Consequently, regular dismissal procedures apply as well. This was an important element of concern for temporary work agencies during the Flexibility and Security legislation process. The concern mainly focussed on dismissal on economic grounds and the accompanying notion of seniority. Business economy as a ground for dismissal is established when after a certain period of looking for suitable employment no such employment can be found (*see* Section 5.5). Seniority here means first in, last out (or last in, first out) when there are several employees with comparable jobs. Dismissal might require the exchange of temporary workers working for different user companies and employed by different branches of the same agency.

The concern over dismissal of temporary workers and 'seniority' was tackled by the StAR in an advice to the Minister of Social Affairs and Employment. The advice was incorporated in the Decree on Dismissals and a separate Appendix B, 'Dismissals in the temporary employment sector' was added to the Decree.[28] The essence for all employers, and so for the temporary work agency as well, is that to determine seniority the agency only has to exchange the 're-employable' temporary worker with comparable workers (if there are any) working for the same branch of the agency. In addition to this, the exchanging of such comparable workers is limited to temporary workers working in comparable functions in the same user enterprise and/or in other user enterprises where at least four temporary workers are working for that enterprise in the comparable function. For both situations, only assignments that will last at least two more months as of the moment that the assignment of the re-employable temporary worker ended have to be taken into account for exchanging. The purpose of exchanging is to dismiss the comparable temporary worker with the least seniority of the branch concerned. However, where there are no possibilities for exchanging or where the user enterprise doesn't want to co-operate, a dismissal permit will be issued by the CWI if the agency gives a convincing explanation why exchanging was not successful. So the seniority rule of 'last in first out' is specially adapted to the needs of both temporary workers and temporary employment agencies.

6.2 European Council Directive on Fixed-term Work[29]

On 8 November 2002, the Act of 7 November 2002 implementing Council Directive 1999/70/EC of 28 June 1999 concerning the framework agreement on fixed-term employment contracts concluded by ETUC, UNICE and CEEP[30] came into force in

27. Buitengewoon Besluit Arbeidsverhoudingen 1945, Decree of 5 October 945, *Staatsblad* F 214 (latest amendment bij Act of 29 November 2001, *Staatsblad* 625) and Ontslagbesluit, Decree of 7 December 1998, *Staatscourant* 238 (latest amendment 6 March 2003, *Staatscourant* 49, p. 24).
28. Decree of the Minister of Social Affairs and Employment of 7 December 1998, *Staatscourant* 238.
29. Council Directive 1999/70/EC of 28 June 1999 Council Directive 1999/70/EC of 28 June 1999 concerning the framework agreement on fixed-term work concluded by ETUC, UNICE and CEEP.
30. *Staatsblad* 2002, 560.

the Netherlands. The act prohibits discrimination between comparable workers on the basis of the type of employment contract. The initial Bill concerning this directive made the non-discrimination principle equally applicable to temporary workers and 'regular' employees. This was a serious point of concern to the temporary work agencies as they considered it would be virtually impossible to comply fully with such a non-discrimination principle. First of all the notion of the comparable worker is not always clear: it is the worker of the user enterprise or the fellow temporary worker at the agency. Furthermore the proposed Bill would create substantial administrative, financial and legal constraints on temporary work agencies since compared to user enterprise workers, the employment conditions of temporary workers would have to change with each new assignment. The competitiveness of the temporary work agency sector might also be blunted by such a non-discrimination principle. For these reasons, as well as the awaited agreement and/or directive on temporary agency work, the framework agreement explicitly excludes temporary workers from the said directive: 'This agreement applies to fixed-term workers with the exception of those placed by a temporary work agency at the disposition of a user enterprise. It is the intention of the parties to consider the need for a similar agreement relating to temporary agency work.'[31] So in the Dutch legislation process the Bill was amended[32] and the temporary employment contract (Article 7:690 CC) was excluded in the definitive Act. And, as mentioned, it now is one of the issues at stake in the (draft) EU Directive on temporary agency work.[33]

6.3 Social Security Contributions and Taxes

Since the introduction of the 1965 Temporary Agency Work Act (*see* Section 2), temporary employees working for temporary work agencies are treated as regular employees of the temporary work agencies under the social security and tax laws. Thus the temporary work agency is required to deduct taxes and social security contributions from the wages of temporary workers as well as to pay the employer's contributions. Although it is primarily the obligation of the temporary work agency, ultimately the user enterprise is also liable for paying the taxes and the social security contributions where the agency does not or cannot fulfil this obligation. This statutory user enterprise liability is regulated by both the Social Security Co-ordination Act[34] and the Collection of State Taxes Act 1990.[35] Until the introduction of the Waadi (1 July 1998), a user enterprise could indemnify itself against this liability by doing business with a licensed temporary work agency and reporting the posting of a temporary worker to the relevant industrial insurance board. This indemnification procedure was not included in the Waadi.

However, since business required some kind of indemnification procedure, the system of a 'frozen account' (*Geblokkeerde rekening*) was introduced, which was already in use in the construction sector. Under this system the temporary work agency concludes a frozen account agreement with the tax authorities and/or the implementation institute for employee insurance schemes (*Uitvoering Werknemersverzekeringen*,

31. Annex to the Council Directive 1999/70/EC, preamble of the ETUC-UNICE-CEEP framework.
32. TK 27 661, 2001–2002, No. 12, Amendment by parliamentarian Weekers c.s.
33. COM (2002)149 def. of 20 March 2002.
34. Coordinatiewet Sociale Verzekering, Act of 24 December 1953, *Staatsblad* 1953, 577 (latest amendment by Act of 12 December 2002, *Staatsblad* 2002, 615).
35. Invorderingswet 1990, Act of 30 May 1990 (latest amendment: *Staatsblad* 2001, 63).

UWV), and the user enterprise pays part of the invoice from the agency into the frozen account. The user enterprise is indemnified against liability for taxes and/or social security contributions for the amount paid into the frozen account. The administrative requirements that have to be fulfilled to make use of the frozen account are dealt with in a separate implementation regulation.[36] Apart from this statutory indemnification procedure, recourse may be had to private regulations, which do not grant statutory indemnification, but do reduce user enterprise liability. The ABU made use of this option to create a private regulation, as the administrative requirements of the frozen account system would have been very costly. On 1 July 1998, the Financial Review Fund (*Stichting Financiële Toetsing*, SFT)[37] came into operation. All ABU members have to join the SFT and to fulfil its requirements. The SFT regularly checks the payment records of its members with the tax authority and UWV and provides unqualified audit opinions to members that comply with the requirements.

7. CONCLUSION

Temporary agency work has been a well-known phenomenon in the Netherlands throughout the past century, though not always readily accepted. Only since January 1999 has the legal position of the temporary worker in the Netherlands been defined by the Civil Code. It took almost seventy years, from the introduction of the 1930 Job Placement Act, and considerable case law on many issues related to temporary work to arrive at a definition in the Civil Code which classified it as a type of employment contract. Development progressed from little regulation between 1930 and the mid-1960s, to an extremely regulated system of public law, including a licensing system (and the conditions connected to it) until the late 1990s. In the Flexibility and Security discussion, deregulation of public law on temporary employment agencies was an important issue, and with the introduction of the Waadi (July 1998) many of the previous regulations were abolished. When the temporary employment contract was defined in Article 7:690 CC, the legal position of the temporary worker was substantially strengthened. Apart form the special provisions regarding the temporary employment contract, all other Civil Code provisions on the employment contract are equally applicable to temporary workers.

Many of the Civil Code provisions that are relevant for temporary agency work are three-quarter-mandatory, making it possible to deviate from the provisions by collective agreement. As was made clear in Section 5 above, the ABU CLA has exercised the option of deviating from many of its articles. In particular, the phases system makes clear how deviation can be used in order to create a more flexible system for temporary agency work. However, in order to be able to make use of the system of three-quarter-mandatory provisions, it is necessary for the employer (and/or employers' federation) to conclude a collective agreement with one or more trade unions. Collective bargaining thus is essential for the temporary work agency sector in the Netherlands.

In conclusion, it can be said that over the years the temporary work agency sector in the Netherlands has reached maturity. The sector has proven valuable to the Dutch labour market, which resulted in the recognition of the temporary work agency as a responsible employer. Most importantly, the temporary work sector employs more workers than any other employment sector in the Netherlands.

36. Decree of 17 Juni 1998, *Staatscourant* 1998, 113, pp. 10–13.
37. *Staatscourant* 1998, 102, p. 4. The NBBU has a similar fund for its members.

SELECT BIBLIOGRAPHY

Goldschmeding, F.J.D., *Flexible work works*, Sinzheimer Lecture 1997, Hugo Sinzheimer Institute 1998, Amsterdam.

Grapperhaus, F.B.J., and Jansen, M., *De uitzendovereenkomst, Monografieën Sociaal Recht 15*, Kluwer, Deventer 1999.

Grapperhaus, F.B.J., and Verburg, L.G., *Employment Law and Works Councils of the Netherlands*, Allen & Overy Legal Practice, Kluwer Law International, The Hague/London/New York 2002.

Grapperhaus, F.B.J., 'De uitzendkracht en gelijke beloning', in *SMA* 2003, No. 1, pp. 6–15, Kluwer.

Heijden, P.F. van der, Slooten, J.M. van, and Verhulp, E. (Eds.), *Arbeidsrecht, Tekst & Commentaar*, 2nd edition, Kluwer, Deventer 2002.

Plessen, W.G.M., 'Ontslag van de vaste uitzendmedewerker, een paradox opgelost', in *Praktijkblad Arbeidsvoorwaarden* 1999, No. 3, pp. 7–8.

European Reports

13. EU Legislation on Temporary Work

Roger Blanpain

NON-TRADITIONAL FORMS OF WORK

Non-traditional forms of work, like temporary work, part-time, fixed term contracts and telework have been some time on the European legislative agenda. Proposals on some of these issues date from the beginning of the 1980s. Their adoption was never immediate; one or other Member State was always keen to veto them.

The first adopted directive concerns temporary work and fixed term contracts and deals with safety and health at work (Directive 91/383 of 25 June 1991).

A second directive relates to the working conditions of temporary workers employed in another member state within the framework of transnational provision of services (Directive 96/71/EC of 16 December 1996 concerning the posting of workers).

Later directives implemented collective agreements concluded by the European social partners on part-time work (Directive 97/81 of 15 December 1997) and on fixed term contracts (Directive 99/70 of 28 June 1999). A European voluntary agreement on telework, to be implemented by the national social partners themselves, was concluded on 16 July 2002.

In addition, the case law of the European Court of Justice concerning the role of private temporary work agencies in the EU should be considered as well as the recent proposal of the European Commission concerning working conditions for temporary workers.

On 20 March 2002, the European Commission put forward a proposal for a Directive on working conditions for temporary workers.[1] An amended proposal was put on the table on 28 November 2002.[2]

The golden thread running through these various European measures on non-traditional forms of work is permitting greater flexibility in the labour market while adequately protecting the workers concerned.

The aims of the proposed Directive on working conditions for temporary workers are:

1. To ensure the protection of temporary workers and to improve the quality of temporary work by ensuring that the principle of non-discrimination is applied to temporary workers and recognizing temporary agencies as employers;

---

1. Proposal for a Directive of the European Parliament and the Council on working conditions for temporary workers COM/2002/0149 final – COD 2002/0072. *See* 'Commission proposes Directive on temporary agency workers', www.eirofound.ie
2. COM (2002), 701 final (2002/0072 COD).

R. Blanpain & R. Graham (eds.), Temporary Agency Work and the Information Society, 249–276

2. To establish a suitable framework for the use of temporary work to contribute to creating jobs and the smooth functioning of the labour market.

Indeed, the underlying idea is that as far as wages and conditions of work are concerned temporary workers have to be treated in the same way as comparable workers with a contract for an indefinite period and/or working on the normal premises of the employer, thus affirming the fundamental principle of non-discrimination.

These various measures also place an emphasis on the role of the social partners. A number of directives in this area emanate from agreements between the European social partners. It is only when the social partners cannot agree on labour law issues which the EU considers important, that directives will be proposed, as in the case of the latest Commission proposal on temporary work.

In our analysis below we limit ourselves to temporary work.

I. HEALTH AND SAFETY AT WORK

On 25 June 1991, the Council adopted Directive 91/383 supplementing measures to encourage improvements in the health and safety at work of workers with a fixed-duration employment relationship or a temporary employment relationship. The directive is based on Article 137 of the EC Treaty. The preamble to the directive reads that 'recourse to forms of employment such as fixed-duration employment and temporary employment has increased enormously' and 'that research has shown that in general workers with a fixed duration employment relationship or temporary employment relationship are, in certain sectors, more exposed to the risk of accidents at work and occupational diseases than other workers'. These additional risks are linked to particular ways in which new workers are integrated into the undertaking and can be reduced through adequate provision of information and training at the start of employment. The specific situation of these workers and the risks they face call for special rules, supplementing the directives on health and safety, notably Directive 89/391 of 12 June 1989, particularly as regards the provision of information, the training and medical surveillance of the workers concerned.

A. Scope

The directive applies to:

1. *Fixed-duration contracts of employment:* 'concluded directly between the employer and the worker, where the end of the contract is established by objective conditions such as: reaching a specific date, completing a specific task or the occurrence of a specific event' (Article 1(1));
2. *Temporary employment:* 'relationships between a temporary employment business which is the employer and the worker, where the latter is assigned to work for and under the control of an undertaking and/or establishment making use of his services' (Article 1(2)).

These definitions are rather broad. In certain legal systems fixed-duration contracts relate exclusively to contracts which specify their duration, and thus are distinguishable from, for example, seasonal contracts or contracts for the performance of a specific task. Also the definition of temporary work may differ from that used in some Member States as certain definitions relate only to certain types of work, such as those of a limited temporary nature and the like. This means that implementation of the directive into national law may be broader than the topics covered suggest.

B. Object: Equal Treatment

The purpose of the directive is to ensure that temporary workers are afforded, as regards health and safety at work, the same level of protection as other workers in the user undertaking and/or establishment (Article 2(1)), namely workers engaged for an indefinite period.

Article 2(2) clearly affirms this principle: 'the existence of an employment relationship as referred to in Article 1 shall not justify different treatment with respect to working conditions inasmuch as the protection of safety and health at work are involved, especially as regards access to personal protective equipment'. Directive 89/391 of 12 June 1989 and the individual directives concerning health and safety apply in full without prejudice to more binding and/or more specific provisions set out in this directive (Article 2(3)).

C. Provision of Information to Workers

Before a worker commences any activity, he is to be informed by the undertaking (and/or establishment) making use of his services of the risks involved. Under this obligation, the undertaking must give the worker clear indications as to:

1. any special occupational qualifications or skills or special medical surveillance required, as defined in national legislation;
2. specific risks, as defined in national legislation, that the job may entail (Article 3).

Regarding *temporary employment*, Member States shall take the necessary steps to ensure that before workers are supplied, a user undertaking shall specify to the temporary employment business, *inter alia*, the occupational qualifications required and the specific features of the job to be filled; the temporary employment business must bring this information to the attention of the worker concerned. The Member States may provide that all details of the information to be supplied to the worker shall appear in a contract of assignment (Article 7).

D. Workers' Training

Member States shall take the necessary measures to ensure that each worker receives sufficient training appropriate to the particular characteristics of the job, account being taken of his qualifications and experience (Article 4).

E. Use of Workers' Services and Medical Surveillance of Workers

Member States have the option of prohibiting workers from being used for certain work which would be particularly dangerous with regard to their safety and health, and to ensure that they are provided with appropriate special medical surveillance, during and after the employment concerned (Article 5).

F. Protection and Prevention Services

Member States shall take the measures necessary to ensure that protection and prevention agencies are informed of the assignment of workers to the extent necessary to carry out adequately their activities on behalf of all workers in the undertaking (Article 6).

G. Temporary Employment: Responsibility

Member States shall take the measures necessary to ensure that, without prejudice to the responsibilities of the temporary employment business as laid down in national legislation, the user undertaking and/or establishment is responsible, for the duration of the assignment, for the conditions governing performance of the work. These conditions are limited to those connected with 'safety, hygiene and health at work' (Article 8).

H. Reporting

Member States have to report to the Commission every five years on the practical implementation of the directive, setting out the points of views of workers and employers. The Commission shall bring the report to the attention of the European Parliament, the Council, the Economic and Social Committee, the Advisory Committee on Safety, Hygiene and Health Protection at Work. The Commission shall submit to the European parliament and the Economic and Social Council a regular report on the implementation of this directive (Article 10).

II. POSTING OF TEMPORARY WORKERS: DIRECTIVE 96/71 OF 16 DECEMBER 1996[3]

Although Directive (96/71) merits applause, it should be clearly stated that this measure combats social dumping only to a certain extent, as not all working conditions are covered, that it does not contribute to greater convergence of working conditions in the Common Market, nor does it simplify the situation for employers.[4]

There is no convergence since the variety of labour regulation systems remains. This does not make matters easier for the employer who will have to be well-informed

3. O.J. C-018, 21 January 1997, 1.
4. 'National legislation which requires an employer, as a person providing a service within the meaning of the Treaty, to pay employer's contributions to the social security fund of the host Member State in addition to the contributions already paid by him to the social security fund of the State where he is established places an additional financial burden on him, so that he is not, so far as competition is concerned, on an equal footing with employers established in the host State.

not only on governmental rules and their interpretation, but also on collective agreements. In practical terms this means that these agreements should be available in all official languages of the Member States. Whether this is really feasible is another matter.

A. Legal Basis

The legal basis of this directive is Article 57(2) EC Treaty, relating to the freedom of services, which allows for a majority vote.

B. Scope of Application

The directive applies to undertakings, established in a Member State, which post workers for a limited period (Article 2(1)) in the framework of transnational services to the territory of a Member State (Article 1(1)) other than the Member State in which the worker normally works (Article 2(1)), in the form of either:

- subcontracting;[5]
- intra-group work;[6]
- temporary work for a user (Article 1(3)), meaning:
  'Being a temporary employment undertaking or placement agency, which hires out a worker to a user undertaking established or operating in the territory of a Member State, provided there is an employment relationship between the temporary employment undertaking or placement agency and the worker during the period of posting' (Article 1(3)(c)).

Member States can provide that temporary workers receive equal treatment compared to other temporary workers active in their territory (Article 3(9)).

The notion of a worker is that which applies in the law of the Member State to whose territory the worker is posted (Article 2(2)).

Merchant navy undertakings are excluded as regards seagoing personnel (Article 1(2)).

The public interest relating to the social protection of workers in the construction industry may, however, because of conditions specific to that sector, constitute an overriding requirement justifying such a restriction on the freedom to provide services. However, that is not the case where the workers in question enjoy the same protection, or essentially similar protection, by virtue of employer's contributions already paid by the employer in the Member State of establishment', which is contrary to Articles 47 and 55 of the EC Treaty (C.O.J., 28 March 1996, *Michel Guiot and Climatec SA*, Case C-272/94, *ECR*, 1996, 1905).

5. This concerns the situation in which undertakings post workers 'to the territory of a Member State on their account and under their direction under a contract concluded between the undertaking making the posting and the party for whom the services are intended, operating in that Member State, provided there is an employment relationship between the undertaking of origin and the worker during the period of posting' (Article 1(3)(a)).

6. This concerns the situation in which undertakings post workers 'to an establishment or to an undertaking owned by the group in the territory of a Member State, provided there is an employment relationship between the undertaking of origin and the worker during the period of posting' (Article 1(3)(b)).

C. Terms and Conditions of Employment

1. Minimum conditions

Working conditions which apply and have to be guaranteed to posted workers, are those laid down by:

1. governmental rules;
2. collective agreements or arbitration awards, which are generally binding,[7] concerning building work;[8] and
3. other collective agreements or arbitration awards, which are generally binding, providing conditions indicated by the Member State (Article 3(10)) other than the minimum conditions specified in the Directive which concern:
   a) working time (maximum work and minimum rest periods);
   b) minimum paid annual vacation;
   c) minimum wage (including overtime);[9]
   d) rules concerning temporary work;
   e) safety, health and hygiene at work;
   f) protection of motherhood, children and youngsters;
   g) equal treatment for men and women and other matters relating to non-discrimination (Article 3(1)).

Though these alone are the minimum conditions applicable to posted workers, they may be improved upon (Article 3(7)(1)).

Prior to implementation of Directive 96/7, the European Court of Justice ruled on the application of normally mandatory conditions to posted workers in a way that influences the interpretation of which of those conditions must apply.

---

7. These are agreements or awards which must be observed by all undertakings in the geographical area and in the profession or industry concerned. In the absence of a system for declaring collective agreements or arbitration awards to be of universal application, Member States may, if they so decide, base their provision of guaranteed working conditions on:
   – collective agreements or arbitration awards which are generally applicable to all similar undertakings in the geographical area and in the profession or industry concerned, and/or collective agreements which have been concluded by the most representative employers and labour organizations at national level and which are applied throughout the national territory, provided that their application to the undertakings referred to in Article 1(1) ensures equality of treatment on matters listed in the first subparagraph of paragraph 1 of this article between those undertakings and the other undertakings referred to in this subparagraph which are in a similar position. Equality of treatment, within the meaning of this article, shall be deemed to exist where national undertakings in a similar position;
   – are subject, in the place in question or in the sector concerned, to the same obligations as posting undertakings as regards the matters listed in the first subparagraph of paragraph 1; and
   – are required to fulfil such obligations with the same effects (Article 3(8)).
8. All building work relating to the construction, repair, upkeep, alteration or demolition of buildings, and in particular the following work: 1) excavation; 2) earthmoving; 3) actual building work; 4) assembly and dismantling of prefabricated elements; 5) fitting out or installation; 6) alterations; 7) renovation; 8) repairs; 9) dismantling; 10) demolition; 11) maintenance; 12) upkeep, painting and cleaning work; 13) improvements.
9. This does not apply to complementary pension schemes (Article 3(1)(iii)). The notion of minimum wage is the wage as defined by law or practice of the posted Member State (Article 3(1) last paragraph). Allocations which go along with the posting are considered to be pay, except when they concern the payment of expenses made, such as for travel, housing and catering (Article 3(7), paragraph 2).

Arblade and Leloup, undertakings situated in France, temporarily carried out works in connection with the construction of a complex of silos, with a capacity of 40,000 tonnes, for the storage of white crystallized sugar on the site belonging to Sucrerie Tirlemontoise at Wanze in Belgium. The question arose under what conditions they could operate in Belgium as far as labour law and related issues were concerned.

The Court answered as follows:

> '1. Articles 59 and 60 of the Treaty do not preclude the imposition by a Member State on an undertaking established in another Member State, and temporarily carrying out work in the first State, of an obligation to pay the workers deployed by it the minimum remuneration fixed by the collective labour agreement applicable in the first Member State, provided that the provisions in question are sufficiently precise and accessible that they do not render it impossible or excessively difficult in practice for such an employer to determine the obligations with which he is required to comply.
>
> 2. These articles preclude the imposition by a Member State of an obligation – even if laid down in public-order legislation – to pay, in respect of each worker deployed, employers' contributions to schemes such as the Belgian *timbres-intempéries* and *timbres-fidélité* schemes, and to issue to each of such workers an individual record, where the undertaking in question is already subject, in the Member State in which it is established, to obligations which are essentially comparable, as regards their objective of safeguarding the interests of workers, and which relate to the same workers and the same periods of activity.
>
> 3. Articles 59 and 60 preclude the imposition by a Member State of an obligation – even if laid down in public-order legislation – to draw up social or labour documents such as labour regulations, a special staff register and an individual account for each worker in the form prescribed by the rules of the first State, where the social protection of workers which may justify those requirements is already safeguarded by the production of social and labour documents kept by the undertaking in question in accordance with the rules applying in the Member State in which it is established. That is the position where, as regards the keeping of social and labour documents, the undertaking is already subject, in the Member State in which it is established, to obligations which are comparable, as regards their objective of safeguarding the interests of workers, to those imposed by the legislation of the host Member State, and which relate to the same workers and the same periods of activity.
>
> 4. Articles 59 and 60 do not preclude the imposition by a Member State of an obligation to keep social and labour documents available, throughout the period of activity within the territory of the first Member State, on site or in an accessible and clearly identified place within the territory of that State, where such a measure is necessary in order to enable it effectively to monitor compliance with legislation of that State which is justified by the need to safeguard the social protection of workers.
>
> 5. Articles 59 and 60 preclude the imposition by a Member State of an obligation – even if laid down in public-order legislation – to retain, for a period of five years after the undertaking in question has ceased to employ workers in the first Member State, social documents such as a staff

register and individual accounts, at the address within that Member State of a natural person who holds those documents as an agent or servant.'[10]

A preliminary reference was also made to the Court in the course of criminal proceedings against Mr. Mazzoleni, in his capacity as manager of Inter Surveillance Assistance SARL (ISA),[11] a company incorporated under French law, and ISA itself, in its capacity as the civilly liable party, for failure to comply with the provisions of Belgian law relating to minimum wages.

The Collective Labour Agreement of 14 June 1993 (the 'CLA'), concluded by the Joint Committee on Private Security Services, concerned the promotion of employment and the fixing of certain conditions of employment for those working as security officers in the private sector was made mandatory by Royal Decree. The CLA is to apply to all private security undertakings carrying out any activity whatsoever on Belgian territory, whether they have their headquarters in Belgium or abroad.

Under the CLA, workers employed by undertakings providing private security services for third parties are to be classified in nine categories on the basis of the type of work carried out, their professional competence, and their degree of independence and responsibility in performing the tasks which are assigned to them. The CLA fixes, in respect of each category of workers, the minimum hourly rate of pay and the amount of various bonuses and allowances.

Between 1 January 1996 and 14 July 1997, ISA, which is based in France, employed 13 workers as security officers at a shopping mall in Belgium. Some of those workers were employed full-time in Belgium, while others were employed there for only some of the time and also worked in France.

The questions raised were the following:

1. In Directive 96/71/EC in the framework of the provision of services, does the term 'period of posting' encompass the part-time period spent, whether randomly or not, by a frontier worker who comes from an undertaking in a Member State, performing, in the course of days, weeks or a month, a part of his services in the adjacent territory or territories of one or more other Member States?
2. Are Articles 59 and 60 of the [EC] Treaty to be interpreted as being infringed where a Member State, for overriding reasons relating to the public interest, requires any undertaking from another Member State employing persons, even temporarily, on the territory of the first State to comply with its legislation or national collective labour agreements relating to minimum wages, where that interest is already protected by the rules of the State in which the service provider is established and workers there are already in a comparable or similar position on the basis not solely of the legislation relating to minimum wages but of the overall position (impact of taxation, welfare protection in relation to illness, including under the obligatory supplementary insurance which applies in France, and to industrial accidents, widowhood, unemployment, retirement and

10. C.O.J., 23 November 1999, Criminal proceedings against Jean-Claude Arblade and Arblade & Fils SARL (C-369/96) and Bernard Leloup, Serge Leloup and Sofrage SARL, C-376/96, ECR, 1999, 8453.

11. C.O.J., 15 March 2001, Criminal proceedings against André Mazzoleni and Inter Surveillance Assistance SARL, C-165/98, ECR, 2001, 2189.

death)? In the same context, put differently: are the temporary national obligations set for employees to be understood as solely the minimum hourly rate of pay without assessing the overall position as regards the welfare protection enjoyed by employees who are required in their work to move from one State to another?

The Court answered:

'Articles 49 and 50 EC do not preclude a Member State from requiring an undertaking established in another Member State which provides services in the territory of the first State to pay its workers the minimum remuneration fixed by the national rules of that State. The application of such rules might, however, prove to be disproportionate where the workers involved are employees of an undertaking established in a frontier region who are required to carry out, on a part-time basis and for brief periods, a part of their work in the territory of one, or even several, Member States other than that in which the undertaking is established. It is consequently for the competent authorities of the host Member State to establish whether, and if so to what extent, application of national rules imposing a minimum wage on such an undertaking is necessary and proportionate in order to ensure the protection of the workers concerned.'

2. *Other conditions*

Member States can impose:
- working conditions relating to public order;[12]
- working conditions contained in generally binding collective agreements, other than construction, as indicated above (Article 3(10)).

Undertakings of the Member States should be treated equally (Article 3(10)). Undertakings from non-Member States cannot be given more favourable treatment than enterprises established in Member States (Article 1(4)).

3. *Exceptions*[13]

Possible exceptions are foreseen as follows:
1. In the case of initial assembly and/or first installation of goods where this is an integral part of a contract for the supply of goods necessary for taking the goods supplied into use and carried out by the skilled and/or specialist workers of the supplying undertaking, the first subparagraph of paragraph 1(b) (*annual holidays*) and (c) (*minimum pay*) shall not apply, if the period of posting *does not exceed* 8 days.
   This exception does not apply to activities in the field of building work.

12. For example, forced labour or labour inspection.
13. The length of the posting is calculated on the basis of a reference period of one month from the beginning of the posting. The duration of posting effected by a posted worker who has been replaced is taken into consideration (Article 3(6)).

2. Member States may, after consulting employers and labour, in accordance with the traditions and practices of each Member State, decide not to apply the first subparagraph of paragraph 1(c) (*minimum pay*) in the cases referred to in Articles 1(3)(a) (*subcontracting*) and (b) (*group*) when the length of the posting *does not exceed one month*.
3. Member States may, in accordance with national laws and/or practices, provide that exemptions may be made from the first subparagraph of paragraph 1(c) (*minimum pay*) in the cases referred to in Articles 1(3)(a) (*subcontracting*) and (b) (*temporary work*) and from a decision by a Member State regarding b. above, by means of generally binding collective agreements concerning one or more sectors of activity, where the length of the posting *does not exceed one month*.
4. Member States may provide for exemptions to be granted from the first subparagraph of paragraphs 1(b) (*annual holidays*) and (c) (*minimum pay*) in the cases referred to in Articles 1(3)(a) (*subcontracting*) and (b) (*group*) on the grounds that the amount of *work to be done is not significant*.

D. Co-operation and Transparency (Article 4)

This covers the following points:

- Member States must indicate one or more liaison offices and inform the other Member States and the Commission accordingly;
- Member States must provide for co-operation between the administrations competent to monitor the working conditions stated in Article 3, especially regarding information on the transnational supply of workers including manifest abuses or possible cases of unlawful transnational activities;
- Member States and the Commission pay close attention to the equal treatment of enterprises;
- Member States must see to it that the information concerning working conditions is 'generally available'.

E. Enforcement (Article 5)

Member States are to take appropriate measures in the event of failure to comply with this directive. They shall in particular ensure that adequate procedures are available to workers and/or their representatives for the enforcement of obligations under this directive.

F. Jurisdiction (Article 6)

In order to enforce the right to the terms and conditions of employment guaranteed in Article 3, judicial proceedings may be instituted in the Member State in whose territory the worker is or was posted, without prejudice to the right, where applicable, under existing international conventions on jurisdiction to institute proceedings in another state.

III. THE ROLE OF PRIVATE EMPLOYMENT AGENCIES IN THE EU: THE JOB CENTRE CASE[14]

In 1997, the European Court of Justice[15] had to examine an Italian Law of 23 October 1960 which lays down a prohibition on acting as an intermediary in employment relationships, whether as an employment agency or as an employment business. Failure to comply with the statute gives rise to penal sanctions.

The question asked was essentially whether the provisions of the Treaty preclude national legislation under which any activity which entails acting as an intermediary between supply and demand in employment relationships is prohibited unless carried on by public employment agencies. The Court ruled in a landmark decision that:

1. placement of employees is an economic activity, even if entrusted to public offices;
2. a body such as a public placement office may therefore be classed as an undertaking for the purposes of the Community competition rules;
3. public placement offices remain subject to competition rules unless and to the extent to which it is shown that their application is incompatible with discharge of their duties;
4. the application of Article 86 of the Treaty cannot obstruct the performance of the particular task assigned to those offices if they are manifestly not in a position to satisfy demand in that area of the market;
5. pursuant to Article 86(b) of the Treaty, such abuse may in particular consist in limiting the provision of a service, to the prejudice of those seeking to avail themselves of it;
6. as the Commission had rightly pointed out, the market in the provision of services relating to the placement of employees is both very extensive and extremely diverse. Supply and demand on that market covers all sectors of production and relates to a range of jobs requiring anything from unskilled labour to the scarcest and most specialized professional qualifications;
7. on such an extensive and differentiated market, which is, moreover, subject to enormous changes as a result of economic and social developments, public placement offices may well be unable to satisfy a significant portion of all requests for services;
8. by prohibiting, on pain of penal and administrative sanctions, any activity as an intermediary between supply and demand on the employment market unless carried on by public placement offices, a Member State creates a situation in which the provision of a service is limited, contrary to Article 86(b) of the Treaty, if those offices are manifestly unable to satisfy demand on the employment market for all types of activity;
9. a potential effect of abusive conduct on trade between Member States is sufficient and arises in particular where the placement of employees by private companies may extend to the nationals or to the territory of other Member States.

---

14. For the text of the Judgment *see* Annex.
15. C.O.J., 11 December 1997, Job *Centre Coop. arl*, Case No. C-55/96, *ECR*, 1997, 7119.

The conclusion of the Court is straightforward and clear. A monopoly on the labour market violates European competition law because:

1. public placement offices are manifestly unable to satisfy demand on the market of all types of activity;
2. the actual placement of employees by private companies is rendered impossible by keeping in force statutory provisions under which such activities are prohibited and non-observance of that prohibition gives rise to penal and administrative sanctions; and
3. the placement activities in question could extend to the nationals or to the territory of other Member States.

In many countries, placement of workers was still by and large monopolized by Public Employment Offices. The general rules, with some exceptions, were still that:

1. placement by fee-charging private employment agencies; and
2. the putting of a worker at the disposal of a user-enterprise were prohibited, except e.g. in the case of temporary work.

Clearly these prohibitions are now both illegal and obsolete. First of all, the monopoly of the Public Employment Office is contrary to the letter and spirit of Convention No. 181 of the ILO (1997) and to European competition law. It is evident that Official Employment Offices can no longer satisfy the demand on the market for all types of activity in a *de facto* manner. They cannot cope with the diversity of the modern labour markets at European level. In conclusion one can say that:

1. any monopoly of Public Employment Offices has to be abolished;
2. enterprises must be able to offer a total package of services on the labour market, vocational training included;
3. the range of possibilities for putting workers at the disposal of user-enterprises must be widened.

IV. AMENDED PROPOSAL FOR A DIRECTIVE ON WORKING CONDITIONS FOR TEMPORARY WORKERS[16]

A. Genesis

On 20 March 2002, the European Commission made a proposal for a Directive on working conditions for temporary workers.[17] This is the third subject to be regulated within the framework of the Commission's September 1995 social partner consultation on 'atypical' work. This process has yielded three agreements negotiated between the social partners at EU level, namely on part-time work, on fixed-term work and on telework. The social partners did not succeed in concluding an agreement on temporary work, the main difficulty being the definition of a 'comparable employee' for the purposes of equal treatment.

Shortly after the breakdown of talks on temporary work, a joint declaration on temporary agency work was signed on 8 October 2001 by Euro-CIETT – the

16. On 28 of November 2002, COM (2002), 701 final (2002/0072 (COD).
17. Proposal for a Directive of the European Parliament and the Council on working conditions for temporary workers COM/2002/0149 final – COD 2002/0072. *See*: 'Commission proposes Directive on temporary agency workers', www.eirofound.ie

European committee of the International Confederation of Temporary Work Businesses – and Uni-Europa – the European regional organization of Union Network International (UNI), which is the international organization grouping services and white-collar worker trade unions. The signatories have forwarded the text to the European Commission, in the hope that it will serve as a basis for a future EU Directive on temporary work.

The declaration underlines that any EU Directive on temporary agency work should have as its fundamental aim to reach a balance between the protection of agency workers and enhancing the positive role that agency work can play in the European labour market. European legislation should be a framework directive, promoting implementation through legislation and/or agreements.

The objectives of the European legislation should be:

1. to reiterate that non-agency employment and open-ended contracts remain the most common forms of employment, although it should also recognize and respect the potential contribution of agency work to the EU's employment and economic objectives;
2. to promote the quality in temporary agency employment and take into account the needs of workers, user companies and agencies, particularly in the areas of flexibility and security;
3. to recognize that agency work may enhance job opportunities and labour market integration, particularly in the case of special and/or disadvantaged groups. This could be achieved by means of training and development;
4. to establish the principle of equal treatment, both in terms of the relationship between the agency and the worker and the relationship between the worker and the user company;
5. to ask Member States to identify, review and, where appropriate, eliminate legal or administrative obstacles to agency work playing a positive role in the labour market. It should also recognize that 'certain prohibitions, restrictions and/or regulations' may be necessary to prevent potential abuses, both in terms of undermining employment conditions or workers in the user company and those of other workers in non-agency employment;
6. to ensure that temporary agency work respects both EU-level and national non-discrimination principles on all issues, and that the 'triangular' nature of agency work 'calls for specific regulations';
7. to ensure that temporary employment agencies do not make workers available to a user company in order to replace striking workers;
8. to ensure that Member States promote the exercise of agency workers' individual and collective rights, which include trade union rights;
9. to state clearly that agency workers are employed by the agency and that these agencies therefore have the obligations of an employer with regard to these workers (agency workers should also be protected by applicable labour legislation);
10. to ensure that agency workers have access to training and development opportunities, which are appropriate, both in the agency and the user company;
11. to ensure that agencies do not charge their workers, either directly or indirectly, for employment services;

12. to encourage the social partners to negotiate on the implementation of the Directive;
13. to recognize that innovations in occupational benefit systems (such as pensions) will be necessary to provide for continuity of rights for temporary agency workers.

On the basis that agency work may play a positive role in the labour market, the sectoral social dialogue will continue to work toward improving the employment and working conditions of agency workers.

B. The Proposal for a Directive

1. The rationale

According to the Commission, the knowledge-based economy is founded on innovation and human capital and requires undertakings and workers to be able to adapt to change more readily. In order to make a success of the transition towards this economy, the co-operation of the social partners must be enlisted in a bid to promote more flexible forms of work organization and reform the regulatory, contractual and legal environment so as to better reconcile flexibility and job security and create more and better jobs.

The proportion of temporary work in the European labour market has been increasing steadily for ten years, with an annual rate of growth estimated at 10 per cent between 1991 and 1998, even though its share of overall employment still remains small (averaging 2.1 million people (expressed in full-time jobs), or 1.4 per cent of total employment in Europe in 1998).

There are four main reasons for this rapid growth, which make temporary work a key element in boosting the capacity of the labour market, undertakings and workers to adapt to changing circumstances:

1. Generally speaking, undertakings have seen an increased need for flexibility in managing their labour force, particularly because of greater and more rapid fluctuations in their order books. Temporary work can thus help to cope with a shortage of permanent staff or a temporary increase in workload. That is particularly important for SMEs, which are more sensitive than other undertakings to the costs of recruiting and laying off permanent staff. But the benefits accruing from temporary work may be curtailed if the sector suffers from poor social standing and job quality. Undertakings, especially SMEs, have an increasing need for qualified workers with a wide range of skills and need them on a temporary basis too. Quality temporary work can thus provide a more effective response to the need for flexibility in today's economy.
2. From the point of view of the temporary workers themselves, this form of employment is often a means of gaining access or returning to the labour market, especially for young people. Depending on the Member States, between 24 per cent and 52 per cent of people who became temporary workers for the first time were not in gainful employment beforehand, because they were either unemployed or still undergoing basic training.

3. More recently, undertakings have been using temporary work because they are short of staff with certain qualifications, especially in occupations related to information technologies.
4. Finally, the legislative framework has become far more flexible: today, the majority of the Member States have put this form of employment on their statute books and many have made their regulations more flexible, whereas just a few years ago it was prohibited in some Member States.

Despite its overall growth, temporary work has spread very unevenly in the Union. According to the above-mentioned study, around 80 per cent of temporary workers in 1999 were employed in four Member States: the Netherlands, France, Germany and the United Kingdom. And its share in total employment differs too: in the Netherlands, temporary workers account for 4.0 per cent of the working population, followed by Luxembourg (3.5 per cent), France (2.7 per cent), the United Kingdom (2.1 per cent), Belgium (1.6 per cent), Portugal (1 per cent), Spain and Sweden (0.8 per cent), Austria, Germany and Denmark (0.7 per cent), Ireland and Finland (0.60 per cent), and Italy (0.2 per cent). These differences are mirrored by differences in the structure of the jobs in question, even though all sectors of activity use temporary work. In the United Kingdom, for example, 80 per cent of the activities of temporary agencies are in the services sector and the public sector, whilst in France 75 per cent are in manufacturing, construction and public works.

The basic common feature of all temporary work is a 'three-way relationship' between a user undertaking, an employee and an agency. Although this applies everywhere, the legal situation varies considerably from one Member State to another. In many Member States, the conditions governing the employment of temporary workers and the activities of temporary agencies are strictly regulated. In others, such as the United Kingdom and Ireland, the legislative and regulatory framework is very flexible.

2. *General provisions*

a. *Scope*

1. This directive applies to the contract of employment or employment relationship between a temporary agency, which is the employer, and the worker, who is posted to a user undertaking to work under its supervision.
2. This Directive applies to public and private undertakings engaged in economic activities whether or not they are operating for gain.
3. Member States may, after consulting the social partners, provide that this directive does not apply to employment contracts or relationships concluded under a specific public or publicly supported training, integration or vocational retraining programme (Article 1).

b. *Aim*

The purpose of this Directive is:

1. To improve the quality of temporary work by ensuring that the principle of non-discrimination is applied to temporary workers;
2. To establish a suitable framework for the use of temporary work to contribute to the smooth functioning of the labour and employment market (Article 2).

c. Definitions

For the purposes of this directive:

1. 'Worker' means any person who, in the Member State concerned, is protected as a worker under national employment law;
2. 'Comparable worker' means a worker in the user undertaking occupying an identical or similar post to that occupied by the worker posted by the temporary agency, account being taken of seniority, qualifications and skills;
3. 'Posting' means the period during which the temporary worker is placed at the user undertaking;
4. 'Basic working and employment conditions' means working and employment conditions relating to:
   a) the duration of working time, rest periods, night work, paid holidays and public holidays;
   b) pay;
   c) work done by pregnant women and nursing mothers, children and young people;
   d) action taken to combat discrimination on the grounds of sex, race or ethnic origin, religion or beliefs, disabilities, age or sexual orientation (Article 3 (1)).[18]

d. Review of restrictions or prohibitions

1. Member States, after consulting the social partners in accordance with legislation, collective agreements and national practices, shall review periodically any restrictions or prohibitions on temporary work for certain groups of workers or sectors of economic activity in order to verify whether the specific conditions underlying them still obtain. If they do not, the Member States should discontinue them.
2. The Member States shall notify the Commission of the result of said review. If the restrictions or prohibitions are maintained, the Member States shall inform the Commission why they consider that they are necessary and justified. The restrictions or prohibitions, which are maintained must be justified on grounds of the general interest regarding, in particular, the protection of workers (Article 4).

3. Employment and working conditions

a. The principle of non-discrimination

1. During their posting, temporary workers shall receive at least as favourable treatment, in terms of basic working and employment

---

18. 'This directive shall be without prejudice to national law as regards the definition of contract of employment or employment relationship. However, Member States shall not exclude from the scope of this Directive contracts of employment or employment relationships solely because they concern:
    a) part-time workers within the meaning of Council Directive 97/81/EC of 15 December 1997;
    b) fixed-term contract workers within the meaning of Council Directive 99/70/EC of 28 June 1999;
    c) persons on a posting at a user undertaking' (Article 3 (2)).

conditions, including seniority in the job, as a comparable worker in the user enterprise, unless the difference in treatment is justified by objective reasons. Where appropriate, the *pro rata temporis* principle applies.

2. Member States may provide that an exemption be made to the principle of 'as favourable treatment' when temporary workers, who have a permanent contract of employment with a temporary agency, continue to be paid in the time between postings.
3. Member States may give the social partners at the appropriate level the option of concluding collective agreements, which derogate from the principle of 'as favourable treatment' as long as an adequate level of protection is provided for temporary workers.
4. Member States may provide that the principle of 'as favourable treatment' shall not apply where a temporary worker works on an assignment or series of assignments with the same user enterprise in a post, which, due to its duration or nature, can be accomplished in a period not exceeding six weeks. (Member States shall take appropriate measures with a view to preventing misuse in the application of this provision.)
5. When this directive calls for a comparison to be made with a comparable worker in the user undertaking but no such worker exists, reference shall be made to the collective agreement applicable in the user undertaking; if no such collective agreement exists, the comparison will be made by reference to the collective agreement applicable to the temporary work agency; if no collective agreement is applicable, the basic working and employment conditions of temporary workers will be determined by national legislation and national practices.
6. The implementing procedures for this article shall be defined by the Member States after consulting the social partners. The Member States may also entrust the social partners at the appropriate level with the task of defining these procedures for this chapter by means of a negotiated agreement (Article 5).

b. Access to permanent employment

1. Temporary workers shall be informed of any vacant posts in the user undertaking to give them the same opportunity as other workers in that undertaking to find permanent employment.
2. Member States shall take any action required to ensure that any clauses banning or having the effect of preventing the conclusion of a contract of employment or an employment relationship between the user undertaking and the temporary worker after the posting are null and void or may be declared null and void.
3. Temporary work agencies shall not charge workers any fees in exchange for arranging for them to be recruited by a user undertaking.
4. Temporary workers shall be given access to the social services of the user undertaking unless there are objective reasons for not doing so.
5. Member States shall take suitable measures or shall promote dialogue between the social partners, in accordance with their national traditions and practices, in order to:
   a) Improve temporary workers' access to training in the temporary work agencies, even in the periods between their postings, in order to enhance their career development and employability;

b) Improve temporary workers' access to training given to the workers of user undertakings (Article 6).

c. Representation of temporary workers
Temporary workers shall count for the purposes of calculating the threshold above which a body representing workers should be formed at the temporary agency in accordance with national and Community legislation. Member States may provide that, under conditions which they define, these workers count for the purposes of calculating the threshold above which bodies representing workers should be formed in the user undertaking in accordance with national and Community legislation (Article 7).

d. Informing workers' representatives
Without prejudice to national and Community provisions which are more stringent and/or more specific on information and consultation, the user undertaking must provide suitable information on the use of temporary workers when providing information on the employment situation in that undertaking to workers' representative bodies set up in accordance with national and Community legislation (Article 8).

4. Final provisions

Articles 9 to 14 contain provisions concerning:
- minimum requirements;
- penalties;
- implementation (two years);
- review by the Commission; and
- entry in to force.

5. Recent developments: 6 March 2003

Ministers gathered in Brussels on 6 March 2003 for the first formal Employment, Social Policy, Health and Consumer Affairs Council under the Greek Presidency. The Council debated a range of issues, including the temporary work proposal.

The proposal is now back with the Council. Given that there are 'divergent views' among the delegations concerning legislation, the degree of regulation and the role of the social partners in this area, in addition to differences in the importance and characteristics of temporary agency work in individual Member States, it was acknowledged that further work is needed in order to reach a 'balanced political compromise' on this issue. It is hoped that agreement of a common position on the draft Directive will be reached at the next Social Policy Council, which will take place on 2–3 June 2003. The outstanding issues are understood to be the following:

1. Review of restrictions and prohibitions on temporary agency work. The text requires Member States to review restrictions and prohibitions on temporary agency working, should it be found that these are no longer justified. Many delegations wish to examine this provision further, as it may have implications for existing national legislation or collective agreements regarding restrictions on the use of temporary agency workers;
2. Application of the principle of equal treatment. The text sets out the principle of equal treatment between temporary agency workers and

those who are directly contracted by the user organization. Currently, an exemption is provided in the text for pay in the case of temporary agency workers on assignments of a maximum period of six weeks. Delegations are questioning this exemption, some opposing it and others calling for a longer maximum period; and

3. Temporary agency work as a labour market instrument. As it currently stands, the text allows Member States not to apply its provisions to employment contracts concluded under special public or publicly-funded programmes which aim to facilitate the integration of long-term unemployed people into the labour market. Some delegations would like the scope of this particular provision to be broader.

'The March Council meeting maintained the momentum in the debate on the draft Directive on temporary agency work. Although there was no concrete outcome, it is clear that there is consensus that this issue is important and should be regulated at Community level. This is a very complex area, characterized as it is by a triangular relationship between the agency, the worker and the user company, and complicated further by the range of practice and regulation current in individual Member States. Nevertheless, there is a political will to reach political agreement on a common position on this text at the June 2003 Council. However, even if this is achieved, there is still some way to go before final adoption, as the EP must then give the text a second reading and agreement on a final text must be reached between the EP and the Council. Thus, it will be some months yet before the text is finalized'.[19]

SOME CONCLUDING REMARKS

The Role of Private Employment Agencies and the Labour Market

The conclusion of the Court in the Job Centre case is straightforward and clear. A monopoly on the labour market violates European competition law. So there is an important role for private employment agencies in the labour market; this is good news as the labour market becomes increasingly diversified and a monopolistic institution is not able to cope with all the demands produced by such a labour market.

But other issues, such as serving the needs of job seekers, have to be addressed. First, the present set of rules governing private employment agencies generally responds to the needs of the employers and the leverage they have. It is completely supply-oriented. The employee has no input. His involvement as an actor in the labour market is mostly reactive rather than proactive. He adapts to developments that occur. Indeed, search, selection and outplacement activities can in many countries only be undertaken on the initiative and at the expense of the employer. An individual job-seeker can merely pass on his name and CV to advertisement agencies, temporary work agencies and job placement agencies, hoping they may act on his behalf. He cannot, however, ask them to act as a service-provider, to look for a job in accordance with his talents and experience, since the agencies cannot charge him any fee.

19. *Andrea Broughton, IRS* 'March employment Council discusses temporary agency work proposal', http://www.eirofound.ie

The job-seeker can resort to the services of the Official Employment Office, which despite its goodwill cannot fulfil all requests it receives. This is certainly the case where a job-seeker is looking for work abroad. For practical purposes, the job seeker has to continue to rely on informal amateurism, resulting in all job-seekers writing the same letters to the same well-known companies, making enquiries through personal contacts, reading newspapers and such like. No professional assistance appears to be available.

Rightly, we all want to protect job-seekers and the unemployed by preventing their exploitation, but we should do more to see to it that they receive professional services which are effectively of the same quality as those available to employers.

We should be more broad-minded than to say that job seekers are not entitled to professional help outside the Public Employment Office since they cannot be charged. Perhaps a kind of insurance system could be set up, as in the case of health services, where one can go to the doctor and have the fee refunded, either totally or partially.

We should also address the issue of contract labour. More and more agencies are becoming talent banks where the self-employed provide their names and skills and the agencies offer opportunities for the self-employed. The agencies match supply and demand for such work. They are in a sense placement agencies for the self-employed. There is obviously plenty of scope for this labour market service, which is growing in importance as the distinction between employee and self-employed becomes increasingly obsolete in outsourced work and in the information society. The question is how to organize contract labour; certainly in a more relaxed and flexible way. Moreover, the gap between employees and the self-employed world should be bridged. Outplacement is currently the only (organized) service on the labour market which can lead to self-employment under official regulation.

A last point concerns vocational training, on which all agree that there should be more, that it should be provided on a permanent basis and should be open to all. Further, training should focus on the 'social skills' needed to operate in a world where teamwork is increasingly important.

In conclusion, it is obvious that we need to take a fresh look at modern labour markets, and at how to match demand and supply for both employment seekers and employers, in a fair way, so that the idea of co-investment can be retained. Adequate and sustained provision of vocational training remains an essential feature of any labour market policy.

The Proposed Directive on Temporary Work

ETUC, the association of European Trade Unions, has welcomed the proposal. UNICE, the European Employers' Association, has indicated that it is not opposed to a Directive which would offer legal protection against discrimination for temporary agency workers, insists that the proposal is 'ill-conceived' and particularly objects to the fact that it uses workers in the user undertaking as comparators, allowing comparison with agency workers only if no user undertaking worker or collective agreement in the user undertaking is available for comparison. Stating that this method is 'unjustified and unnecessarily complicated', UNICE proposes that the two possibilities – taking an agency worker or a worker in the user undertaking as the comparable worker – should be put on an equal footing in the Directive and that Member States should be allowed to choose which comparison to make.

The Confederation of Swedish Enterprises underlines that the Directive would undermine the social dialogue. 'Formally', it says, 'the Directive aims to tackle discrimination against temporary agency workers. The intriguing part, however, is that it establishes that the relevant comparison should be between employees in different companies'. The Commission does indeed extend the principle of non-discrimination to conditions outside the company. As a rule, it wants to prohibit one company, the agency, from providing its employees with salaries and working conditions that are inferior to those in another company.

The Swedish Confederation believes this to be a violation of the right to conclude agreements. Companies and workers in all sectors must be allowed to determine their working conditions according to circumstances in the sector or in the company and in accordance with national negotiating practices. A European directive should not determine the appropriate salary.

The Confederation goes on to underline the diversification in the labour market and that more people work together without sharing the same employer. Their salaries, even if they perform the same or similar tasks, need not be the same. The Directive should respect the autonomy of the social partners in Sweden, regarding pay and working conditions.

Moreover the Directive is said to be contrary to the Treaty, especially Article 137, which excludes pay from its remit, as a matter of social policy.[20]

The most controversial issue of the draft Directive is that the equal treatment principle is, it seems, based on the comparison of a temporary worker with a comparable worker in the user enterprise.

Let us deal first with the argument that the Directive deals with pay, contrary to Article 137(6) of the EC Treaty. This is not a valid argument since the Directive does not actually regulate wages but only deals with equality/non-discrimination, including its effect on pay (as with existing anti-discrimination legislation on men/women, fixed term contracts and part-time workers).

One should also add that the proposed Directive is meant to deal with the triangular relationship in which a worker is employed by one employer (the agency) but is actually working at the workplace of another employer (the user enterprise) alongside workers directly employed by the user. Particularly when clear collective standards exist, this is a core issue for the regulation of industrial relations. The possibility of deviating from the principle of equal treatment where there is a collective agreement providing an adequate level of protection seems to be acceptable.

The exemption for postings less than six weeks seems odd, as does the fact that the Directive does not provide any guidance regarding collective action. Such a provision would not be controversial, since it was a part of the draft agreement of the social partners and it does not contravene Article 137(6) of the EC Treaty which excludes strikes and lock-outs from EU competence. It would not regulate collective action rights but would only specify contexts in which temporary workers could not be used.[21]

20. G. Tunhammer, 'EU Directive on pay would undermine social dialogue', in *F.T.*, 11 April 2002.
21. I. Van den Burg, Committee on Employment and Social affairs of the European Parliament, 27 June 2002, DT/463275EN.doc.

ANNEX

JUDGMENT OF THE COURT (Sixth Chamber)

11 December 1997

(Freedom to provide services – Placement of employees – Exclusion of private undertakings – Exercise of official authority)

In Case C-55/96,

REFERENCE to the Court under Article 177 of the EC Treaty by the Corte d'Appello, Milan, Italy, for a preliminary ruling in the non-contentious proceedings (giurisdizione volontaria) brought before that court by Job Centre Coop. Arl on the interpretation of Articles 48, 49, 55, 56, 59, 60, 62, 66, 86 and 90 of the EC Treaty,

THE COURT (Sixth Chamber), gives the following Judgment

1. By order of 30 January 1996, which was received at the Court on 23 February 1996, the Corte d'Appello (Court of Appeal), Milan, referred to the Court for a preliminary ruling under Article 177 of the EC Treaty three questions on the interpretation of Articles 48, 49, 55, 56, 59, 60, 62, 66, 86 and 90 of the EC Treaty.

2. Those questions were raised in the context of an appeal under Article 2330(4) of the Italian Civil Code against a refusal by the Tribunale Civile e Penale (Civil and Criminal District Court), Milan, to confirm the instrument establishing Job Centre Coop. arl ('JCC').

3. JCC is a co-operative society with limited liability which is in the course of being set up, with its head office in Milan. Under its statutes, its business is to include, in particular, serving as an intermediary between supply and demand on the employment market and providing temporary staff for third parties. Its object is to enable workers and undertakings, whether they are members or not, to draw on such services on the employment market in Italy and the Community.

4. In Italy, the employment market is subject to a mandatory placement system administered by public placement offices and regulated by Law No. 264 of 29 April 1949. Article 11(1) of that Law prohibits the pursuit of any activity, even unremunerated, as an intermediary between supply of and demand for paid employment. Any placement contrary to those rules or engagement of employees through an intermediary other than a placement office gives rise, according to Law No. 264, to penal or administrative sanctions. Furthermore, employment contracts concluded in breach of those rules may be annulled by the courts following a complaint by the placement office, which must be lodged within one year from the engagement of an employee, and at the request of the Public Prosecutor.

5. The first paragraph of Article 1 of Law No. 1369 of 23 October 1960 lays down a prohibition on acting as an intermediary in employment relationships, whether as an employment agency or as an employment business, failure to comply with which gives rise to the penal sanctions provided for in Article 2 thereof. Under the final paragraph of Article 1, any persons employed in breach of the first paragraph of Article 1 are legally regarded in all respects as engaged by the undertaking which has in fact used their services.

6. On 28 January 1994, the chairman of JCC, which was in the course of being set up, applied to the Tribunale Civile e Penale, Milan, for confirmation of the instrument establishing it in accordance with Article 2330(3) of the Italian Civil Code. By order of 31 March 1994, that court stayed the confirmation procedure and submitted to the

Court of Justice for a preliminary ruling two questions concerning various articles of the EC Treaty that it considered relevant to its decision on the application for confirmation of the instrument establishing JCC.

7. In its judgment of 19 October 1995 in Case C-111/94 Job Centre [1995] ECR I-3361, the Court held that it had no jurisdiction to rule on the questions raised by the Tribunale Civile e Penale, Milan, on the ground that when the national court rules under the 'giurisdizione volontaria' procedure on an application for confirmation of the instrument establishing a company with a view to its registration, it is performing a non-judicial function which, in other Member States, is entrusted to administrative authorities. It is exercising administrative authority without being at the same time called upon to settle any dispute.

8. Following that judgment, by decision of 18 December 1995 the Tribunale Civile e Penale, Milan, dismissed the application for confirmation of the instrument establishing JCC submitted by its representative, on the ground that its business objects were incompatible with certain mandatory rules of Italian employment legislation.

9. JCC appealed against that refusal, under Article 2330(4) of the Italian Civil Code, to the Corte d'Appello, Milan, seeking to have the Tribunal's decision set aside and the instrument establishing it confirmed.

10. The Corte d'Appello considered that JCC's appeal raised questions of interpretation of Community law and decided to stay the proceedings and refer to the Court of Justice for a preliminary ruling the following questions:

a. May the provisions of Italian national law contained in Article 11(1) of Law No. 264 of 29 April 1949 and the first paragraph of Article 1 of Law No. 1369 of 23 October 1960, whereby the business of acting as an intermediary and negotiator between supply and demand on the employment market, whether as an employment agency or as an employment business, is prohibited unless carried on by the public offices specified in those provisions, be regarded as relating to the exercise of official authority within the meaning of the combined provisions of Articles 66 and 55 of the EC Treaty in view of the fact that they are treated by Italian law as relating to matters of public policy because their purpose is to protect the interests of workers and the national economy?

b. Must those provisions, in view of their general scope, be regarded as conflicting with the principles of Community law laid down by Articles 48, 49, 59, 60, 62, 66, 86 and 90 of the said Treaty concerning the right to work, freedom of economic initiative, freedom of movement for workers and others, freedom of supply and demand for work and services, free and fair competition between economic agents and the prohibition of abuse of dominant positions?

c. In the event that the abovementioned legislation of the Italian State concerning operation of an employment agency or an employment business is in breach of the principles of Community law mentioned in the foregoing question, must the judicial and administrative authorities of that Member State consider themselves bound to apply those principles directly, allowing public and private bodies and undertakings to act as intermediaries between those offering and those seeking employment and temporary work, provided that the provisions governing employment contracts and mandatory social security are complied with and subject to the controls provided for by law?

11. It appears from the file in the main proceedings that by those questions the national court is asking, essentially, whether the provisions of the Treaty concerning freedom of movement for workers, freedom to provide services and competition preclude national legislation under which any activity as an intermediary between supply and demand in employment relationships is prohibited unless carried on by public placement agencies.

12. JCC is a co-operative society with limited liability in the course of being set up which, in the main proceedings, has claimed the right to act as an intermediary between supply and demand on the employment market and to provide temporary staff.

13. In so far as the questions refer to provisions concerning freedom of movement for workers, it need merely be pointed out that it does not follow from the fact that workers are among the founding members of JCC that Article 48 is applicable, since once JCC has been set up and is in operation it will be an independent legal person.

14. Accordingly, the provisions concerning freedom of movement for workers have no relevance for the dispute in the main proceedings.

15. In so far as the questions refer to Articles 86 and 90 of the Treaty, they raise the problem of the extent of the exclusive right granted to public placement offices, and hence of the prohibition, giving rise to penal and administrative sanctions, of any activity as an intermediary between supply and demand on the employment market by private companies.

16. Consideration must therefore be given first of all to the interpretation of those provisions of the Treaty.

Interpretation of Articles 86 and 90 of the Treaty

17. JCC claims, essentially, that the prohibition of the business of acting as an intermediary between supply and demand on the employment market, unless carried on by public bodies, is contrary to Articles 86 and 90 of the Treaty, since public placement offices are not able to satisfy market demand for such activities. In that connection JCC refers, in particular, to Case C-41/90 *Höfner and Elser* v. *Macrotron* [1991] ECR I-1979.

18. The German and Norwegian Governments, and the Commission, maintain that an exclusive right to place employees should be assessed in the light of the principles that can be extracted from the judgment in Höfner and Elser, cited above.

19. The Italian Government states, first, that the legislation at issue in the main proceedings does not grant any undertaking special or exclusive rights as regards the sub-contracting of employment, but is confined to prohibiting any type of activity as an intermediary in employment relationships. It then considers that, in the light of the particular characteristics and social objectives of the public placement of employees in Italy, it cannot be regarded as an economic activity, and therefore as a business activity. Lastly, it maintains that the public monopoly on placement is not capable of causing the effects referred to in Article 86(b) of the Treaty.

20. Having regard to the foregoing considerations, it is necessary to establish whether public placement offices such as those referred to in Article 11(1) of Law No. 264 may be regarded as undertakings within the meaning of Articles 85 and 86 of the Treaty (*see* Höfner and Elser, cited above, paragraph 20).

21. It must be observed, in the context of competition law, first, that the concept of an undertaking encompasses every entity engaged in an economic activity, regardless of its status and the way in which it is financed and, second, that the placement of employees is an economic activity.

22. The fact that the placement of employees is normally entrusted to public offices cannot affect the economic nature of such activities. Placement of employees has not always been, and is not necessarily, carried out by public entities.

23. The Italian Government further contends that according to Joined Cases C-159/91 and C-160/91 *Poucet and Pistre* v. *Assurances Générales de France and Others* [1993] ECR I-637, a social security body acting under a monopoly system is not an undertaking within the meaning of Article 86 of the Treaty; in paragraphs 18 and 19 of that judgment the Court held that such activity was not an economic activity, since it was based on the principle of national solidarity and was entirely non-profit-making.

24. However, although it is clear from that judgment that administering mandatory social security schemes such as those described in the references for a preliminary ruling in Poucet and Pistre, cited above, does not constitute an economic activity, that conclusion, in paragraph 17, was based on the same criteria as had been applied in Höfner and Elser when it was concluded that employment procurement must be described as a business activity within the meaning of the Community competition rules.

25. A body such as a public placement office may therefore be classed as an undertaking for the purposes of the Community competition rules.

26. Public placement offices entrusted under the legislation of a Member State with the operation of services of general economic interest, such as those envisaged in Article 11(1) of Law No. 264, remain subject to the competition rules pursuant to Article 90(2) of the Treaty unless and to the extent to which it is shown that their application is incompatible with discharge of their duties (*see* Case 155/73 Sacchi [1974] ECR 409, paragraph 15, and Höfner and Elser, cited above, paragraph 24).

27. As regards the operation of public placement offices enjoying an exclusive right, compliance with which is ensured by a prohibition of any activity as an intermediary in employment relationships on pain of penal and administrative sanctions such as those provided for in Laws Nos. 264 and 1369, it must be stated that the application of Article 86 of the Treaty cannot obstruct the performance of the particular task assigned to those offices if they are manifestly not in a position to satisfy demand in that area of the market.

28. Whilst it is true that Article 86 concerns undertakings and may be applied within the limits laid down by Article 90(2) to public undertakings or undertakings vested with exclusive rights or specific rights, the Treaty nevertheless requires the Member States not to take or maintain in force measures which could destroy the effectiveness of that provision (*see* Case 13/77 *Inno* v. *ATAB* [1977] ECR 2115, paragraphs 31 and 32, and Höfner and Elser, cited above, paragraph 26). Article 90(1) provides that the Member States are not to enact or maintain in force, in the case of public undertakings and the undertakings to which they grant special or exclusive rights, any measure contrary to the rules contained in the Treaty, in particular those provided for in Articles 85–94.

29. Consequently, any measure adopted by a Member State which maintains in force statutory provisions that create a situation in which public placement offices cannot avoid infringing Article 86 is incompatible with the rules of the Treaty.

30. In the first place, an undertaking vested with a legal monopoly may be regarded as occupying a dominant position within the meaning of Article 86 of the Treaty (*see* Case 311/84 *CBEM* v. *CLT and IPB* [1985] ECR 3261, paragraph 16), and the

territory of a Member State to which that monopoly extends may constitute a substantial part of the common market (*see* Case 322/81 *Michelin* v. *Commission* [1983] ECR 3461, paragraph 28).

31. Secondly, the mere creation of such a dominant position by granting an exclusive right within the meaning of Article 90(1) is not as such incompatible with Article 86 of the Treaty (*see* CBEM, cited above, paragraph 17; Höfner and Elser, cited above, paragraph 29; Case C-320/91 Corbeau [1993] ECR I-2533, paragraph 11; and Case C-323/93 *Centre d'Insémination de la Crespelle* v. *Co-opérative de la Mayenne* [1994] ECR I-5077, paragraph 18). A Member State will contravene the prohibition contained in those two provisions only if the undertaking in question, merely by exercising the exclusive right granted to it, cannot avoid abusing its dominant position (*see* Case C-387/93 Banchero [1995] ECR I-4663, paragraph 51).

32. Pursuant to Article 86(b) of the Treaty, such abuse may in particular consist in limiting the provision of a service, to the prejudice of those seeking to avail themselves of it.

33. As the Commission has rightly pointed out, the market in the provision of services relating to the placement of employees is both very extensive and extremely diverse. Supply and demand on that market cover all sectors of production and relate to a range of jobs requiring anything from unskilled labour to the scarcest and most specialized professional qualifications.

34. On such an extensive and differentiated market, which is, moreover, subject to enormous changes as a result of economic and social developments, public placement offices may well be unable to satisfy a significant portion of all requests for services.

35. By prohibiting, on pain of penal and administrative sanctions, any activity as an intermediary between supply and demand on the employment market unless carried on by public placement offices, a Member State creates a situation in which the provision of a service is limited, contrary to Article 86(b) of the Treaty, if those offices are manifestly unable to satisfy demand on the employment market for all types of activity.

36. Thirdly, the question of the responsibility imposed on a Member State by virtue of Articles 86 and 90(1) of the Treaty arises only if the abusive conduct on the part of the placement agency concerned is liable to affect trade between Member States. That does not mean that the abusive conduct in question must actually have affected such trade. It is sufficient to establish that it is capable of having such an effect (*see Michelin* v. *Commission*, cited above, paragraph 104).

37. A potential effect of that kind on trade between Member States arises in particular where the placement of employees by private companies may extend to the nationals or to the territory of other Member States.

38. In view of all the foregoing considerations, the reply to the national court must be that public placement offices are subject to the prohibition contained in Article 86 of the Treaty, so long as application of that provision does not obstruct the performance of the particular task assigned to them. A Member State which prohibits any activity as an intermediary between supply and demand on the employment market, whether as an employment agency or as an employment business, unless carried on by those offices, is in breach of Article 90(1) of the Treaty where it creates a situation in which those offices cannot avoid infringing Article 86 of the Treaty. That is the case, in particular, in the following circumstances:

- the public placement offices are manifestly unable to satisfy demand on the market for all types of activity; and

- the actual placement of employees by private companies is rendered impossible by the maintenance in force of statutory provisions under which such activities are prohibited and non-observance of that prohibition gives rise to penal and administrative sanctions; and
- the placement activities in question could extend to the nationals or to the territory of other Member States.

Interpretation of Articles 59 et seq. *of the Treaty*

39. Since the prohibition of any activity as an intermediary between supply and demand on the employment market unless carried on by public placement offices, as referred to in the questions referred to the Court, is contrary to Articles 86 and 90(1) of the Treaty in the circumstances indicated in paragraph 38 of this judgment, there is no need for the Court to give a ruling on the interpretation of Articles 59 *et seq.* of the Treaty.

Public placement offices are subject to the prohibition contained in Article 86 of the EC Treaty, so long as application of that provision does not obstruct the performance of the particular task assigned to them. A Member State which prohibits any activity as an intermediary between supply and demand on the employment market, whether as an employment agency or as an employment business, unless carried on by those offices, is in breach of Article 90(1) of the Treaty where it creates a situation in which those offices cannot avoid infringing Article 86 of the Treaty. That is the case, in particular, in the following circumstances:

- the public placement offices are manifestly unable to satisfy demand on the market for all types of activity; and
- the actual placement of employees by private companies is rendered impossible by the maintenance in force of statutory provisions under which such activities are prohibited and non-observance of that prohibition gives rise to penal and administrative sanctions; and
- the placement activities in question could extend to the nationals or to the territory of other Member States.

14. Temporary Agency Work and Freedom of Services in the European Union

Ronnie Graham[1]

An important element in the development of the Internal Market of late has been European Community law promoting the transnational provision of services in the Member States. The Posted Workers Directive[2] has sought to regulate in part the terms and conditions of employment of workers posted to one Member State by an employer whose undertaking is established in another Member State, and who is exercising the Community right of freedom to provide services. In doing so, the Directive seeks to facilitate the transnational provision of services. However, it also aims at the social protection of workers posted by the service provider. Whether these two objectives are opposed or whether they are complementary is crucial in estimating the effect the Directive may have on the freedom to provide services.

That effect can be gauged by examining both the enforcement of national rules falling within the scope of the Directive which existed prior to its transposition, and potential enforcement of national legislation transposing the Directive. An examination of the enforcement of such national rules and the transposition of the Directive in Belgium is particularly illustrative of the extent to which, in that Member State, the promotion of freedom to provide services and social protection of posted workers are balanced.

Before examining the balancing of those two objectives in the Belgian context, it is first necessary to explain how the Posted Workers Directive provides for their attainment. An outline of the Directive is required, setting out not only its objectives, but also its scope; the terms and conditions to be applied to posted workers and the regulatory forms which they may take; the temporal threshold governing when those terms and conditions can be applied; exemptions from applying them; and how they may be enforced.

AN OUTLINE OF THE POSTED WORKERS DIRECTIVE

I. Aims

It is suggested that the Directive has, in total, four aims, which are not entirely complementary. At the outset, it is worth noting their problematic interrelationship.

---

1. I am very grateful to Mr Stefan Nerinckx, Dr Eeva Kolehmainen and Dr Aukje van Hoek who gave invaluable advice on aspects of this article.

2. Directive 96/71/EC of the European Parliament and of the Council of 16 December 1996 concerning the posting of workers in the framework of the provision of services, OJ L 18/1, 21 January 1997.

R. Blanpain & R. Graham (eds.), Temporary Agency Work and the Information Society, 277–294

Davies' analysis inquires into the extent to which a balance is struck between the two objectives of promoting freedom to provide services and protecting national labour regulation.[3] That inquiry, he maintains, depends on considering two further aims, namely, control of unfair competition and worker protection. Similarly, Grosvenor[4] recognizes that an understanding of the Directive requires 'constant balancing of the issues'. In contrast to Davies, however, he determines that the two objectives which are most important, and which must be balanced, are worker protection and promotion of the freedom to provide services. The balancing of those two objectives, as this Article attempts to show, is clearly demonstrated by the enforcement of regulations relating to posted workers in Belgium.

Even in examining each of the four objectives, a valuable assessment can be made of how, individually, they contribute to the balance between worker protection and the promotion of freedom of services.

Firstly, the Directive seeks to create legal certainty as to which labour regulations apply to posted workers. The Explanatory Memorandum to the Commission's proposal for the Directive states that a clear identification of the working conditions applicable to posted workers is intended.[5] That aim seems inextricable from the objective of co-ordinating the laws of the Member States, to create a list of mandatory rules to be complied with by undertakings which post workers within the Community.[6] Prior to implementation of the Directive, workers posted within the Community could seek to enforce regulations applicable in the host state under Articles 6 and 7 of the Rome Convention.[7] However, that possibility did not determine that any particular conditions were always applicable, so that, without a detailed knowledge of the labour regulations of the home state, both employer and worker would be uncertain which of those would apply.

The limit of the legal certainty created by the Directive should be noted. The substantive content of conditions applicable to posted workers is not given by the list of mandatory rules in Article 3(1). That content continues to be determined by the host state regulations which the Directive determines applicable and which it leaves intact. Eichhorst's description of the Directive as an 'umbrella' regulation is helpful here; it obliges the application of 'certain types of binding provisions' without interfering with the creation of labour regulations in the host state.[8]

The objective of creating legal certainty as to which conditions are applicable to posted workers clearly advances worker protection. For the first time, the posted worker has, in the Directive, a legislative basis on which to enforce specific mandatory rules. On the other hand, benefits for the freedom to provide services are less

3. Davies, 'Posted Workers: Single Market or Protection of National Labour Law Systems', in *Common Market Law Review* 1997, p. 598.
4. 'The Posting of Workers within the Framework of the Provision of Services', http://www.jumper.demon.co.uk/ec1.html, pp. 1–7.
5. Explanatory Memorandum, paragraph 19, as cited in House of Lords Select Committee on the European Communities, Session 1992–1993 5th Report, Protection of Posted Workers, p. 32.
6. The creation of a list of mandatory rules applicable to posted workers is listed as an objective distinct from that of creating legal certainty as to which conditions are applicable in paragraph 19 of the Explanatory Memorandum.
7. Differences in enforcing the applicability of host state regulations under the Rome Convention and under the Directive are beneficially explored with reference to a particular context. This analysis is therefore given below in relation to the Belgian context.
8. Eichhorst, 'European Social Policy between National and Supranational Regulation: Posted Workers in the Framework of Liberalized Services Provision', in *MPIfG Discussion Paper* 98/6, p. 30.

clear. It is possible to argue that greater legal certainty gives employers more confidence to provide services across borders since they would 'know where they stood'.

However, it is not clear how effective will be the obligation, under Article 4(3) of the Directive, on host states to disseminate to employers established in other Member States information concerning their mandatory terms and conditions of employment. Further, the host state's ability, under Article 3(10), to require employers to observe terms additional to those listed in Article 3(1) could undermine employers' confidence as to which host state terms will apply. The list provided by Article 3(1) may become an 'imprecise indicator' of what the host state will require. It would appear premature to expect the increased provision of legal certainty, at which the Directive aims, to translate into encouraging cross-border service provision.

Secondly, the Directive aims at promoting fair competition between undertakings established in the host state and others based in other Member States. That objective addresses the situation where the economy and work force of a host state Member State are disadvantaged by the arrival of workers from other Member States who are governed by a lower standard of social protection.[9] Although not explicitly referred to in the Commission's Explanatory Memorandum, that objective seems implicit in that the Directive seeks to oblige 'foreign undertakings to observe a minimum "hard core" of protective working conditions in force in the host country'.[10]

Once again, this objective appears immediately as one that advances worker protection. Posted workers are to enjoy the same conditions as host state workers in relation to the list in Article 3(1) and will now have a legislative basis for enforcing them. On the other hand, promoting fair competition appears to run counter to the freedom to provide services. Service providers in other Member States must now meet conditions of employment in both the home state and the host state in order that they do not undercut host state providers. If, however, one takes Davies' view that it does not make economic sense to speak of 'undercutting', since the significant issue is labour cost per unit of output,[11] the issue of protecting fair competition does not actually arise. In that view, provision of services, regardless of the provider's origin, must have regard to the efficiency of labour, as well as its cost. It is that efficiency which the receiver of services evaluates in deciding whether to contract with a domestic or a foreign provider. In that view, cross-border provision of services appears unaffected by the aim of promoting fair competition.

Thirdly, the introduction of a list of mandatory rules applicable to posted workers obviously indicates that the Directive aims at worker protection. A more useful inquiry is how much worker protection it allows. In addition to the 'hard core' list of mandatory rules, the Directive allows for extension of the list under Article 3(10) by the host state. The extent of worker protection is thus left open. The host state is thereby given discretion to apply to posted workers additional terms and conditions required by public policy provisions and by certain collective agreements.

9. This phenomenon is often referred to as 'social dumping' (*cf.*, e.g. Grosvenor, p. 1). Davies, by contrast, denies the existence of the phenomenon, claiming that 'labour cost per unit of output ... is the significant issue' and that the origin of the labour is therefore not important. Further, he points out its particular lack of significance in the case of posted workers. They remain within the organizational framework of the home-state enterprise and therefore may not have access to the efficiency enhancing facilities of the host state (*op. cit.*, pp. 599–601).

10. Explanatory Memorandum, *op. cit.*, paragraph 19.

11. *Cf.*, note 7 above.

Regarding which public policy provisions may allow extended worker protection, the Council and Commission originally intended those allowing for the prohibition of forced labour, monitoring compliance with legislation on working conditions, and the legality of industrial action.[12] According to the open phrasing of Article 3(10), host states may seek to apply any public policy provisions to posted workers. It will be the duty of national courts and the European Court of Justice to determine the extent to which public policy provisions may be applied.

As to which collective agreements the host state has discretion to apply to posted workers under Article 3(10), guidance is given by Article 3(8). Where a host state has no universally applicable collective agreements, two other types of collective agreement may be regarded. Collective agreements which are generally applicable to all similar undertakings in the same sector and same state may be applied. Also, collective agreements which are agreed by the most representative employers' and labour organizations, and which are generally applicable in the state, may be applied. The discretion to apply those collective agreements is particularly important given that universally applicable collective agreements are relatively rare in the Member States.[13] Again, it will be for the European Court of Justice, ultimately, to control the extent of worker protection allowed by host states' use of this discretion.

Consequently, it is suggested that actual use of the Article 3(10) discretion and its control will determine the extent of worker protection which the Directive provides. With regard to the aim of the Directive, it can only be said that how much protection it offers has been left deliberately unclear.

Such deliberate vagueness may be connected to conserving freedom to provide services, which is a fourth and a principal aim of the Directive. It may deliberately permit the extent of worker protection allowed to be determined on a case-by-case basis. The analysis attempted below, as to how Belgian labour regulations are applied to posted workers, seeks to show that the extent of protection which they enjoy is continually balanced with the promotion of the freedom to provide services.

The latter, interestingly, is not mentioned in the aims of the Directive as given by the Commission in the Explanatory Memorandum. However, the choice of legal basis indicates that the removal of restrictions on transnational provision of services within the Community is of paramount concern. The Directive has a dual legal basis: Article 47 (2) and Article 55 of the EC Treaty (formerly Articles 57(2) and Article 66). Article 47(2) authorizes the adoption of harmonizing directives promoting 'persons to take up and pursue activities as self-employed persons'. Article 55 applies the Treaty Articles relating to freedom of establishment to the arena of freedom to provide services in Chapter 3 of Title III. Chapter 3 intends that restrictions on the freedom to provide services are progressively abolished. Cross-referencing the two Articles seems to create a legislative competence 'to adopt harmonizing directives for the purpose of removing restrictions on the provision of cross-border services'.[14]

---

12. Biagi, 'Fortune Smiles on the Italian EU Presidency', in *International Journal of Comparative Labour Law and Industrial Relations*, Vol. 12, No. 2, 1997, pp. 97–109, at paragraph 12. The discretion to extend worker protection to include the legality of industrial action was latterly withdrawn from the scope of Article 3(10).
13. This point is made by Ojeda-Aviles in 'European Collective Bargaining and Posted Workers', in *International Journal of Comparative Labour Law and Industrial Relations*, Vol. 13, No. 2, 1997, pp. 127–130, at p. 128.
14. Craig, *op. cit.*, p. 572.

For a Directive whose text so clearly concerns worker protection, it is noticeable that its legal basis does not lie in the social policy provisions of the Treaty. But the fact that worker protection is central to the Directive while its legal basis promotes the freedom to provide services explains why its application must always require a balancing of these two issues.

II. Scope

Three types of undertaking which post workers within the Community are subject to the provisions of the Directive: an undertaking which, in carrying out a contract to provide services, posts workers to another Member State on its account and under its direction; an undertaking which posts workers to one of its subsidiaries established in another Member State, while maintaining its employment relationship with the worker; and a temporary employment agency which hires out a worker to an undertaking in another Member State, while maintaining its employment relationship with the worker.

In view of the context in which this Article has been written, it is worth assessing how far the Directive applies to the category of temporary employment agencies. No definition is given of ‘temporary employment undertaking’. It would appear to be for host states to decide what form of cross-border service provision falls within the category. On the basis of the text, it is not possible to determine precisely which temporary employment agencies are covered by the Directive.

For Member States without legislation providing for protection of temporary workers, the Directive does not affect the position of temporary agency workers hired out by an undertaking established in another Member State. Member States are not obliged to give legal recognition to the existence of temporary work agencies, according to the 19th Recital in the Preamble to the Directive. The Recital intends that where a Member State either has no legislation providing for temporary employment or prohibits the placement of workers, the Directive does not oblige it to allow such employment or placement.[15]

III. Terms and Conditions of Employment Applicable to Posted Workers

A list of types, but not the substantive content, of terms and conditions which are guaranteed to be applicable to posted workers constitutes the ‘hard core’ of worker protection offered by the Directive and is found in Article 3(1). Only those existing in specified regulatory forms, described below, are applicable. The types of terms and conditions to be guaranteed are maximum work periods and minimum rest periods; maximum paid annual holidays; minimum rates of pay; conditions of hiring-out of workers; health, safety and hygiene at work; protective measures relating to the employment of pregnant women, women who have recently given birth, children and young people; and non-discrimination provisions including equality of treatment between men and women.

The selection of terms and conditions listed reflects the fact that the posted workers are employed in the host state in a temporary capacity. Others of a more

15. That intention is found in the Council Minutes relating to discussion of the proposed Directive, as cited by Eeva Kolehmainen, in *The Posted Workers Directive: European Reinforcement of National Labour Protection*, Section 2.2 and note 18.

permanent nature, such as those relating to the form and existence of an employment contract, do not fall within the Directive. The issues arising from applying to posted workers the listed terms and conditions are best examined in a particular context; that examination is, in part, attempted below in relation to the Belgian context.

Significantly, it is immediately clear from the listed terms and conditions that these do not apply in the same way to workers hired out by temporary work agencies. The list includes, at Article 3(1)(d), a specific reference to the applicability of 'conditions of hiring-out of workers, in particular the supply of workers by temporary employment undertakings'. That would appear to render the other listed terms and conditions non-applicable to workers hired out transnationally by temporary work agencies. Another provision of the same Article supports this view. Article 3(9) states that workers hired out undertakings established in other Member States are to be guaranteed the terms and conditions applicable to temporary workers in the host state. Accordingly, it seems that temporary workers posted to another Member State are to be protected by conditions relating only to temporary work in the host state and not by others listed in Article 3(1).

Unlike the two other categories of posted workers, posted temporary agency workers are not guaranteed any specified types of conditions by the Directive. The protection which they receive is to be determined entirely by any host state legislation relating to temporary workers.

IV. Regulatory Forms which Applicable Terms and Conditions Must Take

The above terms and conditions are only applicable to posted workers where they are laid down either by law, regulation or administrative provision or by universally applicable collective agreements. The latter are collective agreements which must be observed in the host state and in the sector concerned. If it is accepted that they are rarely found in the Member States,[16] it appears that the discretion, outlined above, to apply generally applicable collective agreements, or those concluded by the most representative employer and labour organizations, is of greater significance.

V. The 'Zero Threshold'

Undertakings which post workers are to observe the listed terms and conditions from the first day of work in the host state. In its original proposal, the Commission had suggested a threshold of three months' operation, at which time the Directive would apply. However, those Member States who petitioned for 'day one' protection, largely on the grounds that postings in the construction sector were often short and were one of the principal targets of the Directive, succeeded in securing what has

16. Ojeda-Aviles states that only in Spain do collective agreements have the general effectiveness which the Directive requires for their classification as universally applicable ('European Collective Bargaining and Posted Workers: Comments on Directive 96/71', in *International Journal of Comparative Labour Law and Industrial Relations*, Vol. 13/2, pp. 127–130, at p. 128). The absence of universally applicable collective agreements in Germany, for example, is explored in relation to the Directive by Deinert in 'Posting of Workers to Germany – Previous Evolutions and New Influences throughout EU Legislation Proposals', in *International Journal of Comparative Labour Law and Industrial Relations*, Vol. 16, No. 3, 2000, pp. 217–234, at p. 218 and following.

been termed the 'zero threshold'. It is suggested that the zero threshold required the creation of the exemptions in the Directive.

VI. Exemptions

There are three principal exemptions provided for in the Directive. A compulsory exemption applies where the provision of installation or assembly services is an integral part of a contract for the supply of goods; where that provision requires the supplier of the goods to post skilled or specialist workers; and where the posting does not exceed eight days. This compulsory exemption applies only to national rules concerning paid annual holidays and minimum remuneration, and it does not apply in the construction sector. Those national rules cannot be applied in the situation described.

Two permissive exemptions allow, but do not require, host states not to apply minimum pay provisions to postings less than one month in length, and not to apply minimum pay and paid holiday provisions where the work done during posting is not significant.

It is worth noting that these exemptions do not apply where the posted worker has been hired out by a temporary work agency. Importantly, there is therefore no exemption from applying to posted workers legislation relating to minimum pay and minimum paid annual holidays which is applicable to domestic temporary workers.

VII. Enforcement

Prior to enforcement, the host state has a duty under the Directive to make information on the terms and conditions of employment, listed in Article 3(1) generally available. It is the duty of the public authorities of the host state, with the co-operation of public authorities in the home state as required by Article 4(2), to monitor employers' compliance with the listed terms and conditions. To enforce the right to that compliance, the Directive allows proceedings to be brought in the host state. It does not prohibit the right to bring proceedings in the home state under the Rome Convention.

Enforcement of regulations relating to posted workers is best examined in a specific context. The following examination of how such regulations are enforced in Belgium attempts to illustrate whether significant differences arise in the wake of the Directive. In particular, it tries to demonstrate the difference in balance between worker protection and cross-border service provision which has been struck by Belgian regulations prior to implementation of the Directive, and by Community law in the light of the Directive.

BALANCING FREEDOM TO PROVIDE SERVICES AND WORKER PROTECTION: THE BELGIAN CONTEXT

I. Regulations Applying to Posted Workers Prior to the Directive

Prior to implementation of the Posted Workers Directive, workers posted to Belgium enjoyed the protection offered to all employees by national regulations. These consist of national public policy provisions and collective agreements which are universally applicable. Certain sectors concluded such collective agreements to ensure specified terms and conditions of employment were applied without exception. Other collective agreements were concluded on a national level, guaranteeing protection to employees regardless of their sector of work. Those agreements have a statutory basis in the Act of 5 December 1968, which provides that they have a criminal sanction attached to their breach.

National regulations relating to the protection of employees may be relied on by a worker posted to Belgium by an employer whose undertaking is established in a state which is party to the Rome Convention. Article 6 of that Convention states that a choice of law made by the parties to an employment contract cannot deprive an employee of protection offered by mandatory rules otherwise applicable in the absence of choice. Relying on Article 7 of the Rome Convention, a posted worker can claim the protection of mandatory rules, including those of the law of another country with which the situation has a close connection. That provision permits a posted worker to rely on the mandatory rules of the host state, which, in the case of Belgium, include national public policy provisions and universally applicable collective agreements.

II. Stability of the National Regulatory System

Ensuring that all employees, including posted workers, may rely on the protection offered by Belgian national regulations is of benefit to the national regulatory system. It allows such a system a stability undisturbed by exempted categories of workers. The Posted Workers Directive intended to preserve the stability of national regulatory systems. In its Explanatory Memorandum,[17] the Commission stated the Directive aims to co-ordinate, rather than harmonize, national laws relating to posted workers. The Directive identifies not the content of mandatory rules, but simply which rules require compliance by undertakings posting workers to another Member State. However, as the following analysis attempts to show, the enforcement of previously mandatory regulations against undertakings which post workers in Belgium has been restricted in the wake of the Directive. Accordingly, the stability of the national regulatory system has been eroded.

III. The Transposing Law of 5 March 2002 and the Royal Decree of 29 March 2002

In the wake of the Directive, Belgian public policy provisions relating to the protection of posted workers have been supplemented by two regulations. Firstly, the Law of 5 March 2002 transposes the Directive into national law and introduces a simplified system governing tenure of social documents by undertakings posting workers in Belgium. Secondly, the Royal Decree of 29 March 2002 establishes methods of implementing that new system.

Before estimating the effects of enforcing those two regulations in line with the Directive, it is worth noting certain substantive differences between the Law of 5 March and the Directive. That Law goes further than the Directive in three

17. Paragraph 19.

respects. In terms of its scope, the Law of 5 March extends beyond the Directive by applying to all posted workers. Undertakings established outside the European Community which post workers to Belgium fall within the scope of the Law of 5 March. Secondly, as regards mandatory rules applicable to posted workers, the Law of 5 March goes beyond the list given in Article 3(1) of the Directive to include other regulations including those relating to tenure of social documents and universally applicable collective agreements. Thirdly, the Law of 5 March 2002 requires compliance with a regulatory category additional to those detailed in subparagraphs 1 and 2 of Article 3(1) in the Directive: all regulations concerning working conditions which have a criminal sanction attached to their breach.

IV. Enforcing the National Regulations: In Line with the Directive?

Examining the enforcement of the Belgian national regulations, outlined above, illustrates the principal interest of this Article: the balancing of the promotion of freedom to provide services and the social protection of workers. Three elements of the relationship between the Belgian national regulations and the Directive provide a forum for striking that balance, and are considered below. The first element is the application to posted workers of national regulations classified as public policy provisions. The second element is the application to posted workers of Belgian mandatory rules relating to minimum remuneration, which are governed by public policy provisions. The third element is the difference in scope of the Belgian national regulations and the Directive.

A. National regulations classified as public policy provisions

As previously mentioned, Belgian national legislation and universally applicable collective agreements protecting workers are classified as public policy provisions. In a preliminary reference to the European Court of Justice, *Arblade*,[18] a Belgian court sought to ascertain whether applying certain regulations, classified as national 'public-order legislation' (by which should be understood public policy provisions), to posted workers was in breach of Articles 59 and 60 (now, after amendment, Articles 49 and 50) of the EC Treaty enshrining the freedom to provide services. The Posted Workers Directive was not in force at the time. However, the Court's consideration of national regulations applying to posted workers prior to implementation of the Directive are likely to affect its future application and interpretation.[19]

The Court, in *Arblade*, appeared to restrict the applicability of national public-order legislation and collective agreements to posted workers and to promote the freedom to provide services. It implemented a two-stage test for assessing whether the application to posted workers of host state regulations, which restricted the freedom to provide services, was justified. Firstly, such application had to constitute an overriding requirement of public interest.[20] If that condition was

18. Joined Cases C-369/96 and C-376/96 ECR 1999 I-8453.
19. Eeva Kolehmainen, *The Posted Workers Directive: European Reinforcement of National Labour Protection*, Section 4.2.1.4.
20. *Arblade* paragraphs 31 and 36.

satisfied, secondly, it had to be assessed whether that interest was already protected by the regulations of the home state.[21] Only where the posted worker benefited from real additional protection from the application of the host state regulations, could restriction on the freedom to provide services be justified.[22]

The regulations at issue in *Arblade* related to two distinct areas of Belgian labour rules. All had criminal penalties attached to their infringement,[23] and, as regulations providing for the protection of workers, constituted public policy provisions.[24] The first set of regulations concerned minimum remuneration in the construction sector as fixed by the Collective Labour Agreement of 28 March 1991; payment by employers, in relation to their construction workers, of contributions to the '*timbres-intempéries*' and '*timbres-fidélité*' schemes, as determined by the Collective Labour Agreement of 28 April 1988; and, in relation to those contributions, the issue of an individual record, with certain information, to each worker under Royal Decree No. 5 of 23 October 1978.

The second set of regulations at issue concerned obligations to draw up, keep and retain certain social labour documents. Each was enshrined in Belgian national legislation. Importantly, they included an obligation not to hinder surveillance of compliance with the documentary system;[25] retention for five years of the social documents;[26] specification of where the documents should be kept;[27] as well as what they must comprise.[28]

The factual situation in *Arblade* was as follows. The managers of two French companies posting workers to Belgium to work on a construction project were prosecuted at the Tribunal Correctionel de Huy in Belgium for failure to comply with the obligations arising from the two sets of regulations outlined above. The national court asked the European Court of Justice to give a preliminary ruling as to whether enforcement of those obligations was precluded by Articles 59 and 60 (now Articles 49 and 50) of the EC Treaty where the firm was subject to comparable requirements in the home state.[29]

In relation to the first set of regulations, the Court ruled that it was for the national court to determine which provisions, so long as they were sufficiently precise and accessible, establishing minimum remuneration were applicable to the undertaking.[30] Supported by the Opinion of Advocate General Ruiz-Jarabo Colomer, the Belgian government had sought to demonstrate that payment to the '*timbres-intempéries*' and '*timbres-fidélité*' schemes constituted partial payment of the minimum remuneration.[31] By contrast, the Court did not consider that the

21. *Ibid.*, paragraph 39.
22. *Ibid.*, paragraphs 53–54.
23. *Ibid.*, paragraph 17.
24. *Ibid.*, paragraph 18.
25. Royal Decree No. 5 of 23 October 1978 and the Law of 16 November 1972.
26. Articles 22–25 of Royal Decree of 8 August 1980.
27. Articles 8, 9 and 18 of Royal Decree of 8 August 1980.
28. Namely, a copy of binding labour regulations (Law of 8 April 1965); a staff register, individual account, special staff register, and individual document, each containing certain compulsory information (respectively, Articles 3(1), 3(2), 4–7, 10, 11, 13–21 of Royal Decree of 8 August 1980).
29. *Arblade* paragraphs 24 and 27.
30. *Ibid.*, paragraphs 43–44.
31. *Ibid.*, Opinion of Advocate General Ruiz-Jarabo Colomer, paragraphs 74 and 76; written answer by the Belgian Government to a question from the Court, in the Rapport D'Audience in *Arblade*, cited in Kolehmainen, *The Posted Workers Directive: European Reinforcement of National Labour Protection*, Section 4.2.1.4, footnote 121.

advantages to the worker from the '*timbres-intempéries*' and '*timbres-fidélité*' schemes should be considered as part of the minimum remuneration.[32] Further, it found that the employers were, in the home state, under obligations comparable to the contributions to the '*timbres-intempéries*' and '*timbres-fidélité*' schemes which the host state, in addition, had required of them. That requirement therefore constituted a restriction on the freedom to provide services.[33]

At that point, the Court implemented the two-stage test, mentioned above, to determine whether the restriction was justified. It held that, although the public interest relating to the social protection of workers in the construction industry and compliance with related rules could constitute an overriding requirement justifying the restriction, in the present case it did not. That conclusion was made on the basis that the workers enjoyed essentially similar protection to that afforded by the contribution schemes in the home state.[34] With regard to the second stage of the test, the Court concluded that payments to the contribution scheme conferred no social advantage on the workers.[35] The restriction on the freedom to provide services was not justified.

That conclusion demonstrated a narrowing, according to the two-stage test, of which public-order legislation applied to workers posted in Belgium. In other words, it constituted a narrowing of the extent to which posted workers may rely on the social protection offered by host state legislation. On the other hand, it promoted the freedom of an employer established in another Member Sate to provide services in Belgium without additional expense.

In relation to the second set of regulations, the Court's conclusion also favoured the freedom to provide services, and narrowed the application to posted workers of Belgian public policy provisions. The obligations to draw up, keep and retain the specified social and labour documents gave rise to administrative and economic burdens whish were additional to comparable ones imposed on the undertaking in the home state. They were therefore a restriction on the freedom to provide services.[36] Implementing the two-stage test, the Court found that the restriction was not justified. The obligations did not constitute an overriding public interest where the undertaking was under comparable obligations in the home state which adequately enabled the carrying out of controls required in the host state.[37]

Arblade established that applicability of host state's national regulations, where classified as public policy provisions, were caught by a test demanding an overriding requirement of public interest to justify a restriction of the freedom to provide services.[38] That conclusion, it is argued, narrows the social protection applicable to posted workers on the basis of host state mandatory rules, as provided by the Posted Workers Directive. For instance, the application of minimum remuneration rules of the host state to the posted worker is a mandatory rule fundamental to the objective of social protection in the Directive. *Arblade* compromised the application of that mandatory rule by subjecting it to the test demanding an overriding requirement of public interest.

---

32. *Ibid.*, Judgment of the Court, paragraphs 46 and 47.
33. *Ibid.*, paragraph 50 of the judgment.
34. *Ibid.*, paragraph 51.
35. *Ibid.*, paragraph 52.
36. *Ibid.*, paragraphs 58–59.
37. *Ibid.*, paragraphs 60–66.
38. Kolehmainen, *The Posted Workers Directive: European Reinforcement of National Labour Protection*, Section 4.2.1.4.

In explicitly stating that public policy provisions are generally subject to that test, *Arblade* also limited the discretion offered to the host state by Article 3(10) of the Directive. Subsequently, extending the list of applicable mandatory rules to include a public policy provision under Article 3(10) must be an overriding requirement of public interest. In addition, the Court limited the notion of 'public-order legislation' by stating that

> 'that term must be understood as applying to national provisions compliance with which has been deemed so crucial for the protection of the political, social or economic order in the Member State concerned as to require compliance therewith by all persons on the national territory of that Member State and all legal relationships within that State'.[39]

It is suggested that this interpretive guidance also restricts the extension of applicable mandatory rules under the discretion allowed by Article 3(10).

In short, *Arblade* established that the social protection of posted workers offered by Belgian public policy provisions is to be limited where it has the effect of restricting the freedom to provide services.

B. Mandatory rules relating to minimum remuneration

In *Arblade*, the European Court of Justice limited the application to posted workers of Belgian mandatory rules relating to minimum remuneration. That same limitation was increased by the Court in the first preliminary reference which requested an interpretation of the Posted Workers Directive, *Mazzoleni*.[40] Rules concerning minimum remuneration, which constituted a restriction on the freedom to provide services, could be justified only by satisfying a second test. Not only should they amount to an overriding requirement of public interest, conferring real additional protection. They should also be necessary and proportionate to the objective of protecting the workers concerned, in relation to the circumstances at issue.[41]

Introduction of the proportionality test encroaches on the principle, provided by the Posted Workers Directive, that host state rules concerning minimum remuneration are mandatory. The absolute nature of that principle is eroded since, prior to its enforcement, regard must be had to the circumstances in which the service is provided. It is suggested that the proportionality test thus requires the balancing of worker protection and promoting the freedom to provide services.

It should be noted at the outset that *Mazzoleni* concerned the particular posting situation of employees working on both sides of a national frontier. The extent to which its conclusions will be applied to other posting cases is not clear. At issue was the application to posted workers of Belgium's Collective Labour Agreement of 14 June 1993, fixing conditions of employment, including minimum remuneration, for private sector security officers. Those conditions were made mandatory by the Royal Decree of 1 March 1995, and were explicitly stated to refer to private security undertakings with headquarters outside Belgium.[42]

---

39. *Arblade* paragraph 30.
40. C-165/98 2001, ECR I-2189.
41. *Mazzoleni* paragraph 30.
42. *Ibid.*, paragraphs 3–4.

A company, established in France with security officers working in France and Belgium, and its owner were prosecuted before the *Tribunal Correctionel d'Arlon* for failure to pay the minimum hourly wage. That court asked the European Court of Justice, firstly, whether the Posted Workers Directive applied to frontier work. The Court responded that it was not necessary to interpret the Directive for the proceedings since the period prescribed for its implementation had not expired.[43] Secondly, the national court asked whether, to determine if the home state provided comparable protection to that offered by the host state, it was necessary to consider not only minimum remuneration rules, but the overall position of the workers. In that context, 'overall position' referred to all welfare protection.

Before considering whether comparable protection in the home state should be assessed on minimum remuneration rules or the overall position, the Court examined the applicability of the Belgian rules to the workers concerned. At this point, the Court introduced the requirement that, in certain circumstances, the rules must be necessary and proportionate for the protection of the workers concerned. The frontier work at issue apparently constituted such circumstances. Some of the security officers worked for short periods and on a part-time basis, in Belgium, carrying out the rest of their work in France.[44] It was for the national court to consider whether, in those circumstances, application of the mandatory minimum remuneration rules was necessary and proportionate to protecting the workers concerned.

The Court considered that application of the rules to service providers established in a frontier region of the home state could be disproportionate to that objective on two grounds. Firstly, it could create an additional, disproportionate administrative burden in obliging the employer to calculate hourly wages according to which state the worker has carried out his duties. Secondly, employees of the same undertaking, carrying out the same work, could receive different wages. That could result in tension between employees, possibly threatening the cohesion of home state collective agreements.[45]

It is worth observing, in the Court's use here of the proportionality test, the balancing of social protection and promoting freedom to provide services. The first ground indicates that an additional administrative calculation may be a disproportionate burden on a service provider. That conclusion appears to place the protection of the worker rather low in the balance. The second ground refers to respecting social protection, not in the host state but in the home state. However, as Kolehmainen has pointed out,[46] it seems unreasonable to expect home state collective agreements to be threatened because posted workers receive higher wages or request a pay rise on their return. The Court's application of the proportionality test does not appear to favour social protection of the workers concerned in any meaningful way. On the other hand, it appears to attend to the interests of the service provider.

The response as to whether comparable protection in the home state should be assessed on minimum remuneration rules or the overall position in terms of welfare protection also limited application of the mandatory minimum remuneration rule. The Court found that the objective of that rule could be considered met if posted workers enjoyed an equivalent position overall in relation to remuneration,

43. *Ibid.*, paragraph 17.
44. *Ibid.*, paragraphs 9 and 13.
45. *Ibid.*, paragraph 36.
46. Kolehmainen, *The Posted Workers Directive: European Reinforcement of National Labour Protection*, Section 4.2.1.5.

taxation and social security contributions in the host and home states.[47] That conclusion appears to limit the provision in the Posted Workers Directive that host state rules concerning minimum remuneration are mandatory and applicable to posted workers. It also seems to neglect that taxation and social security benefits are outside the scope of the Directive, which is 'the Community measure specifically adopted to regulate the application to posted workers of a host state's minimum terms of employment'.[48]

Mazzoleni addressed the particular posting situation of frontier work, and therefore its effect on the future interpretation of the Posted Workers Directive should not be generalized. However, the applicability of rules relating to minimum remuneration appears hindered by the ruling that it may, in certain circumstances, be dependent on its being proportionate to workers' protection.

The fact that a similar approach was subsequently used in *Finalarte*[49] indicates that this particular application of the proportionality test has been integrated into the Court's method of assessing posting cases. The joined cases in *Finalarte* were more typical posting cases in that they concerned payments into the host state's holiday fund for the construction sector. The host state's mandatory rule providing for holiday pay to be paid by the foreign employer was in that instance enforced by the Court on the grounds that it significantly added to workers' social protection and that it was proportionate to the public interest pursued.[50]

C. *The difference in scope between the Belgian regulations and the Directive*

Both *Arblade* and *Mazzoleni* indicate that the application of Belgian public policy provisions and, particularly, of regulations relating to minimum remuneration is to be restricted in the light of Community law. An obvious, yet significant, observation to be made is that the protection which the Belgian regulations aim to offer to posted workers is, in part, greater than that offered by Community law. It is significant in demonstrating a difference in how the protection of workers and the transnational freedom to provide services are balanced. The difference in protection is worth examining in relation to the applicability of collective agreements, in three respects.

Firstly, Belgian regulations allow for the application of collective agreements to posted workers generally. As noted above, certain of those agreements have been concluded on a national or sector-specific basis so as to be generally applicable. In addition, the Law of 5 March 2002 provides for the application of all regulations, including collective agreements, to posted workers generally.[51] Workers posted from non-Member States are therefore protected by Belgian regulations. They may seek to enforce those agreements against their employers in the home state under Articles 6 and 7 of the Rome Convention.

By contrast, the scope of the Posted Workers Directive is confined to workers posted by undertakings established in a Member State. They enjoy the protection of host state mandatory rules, as limited by *Arblade* and *Mazzoleni*. Therefore, workers

47. *Mazzoleni* paragraph 35.
48. Kolehmainen, *The Posted Workers Directive: European Reinforcement of National Labour Protection*, Section 4.2.1.5.
49. Joined Cases C-49/98, judgment of the Court of 25 October 2001.
50. *Finalarte*, paragraph 53.
51. The Law of 5 March 2002, Articles 3 and 5.

posted from non-Member States may enjoy protection greater than that offered by Community law; the application of Belgian regulations need not constitute an overriding requirement of public interest nor, in certain circumstances, be proportionate to the objective of workers' protection. Workers posted from Member States, on the other hand, benefit from the protection of the Belgian regulations only where the relevant tests under Community law are satisfied.

Consequently, in relation to the workers covered by protective rules, the Belgian regulations have a wider scope than the Posted Workers Directive and appear to provide greater protection than Community law allows. The comparison anticipates a limiting, and a lowered level, of social protection under the Directive for posted workers. On the other hand, employers may benefit from greater freedom to provide services transnationally.

Secondly, the applicability of Belgian collective agreements to posted workers is increased by the Directive due to its absence of a threshold. Prior to implementation of the Directive, workers posted to Belgium could enforce Belgian collective agreements only once habitually employed in the host state. Under the Directive, they may do so from the first day of employment in Belgium. In this respect, the Directive increases the protection of posted workers, and requires service providers to comply immediately with workers' protection regulations for the first time.

A third difference in the protection offered to posted workers by the Belgian regulations and the Directive is worth anticipating, though not yet confirmed by the European Court of Justice. It seems possible that workers posted to Belgium may seek to enforce generally applicable collective agreements providing for remuneration benefits additional to the minimum wage. Examples of such collective agreements are sector-specific agreements providing that salaries be automatically increased in line with a specified cost of living index; and sector-specific agreements providing for year-end bonuses.[52] Other significant collective agreements concern extra pay for shift working and extra holidays. These collective agreements are significant since their enforcement may be of concern to a greater proportion of the workforce than enforcement of agreements governing the minimum wage.

For example, workers posted to Belgium who earn well above the applicable minimum wage may seek to enforce these agreements. In that event, the Court could be obliged to interpret the applicability of the Directive to posted workers who may be considered in lesser need of social protection than those concerned in the posting cases so far decided. In view of the decision in *Arblade*, it is difficult to estimate whether the Court would permit the social protection provided by the latter collective agreements.

They each classify as Belgian public policy provisions, and have a criminal sanction attached to their breach by virtue of the Law of 5 December 1968. That status, following *Arblade*, does not render them automatically applicable. Should their application be considered a restriction on the freedom to provide services, which would seem probable, it could only be justified if constituting an overriding requirement of public interest, and proportionate to the objective of protecting the workers concerned. Where similar benefits existed in the home state, *Arblade* would apparently indicate that their application to posted workers was not justified.

52. Not all sectors provide for year end bonuses. Each sector's Collective Labour Agreement calculates such a bonus differently. One method consists of dividing the annual salary by twelve, multiplying it by thirteen and subtracting from that sum the annual salary to give a 'thirteenth month' bonus.

However, where no such benefits existed in the home state, their application would seem justifiable.

The crucial question, for current purposes, is whether the Court would permit application of such collective agreements, where that would seem to result in a clear hindrance to the freedom to provide services. The answer to that question would provide further guidance as to how worker protection and promoting freedom of services are to be balanced in applying the Directive.

That is only one reason demonstrating why enforcement of the Belgian regulations discussed here, and in particular the Law of 5 March 2002, in going beyond the protection afforded by the Posted Workers Directive, should be closely followed. The present case study has attempted to indicate in what ways the Belgian regulations may oblige the Court to give further interpretation of the extent of worker protection afforded by the Directive, and where that protection must give way to the freedom to provide services. The Belgian context is therefore likely to remain central in leading the Court to prioritize the aims of the Directive in practice.

BIBLIOGRAPHY

Biagi, M., 'Fortune Smiles on the Italian EU Presidency: Talking Half-Seriously About the Posted Workers and Parental Leave Directives', in *International Journal of Comparative Labour Law and Industrial Relations* Vol. 12, No. 2 1996, pp.97–109.

Davies, P., 'Posted Workers: Single Market or Protection of National Labour Law Systems', in *Common Market Law Review* Vol. 34, 1997, pp. 571–602.

Deinert, O., 'Posting of Workers to Germany – Previous Evolutions and New Influences throughout EU Legislation Proposals', in *International Journal of Comparative Labour Law and Industrial Relations*, Vol. 16, No. 3, 2000, pp. 217–34.

Eichhorst, W., 'European Social Policy between National and Supranational Regulation: Posted Workers in the Framework of Liberalized Services Provision', in *MPIfG Discussion Paper* 98/6.

Gronert, V., 'The Posting of Workers in the Framework of the Transnational Provision of Services – New Developments in Germany and in the EU', *Centre for International and European Law on Immigration and Asylum*, http://www.uni-konstant.de/FuF

Grosvenor, R., 'The Posting of Workers within the Framework of the Provision of Services', http://www.jumper.demon.co.uk/ec1.html, pp. 1–7.

Kidner, R., 'Jurisdiction in European Contracts of Employment', in *Industrial Law Journal,* Vol. 27, No. 2 , 1998, pp. 103–120.

Kolehmainen, E., *The Posted Workers Directive: European Reinforcement of National Labour Protection*, Doctoral thesis (unpublished) submitted to the European University Institute, Florence, 2002.

Knofel, S., 'Mandatory Rules and Choice of Law', in *Journal of Business Law*, 1999, pp.239–263.

Ojeda-Aviles, 'European Collective Bargaining and Posted Workers: Comments on Directive 96/71', in *International Journal of Comparative Labour Law and Industrial Relations*, Vol. 13/2, 1997, pp. 127–130.

Streeck, W., 'The Internationalization of Industrial Relations in Europe: Prospects and Problems', in *MPIfG Discussion Paper* 1998.

Proposal for a Council Directive Concerning the Posting of Workers in the Framework of the Provision of Services OJ C 225/6, 30 August 1991.
Amended Proposal for a Council Directive Concerning the Posting of Workers in the Framework of the Provision of Services COM (93) final SYN 346, OJ C 187/5, 9 July 1993.
House of Lords Select Committee on the European Communities 'Session 1992–93 5th Report', *Protection of Posted Workers*, HMSO, London, 1992.

Panel Discussion: European Developments

15A. Report on Negotiations of the European Social Partners Towards an EU-wide Collective Agreement on Temporary Agency Work

Wilfried Beirnaert

WHY THE NEGOTIATIONS ON TEMPORARY AGENCY WORK BROKE DOWN

Determined to exhaust every possibility of reaching a common position on temporary agency work, the European social partners negotiated together for almost a year. Once the customary nine-month negotiation period came to an end, the social partners jointly asked for an extension of three months to continue their efforts. Finally, we agreed on two major issues, but remained divided on a third core point. We reached consensus on the necessity for the Member States to clarify the legal status of the temporary agency worker; and the obligation for the Member States to impose the principle of equal treatment of temporary workers in relation to a comparable worker.

These two points in themselves would have justified an agreement, but a third point – defining the comparable worker – became a stumbling block. According to the European Commission, the social partners were close to consensus on this matter, and the negotiators would have succeeded in agreeing had more goodwill been shown. That assertion tends to overlook the fact that the definition of the comparable worker was an issue fundamental to the overall agreement sought.

For the ETUC, to evaluate equality of treatment in basic work and wage conditions, the comparable worker must be the permanent worker of the user undertaking unless a collective agreement at sector-level provides otherwise. In the employers' view, it was up to the Member States to determine the comparable worker. Since temporary agency work involves a trilateral relationship between temporary worker, agency and user undertaking, no single definition can be given which would be appropriate to the differing employment relationships found across the Member States. In its draft Directive of 20 March 2002, the Commission supported the ETUC's position, with the modification that it should exceptionally be possible to derogate from the rule that temporary workers must be treated equally to permanent employees of the user undertaking.

As subsequently demonstrated by other European bodies, the definition of the comparable worker was a critical issue. The European Economic and Social Committee approved the Commission's proposal which endorses the basic option of the ETUC, though only by a slight majority (83 for; 75 against; 12 abstentions).

R. Blanpain & R. Graham (eds.), Temporary Agency Work and the Information Society, 297–300

A counter-opinion was narrowly defeated (82 for; 90 against; 6 abstentions). The blocking minority in the European Council, which also demands a derogation period longer than six weeks, in fact supports the alternative position that it should be up to the Member States to set down the rules for determining the comparable worker.

DIVERGING VIEWS ON THE NATURE OF THE AGREEMENT

The ETUC wanted to conclude the cycle of negotiations on flexible contracts with an agreement of the same type as the agreement on fixed-term contracts which we had made previously. The underlying rationale for that approach was that the ETUC still tend to consider temporary agency work as lacking job security, like other atypical contracts, and moreover as threatening the position of the permanent worker in the user company. That induced the ETUC to advocate for a restrictive set of circumstances in which the use of temporary agency workers should be permitted.

The ETUC dealt with the dossier by focussing predominantly on the preservation of employment conditions laid down in collective agreements and on the protection of the permanent worker in the user company. UNICE, on the other hand, considered temporary agency work more broadly as an instrument of labour market policy. UNICE considered that temporary agency work was a justifiable form of flexible work. For many jobseekers, it is the point of entry into the labour market. Given the variation in labour market policy across the Member States, a margin of discretion should, according to UNICE, be allowed in the regulation of temporary agency work; only in that way can the Member States ensure that temporary agency work is an effective instrument of their respective labour market policies. It should be up to the Member States to strike the right balance between security and flexibility. The Member States should therefore also be responsible for lifting outdated constraints on temporary agency work.

UNICE's concept of a framework agreement on temporary agency work, laying down basic principles and allowing Member States a wide margin of discretion, diverged markedly from the restrictive agreement proposed by the ETUC.

LESSONS LEARNT FROM THE BREAKDOWN IN NEGOTIATIONS

A breakdown in negotiations need not be catastrophic so long as lessons are learnt from the failure. Rather than marking the end of dialogue, breakdown is integral to its progress. Its effect in this case was, in my view, to contribute to the recognition on both sides that the tactics of the European social dialogue had to be reassessed and given new direction.

The ETUC was inclined to evaluate the results of the European social dialogue by reflecting on the success or failure of negotiating binding collective agreements. Negotiations on temporary agency work had foundered. To save the dialogue we needed to use new methods of negotiation. We agreed that we must design a joint work programme that would be implemented by different forms of agreement. The idea would be that no one form of agreement should predominate, and that in each case we should select which was most appropriate. This approach guided both the framework of action drawn up for lifelong learning (March 2002) and the voluntary agreement we concluded on telework (July 2002). A voluntary agreement is not implemented in compliance with a Directive but is concluded at Member State-level entirely on the basis of national practice.

On 28 November 2002, we approved a joint work programme for the period 2003–2005 containing 19 different initiatives, among them a voluntary agreement on stress at work and harassment. I consider the approval of the work programme to be a milestone in relations between the European social partners.

15B. Agency Work in the European Union

Eva Casado Alarcon

I. AGENCY WORK

Background

Private employment agencies (PrEAs) are an essential part of efficient labour markets. This is because they meet the demands of employers, employees and of national governments, as follows.
PrEAs provide employers with:

- flexibility in times of fluctuating production needs;
- the possibility to fill in for employees who for one reason or another are temporarily absent from work;
- their expertise in matching job descriptions with job applicants.

As regards employees, PrEAs:

- provide work security for agency workers; whereas other so-called 'flexible' employees will be out of work at the end of their contract, an agency worker will have the benefit of having an employer who is pro-actively seeking to ensure that the worker will have work whenever he or she wants;
- keep workers who would otherwise be unemployed in touch with the job market, often providing a springboard to longer term employment;
- provide the kind of work which suits the differing circumstances of many workers, for example, students, retirees and mothers with young children at home;
- provide temporary assignments to workers who find permanent work mundane or repetitive;
- provide training (both on-the-job and off-the-job).

PrEAs satisfy the needs of national governments by:

- contributing to a properly functioning labour market;
- improving the employability of the workforce;
- providing work;
- assisting in the reintegration of disadvantaged people into the labour market;
- improving the national economy through the value of the sector.

That agency work contributes significantly to the employment market is illustrated by the fact that on an average day 8 million agency workers were placed by

R. Blanpain & R. Graham (eds.), Temporary Agency Work and the Information Society, 301–306

employment businesses in 1998, in CIETT countries alone. In Europe, the number of workers employed through an employment business on a given day amounts to over 2.8 million. A total of approximately 7 million people find work through employment businesses each year.

Work through Private Employment Agencies (PrEAs)

The main objective of PrEAs is to find work assignments for their workers, aiming to ensure that they have work whenever they want. They seek to keep the time between assignments for every agency worker to the absolute minimum possible, since every hour a worker is not working is an opportunity cost for the business. On the other hand, the agency worker benefits from the fact that the PrEA is constantly trying to find him/her a new assignment.

PrEAs assist not only young and well-educated workers. An increasing number of the workers who find jobs through agencies are those classified by the OECD as 'outsiders' (long-term unemployed, first time entrants into the labour market, ethnic minorities, etc.).

Work offered by PrEAs can meet the needs of workers who for physical reasons prefer temporary jobs to permanent employment. An increasingly high number of agencies run schemes aimed at providing training and employment to disabled workers.

Other categories that benefit from work through employment businesses are young people, working mothers, and workers who have taken early retirement. For those seeking their first job, agency work can act as a low-threshold point of entry into the labour market. For those seeking flexibility, it offers the opportunity to adapt working patterns to lifestyles.

Training through Private Employment Agencies

In order to meet their clients' demands, PrEAs must be able to supply workers with the required qualifications and skills. Many PrEAs invest significantly in the training of their workers. This is in addition to the on-the-job training opportunities that agency work assignments provide.

This policy enables agency workers to update their skills and to access jobs they would previously have been unable to undertake. This particularly benefits young people who have not yet found a way into the labour market, and the long-term unemployed.

Integration of Workers in the Labour Market (Participation)

This is one of the key areas of the labour market where agency work can make a significant contribution. Research carried out by McKinsey & Co. in 2000 on agency work in the European Union on behalf of CIETT reached a series of conclusions on this issue, most importantly, that:

1. Forty per cent of the workers employed through employment agencies belong to the category defined by the OECD as 'outsiders to the labour

market' (i.e. long-term unemployed, first-time entrants to the labour market, women accessing the labour market, etc.);
2. Agency work acts as a 'stepping-stone' to longer-term employment: 43 per cent of agency workers are in longer-term employment within one year of the start of their first assignment.

II. AGENCY WORK IN THE EUROPEAN UNION

Agency work employed over 7 million workers in the EU in 2001. That is equivalent to an average of 2.8 million workers employed through agencies on any given day or 1.9 per cent of the EU working population. Additionally, the PrEA (Private Employment Agency) industry employs approximately 120,000 full-time employees.[1]

Between 1996 and 1998, the agency work industry increased EU employment by 0.1 per cent accounting for around 11 per cent of total new job creation.[2]

PrEAs are responsible for genuine employment creation: 17 per cent of work done through agencies would not have been carried out had this option not been available; 38% would have been carried out using other flexibility solutions, such as overtime, which do not contribute to employment creation. Only 14 per cent of companies using agency work would have hired permanent workers.

Participation of the agency work industry in the labour market varies significantly among Member States, depending on their legal approach to regulating agency work. Percentages of workers employed through agency work range from 4.5 per cent in the Netherlands, 3.2 per cent in the UK, 2.5 per cent in France, 0.7 per cent in Spain and lower in Italy where the industry was only legalized in 1998.

PrEAs meet a genuine demand for flexible work from workers. Thirty-three of agency workers have a genuine preference for agency work. Only 26 per cent of agency workers work through an agency because they have been unable to find a permanent job.

PrEAs provide both work opportunities and an excellent entry into the labour market for 'outsiders' thus enhancing employment opportunities for workers. Forty per cent of first-time agency workers are 'outsiders'.

PrEAs act as a 'stepping-stone' to longer-term employment. Forty-one per cent of agency workers in the EU are in longer-term employment within one year of their agency work assignment.

The turnover of PrEAs in 1999 was 59 billion Euro, with a total tax contribution of 28 billion Euro. In the UK and the Netherlands, the sector's fiscal contribution is equivalent to 1 per cent of national income.

The Contribution of Agency Work towards the 2010 Lisbon Objectives

Euro-CIETT has called on all European institutions to consider and examine the contribution that agency work can make towards the Lisbon employment creation and integration targets, within the framework of the European Employment Strategy

1. Updated data from the CIETT report *Orchestrating the Evolution of Private Employment Agencies towards a stronger society*, McKinsey, 2000.
2. That is, the use of agency workers to perform tasks that either would not have been performed or would have been performed using internal flexibility solutions that do not increase employment.

and the new broad economic policy guidelines, as indicated by the figures discussed in the previous Section.

Agency work can contribute to the attainment of the EU's three main priorities for a new employment strategy by aiding in:

- achieving the Lisbon targets to raise employment and participation rates;
- improving quality at work and promoting productive jobs; and
- promoting an inclusive labour market.

Additionally, agency work already plays a significant role with regard to social inclusion, providing an effective remedy to some of the 'pervasive weaknesses', mentioned by the European Commission in its Spring 2003 assessment of the European Employment Strategy, by providing an entry into the labour market for outsiders. (i.e. long-term unemployed; female workers; older workers; immigrants, ethnic minorities and workers perceived as disadvantaged).

According to the European Commission, the EU must step up the pace of reform if 15 million new jobs are to be created between now and 2010.

Euro CIETT estimates that the agency work industry could create 4 million new jobs between 1998 and 2010, providing work for up to 18 million people a year. However, the appropriate legal framework needs to be in place for this potential to be realized.

Proposal for a Directive on Working Conditions of Temporary Agency Workers[3]

The European agency work industry and its representative organization Euro-CIETT have expressed concern that the amended proposal for a Directive on agency work will destroy existing agency jobs, will hamper future job creation and will result in increased complexity, administrative burdens and costs.

Agency work already plays an important role in the attainment of the Lisbon objectives on employment creation and participation (integration of workers in labour markets). This contribution is particularly crucial at a time when the European Council has concluded that the EU is lagging behind in the realization of these objectives.

A European Directive on agency work should seek to enhance and not to limit the contribution that agency work can make towards the European Employment Strategy and the Lisbon targets on job creation and participation. The Directive should balance two key objectives: protecting agency workers and enabling the agency work industry to fulfil its job creation potential, in line with the EU employment creation objectives.

The positions of Euro-CIETT on the two elements of the draft Directive which have been the main focus of discussion both in the European Parliament First Reading and in the Council (on Articles 4 and 5) are as follows:

Article 4 – Review of restrictions and prohibitions

As the Commission rightly states in its amended proposal, Article 4 meets the key objective of enabling the agency work industry to fulfil its job creation potential by

3. COM (2002) 701 final. Amended proposal for a Directive of the European Parliament and the Council on working conditions for temporary workers.

providing more flexibility. Therefore, deleting Article 4, either in whole or in part, is equivalent to ignoring completely one of the two stated objectives of the draft Directive.

Any Member State committed to the Lisbon objectives should not object to eliminating unjustified restrictions on agency work and reporting their elimiation to the European Commission. The only reason a Member State would oppose that obligation is if they realize their restrictions on agency work are indeed unjustifiable and are concerned about them being exposed to the European Commission. The EU cannot permit national governments to publicly commit to creating jobs on the one hand (by agreeing to the Lisbon objectives), only to ignore that commitment on the other having deleted the last two sentences of Article 4 of the amended proposal.

Article 4 should clearly state the need to review and eliminate all existing restrictions on agency work. It should also introduce clear time frames for such reviews to take place, as proposed by the European Parliament. Protection of agency workers and health and safety considerations must be the only valid grounds for maintaining a restriction.

Article 5 – The principle of non-discrimination

Part of the second stated objective of the draft Directive is to recognize temporary agencies as employers. As employers, temporary agencies have:

a) the right to determine the working conditions of their employees, the agency workers;
b) a legal obligation not to discriminate between their employees, the agency workers.

It is fundamentally wrong both to remove the agencies' right as employers and to force temporary agencies to introduce discrimination, by obliging them to compare their own employees with those of a different employer, the user undertaking. The only situation where such discrimination can be justified is where it has the full support of the social partners concerned, the temporary agencies and the representative bodies of agency workers, as is the case in some Member States.

In order to recognize these two different approaches to non-discrimination, the principle should be implemented, either at the level of the employer (the temporary agency), or at the level of the user undertaking (assuming this is the preferred approach of representative national social partners). The only other situation where an obligation to establish comparability at the level of the user undertaking is appropriate is where temporary workers are indeed fully integrated in the user undertaking. This can only be the case for temporary workers who have been assigned to the same user undertaking for a certain period of time, which in Euro-CIETT's view should not be less than twelve months.

ANNEX – ABOUT CIETT AND EURO-CIETT

Founded on 17th May 1967 in Paris, CIETT is the International Confederation of Temporary Work Businesses. It brings together the national associations of employment businesses – businesses which supply workers for temporary assignments on their clients' premises – of thirty countries world-wide and six of the largest staffing companies world-wide.

CIETT is the only international organization concerned with the interests of these businesses and is recognized as such by national and international organizations and governments.

Euro-CIETT is the Social Partner for the agency work sector, within the framework of the European Social Dialogue. Euro-CIETT represents the National Federations of Agency Work in all EU Member States, Poland, Romania and six of the largest staffing companies worldwide (Adecco, Kelly Services, Manpower, Randstad, Vedior & USG).

The CIETT and Euro-CIETT mission is to protect and promote the interests of agency work businesses and their national associations, in order to ensure their long term survival and prosperity.

The main objective of CIETT and Euro-CIETT is to seek greater recognition of the contribution made by agency work in relation to overall employment creation, integration in the labour market and economic growth.

Members of CIETT and Euro-CIETT are required to adhere to a Code of Practice adopted in 1971 and designed to protect the interests of their temporary workers and their clients, as well as conforming to their own national laws.

16. Proposal for a Directive of the European Parliament and the Council on Working Conditions for Temporary Workers[1]

(2002/C 203 E/01)

(Text with EEA relevance)

COM(2002) 149 final – 2002/0072(COD)

(Submitted by the Commission on 21 March 2002)

THE EUROPEAN PARLIAMENT AND THE COUNCIL OF THE EUROPEAN UNION

Having regard to the Treaty establishing the European Community and, in particular, Article 137(2) thereof,

Having regard to the proposal from the Commission,

Having regard to the opinion of the Economic and Social Committee,

Having regard to the opinion of the Committee of the Regions,

Acting in accordance with the procedure laid down in Article 251 of the Treaty,

Whereas:

(1) This instrument respects the fundamental rights and complies with the principles recognized by the Charter of Fundamental Rights of the European Union; in particular, it is designed to ensure full compliance with Article 31 of that Charter, which provides that every worker has the right to working conditions which respect his or her health, safety and dignity and to limitation of maximum working hours, to daily and weekly rest periods and to an annual period of paid leave.

(2) Moreover, point 7 of the Community Charter of the Fundamental Social Rights of Workers provides, *inter alia*, that the completion of the internal market must lead to an improvement in the living and working conditions of workers in the European Community; this process will be

1. O.J., 27 August 2002, C 203 E/1/

R. Blanpain & R. Graham (eds.), Temporary Agency Work and the Information Society, 307–314

achieved by harmonizing progress on these conditions, mainly by forms of work other than permanent contracts such as fixed-term contract work, part-time work, temporary work and seasonal work.

(3) The conclusions of the European Council in Lisbon of 23 and 24 March 2000 set the European Union a new strategic target, namely to 'become the most competitive and most dynamic knowledge-based economy in the world, capable of sustained economic growth with more and better jobs and greater social cohesion'.

(4) In accordance with the European Social Agenda, which, on the basis of the communication from the Commission, was adopted by the European Council in Nice of 7, 8 and 9 December 2000, with the conclusions of the European Council in Stockholm of 23 and 24 March 2000 and with the Council Decision of 19 January 2001 on the 2001 employment guidelines, a satisfactory and flexible work organization system has to be put in place, with new flexible contracts offering workers a fair degree of job security and enhanced occupational status, which, at the same time, is compatible with the workers' aspirations and undertakings' needs.

(5) The Commission consulted the social partners on the course of action that could be adopted at Community level with regard to flexibility of working hours and job security of workers on 27 September 1995.

(6) After that consultation, the Commission decided that Community action was desirable and consulted the social partners once again with regard to the content of the planned proposal on 9 April 1996.

(7) In the introduction to the framework agreement on fixed-term work concluded on 18 March 1999, the signatories had indicated their intention to consider the need for a similar agreement on temporary work.

(8) The general cross-sector organizations, i.e. the UNICE, CEEP and ETUC, informed the Commission in their joint letter of their desire to implement the procedure provided for by Article 138(4) of the EC Treaty; in a joint letter they asked the Commission for an extension of the deadline by three months; the Commission granted this request by extending the negotiation deadline until 15 March 2001.

(9) On 21 May 2001, the social partners acknowledged that their negotiations on temporary work had not produced any agreement.

(10) There are considerable differences in the legal situation of temporary workers within the Union.

(11) Temporary work should meet undertakings' needs for flexibility and employees' needs to reconcile their working and private lives and contribute to job-creation and participation and integration in the labour market.

(12) The aim of this directive is to establish a protective framework for temporary workers which also provides temporary agencies operating in the European Community with a consistent and flexible framework which is conducive to their activities, without imposing any administrative, financial or legal constraints which would impede the creation and development of small and medium-sized undertakings.

(13) This Directive shall be implemented in compliance with the Treaty, specifically with regard to freedom to provide services and freedom of establishment and without prejudice to Directive 96/71/EC of the European Parliament and the Council of 16 December 1996[2] concerning the posting of workers in the framework of the provision of services.

(14) Directive 91/383/EEC of 25 June 1991[3] supplementing the measures to encourage improvements in the safety and health at work of workers with a fixed-duration employment relationship or a temporary employment relationship establishes the safety and health provisions applicable to temporary workers.

(15) With respect to basic working and employment conditions, temporary workers should not be treated any less favourably than a 'comparable worker', i.e. a worker in the user undertaking in an identical or similar job, taking into account seniority, qualifications and skills.

(16) However, differences in treatment are acceptable if they are objectively and reasonably justified by a legitimate aim under national law.

(17) In the case of workers who have a permanent contract with their temporary agency, and in view of the special protection such a contract offers, provision should be made to permit exemptions from the rules applicable in the user undertaking.

(18) In view of the need to maintain a certain degree of flexibility in the working relationship, provision should be made for the Member States to be able to delegate to the social partners the task of defining basic working and employment conditions tailored to the specific characteristics of certain types of employment or certain branches of economic activity.

(19) There should be some flexibility in the application of the principle of non-discrimination in cases of missions effected to accomplish a job which, due to its nature or duration, lasts less than six weeks.

(20) An improvement in the minimum protection for temporary workers occasioned by this Directive will enable any restrictions or prohibitions which may have been imposed on temporary work to be reviewed and, if necessary, lifted if they are no longer justified on grounds of the general interest regarding, in particular the protection of workers.

(21) There must be an effective means of safeguarding temporary workers' rights.

(22) In compliance with the principle of subsidiarity and the principle of proportionality under Article 5 of the Treaty, the aims of the action envisaged above cannot be achieved satisfactorily by the Member States, since the goal is to establish a harmonized Community-level framework of protection for temporary workers; owing to the scale and the impact of the action planned, these objectives can best be met at Community level by introducing minimum requirements applicable throughout the European Community; this directive confines itself to what is required for achieving these objectives.

---

2. OJ L 18, 21 January 1997, p. 1.
3. OJ L 206, 29 July 1991, p. 19.

HAVE ADOPTED THIS DIRECTIVE

CHAPTER 1

GENERAL PROVISIONS

Article 1
Scope

1. This Directive applies to the contract of employment or employment relationship between a temporary agency, which is the employer, and the worker, who is posted to a user undertaking to work under its supervision.

2. This directive applies to public and private undertakings engaged in economic activities whether or not they are operating for gain.

3. Member States may, after consulting the social partners, provide that this directive does not apply to employment contracts or relationships concluded under a specific public or publicly supported training, integration or vocational retraining programme.

Article 2
Aim

The purpose of this Directive is:

1. to improve the quality of temporary work by ensuring that the principle of non-discrimination is applied to temporary workers;

2 to establish a suitable framework for the use of temporary work to contribute to the smooth functioning of the labour and employment market.

Article 3
Definition

1. For the purposes of this directive:
   (a) 'worker' means any person who, in the Member State concerned, is protected as a worker under national employment law;
   (b) 'comparable worker' means a worker in the user undertaking occupying an identical or similar post to that occupied by the worker posted by the temporary agency, account being taken of seniority, qualifications and skills;
   (c) 'posting' means the period during which the temporary worker is placed at the user undertaking;
   (d) 'basic working and employment conditions': working and employment conditions relating to:
      (i) the duration of working time, rest periods, night work, paid holidays and public holidays;
      (ii) pay;
      (iii) work done by pregnant women and nursing mothers, children and young people;

(iv) action taken to combat discrimination on the grounds of sex, race or ethnic origin, religion or beliefs, disabilities, age or sexual orientation.

2. This directive shall be without prejudice to national law as regards the definition of contract of employment or employment relationship. However, Member States shall not exclude from the scope of this Directive contracts of employment or employment relationships solely because they concern:
(a) part time workers within the meaning of Council Directive 97/81/EC of 15 December 1997;
(b) fixed-term contract workers within the meaning of Council Directive 99/70/EC of 28 June 1999;
(c) persons on a posting at a user undertaking.

Article 4
Review of restriction or prohibitions

1. Member States, after consulting the social partners in accordance with legislation, collective agreements and national practices, shall review periodically any restrictions or prohibitions on temporary work for certain groups of workers or sectors of economic activity in order to verify whether the specific conditions underlying them still obtain. If they do not, the Member States should discontinue them.

2. The Member States shall notify the Commission of the result of said review. If the restrictions or prohibitions are maintained, the Member States shall inform the Commission why they consider that they are necessary and justified.

The restrictions or prohibitions which could be maintained shall be justified on grounds of the general interest regarding, in particular, the protection of workers.

CHAPTER II

EMPLOYMENT AND WORKING CONDITIONS

Article 5
The principle of non-discrimination

1. Temporary workers during their posting, shall receive at least as favourable treatment, in terms of basic working and employment conditions, including seniority in the job, as a comparable worker in the user enterprise, unless the difference in treatment is justified by objective reasons. Where appropriate, the *pro rata temporis* principle applies.

2. Member States may provide that an exemption be made to the principle established in paragraph 1 when temporary workers who have a permanent contract of employment with a temporary agency continue to be paid in the time between postings.

3. Member States may give the social partners at the appropriate level the option of concluding collective agreements which derogate from the principle established in paragraph 1 as long as an adequate level of protection is provided for temporary workers.

4. Without prejudice to the provisions of paragraphs 2 and 3 above, Member States may provide that paragraph 1 shall not apply where a temporary worker works on an

assignment or series of assignments with the same user enterprise in a post which, due to its duration or nature, can be accomplished in a period not exceeding six weeks.

Member States shall take appropriate measures with a view to preventing misuse in the application of this paragraph.

5. When this directive calls for a comparison to be made with a comparable worker in the user undertaking but no such worker exists, reference shall be made to the collective agreement applicable in the user undertaking; if no such collective agreement exists, the comparison will be made by reference to the collective agreement applicable to the temporary work agency; if no collective agreement is applicable, the basic working and employment conditions of temporary workers will be determined by national legislation and practices.

6. The implementing procedures for this Article shall be defined by the Member States after consultation of the social partners. The Member States may also entrust the social partners at the appropriate level with the task of defining these procedures for this chapter by means of a negotiated agreement.

Article 6
Access to permanent quality employment

1. Temporary workers shall be informed of any vacant posts in the user undertaking to give them the same opportunity as other workers in that undertaking to find permanent employment.

2. Member States shall take any action required to ensure that any clauses banning or having the effect of preventing the conclusion of a contract of employment or an employment relationship between the user undertaking and the temporary worker after his posting are null and void or may be declared null and void.

3. Temporary agencies shall not charge workers any fees in exchange for arranging for them to be recruited by a user undertaking.

4. Temporary workers shall be given access to the social services of the user undertaking unless there are objective reasons against this.

5. Member States shall take suitable measures or shall promote dialogue between the social partners, in accordance with their national traditions and practices in order to:

- improve temporary workers' access to training in the temporary agencies, even in the periods between their postings, in order to enhance their career development and employability;
- improve temporary workers' access to training for user undertakings' workers.

Article 7
Representation of temporary workers

Temporary workers shall count for the purposes of calculating the threshold above which bodies representing workers provided for under national and Community legislation should be formed at the temporary agency.

Member States may provide that, under conditions that they define, these workers count for the purposes of calculating the threshold above which bodies representing workers provided for by national and Community legislation should be formed in the user undertaking.

Article 8
Information of workers' representatives

Without prejudice to national and Community provisions which are more stringent and/or more specific on information and consultation, the user undertaking must provide suitable information on the use of temporary workers when providing information on the employment situation in that undertaking to bodies representing the workers set up in accordance with national and Community legislation.

CHAPTER III

FINAL PROVISIONS

Article 9
Minimum requirements

1. This Directive does not prejudice the Member States' right to apply or introduce legislative, regulatory or administrative provisions which are more favourable to workers or to promote or permit collective agreements concluded between the social partners which are more favourable to workers.

2. The implementation of this Directive shall under no circumstances constitute sufficient grounds for justifying a reduction in the general level of protection of workers in the fields covered by this Directive. This shall be without prejudice to the rights of Member States and/or management and labour to lay down, in the light of changing circumstances, different legislative, regulatory or contractual arrangements to those prevailing at the time of the adoption of this Directive, provided always that the minimum requirements laid down in this Directive are adhered to.

Article 10
Penalties

Member States shall lay down rules on sanctions applicable in the event of infringements of national provisions enacted under this directive and shall take all necessary measures to ensure that they are applied. The penalties provided for must be effective proportionate and disuasive. Member States shall notify these provisions to the Commission by the date given in Article 11 at the latest and any subsequent amendment within good time. They shall, in particular, ensure that workers and/or their representatives have adequate means of enforcing the obligations under this directive.

Article 11
Implementation

1. The Member States shall adopt the laws, regulations and administrative provisions necessary to comply with this directive by [two years after adoption] at the latest, or shall ensure that the social partners introduce the necessary provisions by way of an agreement, whereby the Member States must make all the necessary arrangements

to enable them to guarantee at any time that the objectives of this directive are being attained. They shall forthwith inform the Commission thereof.

2. When Member States adopt these provisions, they shall contain a reference to this directive or shall be accompanied by such a reference on the occasion of their official publication. The methods of making such reference shall be laid down by the Member States.

Article 12
Review by the Commission

(Five years after adoption of this directive) at the latest, the Commission shall, in consultation with the Member States and social partners at Community level, review application thereof with a view to proposing, where appropriate, the necessary amendments to the Parliament and the Council.

Article 13
Entry into force

This directive shall enter into force on the twentieth day after its publication in the *Official Journal of the European Communities*.

Article 14

This directive is addressed to the Member States.

17. Amended Proposal for a Directive of the European Parliament and the Council on Working Conditions for Temporary Workers (Presented by the Commission in Accordance with Article 250(2) of the EC Treaty)

EXPLANATORY MEMORANDUM

1. Introduction

On 20 March 2002, the Commission adopted a proposal for a directive of the European Parliament and the Council on working conditions for temporary workers. This proposal was forwarded to the European Parliament and the Council on 21 March 2002.

On 19 September 2002, the Economic and Social Committee gave its opinion on the Commission's proposal.

The European Parliament gave its opinion at the first reading on 21 November 2002.

2. Amendments

A. The European Parliament's amendments accepted by the Commission

The amended proposal contains two types of amendments; first, to reword the articles or add new provisions in the interests of clarification or precision and, second, to amend the substance and scope of the text by including or deleting important provisions.

The Commission is prepared to accept, in part or in full, all the amendments set out below, which, it thinks, improve the proposal and maintain its aims and political viability:

- Amendment No. 1 (changing the title of the directive): *see* title of the proposal;
- Amendment No. 4 (rewording recital 4): *see* recital No. 4;
- Amendment No. 6 (specifying the links between this proposal and Directive 1999/70 of 28 June 1999 on fixed-term work): *see* recital No. 7;
- Amendment No. 15 (announcing proposed amendments to Article 5.1): *see* recital No. 15;
- Amendment No. 20 (announcing proposed amendments to Article 4): *see* recital No. 19;

R. Blanpain & R. Graham (eds.), Temporary Agency Work and the Information Society, 315–324

- Amendment No. 22 (reinforcing the principle of subsidiarity): *see* recital No. 22;
- Amendment No. 23 (rewording the scope to illustrate more clearly the triangular nature of temporary work): *see* Article 1.1;
- Amendment No. 26 (reinforcing Article 2): *see* Article 2;
- Amendment No. 27 (adding the definition of a temporary worker): *see* Article 3(1)(b);
- Amendment No. 28 (deleting the definition of a comparable worker): deletion of this definition in Article 3;
- Amendment No. 29 (redefining a posting): *see* Article 3(1)(c);
- Amendment No. 30 (adding the definition of a temporary agency): *see* Article 3(1)(d);
- Amendment No. 31 (adding the definition of a user undertaking): *see* Article 3(1)(e);
- Amendment No. 32 (redefining working and employment conditions): *see* Article 3(1)(f) and Article 5(1) second indent;
- Amendment No. 85 (specifying that it is up to the Member States to define pay): *see* Article 3(2);
- Amendment No. 33 (specifying workers who cannot be excluded from the scope of the Directive): *see* Article 3(2);
- Amendment No. 34 (extending the obligation on the Member States to review restrictions or prohibitions pertaining only to certain categories of workers or certain branches to all restrictions or prohibitions; extending the scope of justifications for prohibitions/restrictions): *see* Articles 4(1) and (2);
- Amendment No. 35 (specifying that the provisions in force concerning registration and monitoring of temporary workers are not prohibitions or restrictions within the meaning of the foregoing amendment): *see* Article 4(3);
- Amendment No. 36 (adding a provision stipulating that temporary workers may not replace striking workers in the user undertaking): *see* recital No. 21;
- Amendment No. 87 (acceptance of the part rewording the principle of non-discrimination): *see* Article 5(1) first indent;
- Amendment No. 86 (restricting the exemption to remuneration and requiring consultation of the social partners): *see* Article 5(2);
- Amendment No. 92 (acceptance of the part on prior consultation of the social partners and enabling them to uphold existing collective agreements): *see* Article 5(3);
- Amendment No. 71 (acceptance only of the part restricting exemptions to pay): *see* Article 5(4);
- Amendment No. 43 (deleting Article 5(5)): *see* deleted Article 5(5), previous version;
- Amendment No. 44 (specifying that implementation of Article 5 through an agreement between the social partners should be in line with national practice): *see* Article 5(5);
- Amendment No. 46 (specifying how information on vacancies may be made public): *see* Article 6(1);
- Amendment No. 47 (on clauses prohibiting the conclusion of contracts of employment): *see* Article 6(2);
- Amendment No. 48 (specifying the scope of the prohibition on fees): *see* Article 6(3);

- Amendment No. 49 (specifying social services): *see* Article 6(4);
- Amendment No. 51 (an addition to take account of the fact that workers' representation may be determined by collective agreements): *see* Article 7;
- Amendment No. 52 (introducing a choice of the action open to workers – direct action or action through representatives – if the Directive is not complied with): *see* Article 10.

B. The European Parliament's amendments rejected by the Commission

By contrast, the Commission cannot accept at this stage the other amendments proposed by the Parliament. Some of them do not constitute an improvement to the Directive or are not acceptable from a strictly legal point of view. Others might, in the Commission's view, disrupt the balance of the initial text.

Amended Proposal for a Directive of the European Parliament and the Council on Temporary Work

THE EUROPEAN PARLIAMENT AND THE COUNCIL OF THE EUROPEAN UNION

Having regard to the Treaty establishing the European Community and, in particular, Article 137(2) thereof,

Having regard to the proposal from the Commission,

Having regard to the opinion of the Economic and Social Committee,

Having regard to the opinion of the Committee of the Regions,

Acting in accordance with the procedure laid down in Article 251 of the Treaty,

Whereas:

(1) This instrument respects the fundamental rights and complies with the principles recognized by the Charter of Fundamental Rights of the European Union; in particular, it is designed to ensure full compliance with Article 31 of that Charter, which provides that every worker has the right to working conditions which respect his or her health, safety and dignity and to restriction of maximum working hours, to daily and weekly rest periods and to an annual period of paid leave.

(2) Moreover, point 7 of the Community Charter of the Fundamental Social Rights of Workers provides, *inter alia*, that the completion of the internal market must lead to an improvement in the living and working conditions of workers in the European Community; this process will be achieved by harmonizing progress on these conditions, mainly by forms

of work other than permanent contracts such as fixed-term contract work, part-time work, temporary work and seasonal work.

(3) The conclusions of the European Council in Lisbon of 23 and 24 March 2000 set the European Union a new strategic target, namely to 'become the most competitive and most dynamic knowledge-based economy in the world, capable of sustained economic growth with more and better jobs and greater social cohesion'.

(4) In accordance with the European Social Agenda, which, on the basis of the communication from the Commission, was adopted by the European Council in Nice of 7, 8 and 9 December 2000, with the conclusions of the European Council in Stockholm of 23 and 24 March 2000 and with the Council Decision of 19 January 2001 on the 2001 employment guidelines, a satisfactory and flexible work organization system has to be put in place, including new statutory flexibility arrangements, offering workers a fair degree of job security and enhanced occupational status, and at the same time, reconciling workers' aspirations and undertakings' needs.

(5) The Commission consulted the social partners on the course of action that could be adopted at Community level with regard to flexibility of working hours and job security of workers on 27 September 1995.

(6) After that consultation, the Commission considered that Community action was desirable and consulted the social partners once again with regard to the content of the planned proposal on 9 April 1996.

(7) In the introduction to the framework agreement on fixed-term work concluded on 18 March 1999, the signatories had indicated their intention to consider the need for a similar agreement on temporary work and not to include temporary workers in the Directive on fixed-term work.

(8) The general cross-sector organizations, i.e. the UNICE, CEEP and ETUC, informed the Commission in their joint letter of their desire to implement the procedure provided for by Article 138(4) of the EC Treaty; in a joint letter they asked the Commission for an extension of the deadline by three months; the Commission granted this request by extending the negotiation deadline until 15 March 2001.

(9) On 21 May 2001, the social partners acknowledged that their negotiations on temporary work had not produced any agreement.

(10) There are considerable differences in the legal situation of temporary workers within the Union.

(11) Temporary work should meet undertakings' needs for flexibility and employees' need to reconcile their working and private lives and contribute to job creation and to participation and integration in the labour market.

(12) The aim of this Directive is to establish a protective framework for temporary workers which also provides temporary agencies operating in the European Community with a consistent and flexible framework which is conducive to their activities, without imposing any administrative, financial or legal constraints which would impede the creation and development of small and medium-sized undertakings.

(13) This Directive shall be implemented in compliance with the Treaty, specifically with regard to freedom to provide services and freedom of establishment and without prejudice to Directive 96/71/EC of the European Parliament and the Council of 16 December 1996 concerning the posting of workers in the framework of the provision of services.

(14) Directive 91/383/EEC of 25 June 1991 supplementing the measures to encourage improvements in the safety and health at work of workers with a fixed-duration employment relationship or a temporary employment relationship establishes the safety and health provisions applicable to temporary workers.

(15) The basic working and employment conditions applicable to temporary workers should be at least those which would apply to such workers if they were recruited by the user undertaking to occupy the same job.

(16) In the case of workers who have a permanent contract with their temporary agency, and in view of the special protection such a contract offers, provision should be made to permit exemptions from the rules applicable in the user undertaking.

(17) In view of the need to maintain a certain degree of flexibility in the working relationship, provision should be made for the Member States to be able to delegate to the social partners the task of defining basic working and employment conditions tailored to the specific characteristics of certain types of employment or certain branches of economic activity.

(18) There should be some flexibility in the application of the principle of non-discrimination in cases of assignments effected to accomplish a job which, due to its nature or duration, lasts less than six weeks.

(19) An improvement in the minimum protection for temporary workers occasioned by this Directive will enable any restrictions or prohibitions which may have been imposed on temporary work to be reviewed and, if necessary, lifted if they are no longer justified. They may be justified only on grounds of the general interest regarding, in particular the protection of workers, the requirements of safety and health at work and the need to ensure that the labour market functions properly and abuses are prevented.

(20) The provisions of this Directive on restrictions or prohibitions on temporary work are without prejudice to national legislation or practices prohibiting striking workers being replaced by temporary workers.

(21) There must be an effective means of safeguarding temporary workers' rights.

(22) In compliance with the principle of subsidiarity and the principle of proportionality under Article 5 of the Treaty, the aims of the action envisaged above cannot be achieved satisfactorily by the Member States, since the goal is to establish a harmonized Community-level framework of protection for temporary workers; owing to the scale and the impact of the action planned, these objectives can best be met at Community level by introducing minimum requirements applicable throughout the European Community in order to provide the Member States with a common framework to facilitate the integration of European labour markets and cross-border mobility of workers,

especially in border regions; this Directive confines itself to what is required for achieving these objectives

HAVE ADOPTED THIS DIRECTIVE

CHAPTER I

GENERAL PROVISIONS

Article 1
Scope

1. This Directive applies to workers with a contract of employment or employment relationship with a temporary agency, who are posted to user undertakings to work temporarily under their supervision.

2. This Directive applies to public and private undertakings engaged in economic activities whether or not they are operating for gain, and which are temporary agencies or user undertakings.

3. Member States may, after consulting the social partners, provide that this Directive does not apply to employment contracts or relationships concluded under a specific public or publicly supported vocational training, integration or retraining programme.

Article 2
Aim

The purpose of this Directive is:
1. to ensure the protection of temporary workers and to improve the quality of temporary work by ensuring that the principle of non-discrimination is applied to temporary workers and recognizing temporary agencies as employers;

2. to establish a suitable framework for the use of temporary work to contribute to creating jobs and the smooth functioning of the labour market.

Article 3
Definition

1. For the purposes of this Directive:
(a) 'worker' means any person who, in the Member State concerned, is protected as a worker under national employment law;
(b) temporary worker: a person with a contract of employment or an employment relationship with a temporary agency with a view to being posted to a user undertaking to work temporarily under its supervision;
(c) 'posting' means the period during which the temporary worker is placed at the user undertaking to work temporarily under its supervision;
(d) 'temporary agency' means any natural or legal person who, in compliance with national law, concludes contracts of employment or employment relationships

with temporary workers in order to post them to user undertakings to work there temporarily under their supervision;

(e) 'user undertaking' means any natural or legal person for whom and under the supervision of whom a temporary worker works temporarily;

(f) 'basic working and employment conditions': working and employment conditions laid down by legislation, regulations, administrative provisions, collective agreements and/or other general provisions relating to:

   (i) the duration of working time, overtime, work breaks, rest periods, night work, paid holidays and public holidays;

   (ii) pay.

2. This Directive shall be without prejudice to national law as regards the definition of pay, contract of employment or employment relationship or worker.

Member States shall not exclude from the scope of this Directive workers, contracts of employment or employment relationships solely because they relate to:

- part-time workers;
- fixed-term contract workers; or
- persons with a contract of employment or employment relationship with a temporary agency.

Article 4

Review of restrictions or prohibitions

1. Prohibitions or restrictions on the use of temporary work are justified only on grounds of general interest relating in particular to the protection of temporary workers, the requirements of health and safety at work and the need to ensure that the labour market functions properly and abuses are prevented.

2. The Member States, after consulting the social partners in accordance with national legislation, collective agreements and practices, shall review any restrictions or prohibitions mentioned above in order to verify whether they are justified on the grounds given in paragraph 1. If not, the Member States shall discontinue them. The Member States shall inform the Commission of the results of that review.

3. Paragraphs 1 and 2 are without prejudice to national requirements with regard to registration, licensing, certification, financial guarantees or monitoring of temporary agencies.

CHAPTER II

EMPLOYMENT AND WORKING CONDITIONS

Article 5

The principle of non-discrimination

1. The basic working and employment conditions of temporary workers shall be, for the duration of their posting at a user undertaking, at least those that would apply if they had been recruited directly by that enterprise to occupy the same job.

When applying the above paragraph, the rules in force in the user undertaking on:

(i) protection of pregnant women and nursing mothers and protection of children and young people and

(ii) equal treatment for men and women and any action to combat any discrimination based on sex, race or ethnic origin, religion, beliefs, disabilities, age or sexual orientation

must be complied with as established by legislation, regulations, administrative provisions, collective agreements and/or any other general provisions.

2. As regards pay, Member States may, after consulting the social partners, provide that an exemption be made to the principle established in paragraph 1 when temporary workers who have a permanent contract of employment with a temporary agency continue to be paid in the time between postings.
3. Member States may, after consulting the social partners at the appropriate level, give them the option of upholding or concluding collective agreements which derogate from the principle established in paragraph 1 as long as an adequate level of protection is provided for temporary workers.
4. Without prejudice to the provisions of paragraphs 2 and 3 above, Member States may, with regard to pay, provide that paragraph 1 shall not apply where a temporary worker works on an assignment or series of assignments with the same user enterprise in a post which, due to its duration or nature, can be accomplished in a period not exceeding six weeks.

   Member States shall take appropriate measures with a view to preventing misuse in the application of this paragraph.
5. The implementing procedures for this article shall be defined by the Member States after consultation of the social partners. The Member States may also entrust the social partners at the appropriate level with the task of defining these procedures for this chapter by means of a negotiated agreement, in accordance with national practices.

Article 6
Access to permanent quality employment

1. Temporary workers shall be informed of any vacant posts in the user undertaking to give them the same opportunity as other workers in that undertaking to find permanent employment. Such information may be provided by a general announcement in a suitable place in the undertaking for which and under whose supervision temporary workers are engaged.

2. Member States shall take any action required to ensure that any clauses prohibiting or having the effect of preventing the conclusion of a contract of employment or an employment relationship between the user undertaking and the temporary worker after his posting are null and void or may be declared null and void.

This paragraph is without prejudice to provisions under which temporary agencies receive a reasonable level of recompense for services rendered to user undertakings for posting, recruitment and training of temporary workers.

3. Temporary agencies shall not charge workers any fees, especially in exchange for arranging for them to be recruited by a user undertaking, or for concluding a contract of employment or an employment relationship with a user undertaking after carrying out a posting in that undertaking.

4. Temporary workers shall be given access to the amenities or collective services of the user undertaking especially canteen, child care and transport services under the same conditions as workers employed directly by the undertaking, unless there are objective reasons against this.

5. Member States shall take suitable measures or shall promote dialogue between the social partners, in accordance with their national traditions and practices in order to:

- improve temporary workers' access to training in the temporary agencies, even in the periods between their postings, in order to enhance their career development and employability;
- improve temporary workers' access to training for user undertakings' workers.

Article 7
Representation of temporary workers

Temporary workers shall count, under conditions established by the Member States, for the purposes of calculating the threshold above which bodies representing workers provided for under Community and national law and collective agreements are to be formed at the temporary agency.

Member States may provide that, under conditions that they define, these workers count for the purposes of calculating the threshold above which bodies representing workers provided for by Community and national law and collective agreements are to be formed in the user undertaking, in the same way as if they were workers employed directly for the same period of time by the user undertaking.

Article 8
Information of workers' representatives

Without prejudice to national and Community provisions on information and consultation which are more stringent and/or more specific, the user undertaking must provide suitable information on the use of temporary workers when providing information on the employment situation in that undertaking to bodies representing the workers set up in accordance with national and Community legislation.

CHAPTER III

FINAL PROVISIONS

Article 9
Minimum requirements

1. This Directive does not prejudice the Member States' right to apply or introduce legislative, regulatory or administrative provisions which are more favourable to workers or to promote or permit collective agreements concluded between the social partners which are more favourable to workers.

2. The implementation of this Directive shall under no circumstances constitute sufficient grounds for justifying a reduction in the general level of protection of workers in the fields covered by this Directive. This shall be without prejudice to the rights of Member States and/or management and labour to lay down, in the light of changing circumstances, different legislative, regulatory or contractual arrangements

to those prevailing at the time of the adoption of this Directive, provided always that the minimum requirements laid down in this Directive are adhered to.

Article 10
Penalties

Member States shall lay down rules on penalties applicable in the event of infringements of national provisions enacted under this Directive and shall take all necessary measures to ensure that they are applied. The penalties provided for must be effective, proportionate and dissuasive. Member States shall notify these provisions to the Commission by the date given in Article 11 at the latest and any subsequent amendment within good time. They shall, in particular, ensure that workers and their representatives have adequate means of enforcing the obligations under this Directive.

Article 11
Implementation

1. The Member States shall adopt the laws, regulations and administrative provisions necessary to comply with this Directive by [two years after adoption] at the latest, or shall ensure that the social partners introduce the necessary provisions by way of an agreement, whereby the Member States must make all the necessary arrangements to enable them to guarantee at any time that the objectives of this Directive are being attained. They shall forthwith inform the Commission thereof.

2. When Member States adopt these provisions, they shall contain a reference to this Directive or shall be accompanied by such a reference on the occasion of their official publication. The methods of making such reference shall be laid down by the Member States.

Article 12
Review by the Commission

(Five years after adoption of this Directive) at the latest, the Commission shall, in consultation with the Member States and social partners at Community level, review application thereof with a view to proposing, where appropriate, the necessary amendments to the Parliament and the Council.

Article 13
Entry into force

This Directive shall enter into force on the twentieth day after its publication in the *Official Journal* of the European Communities.

Article 14
This Directive is addressed to the Member States

Done at Brussels,

For the European Parliament — For the Council

The President — The President

18. Report on the Proposal for a European Parliament and Council Directive on Working Conditions for Temporary Workers

COM(2002) 149–C5-0140/2002 – 2002/0072(COD)

Committee on Employment and Social Affairs
(Rapporteur: Ieke van den Burg)

In amendments by Parliament, amended text is highlighted in ***bold italics***. Highlighting in *normal italics* is an indication for the relevant departments showing parts of the legislative text for which a correction is proposed, to assist preparation of the final text (for instance, obvious errors or omissions in a given language version). These suggested corrections are subject to the agreement of the departments concerned.

CONTENTS

PROCEDURE

By letter of 21 March 2002 the Commission submitted to Parliament, pursuant to Article 251(2) and Article 137(2) of the EC Treaty, the proposal for a European Parliament and Council Directive on Working Conditions for Temporary Workers (COM(2002) 149 – 2002/0072 (COD)).

At the sitting of 8 April 2002 the President of Parliament announced that he referred this proposal to the Committee on Employment and Social Affairs as the

R. Blanpain & R. Graham (eds.), Temporary Agency Work and the Information Society, 325–370

committee responsible and the Committee on Citizens' Freedoms and Rights, Justice and Home Affairs, the Committee on Economic and Monetary Affairs, the Committee on Legal Affairs and the Internal Market and the Committee on Women's Rights and Equal Opportunities for their opinions (C5-0140/2002).

The Committee on Employment and Social Affairs appointed Ieke van den Burg rapporteur at its meeting of 23 April 2002.

It considered the Commission proposal and draft report at its meetings of 28 May 2002, 19 June 2002, 10 September, 30 September 2002 and 21 October 2002.

At the last meeting it adopted the draft legislative resolution by 30 votes to 13, with 1 abstention.

The following were present for the vote: Theodorus J.J. Bouwman, chairman; Marie-Hélène Gillig, vice-chairperson; Winfried Menrad, vice-chairman; Marie-Thérèse Hermange, vice-chairperson; Ieke van den Burg, rapporteur; Sylviane H. Ainardi, Jan Andersson, Elspeth Attwooll, Regina Bastos, Philip Bushill-Matthews, Chantal Cauquil (for Ilda Figueiredo), Alejandro Cercas, Luigi Cocilovo, Brian Crowley (for Nello Musumeci), Proinsias De Rossa, Harald Ettl, Jillian Evans, Carlo Fatuzzo, Fiorella Ghilardotti (for Enrico Boselli), Anne-Karin Glase, Lisbeth Grönfeldt Bergman (for Enrico Ferri), Roger Helmer, Anne Elisabet Jensen (for Daniel Ducarme), Karin Jöns, Anna Karamanou, Ioannis Koukiadis (for Elisa Maria Damião), Rodi Kratsa-Tsagaropoulou, Arlette Laguiller, Elizabeth Lynne, Toine Manders (for Marco Formentini), Thomas Mann, Mario Mantovani, Franco Marini (for James L.C. Provan, pursuant to Rule 153(2)), Claude Moraes, Ria G.H.C. Oomen-Ruijten (for Raffaele Lombardo), Bartho Pronk, Lennart Sacrédeus, Herman Schmid, Peter William Skinner (for Stephen Hughes), Miet Smet, Bruno Trentin (for Helle Thorning-Schmidt), Anne E.M. Van Lancker, Barbara Weiler, Sabine Zissener (for Mario Clemente Mastella).

The opinions of the Committee on Legal Affairs and the Internal Market and the Committee on Women's Rights and Equal Opportunities are attached; the Committee on Citizens' Freedoms and Rights, Justice and Home Affairs and the Committee on Economic and Monetary Affairs decided on 14 May 2002 and on 13 May 2002 not to deliver opinions.

The report was tabled on 23 October 2002.

DRAFT LEGISLATIVE RESOLUTION

European Parliament legislative resolution on the proposal for a European Parliament and Council Directive on Working Conditions for Temporary Workers (COM(2002) 149 – C5-0140/2002 – 2002/0072(COD))

(Co-decision procedure: first reading)

The European Parliament,

- having regard to the Commission proposal to the European Parliament and the Council (COM(2002) 149*),
- having regard to Article 251(2) and Article 137(2) of the EC Treaty, pursuant to which the Commission submitted the proposal to Parliament (C5-0140/2002),
- having regard to Rule 67 of its Rules of Procedure,

---

* OJ C 203 E, 27 August 2002, p. 1.

– having regard to the report of the Committee on Employment and Social Affairs and the opinions of the Committee on Legal Affairs and the Internal Market and the Committee on Women's Rights and Equal Opportunities (A5-0356/2002),

1. Approves the Commission proposal as amended;
2. Asks to be consulted again should the Commission intend to amend the proposal substantially or replace it with another text;
3. Instructs its President to forward its position to the Council and Commission.

Text proposed by the Commission	Amendments by Parliament

Amendment 1
Title

Proposal for a Directive of the European Parliament and the Council on ***working conditions for temporary workers***.	Proposal for a Directive of the European Parliament and the Council on ***temporary agency work***.

Justification

Firstly, the aims and content of the Directive are broader than just 'working conditions', extending to cover the promotion and regulation of the temporary work agency sector. Secondly, it is more consistent with the titles of the previous Directives on part-time work and fixed-term work. Finally, the term 'temporary workers' risks confusion between temporary agency workers and other temporary workers such as those on a fixed-term contract (see also amendments to Article 3).

Amendment 2
Recital 1 a (new)

	Article 21(1) of the Charter of Fundamental Rights of the European Union prohibits discrimination based on any ground, including sex. Article 23 of the Charter of Fundamental Rights of the European Union stipulates that equality between men and women must be ensured in all areas, including employment, work and pay. Article 141 of the EC Treaty establishes the legal basis for prohibiting discrimination between men and women for work of equal value. Furthermore, Articles 2 and 3(2) of that Treaty stipulate respectively that promoting equality between men and women and eliminating all inequalities between men and women are goals of the Community.

Justification

Articles 2 and 3 of the Treaty should be included among the references for policies and actions by the European Union to promote equality between men and women.

Amendment 3
Recital 2 a (new)

This directive builds on the Private Employment Agencies Convention (C181) and Recommendation (R188) adopted by the International Labour Conference in 1997 with the full support of the Employers' and Workers' Groups and EU Member State governments; these ILO instruments constituted a major step forward in the recognition of the positive role that private temporary work agencies may play in a well- functioning labour market whilst taking account of the need to protect workers from abuse.

Justification

These ILO instruments are major reference points for the Member States (who have ratified them or are in the process of doing so) and thus should be referred to in this proposal for a Directive and be taken into account in the drafting.

Amendment 4
Recital 4

In accordance with the European Social Agenda, which, on the basis of the communication from the Commission, was adopted by the European Council in Nice of 7, 8 and 9 December 2000, with the conclusions of the European Council in Stockholm of 23 and 24 March 2000 and with the Council Decision of 19 January 2001 on the 2001 employment guidelines, a satisfactory and flexible work organization system has to be put in place, ***with new flexible contracts*** offering workers a fair degree of job security and enhanced occupational status, ***which, at the same time, is compatible with*** the workers' aspirations and undertakings' needs.

In accordance with the European Social Agenda, which, on the basis of the communication from the Commission, was adopted by the European Council in Nice of 7, 8 and 9 December 2000, with the conclusions of the European Council in Stockholm of 23 and 24 March 2000 and with the Council Decision of 19 January 2001 on the 2001 employment guidelines, a satisfactory and flexible work organization system has to be put in place, ***in particular through new forms of regulated flexibility*** offering workers a fair degree of job security and enhanced occupational status, ***while, at the same time, ensuring that*** workers' aspirations and undertakings' needs ***are compatible.***

Justification

New forms of regulated flexibility do not necessarily coincide with new flexible contracts.

Amendment 5
Recital 4 a (new)

	On 29 June 1990, the Commission proposed a set of three draft Directives on atypical work underpinned by different legal bases. Only the proposal relating to health and safety was adopted, becoming Directive 91/383/EEC of 25 June 1991, as the Council could not reach consensus on the other proposals. For its part, the European Parliament adopted several elaborate and detailed resolutions on the subject of atypical work.

Justification

It is strange that the Commission chooses to describe the history of the atypical work dossiers as starting only in 1995. This amendment fills in the background of activities during the early 1990's and notes the significant and comprehensive work of the European Parliament at that time.

Amendment 6
Recital 7

In the introduction to the framework agreement on fixed-term work concluded on 18 March 1999, the signatories had indicated their intention to consider the need for a similar agreement on temporary work.	In the introduction to the framework agreement on fixed-term work concluded on 18 March 1999, the signatories had indicated their intention to consider the need for a similar agreement on temporary ***agency*** work ***and not yet deal with temporary agency workers in the Fixed-Term Work Directive. The exclusion from that Directive of fixed-term workers assigned by a temporary work agency to a user undertaking may be lifted on adoption of this new directive. Nevertheless, it should be ensured that when a temporary work agency, in line with the new directive, treats its temporary agency workers differently due to differences between user undertakings' conditions, that this constitutes an objective reason for such different treatment and therefore does not contravene other national and Community anti-discrimination provisions.***

Justification

This amendment clarifies the way the new Directive should inter-relate with the Fixed-Term Work Directive and pre-empts any perception of conflict between the new Directive and other non-discrimination provisions.

Amendment 7
Recital 9 a (new)

The European level social partner organizations covering the temporary work agency sector, Euro-CIETT and Uni-Europa, in their Joint Declaration concluded and published in October 2001, asked for a framework directive and gave as their view that the Directive should have the fundamental aim of reaching a fair balance between the protection of temporary agency workers and enhancing the positive role that temporary work agencies may play in the European labour market.

Justification

Since the sectoral organizations of employers and workers in the temporary work agency sector have always been particularly involved and interested in the development of the Directive, it is important to refer to their joint declaration which outlines the major elements of what they believe the Directive should comprise.

Amendment 8
Recital 11

Temporary work should meet undertakings'needs for flexibility and employees' need to reconcile their working and private lives ***and contribute to*** job creation and participation and integration in the labour market.

Temporary ***agency*** work should ***promote the European Union's economic, social and employment objectives by helping to*** meet undertakings' needs for flexibility and employees' need to reconcile their working and private lives. ***Temporary agency work should also promote*** job creation, participation and integration in the labour market ***both by providing opportunities for training and professional experience and by supporting user undertakings, especially small and medium-sized undertakings, with a view to increasing permanent job opportunities, particularly for women***.

Justification

The potential and real advantages of a healthy temporary work agency sector should be mentioned in greater detail.

Amendment 9
Recital 12a (new)

The triangular character of temporary agency work should be taken into account and may lead to the need for specific measures and regulations to safeguard the overall and proper functioning of the labour market. Such measures might, for instance, ensure that temporary work agencies' activities are not to the detriment of systems and traditions of industrial relations in the user undertakings and sectors, including in circumstances of industrial conflict.

Justification

This amendment would give due emphasis to the measures that may need to be taken to ensure that the activities of temporary work agencies do not cut across existing standards and industrial relations benefiting workers in the user companies/sectors.

Amendment 10
Recital 12b (new)

Notwithstanding that social security protection is not an explicit part of the provisions of this Directive, it should be recalled that social protection systems should be made capable of adaptation to new patterns of work and to provide adequate protection to those engaged in such work. In particular, attention should be given to the problems that arise for temporary agency workers as a result, for example, of the impact of broken work histories, multiple employment situations and short contracts on the continuity of employment rights.

Justification

This issue has been raised several times in recent years by the European social partners, including in their framework agreement on fixed-term work. The Commission is also showing itself to be more willing to look at this question. Therefore, although not covered in this Directive as such, it is relevant to reiterate here that social protection systems must become more adaptable to new forms of work.

Amendment 11
Recital 14

Directive 91/383/EEC of 25 June 1991* supplementing the measures to encourage improvements in the safety and health at work of workers with a fixed-duration employment relationship or a temporary employment relationship establishes the safety and health provisions applicable to temporary workers.	Directive 91/383/EEC of 25 June 1991** supplementing the measures to encourage improvements in the safety and health at work of workers with a fixed-duration employment relationship or a temporary employment relationship establishes the safety and health provisions applicable to temporary ***agency*** workers. ***However, some room for improvement has been identified, in particular to better specify the responsibilities of the temporary work agency and the user undertaking as regards training.***

Justification

The Directive on health and safety at work for temporary agency workers does not properly specify the respective responsibilities of the agency and user company as regards training; the resultant problems and high level of health and safety incidents amongst temporary agency workers were identified in the Dublin Foundation's recent report on 'Temporary agency work in the EU' (p. 68).

Amendment 12
Recital 14a (new)

	As stressed by the European-level social partners in the context of the Directives on part-time and fixed-term contract work, as well as in the Joint Declaration of the sectoral social partners, Euro-CIETT and Uni-Europa, direct employment contracts of an indefinite duration are, and will continue to be, the general form of employment relationship between employers and workers.

Justification

The Directive should recognize, as do other such initiatives, the importance of direct and open-ended employment contracts as a kind of benchmark in the labour market.

* OJ L 206 of 29 July 1991, p. 19.
** OJ L 206 of 29 July 1991, p. 19.

Amendment 13
Recital 14b (new)

In the context of social dialogue as an objective of the Community and the Member States (Article 136 TEC), the further development of social dialogue in the temporary work agency sector and the conclusion of collective agreements with respect to temporary agency work should be encouraged and stimulated, including with a view to improving the acceptance of temporary agency work throughout the European Union.

Justification

The social dialogue should be explicitly referred to, both as a Community objective and as a tool for the regulation of temporary agency work and its proper recognition as a legitimate part of the labour market.

Amendment 14
Recital 14c (new)

Directive 92/85/EEC on the introduction of measures to encourage improvements in the safety and health at work of pregnant workers and workers who have recently given birth or are breastfeeding and equal treatment in statutory and occupational social security schemes applies to all employees. The Charter of Fundamental Rights enshrines respect for the entitlement to social security benefits, including childcare facilities and social security provision for maternity, illness or industrial accident. Furthermore, Article 33(2) of the Charter stipulates that, in order to reconcile family and professional life, everyone has the right to protection from dismissal and the right to paid maternity leave or parental leave following the birth or adoption of a child. In particular, the amendment of Directive 76/207/EEC on the implementation of the principle of equal treatment for men and women as regards access to employment, vocational training and promotion, and

	working conditions, prohibits any discrimination on the grounds of sex, including sexual harassment, and enshrines the right to maternity, paternity and parental leave.

Justification

It seems necessary to mention the amendment of Directive 76/207/EEC, under which the principle of non-discrimination on grounds of sex at the workplace is extended to include protection against direct and indirect discrimination, harassment and sexual harassment and protection of the right to maternity, paternity and parental leave (aimed at reconciling family and professional life) and provides for the promotion of positive actions and for enterprises to be asked to draw up plans to promote equality.

Amendment 15
Recital 15

With respect to basic working and employment conditions, temporary workers should ***not*** be ***treated any less favourably than a 'comparable worker', i.e. a worker in*** the user undertaking ***in an identical or similar job***, taking into account ***seniority***, qualifications and skills.	***The*** basic working and employment conditions ***applicable to*** temporary ***agency*** workers should be ***at least those that would apply to temporary workers directly employed by*** the user undertaking ***for the same duration to perform the same or similar work***, taking into account qualifications and skills.

Justification

To make the Recital consistent with the amendment made to Article 5.1.

Amendment 16
Recital 16

However, differences in treatment are acceptable if they are objectively and reasonably justified by a legitimate aim under national law.	However, differences in treatment are acceptable if they are objectively and reasonably justified by a legitimate aim under national law. ***They must be compatible with the Charter of Fundamental Rights and with the EU Treaties, regulations and all directives governing the principle of non-discrimination.***

Justification

It is important to include reference to the various European regulations and directives which enshrine and regulate the principle of non-discrimination in general terms.

Amendment 17
Recital 17

In the case of workers who have a permanent contract with their temporary agency, and in view of the special protection such a contract offers, provision should be made to permit exemptions from the rules applicable in the user undertaking.

In the case of workers who have a permanent contract ***or a contract of at least 18 months*** with their temporary ***work*** agency, and in view of the special protection such a contract offers, provision should be made to permit exemptions from the rules applicable in the user undertaking. ***The contract should offer the temporary agency worker the protection normally afforded, according to national law and practice, by permanent contracts or contracts of similar duration entered into by other categories of worker***.

Justification

In addition to the amendment to Article 5.2, it should be clear that the contract should really be a full fledged employment contract with all the normal labour law and social security rights linked to it.

Amendment 18
Recital 18

In view of the need to maintain a certain degree of flexibility in the working relationship, provision should be made for the ***Member States*** to be able to ***delegate to the social partners the task of defining*** basic working and employment conditions ***tailored to the specific characteristics of certain types of employment or certain branches of economic activity***.

Provision should be made for the ***social partners*** to be able, ***at an appropriate level and in accordance with national legislation and practice***, to ***negotiate and define*** basic working and employment conditions ***for temporary agency workers to apply in the event of a departure from the principle of non-discrimination***.

Justification

This directive should not restrict the ability of employers and employees to act independently but should encourage it along with good industrial relations in accordance with the provisions of the Treaty.

Amendment 19
Recital 19

There should be some flexibility in the application of the principle of non-discrimination in cases of missions effected to accomplish a job which, due to its nature or duration, lasts less than six weeks.

Deleted

Justification

In the line with the deletion of Article 5.4.

Amendment 20
Recital 20

An improvement in the minimum protection for temporary workers occasioned by this Directive will enable any restrictions ***or*** prohibitions which may have been imposed on temporary work to be reviewed and, if necessary, lifted if they are no longer justified on grounds of the general interest ***regarding, in particular the protection of workers***.	An improvement in the minimum protection for temporary ***agency*** workers occasioned by this Directive will enable any restrictions, prohibitions ***or specific administrative provisions*** which may have been imposed on temporary ***agency*** work to be reviewed and, if necessary, lifted if they are no longer justified. ***They can only be justified*** on grounds of the general interest ***e.g. health and safety, other risks to particular groups or sectors, labour market functioning and the need to prevent abuse***.

Justification

To bring this Recital into line with changes made to Article 4.

Amendment 21
Recital 21

There must be an effective means of safeguarding temporary workers' rights.	There must be an effective means of safeguarding temporary ***agency*** workers' rights. ***In addition to being fully covered by national and Community provisions for information, consultation and participation of employees, in both temporary work agencies and user undertakings, this means temporary agency workers should have access to internal procedures and provisions for complaints in the user undertaking***.

Justification

This amendment brings the Recital into line with amendments made to Article 7.

Amendment 22
Recital 22

In compliance with the principle of subsidiarity and the principle of proportionality under Article 5 of the Treaty, the aims of the action envisaged above cannot be achieved satisfactorily by the Member States, since the goal is to	In compliance with the principle of subsidiarity and the principle of proportionality under Article 5 of the Treaty, the aims of the action envisaged above cannot be achieved satisfactorily by the Member States, since the goal is to

establish a harmonized Community-level framework of protection for temporary workers; owing to the scale and the impact of the action planned, these objectives can best be met at Community level by introducing minimum requirements applicable throughout the European Community; this directive confines itself to what is required for achieving these objectives,	establish a harmonized Community-level framework of protection for temporary ***agency*** workers; owing to the scale and the impact of the action planned, these objectives can best be met at Community level by introducing minimum requirements applicable throughout the European Community ***to provide for a common framework for Member States that may facilitate the integration of European labour markets and cross-border labour mobility particularly in border regions***; this directive confines itself to what is required for achieving these objectives

Justification

To strengthen the explanation of how the Directive is consistent with the principle of subsidiarity and why such action is needed at EU level.

Amendment 23
Article 1.1

1. This directive applies to ***the contract of employment or employment relationship between a temporary agency, which is the employer, and the worker, who is posted to a user undertaking to work under its supervision***.	This directive applies to ***all situations in which, on the basis of an employment contract or employment relationship between the temporary work agency and the temporary agency worker, an agency assigns a worker to work under the direction and supervision of a user undertaking***.

Justification

To better reflect that the Directive deals with the triangular relationship inherent to temporary agency work and not only with the relationship between the agency and the worker. The expression 'direction and supervision', drawn from the Posting of Workers Directive, is intended to express a relationship of authority-dependency.

Amendment 24
Article 1.2

2. This directive applies to public and private undertakings engaged in economic activities whether or not they are operating for gain.	2. This directive applies to public and private undertakings ***that are*** engaged in economic activities ***and that are operating as temporary work agencies***, whether or not they are operating for gain.

This directive also applies to public and private user undertakings whether or not they are engaged in economic activities and whether or not they are operating for gain.

Where customary in national law and practice, Member States may exempt from the provisions in Article 5 of this Directive specific public and private undertakings engaged in non-profit-making economic activities.

Justification

This aims to put beyond doubt that all *organizations operating as temporary work agencies and* all *users of temporary agency workers are to be covered by the directive, including e.g. public administrations and voluntary/charitable organizations. The last paragraph makes it possible for Member States to exempt certain non-profit-making organizations from the provisions of Article 5, where such exemptions would reflect existing law and practice.*

Amendment 25
Article 1.3

Member States may, after consulting the social partners, provide that this directive does not apply to employment contracts or relationships concluded under a specific public or publicly supported training, integration or vocational retraining programme.

Member States may, after consulting the social partners, provide that this directive does not apply to employment contracts or relationships concluded under ***a specific training programme or*** a specific public or publicly supported integration or vocational retraining programme.

Justification

It needs to be made clear that trainees in general should not fall within the scope of the directive. For instance, there are special training support programmes geared to integrating problem groups into the labour market, under which a training group concludes a contract with a trainee. The latter then receives his/her training in a member firm on different terms from those applicable to a trainee employed directly in that firm. Such programmes are purely private initiatives, and would be at serious risk if the proposed directive were to apply to them.

Amendment 26
Article 2

The purpose of this Directive is:

a) to improve the quality of temporary work by ensuring that the principle of non- discrimination is applied to temporary workers;

The purpose of this Directive is:

a) ***to provide for the protection of temporary agency workers and*** to improve the ***appeal and*** quality of temporary ***agency*** work by ***recognizing temporary agency workers as workers of the agency, adequately covered by statutory employment rights and social***

	protection, and by ensuring that the principle of non-discrimination is applied to temporary ***agency*** workers;
b) to establish a suitable framework for the use of temporary work to contribute to the smooth functioning of the labour and employment market.	b) to establish a suitable framework for the ***development and*** use of ***the*** temporary ***agency*** work ***sector in order*** to contribute to ***job creation and*** the smooth functioning of thc labour and cmploymcnt markct ***by providing user undertakings in a flexible manner with temporary human resources with-out detrimental effects on existing permanent workforces***;
	c) to recognize temporary work agencies as employers, taking into account their triangular relationships with temporary agency workers and user undertakings, while ensuring respect for the principle of non-discrimination and thereby for the established working conditions in user undertakings and sectors.

Justification

This amendment makes explicit some of the balanced aims of the Directive, in particular in respect of protecting temporary agency workers and the interests of existing permanent workforces, while promoting the development of the sector and thereby job creation.

New wording is also added in the first part to reflect the provisions of the new article that has been inserted before Article 5, setting out the need for changes so that temporary agency workers enjoy basic statutory employment right and social protection.

A further change is to insert a third objective of the Directive which is to recognize the legitimacy of temporary work agencies whilst ensuring that their activities do not compromise existing standards in user companies and sectors.

Amendment 27
Article 3.1(aa) (new)

	(aa) 'temporary agency worker' means any person who enters into a contract of employment or employment relationship of indefinite or fixed duration with a temporary work agency, to be assigned temporarily in a user undertaking to work under the direction and supervision of that user undertaking;

Justification

It seems inappropriate to leave a Directive on temporary agency work without a definition of a temporary agency worker. The formulation 'direction and supervision' relates to the amendment made to Article 1.1, drawing on the Posting of Workers Directive.

Amendment 28
Article 3.1(b)

(b) 'comparable worker' means a worker in the user undertaking occupying an identical or similar post to that occupied by the worker posted by the temporary agency, account being taken of seniority qualifications and skills.	***Deleted***

Justification

This amendment is consequential on the re-formulation of Article 5.1.

Amendment 29
Article 3.1(c)

(c) ***'posting'*** means the period during which the temporary worker is ***placed at*** the user undertaking;	(c) '***assignment***' means the period during which the temporary ***agency*** worker is ***assigned to work under the direction and supervision of*** the user undertaking;

Justification

'Assignment' is preferred here and throughout the Directive to the term 'posting' in order to avoid any confusion with the Posting of Workers Directive (which covers a broader category of workers than just temporary agency workers). The second change is for consistency with other amendments.

Amendment 30
Article 3.1(ca) (new)

	(ca) 'temporary work agency' means any natural or legal person entering into employment contracts or employment relationships with temporary agency workers with a view to assigning them to work temporarily under the direction and supervision of user undertakings;

Justification

It seems inappropriate to leave a Directive on temporary agency work without a definition of a temporary work agency.

Amendment 31
Article 3.1(cb) (new)

	(cb) 'user undertaking' means any natural or legal person to whom and under whose direction and supervision temporary agency workers are assigned to work temporarily;

Justification

For completeness, given how critical the term is to the previous definitions, it seems appropriate to have a definition of 'user undertaking'.

Amendment 32
Article 3.1(d)

(d) 'basic working and employment conditions': working and employment conditions relating to: i) ***the duration of*** working time, rest periods, ***night work, paid holidays and public holidays***; ii) ***pay***; iii) ***work done by pregnant women and nursing mothers, children and young people***; iv) ***action taken to combat discrimination on the grounds of sex, race or ethnic origin, religion or beliefs, disabilities, age or sexual orientation***.	(d) 'basic working and employment conditions': working and employment conditions, ***as set out in legislation, collective agreements and other company-related provisions,*** relating to: (i) working time ***and*** rest periods; (ii) ***paid holidays***; (iii) ***pay, including overtime pay***; (iv) ***health, safety and hygiene at work***; (v) ***protective measures with regard to the terms and conditions of employment of pregnant women or women who have recently given birth, of children and of young people, as well as provisions relating to parental leave***; (vi) ***equality of treatment between men and women and action taken to combat discrimination and harassment on the grounds of sex, race or ethnic origin, religion or beliefs, disabilities, age or sexual orientation***.

Justification

The amendment draws on the terms for basic employment and working conditions used in the Posting of Workers Directive Article 3.1, adapted here to be in line with the structure of Article 5, the latter being similar to the Part-Time and Fixed-Term Work Directive which do not contain such a general definition. Other changes make it clear that the conditions referred to are those derived from legislation, collective agreements or other workplace provisions, as well as making explicit references to parental leave provisions and action to combat harassment.

Amendment 33
Article 3.2(c)

(c) persons ***on a posting at a user undertaking***.	(c) persons ***with an employment contract or an employment relationship with a temporary work agency***.

Justification

This is to broaden the group of workers that 'Member States shall not exclude from the scope of this Directive', in particular by not restricting the provision to workers on a posting. This is partly because 'assignment' should be used instead of 'posting'; but a further reason for the change is so as not to exclude workers who work in a user undertaking under a leasing or other (often longer-term but nevertheless 'temporary') arrangement involving a temporary work agency.

Amendment 34
Article 4

1. Member States, after consulting the social partners in accordance with legislation, collective agreements and national practices, ***shall review periodically any restrictions or prohibitions on temporary work for certain groups of workers or sectors of economic activity*** in order to verify whether the specific conditions underlying them still obtain. If they do not, the Member States should discontinue them.	1. Member States, after consulting the social partners in accordance with legislation, collective agreements and national practices, ***may, where justified, prohibit or restrict temporary agency work. Where national practice makes it more appropriate, Member States may give the social partners at the appropriate level the option of doing so directly.*** ***1a (new) Member States shall, within two years of the adoption of this directive and every 5 years thereafter, after consulting the social partners in accordance with legislation, collective agreements and national practices, review all existing restrictions, prohibitions and specific administrative provisions on temporary agency work***, in order to verify whether the specific conditions underlying them still obtain. If they do not, the Member States should discontinue them.
2. The Member States shall notify the Commission of the result of said review. If the restrictions or prohibitions are maintained, the Member States shall inform the Commission why they consider that they are necessary and justified. The restrictions or prohibitions which could be maintained shall be justified on grounds of the general interest regarding, in particular, the protection of workers.	2. The Member States shall notify the Commission of the result of said review. If the restrictions or prohibitions are maintained, the Member States shall inform the Commission why they consider that they are necessary and justified. The restrictions or prohibitions which could be maintained shall ***only*** be justified on grounds of the general interest regarding, in particular, the protection of ***temporary agency*** workers, ***the health and safety and other risks posed to certain groups of workers or sectors of economic activity, the proper functioning of the labour market and the need to prevent potential abuses***.

Justification

The first change is to split the existing paragraph 1 into two parts: the first puts beyond doubt that restrictions and prohibitions on the use of temporary agency work can be maintained and/or introduced in certain circumstances (in line with ILO Convention 181 Article 4); the second strengthens the provision for Member States' reviews of such restrictions, prohibitions and specific administrative provisions, including by inserting a deadline for the first such review and timing for subsequent reviews.

The second part of paragraph 2 is amended to make more explicit the only possible justifications for restrictions or prohibitions to be maintained and/or introduced: the text echoes the three objectives of the Directive (see amendment to Article 2) as well as, in the last part, drawing on the Joint CIETT-UNI-Europa Declaration.

Amendment 35
Article 4.3 (new)

3. This provision is without prejudice to reasonable arrangements for the registration, licensing, certification, guaranteeing or monitoring of temporary agency work, as long as they do not place disproportionate administrative burdens on the undertakings and persons involved.

Justification

This provision puts beyond doubt that reasonable administrative arrangements for the registration and monitoring of temporary work agencies will not be considered as restrictions or prohibitions.

Amendment 36
Article 4.4 (new)

4. Restrictions or prohibitions shall be maintained or, where necessary, introduced, to prevent temporary agency workers being assigned to user undertakings or sectors where workers are engaged in collective action.

Justification

This provision would ensure temporary agency workers were not used to e.g. break a strike. As such, it is in line with the ILO provisions and was part of the consensus that existed during the social partner negotiations on temporary agency work in 2000–2001.

Amendment 37
New article before Article 5

Member States shall ensure that temporary agency workers are not treated less favourably with regard to basic

statutory employment rights and social protection than other categories of worker.

Member States shall, within two years of the adoption of the directive and after consultation with the social partners, review existing labour and social legislation, collective agreements and national practices, in order to verify if temporary agency workers are adequately covered.

Member States shall, after consultation with the social partners, clarify the legal status of temporary agency workers with a view to recognizing them as employees of temporary work agencies and to ensuring and, where necessary extending, the scope of labour legislation and social protection to cover them.

Member States shall determine and allocate, in accordance with Community and national law and practice, the respective responsibilities of temporary work agencies and user undertakings with regard to the rights and obligations covered by this provision.

Justification

This is designed to require Member States to review and where necessary improve temporary agency workers' basic employment rights as a somewhat separate issue from the non-discrimination and other provisions in the Directive.

Amendment 38
Article 5.1

Temporary workers during their posting, shall receive at least as favourable treatment, in terms of basic working and employment conditions, including seniority in the job, as a comparable worker in the user enterprise, unless the difference in treatment is justified by objective reasons. Where appropriate, the *pro rata temporis* principle applies.

The basic working and employment conditions applicable to a temporary agency worker shall be at least those which apply or would apply to a worker directly employed by the user undertaking on a contract for the same duration, performing the same or similar tasks, taking into account qualifications and skills, unless the difference in treatment is justified by objective reasons. Where appropriate, the *pro rata temporis* principle applies.

Justification

This re-formulation makes it clear that temporary agency workers' conditions are to be at least equivalent to those that would be enjoyed by workers directly employed by the user undertaking for the same duration (regardless of the type of contract and – because of 'would' – whether or not such workers actually exist in the particular user undertaking).

Amendment 39
Article 5.1 a (new)

	Basic protection as regards essential working conditions and employment protection which is mainly of interest to women and employees with family responsibilities, as well as protection against discrimination and intimidation, maternity protection and maternity and parental leave, must be available from day one for all temporary agency workers, whatever type of contract they have.

Justification

In order to ensure equal treatment for all employees in the same workplace and to provide proper protection for temporary agency workers, appropriate basic protection must be offered from day one of the employment contract, inter alia as regards parental leave and discrimination.

Amendment 40
Article 5.2

Member States may provide that an exemption be made to the principle established in paragraph 1 when temporary workers ***who*** have a ***permanent*** contract of employment with a temporary agency ***continue to be paid in the time between postings***.	***With regard to pay or specific pay elements***, Member States may, ***where appropriate after consultation of the social partners***, provide that an exemption be made to the principle established in paragraph 1, when temporary ***agency*** workers have a permanent contract of employment ***or a contract of employment of at least 18 months*** with a temporary ***work*** agency ***that guarantees them adequate and continuous payment whether or not they are on an assignment***. ***Member States shall take appropriate measures with a view to preventing misuse in the application of this paragraph***.

Justification

The exemption for permanent employment contracts should be restricted to only pay or specific pay elements to avoid major discrepancies with workers in the user undertaking. The description of the continuation of payment between assignments should be more precise.

This amendment recognizes that non-permanent contracts of a certain duration provide similar stability of income etc to permanent contracts.

The amendment to Recital 17 is also relevant here.

Amendment 41
Article 5.3

Member States may give the social partners at the appropriate level ***the option of concluding*** collective agreements which derogate from the principle established in paragraph 1 ***as long as an adequate level of protection is provided for temporary workers***.	***The social partners may*** at the appropriate level ***continue with or conclude*** collective agreements which derogate from the principle established in paragraph 1.

Justification

The possibility of the social partners concluding agreements which depart from the principle of non-discrimination should not require the Member States' authorization but should rather follow directly from the directive. To avoid interference with existing collective agreements which depart from the principle of non-discrimination, it should be possible to continue with them unchanged after the directive is adopted. Once the social partners have concluded such an agreement at the appropriate level, neither of the parties should be able to create uncertainty about the agreement by appealing to the Court of Justice to set aside the agreement on grounds of inadequate protection.

Amendment 42
Article 5.4

Without prejudice to the provisions of paragraphs 2 and 3 above, Member States may provide that paragraph 1 shall not apply where a temporary worker works on an assignment or series of assignments with the same user enterprise in a post which, due to its duration or nature, can be accomplished in a period not exceeding six weeks. Member States shall take appropriate measures with a view to preventing misuse in the application of this paragraph.	***Deleted***

Justification

Given the comparison with temporary workers employed directly by the user undertaking, this exemption is not justified because the principle of non-discrimination must be guaranteed for work of equal duration from the first day of the work relationship and throughout its duration.

Amendment 43
Article 5.5

When this directive calls for a comparison to be made with a comparable worker in the user undertaking but no such worker exists, reference shall be made to the collective agreement applicable in the user undertaking; if no such collective agreement exists, the comparison will be made by reference to the collective agreement applicable to the temporary work agency; if no collective agreement is applicable, the basic working and employment conditions of temporary workers will be determined by national legislation and practices.	***Deleted***

Justification

This deletion is consequential on the deletion of the 'comparable worker' definition in Article 3.1(b)

Amendment 44
Article 5.6

The implementing procedures for this article shall be defined by the Member States ***after consultation of the social partners***. The Member States may also entrust the social partners at the appropriate level with the task of defining these procedures for this chapter by means of a negotiated agreement.	The implementing procedures for this article shall be defined by the Member States. The Member States may also entrust the social partners at the appropriate level with the task of defining these procedures for this chapter by means of a negotiated agreement ***in accordance with national practices***.

Justification

The importance of differing national practices in differing Member States should be explicitly recognized.

Amendment 45
Article 5.6 (a) (new)

	The same provisions as regards safety, health, hygiene and occupational health shall apply to workers on assignments as to workers in the user undertaking. Special attention shall be paid to training assigned workers in safety matters, given the temporary nature of their work and the fact that they may carry out different types of work in the various user enterprises.

Justification

Reasons stemming from equal treatment and equal rights for all those working in the undertaking and particular consideration for the temporary nature of the work, which is frequently of very short duration, as well as the fact that, in many cases, temporary agency workers carry out different tasks in the various user enterprises for which they work.

Amendment 46
Article 6.1

Temporary workers shall be informed of any vacant posts in the user undertaking to give them the same opportunity as other workers in that undertaking to find permanent employment.	Temporary ***agency*** workers shall be informed of any vacant posts in the user undertaking to give them the same opportunity as other workers in that undertaking to find permanent employment. ***Such information may be provided via a general announcement in a suitable place in the undertaking to which a temporary agency worker is assigned.***

Justification

The additional text, drawn from the Fixed-Term Contracts Directive, is intended to make the text more 'operational'; it also indicates that user undertakings will need to be involved in complying with this provision.

Amendment 47
Article 6.2

Member States shall take any action required to ensure that any clauses banning or having the effect of preventing the conclusion of a contract of employment or an employment relationship between the user undertaking and the temporary worker after his ***posting*** are null and void or may be declared null and void.	Member States shall take any action required to ensure that any clauses banning or having the effect of preventing the conclusion of a contract of employment or an employment relationship between the user undertaking and the temporary ***agency*** worker after his ***assignment*** are null and void or may be declared null and void. ***This paragraph is without prejudice to arrangements under which temporary work agencies receive a reasonable level of recompense for services rendered to the user undertaking in respect of the assignment, recruitment and training of temporary agency workers.***

Justification

This amendment aims to ensure that the practice of 'temp-to-perm fees' in e.g. the UK is not affected by this article.

Amendment 48
Article 6.3

Temporary agencies shall not charge workers any fees in exchange for arranging ***for them to be recruited by a user undertaking***.	Temporary ***work*** agencies shall not charge workers any fees, ***in particular*** in exchange for arranging ***assignments in the user undertakings or in case they enter into a contract of employment or an employment relationship with the user enterprise after their assignment in the respective user enterprise***.

Justification

Agency workers themselves should not be charged if they move on to the user enterprise they were assigned to.

Amendment 49
Article 6.4

Temporary workers shall be given access to the ***social services*** of the user undertaking unless there are objective reasons against this.	Temporary ***agency*** workers shall be given ***the same*** access to the ***collective facilities*** of the user undertaking, ***for example childcare facilities, as apply or would apply to workers directly employed by the user undertaking for the same duration*** unless there are objective reasons against this.

Justification

This amendment carries forward the re-formulation of Article 5.1 into Article 6.4. It also aims to make more explicit what services/facilities are covered by this provision.

Amendment 50
Article 7, new paragraph before 1st paragraph.

	Member States and social partners shall provide that temporary agency workers benefit in the same way as other workers from provisions in national and Community legislation for the information, consultation and participation of employees, in respect of both temporary work agencies and user undertakings. They shall also provide that temporary agency workers can be represented by the workers' representative body in the user undertaking and have access to any internal procedures and provisions for complaints, whether these are initiated by or against the temporary agency worker.

Justification

This new paragraph addresses the fact that the Commission's draft of Article 7 only provides for temporary agency workers to count in working out whether or not national and/or Community information, consultation and participation procedures are triggered as regards a particular company. The change would ensure they also benefit as other employees from the actual procedures where triggered and implemented – in other words, that they should be informed and consulted along with the rest of the workforce. Finally, it also addresses the fact that temporary agency workers are particularly vulnerable to unsubstantiated complaints from a user company, whilst also often being precluded from using internal procedures to initiate e.g. sexual harassment complaints.

Amendment 51
Article 7

Temporary workers shall count for the purposes of calculating the threshold above which bodies representing workers provided for under national and Community legislation should be formed at the temporary agency.	Temporary ***agency*** workers shall count for the purposes of calculating the threshold above which bodies representing workers provided for under national and Community legislation ***or collective agreements*** should be formed at the temporary agency.
Member States may provide that, under conditions that they define, these workers count for the purposes of calculating the threshold above which bodies representing workers provided for by national and Community legislation should be formed in the user undertaking.	Member States may provide that, under conditions that they define, these workers count, ***as do or would workers directly employed by the user undertaking for the same duration***, for the purposes of calculating the threshold above which bodies representing workers provided for by national and Community legislation ***or collective agreements*** should be formed in the user undertaking.

Justification

The amendment takes account of the fact that workers' representation may also be determined by collective agreements. The longer addition to the second paragraph carries forward the re-formulation of Article 5.1 into Article 7.

Amendment 52
Article 10

Member States shall lay down rules on sanctions applicable in the event of infringements of national provisions enacted under this directive and shall take all necessary measures to ensure that they are applied. The penalties provided for must be effective proportionate and dissuasive Member States shall notify these provisions to the	Member States shall lay down rules on sanctions applicable in the event of infringements of national provisions enacted under this directive and shall take all necessary measures to ensure that they are applied. The penalties provided for must be effective proportionate and dissuasive Member States shall notify these provisions to the

Commission by the date given in Article 11 at the latest and any subsequent amendment within good time. They shall, in particular, ensure that workers and/***or*** their representatives have adequate means of enforcing the obligations under this directive.

Commission by the date given in Article 11 at the latest and any subsequent amendment within good time. They shall, in particular, ensure that workers and their representatives have adequate means of enforcing the obligations under this directive.

Justification

Member States should ensure that both *workers* and *their representatives are equipped to press the provisions of the Directive in order that workers have an effective choice between acting directly or through their representatives.*

Amendment 53
Article 11.1

The Member States shall adopt the laws, regulations and administrative provisions necessary to comply with this directive by [two years after adoption] at the latest, or shall ensure that the social partners introduce the necessary provisions by the way of an agreement, whereby the Member States must make all the necessary arrangements to enable them to guarantee at any time that the objectives of this directive are being attained. They shall forthwith inform the Commission thereof.

The Member States shall adopt the laws, regulations and administrative provisions necessary to comply with this directive by [two years after adoption] at the latest, or shall ensure that, ***where applicable in accordance with their national legislation or practices***, the social partners introduce the necessary provisions by the way of an agreement, whereby the Member States must make all the necessary arrangements to enable them to guarantee at any time that the objectives of this directive are being attained. They shall forthwith inform the Commission thereof.

Justification

This Directive purports to make temporary agency work more attractive: the differing circumstances pertaining in each Member States should determine how the best implementation method to ensure this goal is achieved, and this provision should therefore allow a wide degree of flexibility in transposition.

Amendment 54
Article 11.3 (new)

They should transpose these provisions in a manner consistent with promoting job creation and making temporary agency work more attractive, recognising the different circumstances pertaining to their own Member State.

Justification

Explicitly recognizes the importance of national legislation and practices in the context of the overall objectives of the Directive.

EXPLANATORY STATEMENT

In preparing her draft report, the rapporteur has been in regular contact and has had in-depth discussions with the whole range of interested parties, both in public and private. In addition to working visits to the 'coal face' and talks with temporary agency workers and agency staff, this work has included:

- the seminar organized in the European Parliament by the European Policy Centre on 8 May 2002;
- the ***mini-hearing*** organized by the rapporteur in Committee on 28 May with interventions from key social partner representatives and researcher Donald Storrie; this first discussion in Committee was supported by the rapporteur's ***first working document dated 14 May 2002 (PE 316.344)***;
- a further exchange of views in Committee on 19 June and bilateral discussions with shadow rapporteurs and the draftspersons for the FEMM and JURI Committees, including on the basis of the rapporteur's ***second working document dated 27 June 2002 (PE 316.355)***;
- contacts and discussions with interested parties including European, national and sectoral social partner organizations, but also with Member State representatives, the Commission, the Council secretariat and the Danish Presidency.

These preparations have fed into the rapporteur's draft report, which covers a considerable number of amendments. The rapporteur would like to underline, however, that this in no way means that the main line and the core message set out in the Commission's proposal are not followed. She is still fully convinced of the need and importance of the Directive but, over recent weeks, has become all the more convinced of the complexity of the issue.

The Main Reasons for Changes

The reasons for the number of amendments (of which many are rather technical in nature) are:

- to formulate more clearly the aims and objectives of the Directive on the basis of the threefold approach set out in the rapporteur's first working document, inspired, *inter alia,* by the Dublin Foundation's report* and other studies;
- to build more precisely on what was discussed in the social partners' negotiations, as well as on existing European and ILO instruments, in order to facilitate the consistent interpretation and implementation of the new Directive;
- to focus on and prioritize basic protection for temporary agency workers as a separate, but no less important, issue from the provision not to treat a temporary agency worker less favourably than a comparable worker in the user company as regards working and employment conditions (the 'non-discrimination provision');

---

* 'Temporary agency work in the EU' published by the Dublin Foundation in April 2002 (http://www.eurofound.eu.int/workking/working.htm).

- to take account of the different situations that exist in Member States, particularly with respect to the need for possible exemptions from the non-discrimination provision.

The Threefold Objectives

There was broad support in the various discussions in and outside Committee for the three objectives or levels of equal treatment that were identified in the first working document:

- equal treatment for agency workers compared with other workers *as regards employment status and security*;
- respect for established social standards in user firms *through equal treatment as regards pay and conditions between agency workers and comparable workers in user firms*;
- recognition of the temporary agency sector as legitimate and professional business *by removing unnecessary restrictions and permits/bans*.

The rapporteur proposes to reflect these in the recitals and the articles of the Directive, underlining the need for a delicate balance between them and for due attention to be paid to the triangular character of temporary agency work.

Without broadening the provisions to issues for which the EU is not competent or for which the legal basis and the decision-making procedures would have to be extended, her additions on basic statutory employment protection are intended to provide a more complete framework and a better balance in the provisions that are relevant for the different parties involved.

Building on Existing Regulatory Texts and Consensus

Unfortunately, the Commission has not taken every opportunity to build on existing regulatory texts and its references are therefore somewhat incomplete. The rapporteur has taken inspiration not only from the Directive based on the Fixed Term Work agreement concluded by the European social partners (99/70/TEC) (which in turn is based to a large extent on the Part Time Work Directive 97/81/TEC), but also from the Posting of Workers Directive (96/71/TEC) and the ILO Convention (C181) and Recommendation (R188) that were adopted in the tripartite International Labour Conference in 1997 with overwhelming support and consensus between the parties.

Like the Commission, the rapporteur regrets that the European social partners did not reach an agreement for a directive on temporary work agencies and also wishes to build on the consensus reached in the negotiations in the beginning of 2001. Furthermore, in October 2001, the European social partner organizations covering the temporary work agency sector, Euro-CIETT and Uni-Europa, concluded a Joint Declaration outlining the main elements of a proposal for a Directive that they would like to see the Commission present. Strangely, the Commission has not referred to that text. The rapporteur proposes such a reference and indeed has lifted several formulations in her amendments directly from this Joint Declaration.

Similar 'plagiarism' is committed in amending articles and terms proposed by the Commission that were close to, but somewhat different from, for instance, the provisions in the Fixed Term Work and Posting of Workers Directives or the

ILO Convention. Such discrepancies in legal texts may cause a good deal of interpretative problems and barriers in implementation, application and jurisdiction. It therefore seems wise to bring definitions and obligations more into line.

With a similar concern, the rapporteur has also chosen to use the terms 'temporary agency worker', 'temporary work agency' and 'user undertaking' throughout the Directive, based on clear definitions of these terms in Article 3 to avoid confusion. Furthermore, the term 'posting' has been replaced by 'assignment' to avoid confusion with the Posting of Workers Directive. Although that Directive deals with cross-border posting of temporary agency workers (for which the main provision is for the application of the law and collective agreements current in the Member State in which the work is carried out), it primarily deals with posted workers who continue to work under the direction of their employer in the Member State of origin. An essential element of the definition of an 'assignment' in this new Directive should be that the temporary agency worker works under the direction and supervision of the user undertaking. To underline this and avoid confusion, the term 'assignment' is used throughout. It is, of course, important that these specific terms are precisely formulated in all the language versions. Finally, the definition of employment and working conditions has been adapted to Article 3 of the Posting of Workers Directive, taking into account that the latter does not deal with an equal treatment provision but with the application of the employment and working conditions that pertain in the new workplace.

Basic Protection – the First Priority

Whilst the Commission's proposal focuses almost exclusively on the non-discrimination clause, this obligation not to treat temporary agency workers less favourably than comparable workers in the user undertaking is not the only issue in the rapporteur's proposals. She emphasizes firstly the need for basic protection and immediately adds that basic protection has to be provided from day one and cannot, under any condition, be exempted or derogated from! This notion has received full support from the whole range of interested parties in the rapporteur's preparatory discussions. Amendments have thus been introduced to make clear that temporary agency workers should have the right to basic protection from day one.

Such basic protection includes labour law and social security protection. Without going into details or prescribing specific forms of protection, a new recital proposes that Member States should check and review whether their temporary agency workers are adequately covered by labour law and social protection. Furthermore, in the definitions, there is a deliberate reflection of the fact that only in a few Member States is it not (yet) evident that temporary agency workers have employee status or equivalent basic protection. The scope of the Directive covers not only those with employment contracts but also those in other employment relations (where the decisive factor is whether they work in a relation of dependency on, and under the direction and supervision of another person,) but nevertheless the rapporteur would clearly like to promote the idea that the Directive will be a step towards full employee rights for temporary agency workers and other 'atypical workers'.

The provision to not treat temporary agency workers less favourably than comparable workers in the user undertaking has been amended to bring it as far as possible into line with the Part-Time and Fixed-Term Work Directive. The situations in which user undertakings make recourse to temporary agency work differ considerably: sometimes a 'temp' is hired to replace a permanent worker on leave; in other cases, they are hired for a specific project for which extra manpower is needed. In the first instance, it is not so difficult to find a comparable worker; in the second, it may be more complicated. If the user undertaking had opted for the direct recruitment of a temporary worker (e.g. on a fixed term contract), he or she would have set wage levels and other conditions on the basis of tradition and existing standards. Therefore, even in cases where there is no concrete existing comparable worker, a notional comparison is possible. In her amendments, the rapporteur shifts the emphasis from individual comparisons to this more generic approach and the reference to collective standards.

The Exemptions from the Non-Discrimination Provision

The rapporteur has made it very clear from the outset that she was not happy with the exemptions from the non-discrimination provision proposed in the Directive, particularly the last one that intends to exempt assignments that last up to 6 weeks:

- the derogation by collective agreement in Article 5.3 is an accepted and – in the eyes of the rapporteur, but also in the light of the European support for social dialogue and of commitments made by Member States in the International Labour Organization – commendable approach which would facilitate tailor-made solutions to widely differing situations;
- the exemption for temporary agency workers with a permanent employment contract in Article 5.2 underlines the preference for permanent and continuous employment – but has to be clearly qualified, particularly because the precise guarantees and conditions linked to that status depend on national law and practice;
- finally, the exemption in Article 5.4, in the view of the rapporteur, in fact does not fit in the Directive at all and would, if adopted as presently formulated, completely undermine the impact and effectiveness of the whole approach. Although the rapporteur was seriously intending to promote deletion of that exemption, she has noted the vigorous appeals from particular Member States who fear that, without such a provision, they will have major problems in implementing the Directive. She proposes to take such serious concerns into consideration but only in specific situations, so as not to make the exemption attractive for situations in which there are absolutely no grounds for it. Another qualification that for many of the consulted parties appears to be acceptable is the limitation of this exemption to pay. They all agree that with respect to other basic working and employment conditions, temporary agency workers should get basic protection from day one. With all the reservations that she still has, the rapporteur asks the Committee to judge whether, under the proposed conditions, this exemption can be accepted for the period up to the planned evaluation and review of the Directive.

11 September 2002

OPINION OF THE COMMITTEE ON LEGAL AFFAIRS AND THE INTERNAL MARKET

for the Committee on Employment and Social Affairs

on the proposal for a directive of the European Parliament and the Council on working conditions for temporary workers

(COM(2002) 149 – C5-0140/2002 – 2002/0072(COD))

Draftsman: Giuseppe Gargani

PROCEDURE

The Committee on Legal Affairs and the Internal Market appointed Ioannis Koukiadis draftsman at its meeting of 22 May 2002. However, following the vote on 10 September 2002, Mr Ioannis Koukiadis stepped down as draftsman and Mr Giuseppe Gargani was appointed in his place.

It considered the draft opinion at its meeting(s) of 4 June, 20 June and 10 September 2002.

At the last meeting it adopted the following amendments by 14 votes to 13, with 0 abstentions.

The following were present for the vote: Giuseppe Gargani chairman and draftsman; Willi Rothley, vice-chairman; Ioannis Koukiadis, vice-chairman; Bill Miller, vice-chairman; Paolo Bartolozzi, Maria Berger, Ward Beysen, Michel J.M. Dary, Enrico Ferri, Janelly Fourtou, Marie-Françoise Garaud, Evelyne Gebhardt, José María Gil-Robles Gil-Delgado, Malcolm Harbour, The Lord Inglewood, Othmar Karas (for Bert Doorn), Hans Karlsson, Piia-Noora Kauppi (for Rainer Wieland), Kurt Lechner, Klaus-Heiner Lehne, Neil MacCormick, Arlene McCarthy, Toine Manders, Linda McAvan, Manuel Medina Ortega, Pasqualina Napoletano (for Fiorella Ghilardotti pursuant to Rule 153(2)), Angelika Niebler (for Joachim Wuermeling), Anne-Marie Schaffner, Marianne L.P. Thyssen, Diana Wallis, and Stefano Zappalà.

SHORT JUSTIFICATION

General

Of the three forms of atypical employment, namely fixed-term contract work, part-time work and temporary work, the first two have been the subject of Community regulation, with directives which were concluded by means of collective agreements. For the third, however, difficulties have arisen and agreement has not been reached. These obstacles to regulating the issue, together with the persistence shown in seeking a solution, demonstrate the problem's dimensions.

Temporary employment agencies appeared several decades ago. Initially there were doubts as to their legality, because it was thought that their operations ran counter to the prohibition set out by the ILO's international conventions. Later, these doubts evaporated when it became clear that temporary employment firms are not financed by the workers.

Since then, the agencies have grown significantly and spread to all the European Union countries, since they fulfil the new economy's basic needs. There is no doubt that they have contributed to an increase in the active population, mainly by facilitating the entry of women and young people into the employment market. They have also assisted significantly in the improvement of businesses' competitiveness.

However, this form of atypical employment is, of all the atypical forms of employment, the one that lends itself most to infringements of Community legislation and the exploitation of labour. It is no accident that in many countries the practice is referred to in terms of borrowing or hiring out employees, viewing workers as objects. In addition, allegations concerning the use of temporary employment agencies as a means to promote illegal immigration are common. However, there are also dangers for the other workers. For these reasons, many European countries, specifically nine of the 15, undertook to pass legislation to introduce restrictions and, in many cases, prohibitions. It is therefore clear that the status of agencies in the EU Member States is particularly heterogeneous, ranging from operation without any restrictions to exhaustive regulation, and that this has an impact on the competitiveness of businesses and on the operation of the internal market.

It should, however, be said that the proposed directive does not aim to lay down new employment conditions, but to ensure that existing legal protection for this category of temporary worker is implemented, in order, so far as possible, to ensure that there is no unjustifiable discrimination in the treatment of temporary workers as compared with other workers. The proposal is an attempt to ensure that legislation which has already been published is applied, including Directive 96/71 concerning the posting of workers in the framework of the provision of services.

The starting point for all the problems which this form of employment engenders is that instead of the traditional bilateral relationship between an employee and employer, we have a three-way relationship with the following strange consequences: businesses which hire employees but do not employ them themselves (employers without employees), and businesses which employ employees but are not considered to be employers (employees without employers). This concept was quickly combated by the various national legislations: they accepted that the employer could have a split identity and divided responsibilities between the two employers; this was also accepted by International Labour Convention No. 181 in 1997.

Commission's Proposal

The draft directive put forward by the Commission introduces two important elements. The first is the introduction, in Article 5, of a general principle prohibiting discrimination in working conditions between temporary workers and comparable workers in the user enterprise. However, it should be noted that this article introduces two exceptions, in paragraphs 2 and 4. The second important element of the proposal for a directive is Article 4, which refers to the review of restrictions and prohibitions by the Member States.

Legal Basis

The legal basis chosen by the Commission for this proposal is Article 137, together with Article 136 of the Treaty. Clearly, the need for action with regard to the employment of temporary employees is adopted as a complement to the Member States' legislation in order to avoid unfair discrimination between temporary employees, and to strengthen the protection of minimum rights for those who are employed on a temporary basis, in order to achieve the objectives set out in Article 136 on the promotion of employment, in conjunction with the flexibility sought by undertakings in managing the labour market, and appropriate social protection.

According to Article 137(6), the provisions of that Article shall not apply to pay, but this exception applies to the issue of setting pay levels and not to cases where it is merely a question of ensuring respect for the principle of non-discrimination regarding identical work. For this reason, moreover, in the previous directives on fixed-term contracts and part-time employment, which were drawn up by consensus, it is acknowledged that under point 7 of the Community Charter of the Fundamental Social Rights of Workers it is essential for working conditions to be harmonized in all three forms of atypical employment, namely part-time employment, fixed-term contract work and temporary work, while Article 6 of the EU Treaty also stipulates that the Union shall respect fundamental rights. In general, the directive aims merely to ensure legal certainty. The same idea prevails with regard to cross-border temporary work in Directive 96/71 on the posting of workers.

AMENDMENTS

The Committee on Legal Affairs and the Internal Market calls on the Committee on Employment and Social Affairs, as the committee responsible, to incorporate the following amendments in its report:

Text proposed by the Commission*	Amendments by Parliament
Amendment 1 Article 2, point (c) (new)	
	(c) to lay the foundations for further development of the temporary work sector, in order to promote job creation and make agency work more attractive.

Justification

Explicitly includes the objectives of the Directive in a substantive article.

* OJ C 203 E, 27 August 2002, p. 1.

Amendment 2
Article 3, paragraph 1, point (b)

(b) 'comparable worker' means ***a*** worker ***in the user undertaking*** occupying an identical or similar post to that occupied by the worker posted by the temporary agency, account being taken of seniority, qualifications and skills;	(b) 'comparable worker' means ***another agency*** worker ***in the same or a comparable organization*** occupying an identical or similar post to that occupied by the worker posted by the temporary agency, account being taken of seniority, qualifications and skills;

Justification

Redefines 'comparable worker' in a realistic manner, in relation to the overall objectives of the Directive to encourage high quality agency work.

Amendment 3
Article 3, paragraph 1, point (d), (i)

(i) the duration of working time, rest periods, night work, ***paid*** holidays and public holidays;	(i) the duration of working time, rest periods, night work, holidays and public holidays;

Justification

Holidays can be paid or unpaid.

Amendment 4
Article 3, paragraph 1, point (d), (ii)

(ii) pay;	***Delete***

Justification

Pay should not be covered by this Directive.

Amendment 5
Article 5, paragraph 4

4. Without prejudice to the provisions of paragraphs 2 and 3 above, Member States may provide that paragraph 1 shall not apply where a temporary worker works on an assignment or series of assignments with the same user enterprise in a post which, due to its duration or nature, can be accomplished in a period not exceeding ***six weeks***.	4. Without prejudice to the provisions of paragraphs 2 and 3 above, Member States may provide that paragraph 1 shall not apply where a temporary worker works on an assignment or series of assignments with the same user enterprise in a post which, due to its duration or nature, can be accomplished in a period not exceeding ***twelve months***.

Justification

A cut-off point of twelve months allows agency workers to be used to add value to an enterprise and to provide extra flexibility to develop new activities. Twelve months will also allow a full period of maternity leave to be covered by a temporary worker.

The six-week proposal is entirely unrealistic and undermines the objectives of the Directive.

Amendment 6
Article 5, paragraph 5

5. When this directive calls for a comparison to be made with a comparable worker in the user undertaking but no such worker exists, reference shall be made to the collective agreement applicable in the user undertaking; if no such collective agreement exists, the comparison will be made by reference to the collective agreement applicable to the temporary work agency; if no collective agreement is applicable, the basic working and employment conditions of temporary workers will be determined by national legislation and practices.	***Delete***

Justification

It should not be for an EU Directive to determine prescriptive details about comparability of workers within such a diverse sector of 'atypical' workers in different Member States.

Amendment 7
Article 5, paragraph 6

6. The implementing procedures for this article shall be defined by the Member States ***after consultation of the social partners***. The Member States may also entrust the social partners at the appropriate level with the task of defining these procedures for this chapter by means of a negotiated agreement.	6. The implementing procedures for this article shall be defined by the Member States. The Member States may also entrust the social partners at the appropriate level with the task of defining these procedures for this chapter by means of a negotiated agreement ***in accordance with national practices***.

Justification

The importance of differing national practices in differing Member States should be explicitly recognized.

Amendment 8
Article 6, paragraph 3

3. Temporary agencies shall not charge workers any fees in exchange for arranging for them to be recruited by a user undertaking.	***Delete***

Justification

It should not be for an EU Directive to determine whether and how fees should be charged by Temporary Agencies in differing Member States.

Amendment 9
Article 7, paragraph 2

Member States may provide that, under conditions that they define, these workers count for the purposes of calculating the threshold above which bodies representing workers provided for by national and Community legislation should be formed in the user undertaking.	***Delete***

Justification

Self-explanatory.

Amendment 10
Article 11, paragraph 1

1. The Member States shall adopt the laws, regulations and administrative provisions necessary to comply with this directive by [two years after adoption] at the latest, or shall ensure that the social partners introduce the necessary provisions by the way of an agreement, whereby the Member States must make all the necessary arrangements to enable them to guarantee at any time that the objectives of this Directive are being attained. They shall forthwith inform the Commission thereof.	1. The Member States shall adopt the laws, regulations and administrative provisions necessary to comply with this directive by [two years after adoption] at the latest, or shall ensure that, ***where applicable in accordance with their national legislation or practices***, the social partners introduce the necessary provisions by the way of an agreement, whereby the Member States must make all the necessary arrangements to enable them to guarantee at any time that the objectives of this directive are being attained. They shall forthwith inform the Commission thereof.

Justification

This Directive purports to make agency work more attractive: the differing circumstances pertaining in each Member States should determine how the best implementation method to ensure this goal is achieved, and this provision should therefore allow a wide degree of flexibility in transposition.

Amendment 11
Article 11, paragraph 3 (new)

	3. They should transpose these provisions in a manner consistent with promoting job creation and making agency work more attractive, recognising the different circumstances pertaining to their own Member State.

Justification

Explicitly recognizes the importance of national legislation and practices in the context of the overall objectives of the Directive.

29 August 2002

OPINION OF THE COMMITTEE ON WOMEN'S RIGHTS AND EQUAL OPPORTUNITIES

for the Committee on Employment and Social Affairs

on the proposal for a Council directive on Temporary work: protective framework for workers, relationship with the temporary agency

(COM(2002) 149 – C5-0140/2002 – 2002/0072(COD))

Draftsperson: Thomas Mann

PROCEDURE

The Committee on Women's Rights and Equal Opportunities appointed Thomas Mann draftsperson at its meeting of 18 April 2002.

It considered the draft opinion at its meetings of 9 July 2002 and 27 August 2002.

At the last meeting it adopted the following amendments by 20 votes, with 3 abstentions.

The following were present for the vote: Anna Karamanou chairperson; Olga Zrihen Zaari vice-chairperson; Thomas Mann draftsperson; María Antonia Avilés Perea, María del Pilar Ayuso González, Regina Bastos, Armonia Bordes, Lone Dybkjær, Ilda Figueiredo, Fiorella Ghilardotti, Koldo Gorostiaga Atxalandabaso, Lissy Gröner, María Izquierdo Rojo, Hans Karlsson, Rodi Kratsa-Tsagaropoulou, Maria Martens, Emilia Franziska Müller, Elena Ornella Paciotti, Christa Prets, Patsy Sörensen, Joke Swiebel, Elena Valenciano Martínez-Orozco and Lousewies van der Laan.

SHORT JUSTIFICATION

In March 2000, the European Council meeting in Lisbon adopted the strategy to make the Union the most competitive and dynamic knowledge-based economy in the world capable of sustained economic growth with more and better jobs and greater social cohesion.

The aim of the strategy is to achieve full employment by 2010, i.e. a rate of employment of 70 per cent overall, at least 60 per cent for women and 50 per cent for older workers. The employment policy guidelines for 2001 and the broad guidelines for economic policy for 2001 therefore recommend the development of diversified and flexible forms of employment relationships and labour contracts, e.g. temporary work.

The European Union must promote more flexible forms of work and reform legal provisions and contractual agreements to create more and qualitatively better jobs. This also applies to the temporary sector, the main feature of which is a 'three-way relationship' between an agency, an employee and a user undertaking.

Different national rules apply throughout the EU in regard to both the activities of temporary agencies and working conditions for temporary workers. The Commission's main concern is to establish non-discrimination for temporary workers in relation to comparable, permanently employed workers. Factors to be taken into account include working time, paid holiday, night work and working hours for pregnant women and nursing mothers. Exceptions are pension entitlements and special payments such as Christmas bonuses. The minimum period of employment to qualify for equal status is six weeks.

As regards the equal status of men and women, the picture varies widely in relation to temporary work between the Member States. According to the Commission, in some countries more than three quarter of temporary workers are men, while in others the division is more or less equal or women are in the majority. The industry, construction and public works sectors are dominated by men, e.g. Austria (87 per cent), Germany (80 per cent), France (74 per cent), Luxembourg (77 per cent), Spain (62 per cent) and Belgium (60 per cent). In the Netherlands, Portugal and the United Kingdom, there is a relative balance between the two sectors. In Finland and Sweden, however, women are in the majority, accounting for some 80 per cent of all temporary workers.

Your draftsperson has devoted particular attention to the situation of women on the employment market in general and the temporary market in particular. In order to take greater account of the situation of women, it would seem valid to make frequent reference to gender on certain points.

One of the reasons for the absence of women from the labour market is the difficulty of combining family life and employment. According to Eurostat, the EU's statistical office, the current rate of employment for couples without children is 42 per cent in Spain and 79 per cent in the United Kingdom. For couples with children, the employment rate ranges from 43 per cent in Spain to 74 per cent in Portugal.

Temporary work can serve to offset a shortage of permanent staff or a temporary increase in the workload. It offers the lesser qualified and women, in particular, who have been absent from the labour market for a good length of time, an opportunity to step back into working life.

Temporary workers should not, however, be regarded as 'rationalization factors'. There is an inherent risk that by employing them, the more costly permanent workforce is cut back. The advantage of hiring temporary workers is possibly undermined in that social acceptance, payment or the quality of the temporary work falls short of expectations. As regards working conditions, job offers and women's pay, there is a need for great improvement in this sector.

AMENDMENTS

The Committee on Women's Rights and Equal Opportunities calls on the Committee on Employment and Social Affairs, as the committee responsible, to incorporate the following amendments in its report:

Text proposed by the Commission*	Amendments by Parliament

* OJ C 203 E, 27 August 2002, p. 1.

Amendment 1
Recital 1a (new)

***(1a) Article 21(1) of the Charter of Fundamental Rights of the European Union prohibits discrimination based on any ground, including sex. Article 23 of the Charter of Fundamental Rights of the European Union stipulates that equality between men and women must be ensured in all areas, including employment, work and pay. In the European Community, in 1957 Article 119 of the Treaty of Rome enshrined the principle that men and women should receive equal pay for equal work. Article 141 of the EC Treaty establishes the legal basis for prohibiting discrimination between men and women for work of equal value. Furthermore, Articles 2 and 3(2) of the Treaty on European Union stipulate respectively that promoting equality between men and women and eliminating all inequalities between men and women are goals of the Community*.**

Justification

Articles 2 and 3 of the Treaty of Amsterdam should be included among the legal bases for policies and actions by the European Union to promote equality between men and women.

Amendment 2
Recital 3

(3) The conclusions of the European Council in Lisbon of 23 and 24 March 2000 set the European Union a new strategic target, namely to 'become the most competitive and most dynamic knowledge-based economy in the world, capable of sustained economic growth with more and better jobs and greater social cohesion'.

(3) The conclusions of the European Council in Lisbon of 23 and 24 March 2000 set the European Union a new strategic target, namely to 'become the most competitive and most dynamic knowledge-based economy in the world, capable of sustained economic growth with more and better jobs and greater social cohesion'. ***The Union will thus put itself in a position to achieve full employment, i.e. a rate of employment of 70 per cent overall, at least 60 per cent for women and 50 per cent for older workers, by 2010*.**

Justification

The figures clarify the Lisbon targets.

Amendment 3
Recital 11

(11) Temporary work should meet undertakings' needs for flexibility and employees' need to reconcile their working and private lives and contribute to job creation and participation and integration in the labour market.	(11) Temporary work should meet undertakings' needs for flexibility and employees' need to reconcile their working and private lives and contribute to job creation and participation and integration in the labour market ***by increasing job opportunities, particularly for women***.

Amendment 4
Recital 14a (new)

	(14a) Directive 92/85/EEC on the introduction of measures to encourage improvements in the safety and health at work of pregnant workers and workers who have recently given birth or are breast-feeding and equal treatment in statutory and occupational social security schemes applies to all employees, as established by Article 33(1) of the Charter of Fundamental Rights. The Charter also enshrines respect for the entitlement to social security benefits, including childcare facilities, and social security provision for maternity, illness or industrial accident. Furthermore, Article 33(2) of the Charter of Fundamental Rights stipulates that, in order to reconcile family and professional life, everyone has the right to protection from dismissal and the right to paid maternity leave or parental leave following the birth or adoption of a child. In particular, the amendment of Directive 76/207 on the implementation of the principle of equal treatment for men and women as regards access to employment, vocational training and promotion, and working conditions, prohibits any discrimination on the grounds of sex, including sexual harassment, and enshrines the right to maternity, paternity and parental leave.

Justification

It seems necessary to mention the amendment of Directive 76/207/EEC, under which the principle of non-discrimination on grounds of sex at the workplace is extended to include protection against direct and indirect discrimination, harassment and sexual harassment and protection of the right to maternity, paternity and parental leave (aimed at reconciling family and professional life) and provides for the promotion of positive actions and for enterprises to be asked to draw up plans to promote equality.

Amendment 5
Recital 15

(15) With respect to basic working and employment conditions, temporary workers should not be treated any less favourably than a 'comparable worker', i.e. a worker in the user undertaking in an identical or similar job, taking into account seniority, qualifications and skills.	(15) With respect to basic working and employment conditions, temporary workers should not be treated any less favourably than a 'comparable worker', i.e. a worker in the user undertaking in an identical or similar job, taking into account seniority, qualifications and skills ***and with no discrimination on grounds of sex***.

Amendment 6
Recital 16

(16) However, differences in treatment are acceptable if they are objectively and reasonably justified by a legitimate aim under national law.	(16) However, differences in treatment are acceptable if they are objectively and reasonably justified by a legitimate aim under national law. ***They must be compatible with the Charter of Fundamental Rights and with the EU Treaties, regulations and all directives governing the principle of non-discrimination***.

Justification

It is important to include reference to the various European regulations and directives which enshrine and regulate the principle of non-discrimination in general terms.

Amendment 7
Recital 19

(19) There should be some flexibility in the application of the principle of non-discrimination in cases of missions effected to accomplish a job which, due to its nature or duration, lasts less than six weeks.	***Deleted***

Amendment 8
Recital 21

Not applicable to English version

Amendment 9
Recital 22a (new)

(22a) In the Member States of the EU, there is still gender-specific pay discrimination between men and women performing the same work or work of equal value.

Justification

Clarification of pay discrimination. According to statistics provided by the European Community Household Panel (ECHP) and figures provided by the Structure of Earnings Survey (SES), in 1995 women earned only between 72 per cent and 83 per cent of men's pay, despite performing equal work or work of equal value. The biggest disparities are in the United Kingdom, Greece and the Netherlands; the lowest wage differentials are in Sweden, Belgium and Luxembourg. More recent figures soon to be published by Eurostat, the European Union's Statistical Service, show no improvement – on the contrary, in Austria, for example, pay discrimination has increased in certain sectors.

Amendment 10
Article 3, paragraph 1, point b

b) 'comparable worker' means a worker in the user undertaking occupying an identical or similar post to that occupied by the worker posted by the temporary agency, account being taken of seniority, qualifications and skills.	b) 'comparable worker' means a worker in the user undertaking occupying an identical or similar post to that occupied by the worker posted by the temporary agency, account being taken of seniority, qualifications and skills, ***and with no discrimination on grounds of sex***.

Amendment 11
Article 4, paragraph 2a (new)

2a. Temporary workers shall not be employed to replace regular employees during industrial action or disputes.

Justification

This provision was already included in the draft agreement between the social partners and did not give rise to any disagreement.

Amendment 12
Article 5, paragraph 1a (new)

1a. Basic protection as regards essential working conditions and employment protection which is mainly of

	interest to women and employees with family responsibilities, as well as protection against discrimination and intimidation, maternity protection and maternity and parental leave, must be available from day one for all temporary workers, whatever type of contract they have.

Justification

In order to ensure equal treatment for all employees in the same workplace and to provide proper protection for temporary workers, appropriate basic protection must be offered from day one of the employment contract, inter alia as regards parental leave and discrimination.

Amendment 13
Article 5, paragraph 2

2. Member States may provide that an exemption be made to the principle established in paragraph 1 when temporary workers ***who*** have a permanent contract of employment with a temporary agency ***continue to be paid*** in the time between postings.	2. Member States may provide that an exemption be made to the principle established in paragraph 1 when temporary workers have a permanent contract of employment with a temporary agency ***and full pay and social protection are also provided*** in the time between postings.

Justification

When temporary workers are bound to an employment agency by a permanent contract their income and social protection should be guaranteed.

Amendment 14
Article 5, paragraph 4

4. Without prejudice to the provisions of paragraphs 2 and 3 above, Member States may provide that paragraph 1 shall not apply where a temporary worker works on an assignment or series of assignments with the same user enterprise in a post which, due to its duration or nature, can be accomplished in a period not exceeding six weeks. Member States shall take appropriate measures with a view to preventing misuse in the application of this paragraph.	***Deleted***

Justification

This exemption clause conflicts with the very nature of temporary work, which can by definition be very limited in time. This provision could open the way to abuse, as the Commission itself admits in its second paragraph. This clause should therefore be deleted.

Amendment 15
Article 7, first subparagraph

Temporary workers shall count for the purposes of calculating the threshold above which bodies representing workers provided for under national and Community legislation should be formed at the temporary agency.	Temporary workers shall count for the purposes of calculating the threshold above which bodies representing workers provided for under national and Community legislation should be formed at the temporary agency. ***Women, in particular, are called upon to take an active part in this process in application of the principle of equality and to enjoy positive measures aimed at promoting a balance between men and women within trade union organizations at all levels*.**

Justification

The amendment is designed to support representation of women within trade unions (and is in line with the own-initiative report by the Committee on Women's Rights and Equal Opportunities on representation of women among social partners in the European Union).

19. Concluding Remarks

Roger Blanpain

First of all, a word of thanks to the Royal Flemish Academy, for hosting and supporting this conference as well as to all participants, especially to the speakers and those who have participated in our very lively discussions.

For sure, private employment agencies, including temporary work agencies, are fully fledged actors in labour markets, providing, like any other company, a service or offering a product.

The Fordist model of the enterprise lies behind us. Today and tomorrow, we have to deal with highly diversified labour markets and varying needs of employees and employers.

However, distinctions between the various activities of private agencies are not easy to make. One example from our discussions is that clearly we are no longer sure about the meaning of the term 'subcontracting': putting workers at the disposal of a user without delegation of authority, or with delegation of authority but at the same time providing a service as an entity and in an organized way. We will have to follow closely the meaning attributed to notions used by lawyers to describe the functioning of labour markets.

In sum, we discussed the question of whether the temporary work agency is a company like any other enterprise, or whether it should be equipped with distinctive rules as discussed below.

1. Recognition by the Member State

Is such recognition, as a licence to operate, necessary or not? We noted divergent points of view and various solutions at national level. For example, there is no longer recognition in the Netherlands and Sweden; recognition persists in Belgium and Germany.

2. The Equal Treatment Principle

The right of the temporary work agency to negotiate its own wage and working conditions was discussed and remains open. Companies in general indicate that the principle of equal treatment – a fundamental EU principle, as indicated above – is unworkable, while many Governments and trade unions defend the principle.

3. Status of the Agency Workers

In all EU Member states, the temporary worker is looked upon as a fully fledged employee, while in the UK he is in general considered as self-employed. In some

R. Blanpain & R. Graham (eds.), Temporary Agency Work and the Information Society, 371–372

countries such as Belgium, temporary workers are fixed-term workers, while in other countries, like Germany, they are considered to be engaged for an indefinite period. Would it not be preferable to leave it to the contracting parties to decide upon the nature of their agreement, according to their respective needs and possibilities?

4. Workers' Participation

The fear was expressed that too many temporary workers might undermine the existing systems of workers' participation and the role of the works councils, while at the same time the information and consultation possibilities for temporary workers might be inadequate. This is a further point for attention.

5. Freedom of Services

Another difficult issue concerns the trans-border activities of temporary work agencies. How to reconcile the freedom to provide services in the EU and the recognition – licence requirement in a number of countries? Should a UK temporary work agency be obliged to obtain a licence in Belgium before engaging in temporary work activities in that country?

Would a German licence suffice to operate in another EU Member State?

Again, opinions diverged. Personally, it seems to me that a licence requirement, imposing tame-consuming administrative requirements on employers, is contrary to the freedom to provide services. One objective of a licence, namely the protection of workers against the malpractice of an employer can be addressed by other means, by mere registration and adequate inspection by public authorities.

What is quite sure is that private employment agencies are assuming an active role in the labour market. This should be welcomed. Again, it is a question of rights and obligations and of balancing them: favouring private initiative while maintaining fundamental social standards. After all, humanity is the core. As my Master, Professor Zeger Van Hee told me over and over again: *omnia pro homine.*